PUBLIC GOVERNANCE IN THE AGE OF GLOBALIZATION

Public Governance in the Age of Globalization

Edited by

KARL-HEINZ LADEUR
University of Hamburg, Germany

ASHGATE

Published by
Ashgate Publishing Limited
Gower House
Croft Road
Aldershot
Hants GU11 3HR
England

Ashgate Publishing Company
Suite 420
101 Cherry Street
Burlington, VT 05401-4405
USA

Ashgate website: http://www.ashgate.com

British Library Cataloguing in Publication Data
Public governance in the age of globalization
   1. International and municipal law - Congresses
   2. Globalization - Political aspects - Congresses 3. State,
   The - Congresses 4. Globalization - Economic aspects -
   Congresses
   I. Ladeur, Karl-Heinz
   341'.04

Library of Congress Cataloging-in-Publication Data
Public governance in the age of globalization / edited by Karl-Heinz Ladeur.
   p. cm.
   Includes bibliographical references and index.
   ISBN 0-7546-2368-8
   1. Public administration. 2. Globalization. 3. Democracy. I. Ladeur, Karl-Heinz.

JF1351.P822 2003
327.1--dc22

2003058363

ISBN 0 7546 2368 8

Printed and bound in Great Britain by MPG Books Ltd, Bodmin, Cornwall

Contents

Part IV: The New Forms of War in a Global Society

Part V: The Economy and Global Public Governance

List of Contributors

Joshua Cohen, Goldberg Professor of the Humanities, Massachusetts Institute of Technology

Martin van Creveld, Professor of Military History, Hebrew University, Jerusalem

Lawrence M. Friedman, Marion Rice Kirkwood Professor of Law, Stanford University

Mark Van Hoecke, Rector of the Catholic University, Brussels

Karl-Heinz Ladeur, Professor of Public Law, University of Hamburg

Jean-Jacques Rosa, Professor of Economics at the Institut d'Etudes Politiques, Paris

Charles F. Sabel, Professor of Law and Sociology, Columbia University

Saskia Sassen, Ralph Lewis Professor of Sociology, University of Chicago

Anne-Marie Slaughter, Dean, Woodrow Wilson School of Public and International Affairs, Princeton University

Pedro Gustavo Teixeira, Researcher, Law Department of the European University Institute, Italy

Gunther Teubner, Professor of Private Law, University of Frankfurt/Main

Joel P. Trachtman, Professor of International Law, Tufts University

Thomas Vesting, Professor of Public Law, University of Frankfurt/Main

Foreword

The articles are based on a conference which was held in March 2001 at the European University Institute in Florence. All papers presented during this conference have been revised and edited in the meantime. I thank my collaborators in Florence, Alexandra George and Alessandra Chirico, and at the University of Hamburg, Sylvia Kunz and Heiko Siebel-Huffmann, for their careful work on the preparation of this volume.

The financial support of the Law Department of the European University Institute is gratefully acknowledged.

Karl-Heinz Ladeur, Florence/Hamburg, January 2004

Chapter 1

Globalization and Public Governance – A Contradiction?

Karl-Heinz Ladeur

I.   Globalization and its Discontents

This book is devoted to the analysis of the difficult relationship between 'globalization' and 'public governance'. Both concepts may appear to be so all embracing and 'global' that their use might, in itself, require an explanation.[1] The chapters of this book try first to explain what, with respect to 'public governance', 'globalization' is not: it is not the invocation of a chaotic unstructured process of dissolution of public order as it has been conceived of in the context of the 'Westphalian System' as established in 1648.[2] Nor is it equivalent to a take-over of political power by multi-national 'stateless' enterprises with a corresponding tendency towards abolishing state-based democracy. Many phenomena which are attributed to the process of globalization, in particular the crisis of the welfare-state, do not have much to do with a challenge of the sovereignty of the state by multi-nationals that look for new opportunities for capital investment and orient their decision-making at global markets.

With good reasons, P. Krugman[3] has argued that the effective influence of globalization on the nation state is still negligible when compared to national economic factors: major sectors of the economies of the leading industrial countries develop without the underlying major impact of the world economy.

In spite of this request for a more balanced and differentiated judgement, we have to register that the important phenomenon of 'globalization' is taking place.[4]

---

1   Cf. Wolfgang H. Reinicke, *Global Public Policy: Governing without Government* (Cambridge, Mass.: The Brookings Institution Press, 1998).

2   Cf. in particular Linda Weiss, *The Myth of the Powerless State* (Ithaca: Cornell University Press, 1998).

3   Cf. Paul Krugman, *Pop Internationalism* (Cambridge, Mass.: MIT Press, 1996).

4   Cf. John W. Meyer et al., *World Society and the Nation State*, 103 AMERICAN JOURNAL OF SOCIOLOGY 1998, p.144; David Held et al., *Global Transformations: Politics,*

However, this development is deployed in a much more institutionalized way than many critics would have it. There are important transnational (international and inter-societal) and supra-national elements of a new public order, which remain, however, beyond the traditional borders of the state but not completely beyond the state as such. New organizations and institutions are brought to bear on economic processes that impose a legal and political structure on global economic processes. The crises on the global financial markets[5] do not call this hypothesis into question; they do, however, demonstrate that there is no harmoniously fine-tuned co-ordination between economic and legal-political evolutions.

In spite of the fact that, in a sense, we also had a global economy before World War I, new phenomena, which may justify the use of the concept of 'globalization', are to be taken into account by virtue of the increasing importance of 'transnational' forms of economic exchanges.

'Transnational', in this sense, means processes which develop beyond the impact of the well known international government-based treaties. This is, in fact, an important element of the transformation of economic transactions on world markets. At the end of the day, one should, of course, not forget that the economic systems at the beginning of the 20th century were the object of a deeply rooted process of internationalization. However, former processes of globalization were much more closely related to the forms of the traditional nation state and its legal forms of mediation between internal and external relationships. The state itself has never been a closed form, but its sovereignty was demonstrated by the fact that, even in liberal states which recognized freedom of internal competition, the state used to control the external economic relations with firms in other countries very intensely/strictly. This earlier form of globalization was much more closely linked with the international state-system and the ideas on the mutual advantages of international economic relationships.

II.   Globalization in the 1920s – a Lesson which has to be Learned

It is necessary to remember this past epoch of economic history if one wants to do justice to recent evolutions of the globalized economy. This is all the more so because the first World War between the major industrialized countries of the time and, moreover, the crisis of the world economy in the 1920s as well as the reactions it provoked from governments should commend us not to consider it as a simple

---

Economics and Culture (Stanford: Stanford University Press, 1999); Gunther Teubner (ed.), *Global Law without a State* (Aldershot: Dartmouth, 1997).

5   Cf. Robert O. Keohane/Joseph S. Nye Jr., Introduction, in Joseph S. Nye and John D. Donahue (eds.), *Governance in a Globalizing World* (Cambridge, Mass.: The Brookings Institution Press, 2000), p.1.

confrontation of national (i.e., democratic) versus transnational (global, undemocratic). The re-nationalization of economic policies produced devastating consequences which may shed some new light on the sometimes chaotic reactions of emerging global institutions such as the World Bank and the IMF, which try to tackle crises as global phenomena, while nation states try to avoid protectionist state-oriented policies.[6] The rise of fascist and national socialist movements, as well as anti-Semitism, were the phenomena that accompanied earlier anti-globalization movements which regarded cosmopolitan Jews as the core of a conspiracy against nations and their autonomy.

The proliferation of crises in the global financial economy is not a new phenomenon, either: the 'Black Monday' on Wall Street in 1929 and the breakdown of the Austrian bank 'Österreichische Creditanstalt' in 1930 provoked worldwide crises.[7] And one should not forget that reactions of nation states consisted of a re-nationalization of economic policies and a reduction of international co-operation. Instead, states focused on protectionist measures as compensation for the destabilization of the world economy. The political and economic consequences of this policy are well known. The management potential of European states in reacting to global crises should not be overestimated. One cannot simply assume that the management potential has much improved and the potential of a Keynesian policy of stimulation of consumption has more or less been exhausted. In comparison to the crisis of the late 1920s and early 1930s, the last major financial crisis, which began in 1997 in Thailand and which, fuelled by panic reactions in many countries, proliferated all over the world, turned out to be rather harmless. This shows that international institutions for the control of financial markets work – this does not exclude that they need to be improved, but it demonstrates that they can be improved. Thus it is not at the level of states but at transnational level that solutions have to be found.

The present anti-globalization movements have not produced aggressive ideologies, which might be compared to the ideologies of their counterparts in the 1920s. However, beyond their very concrete, but politically controversial, claim for a Tobin tax[8] in order to help cool on global speculation – an idea which is not even accepted by the researcher who has given his name to this type of tax – the ideas of the anti-globalization movements remain vague. The movements themselves seem to

---

6   Cf. Keohane and Nye, *supra* n. 5, p.10.

7   *The Economist*, 18 October 1997; cf. for this earlier period of globalization Harold James, *The End of Globalization. Lessons from the Great Depression* (Cambridge/Mass: Harvard University Press, 2001), who is more optimistic with respect to the new wave of globalization because technological and economic needs are more pressing and because of the relative strength of present international organizations.

8   Cf. James Tobin, Interview, *Der Spiegel*, 2 September 2001; for a critique of the illusions about the Tobin Tax cf. also Olivier Storch, *La Taxe Tobin: Revue de la pensée magique*, manuscript 2001.

feed on an antithetical distance from globalization rather than on a creative idea of how to impose a rational structure onto it. Fighters against globalization seem to be driven more by resentment than by reason. They differ from the rather nationalistic militancy of their predecessors in the 1920s by their passive approach: they seem to project their search for authenticity and identity within the nation state (which, on different occasions, is an object of fight itself) and on peoples of Third World countries. The contribution of Karl-Heinz Ladeur tries to question some of the arguments which are put forward by anti-globalization movements. Moreover, the search for new institutions and paradigms that might introduce more structure and homogeneity in globalization is a general focus of this volume.

This introduction is only meant to draw attention to the fact that globalization is such a heterogeneous, provocative, irritating and all-embracing phenomenon that more hidden causes of economic, political and cultural crises might not obtain sufficient attention in public discussion. This is also due to the fact that the deep structure of public rationality is centred on the state, and this goes far beyond the agenda of public decision-making; it has constituted the Western hierarchical view of society including the self-image of the citizen as a 'public person' being modelled on the sovereign 'Westphalian' state with both its distinctions and abstractions, and the movement of self-transformation of the 'subject' beyond the linkages of history and tradition in particular. This basic relationship permits the tendency to project the causes for the challenge of this development as being on the outside, being caused by the multinationals, etc. This relationship between both the state and the citizen as 'subjects' should be deconstructed. Moreover, the presupposition that the state is, almost necessarily, the instrument of democratic self-determination should be called into question as well. This is all the more so if one takes into consideration the character of so many Third World states which are looked at in a purely hypothetical way, instead of taking into consideration their functioning in a more realistic way.

III. Globalization – Whether Good or Bad – Should not be Overestimated

The contributions to this volume take a more detached view: they do not presuppose that globalization is the pre-eminent characteristic of the transformation of the economic system that we have witnessed in recent times, nor do they presuppose that globalization takes place in a chaotic unstructured way without any institutionalization or rationality. However, globalization is actually taking place, and it provokes fundamental transformations of the economic, legal and political systems. This is all the more so if one takes into consideration the changes which are derived from the technological innovations which cannot be identified with the phenomenon of globalization as such, though both evolutions are interdependent and mutually reinforcing.

Globalization, as opposed to former developments of internationalization of the economy, is definitely characterized by its transnational form, i.e., it is based on exchange processes which, more or less, bypass both the state and the traditional international character of the world economy in the past. It is an important characteristic of the globalization process that it produces more spontaneously self-generating flexible ways of co-ordination and co-operation among firms, instead of following the established tracks of international co-operation among states, even if they were established in the interest of firms. But in the past, the public forms and instruments including international treaties between states were much more important as institutions for the mediation and the establishment of a legal basis for private contracts and transactions. The new forms of co-ordination are generated in a bottom-up, instead of a top-down, approach; they create self-stabilizing networks of inter-relationships from which expectations which help orient participants to develop trust can emerge[9] – a version of trust in the continuity of the network itself, not just in the personal reliability of the partners about which one could collect personal experience[10] (note that this was the basis of the famous *lex mercatoria* in mediaeval ages). The generation of flexible institutions takes places beyond the state; it follows from the shared interest in establishing stable co-ordination patterns which is made possible by the increasing interest in the quality of complex products, the reliability of relationships, the broadening of the perspectives of the participants through the commonality of interchanging roles (participants change from the role of sellers to that of buyers and *vice versa* on regular terms),[11] the importance of trust, the complexity of contracts, and the diminishing impact of state law on practices of contract-making.

IV.   The Emergence of Networks and of a New 'Paradigm'?

All this is the reason why the contributors to this volume often refer to the concept of 'network' which – in spite of the fact that it is fashionable now – is crucial in the sense of referring to the rise of a new 'relational rationality' (McClennen), as opposed to a traditional rule-based universal rationality linked to the rise of the

---

9   Cf. Keohane and Nye, *supra* n. 5, p.12.

10   Cf. Jean-Marie Guéhenno, *The End of the Nation State* (Ann Arbor: Michigan University Press, 1995).

11   Cf. Teubner, *supra* n. 4; Christoph Möllers, Globalisierte Jurisprudenz: Einflüsse relativierter Nationalstaatlichkeit auf das Konzept des Rechts und die Funktion seiner Theorie, in Michael Anderheiden, Stefan Huster and Stephan Kirste (eds.), *Globalisierung als Problem der Gerechtigkeit und der Steuerungsfähigkeit des Rechts*, ARCHIV FÜR RECHTS- UND SOZIALPHILOSOPHIE, BEIHEFT 79 (2000), 41-60.

modern state and modern law.[12] Traditional forms of 'situational' patterns of co-ordination had been linked to local parochial practices of co-operation; they had excluded foreigners whereas the new forms of 'relational' heterarchical co-ordination are global: they allow for stability under conditions of complexity and may establish trust among strangers. This spontaneous generation of norms has occurred at all times, especially in the economic system, but it has been brought about much more slowly:[13] economic practice has produced '*boni mores*', commercial habits, private standards, general experience, etc., which were always the necessary basis for the interpretation and transformation of state-based domestic and international law. They were needed for the specification of private law in particular.

However, private networks of inter-relationships nowadays are much more dynamic, and they allow for much more self-stabilization than in the past, because participants can no longer just presuppose the general standards of expectations enshrined in *boni mores* habits, etc., they have to include more general interests in contract-making, they have to broaden the horizon of decision-making and, at the same time, they have to change relationships continuously. This is why participants can neither wait for the state to come up with new rules, nor for new private standards (new experience) to be brought about spontaneously. Private exchange relationships have to integrate an element of institution building which opens the way for new options, without doing away with all legal constraints.[14] It is a kind of hybrid linkage between individual exchange and the generation of flexible situational constraints and expectations, which allows for new relations to be brought about. The evolution of spontaneously generated patterns of behaviour and co-ordination has to be monitored, evaluated, varied and renewed, because state law is not flexible enough to adapt to the new requirements of a globalized and, above all, dynamic economy. Reflexive, strategic and procedural constraints of rule- making are increasingly important. This is also why the international, but still state-based, law-making treaties lose their importance.

However, it has to be recalled that this is just a repercussion of a development, which takes place within the domain of domestic law, as well. In both domestic and transnational legal relationships, it can no longer be presupposed that the judge will be able to provide sufficient specialized knowledge and competence so as to come up with adequate legal solutions for such highly complex cases. And this is another reason why the common interest of transnational firms in establishing a reliable legal basis for innovative complex contracts, etc., increases. And, at the same time,

---

12 Cf. Stefan Weber, *Medien – Systeme – Netze. Elemente einer Theorie der Cyber-Netzwerke*, Bielefeld: transkript 2001, p.47s.
13 Cf. Teubner, *supra* n. 4.
14 Cf. Keohane and Nye, *supra* n. 5; Jane E. Fountain, *Building the Virtual State* (Washington D.C.: The Brookings Institution Press, 2001), pp.74ff.

this is the basis for the productivity of the network concept that, above all, indicates the rise of a new logic which accepts the potential of heterarchical inter-relationships to generate 'emergent' patterns of co-ordination which may replace universal rules imposed from above. If one takes into consideration this intertwinement of domestic and transnational forms of new elements of spontaneous law, the rise of global forms of co-ordination beyond public international law can no longer be regarded as anomalous deviations from the right way of state-based law, but as the expression of an evolutionary step towards new forms of the self-organization of societal norms which go beyond the official legal system.

V.   Against Simplifications which are Far Spread among Anti-Globalists

The contributions to this volume draw on the traditional forms of linkages between law and the spontaneous generation of rules and standards, such as experience, which was closely related to state law. On the other hand, they go further in the analysis of post-modern forms of institutions and law beyond the state in order to discover new patterns of self-organization which introduce more reflexivity and potential for self-observation and self-transformation of relationships into legal practices. In a first step, it should be retained that transnational legal forms do not just oppose state sovereignty and the requirements of justice hammered out in state law from outside, but that they react to a fundamental transformation in the economic system, which is due to increasing levels of complexity and the rise of a new paradigm of 'relational rationality' which is based on the assumption of the creative potential of heterarchical patterns of the inter-relationships emerging from transnational new dynamic economic practices.

If one takes into consideration this evolution of a modern version of transnational self-organized patterns of co-ordination, which are, at the very least, a functional equivalent of the law and its classical role of stabilizing expectations, one has to accept from the outset that globalization cannot be reduced to the arbitrary economic behaviour of some multinationals which have 'gone wild' simply because they undermine the democratic legitimacy of both the law and the state, and create chaos in the world economy. On the contrary, there is a new set of transnational, international and state-based institutions whose contradictions have certainly not yet been managed, but whose potential, first of all, has be realized and described in terms which do not just reduce the new phenomena to deviations from a fixed set of 'normal' institutions. The simplified antithetical schematic confrontation of 'the' state and multinationals, which has been widely diffused among groups of the anti-globalization movement is problematic in the following two ways. On the one hand, the new institutions are either not taken into account at all, or they are reduced to empty shells open to be exploited by multinationals. On the other, they are evaluated in a one-sided way and are held responsible for all kinds of perverse effects (aggravation of social conditions of workers, children, and deterioration of the environment).[15] The assumption that globalization has an inevitably negative impact on both living conditions and the environment is far from being obvious and needs to be reconsidered.

The incompatibility of globalization and environmental protection is equally doubtful. Environmental protection, as many environmentalists conceive it, is inefficient and expensive,[16] and the decline in concern for the environment (a phenomenon that can be observed in most countries) is, at least partly, due to the fact that it is ideology, and not a rational strategy taking economic constraints into consideration, that dominates the international discussion. Environmental problems in Third World countries do not seem to have their primary cause in globalization; on the other hand, the diverging priorities in Western and underdeveloped countries have to be considered. The legitimate concern that the economic model that has evolved in the Western world could not be expanded to a global economy may be confronted with the counter-argument that the exclusion of the Third World from the world economy altogether would have devastating effects, as well. Moreover, behind the criticism of a shift of work-intensive production to Third World countries, there is often an unwillingness to accept the constraints that the First World is exposed to, and no concern for the future of the Third World. The same is valid for 'social standards', the imposition of which might replace bad working conditions by no work at all. The rise of the knowledge economy in developed countries, which includes the integration of Third World countries into a distributed network of production, will have a spill-over effect even if, at a first stage, only work-intensive production is transferred to underdeveloped countries. This step towards an integration of the world economy will necessarily spread new working experience in the non-industrialized world.

The argumentation of the critics in the anti-globalization movement is also characterized by other contradictions, in particular, by an illegitimate combination of normative and factual views with regard to the relevance of democracy. First of all, the abstract potential of democratic government is identified with the essence of the state, whereas the reality of anti-democratic government is regarded as but one of the phenomena of globalization. Globalization, in this view, undermines the immanently democratic substance of the state. Most Third World countries do not have democratic governments, the reinforcement of which might exercise a benevolent influence on the living conditions of their populations. On the contrary, it is to be assumed that the opening of such states towards the world economy might instead have a healthy influence on their social structure because it may limit the destructive exercise of public power. However, even with regard to developed and

---

15 Cf. Björn Lomborg, *The Skeptical Environmentalist* (Cambridge: Cambridge University Press, 2001).

16 *The Economist*, 29 September 2001.

democratic states, the same illusions concerning the action potential of governments are widespread.

VI. The Limits of the Nation State in Managing Complex Problems

The potential and real consequences of globalization are not denied by its protagonists but the steering potential of the democratic state under conditions of uncertainty is sometimes no more than a myth. It is wishful thinking to assume that a democratic state might be able to 'steer' a modern economy whose success was based on its autonomy, its independence from state influence and the 'good intentions' that it might also be based on. A liberal democracy presupposes the priority of individual 'negative liberties' over public planning of economic development and the high value attributed to the possibility of binding uncertainty by establishing a distributed system of rights.[17] The normative limits of this system of trial and error have to be determined by democratic laws. However, critics of globalization are often not very explicit about the role attributed to the state in guaranteeing 'justice' in a society, which is continuously involved in a process of self-transformation. It has to be recognized that globalization may have detrimental effects because of the dynamic of change that it imposes on countries which may not be well prepared for it. However, one should not forget the disastrous consequences, which have been produced by approaches to overcome the autonomy of the economic system.

At this point, a look at the limited potential of nation states to formulate 'policies of justice' might be helpful: the overestimation of the phenomenon of globalization may also be due to the fact that the causes of the growing importance of global networks of transnational inter-relationships which are to be seen in the rise of the 'knowledge economy' have a strong internal effect, as well. The intertwining of different complex paths of evolution has to be taken into consideration, but this should not be misunderstood as referring to the assumption that political processes are being subjugated to the economic system. Many disruptive evolutions that we have been able to observe would also have taken place within a closed economy. The potential of the nation state to impose rules on a dynamic economic system is – even without a globalization process – rather limited. But this is mainly due to the process of devaluation of public knowledge (experience which is open to everyone, etc.) and the transformation of hierarchical inter-relationships in organizations, as well as the growing importance of the future-oriented strategies of enterprises as opposed to path-dependent search processes. This evolution is accompanied by the increasing importance of knowledge as an economic resource. As a consequence,

17 Cf. Karl-Heinz Ladeur, *Negative Freiheitsrechte und gesellschaftliche Selbst-organization* (Tübingen: Mohr, 2000).

the traditional instruments of sovereign state power lose their impact on the economic system. The public interest can no longer be formulated and put into practice by general norms. Instead, it is increasingly important to use public-private partnerships, the 'regulation of self-regulation' and other indirect forms of stimulating the productive exercise of state power in order to allow for an experimental, proactive and open conception of private intervention. The crisis of the welfare state is a home-made one. Moreover, it does not have much to do with globalization.

VII. Government and Governance

When the authors of this volume talk about 'public governance', they always bear in mind that globalization should not be regarded as a tendency which undermines state sovereignty from outside, and that this development could be compensated only by either strengthening the nation state (and, at the same time, blocking globalization) or by establishing the state model itself at global level. It is the new patterns of networks of inter-relationships, and not the limited exchange contracts mediated by international law which emerge beyond the state – both within regional economies and without (at global level) – that should stimulate the search for a corresponding form of public governance beyond the sovereign state and its monopoly of imposing binding-decisions on every citizen. It should be possible to find new, more open forms of public governance, which cannot be reduced to a kind of secondary modelling of the nation state at global level. This experimental approach is a first justification for the use of the concept of 'governance', instead of 'government' which is closely associated with the sovereign state even if it includes certain non-state forms of exercising political power. However, the concept of 'government' focuses on binding decision-making, at least as the outcome of a political process. The concept of 'governance', which might be criticized for its vagueness, also comprises, and not by chance, private forms of management ('corporate governance').

The concept takes up the new forms of permeability of the state, which establish themselves beyond the more structured relationships between state and society in the 'corporate state' which has stable relationships with large/major 'representative' organizations. The new paradigm of 'openness' of governmental decision-making procedures towards societal influences is much less structured than it used to be in the past.[18] The search for new forms of governance has to focus on both internal and

---

18 Cf. Keohane and Nye, *supra* n. 5; Stephan Hobe, *Der kooperative offene Verfassungsstaat*, 34 DER STAAT 1998, p.521; Udo Di Fabio, *Das Recht offener Staaten* (Tübingen: Mohr, 1998); Peer Zumbansen, *Die vergangene Zukunft des Völkerrechts*, 34 KRITISCHE JUSTIZ 2001, p.46; id., Spiegelungen von 'Staat und Gesellschaft'- Governace-Erfahrungen in der Globalisierungsdebatte, in Michael Anderheiden, Stefan

transnational networks of relationships which emerge beyond both the individual and the group-based legal relationships which were characteristic for the welfare state. The contributions in this volume show that these new processes are not complete unstructured and chaotic, but that new patterns of co-ordination which may be modelled with a view to the creation of a more adaptive and productive model of public governance can be observed. Such an approach would not just regard transnational processes of networks as a threat to government and democracy, but, on the contrary, as an incentive for the development of responsive forms of heterarchical decentred forms of governance which might develop their own reflexive potential *vis-à-vis* the evolution of a 'society of networks'.

If one takes into consideration the possibility of a generation of self-stabilizing patterns of network formation, the state could step in by introducing new flexible public reflexive forms of procedures which might be regarded as a functional equivalent to traditional forms of formulation of the public interest and its implementation. As soon as one tries to take this view, one becomes aware of the fact that globalization does not abolish the state, but transforms it by making it more permeable for the observation and registration of the discontinuous effects emerging in a world economy which can no longer be 'steered' by supposedly stable and continuous international treaties which allow for stable exchange between otherwise separate economies. In the same vein, just as the state has to open towards new patterns of 'networking' within regional societies, it has also to observe the evolution of patterns of relationships at global level. Both aspects correspond with one another: borders are no longer defined by political geography. They become less stable and less visible as the central instrument of state government, unilateral decision based on territorial sovereignty, loses its importance. Political powers overlap in the same way as societal networks of inter-relationships do.[19] This evolution can neither be described as the abolition of all forms of public power, nor as a non-political reign of technocracy which finds its institutionalization in the WTO, IMF, World Bank, etc., which have become emancipated from state-based public control.[20]

Huster and Stephan Kirste (eds.), *Globalisierung als Problem von Gerechtigkeit und Steuerungsfähigkeit des Rechts* (Stuttgart: Steiner, 2001), p.13; Michael J. Sandel, *Democracy and its Discontents* (Cambridge: Harvard University Press, 1996), p.338s; Michael Reisman, *Designing and Managing the Future of the State*, 8 EJIL 1998, p.409-420; John Hoffman, *Beyond the State* (Cambridge, Mass.: Polity, 1995), p.212.

19 Cf. Reinicke, *supra* n. 1; for the fading boundaries between international law (as a body of law concerning external legal relations of the state) and constitutional (as a law concerning the internal structure of the state) cf. Anne Peters, *Elemente einer Theorie der Verfassung Europas* (Berlin: Duncker & Humblot, 2001); Robert Uerpmann, *Internationales Verfassungsrecht*, JURISTENZEITUNG 2001, 565-573.

20 Cf. Joseph H.H.Weiler (ed.), *The EU, the WTO and the NAFTA*, Academy of European Law (Oxford: Oxford University Press, 2000); Gunther Teubner, *Das Recht der globalen*

This view turns out to be fixated on the nation state as the one and only form of public legitimate government which might (real)/could-can (hypothetical) be expanded to world level but not be replaced by new, less-hierarchical, network-like, overlapping structures of public governance, which might combine different institutions and political logic. The Westphalian sovereign state seems to be the normal form of public governance. The contributions to this volume try to be more precise and to ask whether and how a new form of public governance adapted to the new 'relational rationality' might be imaginable. They ask whether the evolution of networks might be the basis for a new viable paradigm, which might bring new life into public governance once one has accepted that the 'good old state' has already undergone a lot of changes and that its achievements in the past are much more ambivalent if one separates the democratic ideal from the reality of the state. A more realistic and pragmatic approach might come to the conclusion that giving up this ideal might even help find more finely-tuned productive forms of governance, even if they do not conform to the more or less fictitious chain of delegation of power from the single decision made by a civil servant whose accountability is, in practice, rather doubtful. Instead, one might take into consideration the emergence of a global society whose dynamics and fluidity might not fit into a reconstruction of the state at world level. We know that this evolution towards a world society beyond stable geographical borders (see the contribution of Lawrence Friedman) does not exclude public intervention, and that, on the other hand, the autonomy of economic evolution – which has been the basis for the success of Western societies – has always imposed limits on state intervention even though they were the self-imposed limits of a sovereign state which was not bound by traditions but only by state law.

VIII. The Permeability of the State under Post-Modern Conditions of Uncertainty

In the same way that the state was supplemented by the especially procedural implications of private organizations in the period of the welfare state, the generation of a collective order is now supplemented by external expansive engagements of the state and, at the same time, an overlapping influence of other states and new international and transnational networks of inter-relationships.[21]

Zivilgesellschaft, FRANKFURTER RUNDSCHAU No.253, 31st October 2000, p.20; Ernst Ulrich Petersmann, *The Transformation of the World Trading System through the 1994 Agreement stabilizing the World Trade System*, 6 EUROPEAN JOURNAL OF INTERNATIONAL LAW 1995, 161-221.

21   Cf. Karsten Ronit, *Institutions of Private Authority in Global Governance*, ADMINISTRATION AND SOCIETY 2001, p.555, 557; id./Volker Schneider, *Global Governance through Private Organizations*, 12 GOVERNANCE 1999, p.243; Paul Hirst and Grahame Thompson (eds.), *Globalization in Question. The International Economy*

There seems to be a parallel between public and private forms of governance which might be developed in a fruitful way by creating new forms of institutions. These new institutional forms are not primarily focused on rule-making and decision-making in the traditional sense of liberal state activities – a model which has already been transformed by the welfare state and which might undergo a new wave of transformation which cannot be regarded as destructive. In this respect, we should remind ourselves of the criticism, which the evolution towards the welfare state provoked in the 1920s. This development towards a permeability of the public institutions for societal influences has been recently regarded by many authors as the end of the state as such. And again, one should bear in mind that the reaction to this evolution had in the past devastating effects not only for the world economy but also for the stability of states and liberal societies.

It might seem completely rational that states create organizations such as those mentioned above. This does not conflict with the function of public governance once one accepts that states are more and more permeable in several ways and directions. This might be regarded as a productive form of co-ordinated, flexible and innovative co-operation of states which, from the outset, is not incompatible with the logic of public governance – this does not imply that the practice of these institutions is beyond doubt but that one has to bear in mind that this complex evolution towards networks of overlapping networks imposes the necessity to observe complex processes of creation of new patterns which might be influenced by public decison-making; this presupposes learning and the search for best practices. However, the institutions as such might be regarded as adequate for the establishment of a reflexive procedure for the monitoring and evaluation of the experimental logic that is evolving. Anyhow, the IMF, the World Bank and the WTO are far from being beyond the reach of states.[22] But when an economic relationship expands in transnational networks beyond state borders, the state also has to be 'externalized' in a new way. This does not mean the geographical expansion of the state as it did in the past, but expansion of the co-operative logic of the states, which have already developed within states. The establishment of these new international organizations, which develop the continuous activity of intervening in global economic processes and legal orders, do not follow the usual modal of separating rule-making (at the international level) from implementation (at the national level).

and the Possibility of Governance (Cambridge, Mass.: Polity, 1996); Robert O. Keohane and Helen V. Milner (eds.), *Internationalization and Domestic Politics* (Cambridge: Cambridge University Press, 1996); Christine Chinkin, *A Critique of the Public/Private Dimension*, 10 EJIL 1999, p.387.

22 Cf. John H. Jackson, *The WTO, Constitution and Proposed Reform*, 4 JOURNAL OF INTERNATIONAL ECONOMIC LAW 2001, p.67.

IX.   The New 'Hybrids' – Piercing the Veil of Sovereignty: Towards Multi-polarity

The new forms of the co-ordination of states in the WTO, etc., are 'hybrid' in the sense of deploying an institutional rationality of their own, which cannot be reduced to international co-ordination among governments. Such a traditional form of agreement among sovereign states which accept mutual obligations on a limited case by case approach, thus opening the veil of sovereignty in a self-controlled manner, would be much too cumbersome for the new global economy. In this respect, the evolution of a new kind of 'bindingness' which is not derived from established stable rules but emerges from a logic of its own may be observed.

The reservations that Member States had when joining the WTO, and the different regional conflicts which emerge within WTO procedures, show that this institution is not just beyond reach of states. They reveal the openness of states whose internal and external relations can no longer be kept separate.[23] But even the decision-making procedures for dispute settlements which, in the long run, may evolve towards a quasi-judicial function, cannot just be referred to a new unaccountable international institution. The states themselves have established a kind of experimental search procedure for the balancing of conflicts which fit into the new hybrid institutions which do not follow a clear design, but are meant to search for satisfactory procedures and best practices which cannot be established in a top-down approach beforehand. They have to be set in motion with the task of testing an experimental design, which will try and find a self-stabilizing pattern of co-ordination in a bottom-up approach.

The evolution of EC institutions towards supra-national elements can be described in the same vein: at a certain moment (Van Gend en Loos), the ECJ imposed the new logic of direct effect of EC law, which had certainly not been intended by the Member States, but which followed a logic of intensification of legal integration beyond a certain point which appeared to be incompatible with the more international logic of co-ordination among states. And this was the situation in which the ECJ pierced the veil of sovereignty and introduced the direct effect of EC law (beyond the traditional logic of implementation of international treaties). However, this does not mean that the EC is on its way to becoming a European Superstate: it has all the characteristics of a hybrid organization itself, and there is a certain rationality behind this linkage of national, transnational (mutual recognition), intergovernmental (the Council) and supra-national (the ECJ, the Commission, the European Parliament) institutional elements. This is not just an awkward type of compromise but the outcome of an open process of integration, which is adapted to the heterogeneity of economic and legal relationships in a 'society of networks'. It is a multi-polar network-like structure of public governance operating with different

23   Cf. Jackson, *supra* n. 22.

logic. This approach might raise some doubts about the adequacy of the concept of 'multi-level governance'[24] which still alludes to the kind of hierarchical structure that we already know from federalism. In this respect, the English reluctance to accept 'federalism' as the pivotal frame of reference for the institutional reform of the EC has a certain logic: federalism is, of course, based on decentralization of competences, but, at the same time, it presupposes that, in reality, the highest level has appropriated the sovereignty which is characteristic for the state.[25]

It is far from evident that the EU should have sovereignty in the traditional sense. The multi-*polarity* of the EC without a clearly defined top level of hierarchy might be a much more adequate design for such a new institutional co-operative setting, especially if one bears in mind that the Member States themselves have 'disaggregated' their sovereignty – to use a concept introduced by Anne-Marie Slaughter – also within their uncontested competences by accepting private norm-making, public-private partnerships, and regulated self-regulation (instead of imposing state norms) to name but a few of the phenomena of the emerging network-like decentred conceptions of the state. So, why not reproduce this pattern at European and even at global level? Whatever the answer, the evolution of government at global level should not be treated separately from the internal processes of the 'disaggregation' of states, which is a consequence of the breakdown of borders between the private and public spheres. One should bear in mind that the recent anti-Europeanism might have the same basis as the diffuse anti-globalization movement.

X.   The Open State

It could be a challenge to develop a conception of the 'open state'[26] which should be regarded as a political form in its own right and not as deficient *vis-à-vis* either the traditional nation state or a utopian world state.[27] Conceptions of 'globalization' and 'global governance' should not provoke superficial analogies with the 'state' or with 'government'.[28] This does not mean that the productive element of 'statehood', namely, the inclusion of all citizens into a common public order, should be given up

---

24   Cf. EC Commission, *European Governance, A White Paper*, 25 July 2001, COM (2001) 428.

25   Cf. generally Andrew Moravcsik, *The Choice for Europe. Social Purpose and State Power - From Messina to Maastricht* (Ithaca: Cornell University Press, 1998).

26   Cf. Di Fabio and Hobe, *supra* n. 18.

27   Cf. Sandel, *supra* n. 18, p.338s.

28   Cf. Jürgen Habermas, *Die postnationalistische Konstellation* (Frankfurt: Suhrkamp, 1998), p.91s; id., *Does Europe Need a Constitution?*, NEW LEFT REVIEW No.11, 2001, p.5 (with a view to the European Unification as an alternative to globalization); Keohane and Nye, *supra* n. 5, p.28.

altogether. Instead, it is the fine-tuning and co-ordination of different components of national, transnational, international/intergovernmental and supra-national origin which is at issue. We should venture to design a new network-related model which links different public and private actors beyond and within the state in a productive way. Such a model should not do away with the state but it should try to learn from former transformations of the state and try to discover a pattern of transformation, which might be referred to also when thinking about the multi-polar network of public governance. A more differentiated analysis of different forms and functions might be helpful to avoid the vagueness of the concept of governance which is, in fact, problematic if it cannot be supplemented with a more detailed 'infrastructure'. The concept as such is nothing but a programme which needs more concreteness. However, some more procedural and methodological principles might help overcome concerns about this lack of structure: first of all, one has to bear in mind that the concepts of state and government did not imply a political programme for public policies either, but they could presuppose and invoke a certain formal structure of public interest and rules which should have a universal and inclusive character with respect to all citizens.

This idea is also at the basis of the hierarchy of public interest over private interests. In a network-like structure of public governance, this separation and hierarchization can no longer be taken for granted. On the other hand, the harmonious identity of public and private interests is certainly not an idea which is at the basis of a liberal conception of state and government. In a network-like structure, at least the hierarchy of government can no longer be presupposed, albeit because of the epistemological difficulties in defining what the public interests are. The procedure of representation which is meant to aggregate the public interest can no longer be trusted because of the increasing heterogeneity of interests, the necessity to introduce an element of design and experimentation into public policy, and the intransparence of a complex society. In this respect, the element of procedure which is already at the basis of parliamentary deliberation might be referred to and remodelled in the sense of a more experimental design and search process intended to find 'best practices' also by comparing public governance and its instruments in different governmental regimes. This idea might draw on the concept of benchmarking, which is used in modern management processes and which presupposes that established practices and common knowledge can no longer be trusted and have at least to be supplemented by explicit search processes. Private and public actors may take action to tackle problems alike and there should be the possibility of creating procedures (both public and private) in order to design strategies, observe and evaluate consequences, and compare them to results found elsewhere. In this way, public actors might rearrange participation (e.g. in standard setting processes, impose selective giving-reasons requirements, introduce public hearings) but they can no longer impose models of 'behavioural steering'[29] once the new addressees of law or other public decisions are no longer persons but networks of inter-relationships where concrete responsibilities can no longer be defined.

In the same vein, a concept like the 'networked minimum', which has been proposed by Keohane and Nye,[30] might be understood: 'Networked because globalism is best characterized as networked, rather than as a set of hierarchies. Minimal because governance at global level will only be acceptable if it does not supersede national governance and if its intrusions into the autonomy of states and communities are clearly justified in terms of co-operative results'.

XI. The Change of Social Epistemology and the Necessity for Co-operation of Private and Public Actors

It is against this background that the rise of the concept of governance is to be understood: it takes into account that, both at national and at transnational level, there is no clear separation between public and private, and that forms of public and private ordering both overlap and become exchangeable. This is visible, for example, with respect to safety standards. They can be public but can – at the same time – be based on private expertise, and they may be private and then be open to limited public control – limited because the lack of expertise in government remains the same. The example demonstrates that this evolution does not end up in complete freedom for private actors and a loosening of public legal impact on industry. But the reason for a more heterarchical relationship between private and public actors comes to the fore. And, at the same time, the necessity for co-operation is made visible. 'Co-operation', as such, is again a vague idea, but, if it is linked to the transformation of the 'social epistemology' – the rules which allow for construction and transformation of social reality at a certain time – it might get more contours in the sense of a more open design-based approach to the private and public management of problems and of decision-making once the common knowledge (experience) has been devaluated. The state can no longer deliver stable rules of guidance for private actors – rules which are not in themselves supposed to underlie change produced by their private application – but it has to fine-tune limited interventions in the process of private management and the regulation of complex problems linked to growing levels of uncertainty. In this sense, the possibilities generated from private action create a domain of options which is, at the same time, the pre-structure on which public regulation has to draw.

A new model of 'public governance' for both national and transnational levels could try and find a functional equivalent to the institutions of liberal government

29 Cf. Keohane and Nye, *ibid.*
30 Cf. Keohane and Nye, *supra* n. 5, p.14.

and law at a more abstract level. In this respect, procedure – as mentioned above – could be a productive element, not in the sense of just replacing substantive, material decision-making by procedure in the legal sense, but by drawing our attention to the cognitive conditions of decision-making which have to be generated in the decision-making process itself, and which, indeed, can no longer be presupposed, as was the case under the conditions of 'substantive rationality' in the sense of H.A. Simon. This could imply a shift from substantive rules to procedural meta-rules which would have their focus more on the modelling of reality, the monitoring of the implementation of norms, the evaluation of the consequences of the implementation of a certain decision, etc.[31]

The link with the traditional social epistemology of liberalism could consist in the requirement of structure and the exclusion of responsibility for far-reaching indirect consequences of action. At transnational level, this could imply a principle of competition of institutions. Public governance could then consist in both new approaches to, and management of, complexity which, from the outset, would have to be reflected by decision-making strategies, and should only allow for public strategies which reflect uncertainty in their own design. This conception draws on the assumption that the construction of institutions is responsive to an infrastructure of societal knowledge, forms practices, expectations, management and decision-making, which underlies a trans-subjective process of transformation which is beyond the reach of both private and public actors in spite of being an intended consequence of individual decisions.

XII. The Rise of a New 'Relational Rationality' *vis-à-vis* Hierarchical Institutions

On the background of the assumptions that have been sketched in this introduction, the widespread complaint about the 'democratic deficit' of both the EC and global institutions such as the WTO, the IMF and the World Bank appears to be problematic. It is due to a superficial analogy to state institutions whose rationality cannot be immediately transposed to the complex networks of transnational inter-relationships. The latter cannot just be dissolved into individual acts which, in some way, might be controlled by rules in the traditional sense. The networks generate their own 'relational rationality' based on overlapping situations, and the creation of expectations and constraints which do not follow traditional models based on a clear separation of general knowledge, experience and habits, but which have to refer to

---

31   Cf. Adrienne Héritier, *Composite Democratic Legitimation in Europe: The Role of Transparency and Access to Information*, Max-Planck-Project Group Preprint 2001/6.

an element of design, of producing possibilities and opening up new domains of options (high technology).[32]

Instead of referring to a stable idea of reality and normality, 'public governance' does not presuppose the traditional clear-cut separations between private and public, the universal and the specific, general (norm) and concrete (decision). As mentioned above, this does not lead to the delegation of public power to private actors, the element of 'public' responsibility and accountability is not given up. However, its contours cannot be presupposed any longer; they have to be reconstructed both at national and at international level. And the search process, which has been invoked here several times, should not be so irritating if one bears in mind that the conception of the liberal democratic state has not been developed without a long trial and error process either. In this respect, the new logic of 'public governance' beyond the state follows the classical liberal example. It searches for a new multi-polar (not a multi-level) public order which is not separate from private ordering (producing patterns of inter-relationships)[33] and not just decisions which do not have further impact on the normative order as such. Public governance is to be distinguished from private governance in as much as it focuses, above all systematically, on external effects produced as the unintended consequences of private actions, though not, primarily, taking responsibility in compensation for privately produced detrimental effects. Instead, it tries to stimulate more responsive strategies by private networks of interactions bringing in incentives to develop long-term horizons of decision-making.[34] In this respect, it exercises indirect influence although it does not directly intend to change societal networks. In this respect, it follows the example of classical liberal states, which also developed indirect norm-based responsibility, but tried to avoid broadening the domain of state responsibility because of fear of producing perverse effects in blocking private initiative. This openness again follows the classical liberal example, which does not define public tasks in a positive way, but, in its 'negative' focus on imposing limits to private action, presupposes the creativity of the self-organizing potential of liberal society.

The contributions to this volume clearly do not follow all the same track of analysis, but, as the reader will be able to observe, they have a common interest focusing on the necessity to develop a new logic of experimenting with new forms of public governance at global level. This is an intellectual strategy which tries to avoid a mere positivistic registration of 'what happens' in reality and with a blind

---

32   For new problems of complexity in antitrust regulation in the new economy cf. Gary Minda, *Antitrust Regulability and the New Digital Economy. A Proposal for Integrating 'Hard' and 'Soft' Regulation*, THE ANTITRUST BULLETIN XLVI/3 (2001), p.439, 458.

33   Cf. Christine Chinkin, *A Critique of the Public/Private Dimension*, 10 EJIL (1999), 387-395; Alfred A. Aman Jr., *The Globalizing State: A Future-Oriented Perspective on the Public/Private Distinction, Federalism and Democracy*, 31 VANDERBILT JOURNAL OF TRANSNATIONAL LAW 1998, 769, 802.

34   Cf. Meyer, *supra* n. 4.

attempt to adapt institutions to reality, and an abstract lament blaming multi-nationals for their strategies of destroying the nation state as the bearer of democracy. This is why the polarization of a 'moral point of view that accepts cleavages and exclusion', the 'neo-liberal approach', on the one hand, and the creation of a 'public sphere' for the mutual exchange of claims for 'recognition',[35] on the other hand, cannot do justice to a complex self-transformation of all public and private institutions.

XIII. Overview of the Contributions

Thomas Vesting takes the view that Niklas Luhmann's systems theory, which regards societies as composed of communications and not of individuals, might be helpful in understanding the emergence of new legal forms for transnational economic transactions. According to this theory, the legal system has to strengthen its own rationale as an autonomous system. This idea can be productive as a starting point for the observation of the phenomenon of overlapping networks of legal inter-relationships which call into question the 'spatial' basis of the traditional state-related legal system which invokes the autonomy of the sovereign will power of the state, but also fit well into the open logic of a legal system which is regarded as being composed of communicative and flexible inter-relationships developing freely beyond the borders of the state.

Saskia Sassen ventures the idea that states are not the only or the most powerful strategic actors in the new transnational order, and, in addition, that states have undergone a process of denationalization which consists in the expansion of their influence beyond their territory. This might be regarded as a countervailing element with regard to the decreasing weight of the exclusivity of sovereignty. In the same vein, the state can be seen as 'incorporating the global project' in its own action potential. This opening up of the state is a reaction to the decreasing role of borders in the global economy.

Lawrence Friedman demonstrates to what extent the globalization of law has found its repercussion also in 'local' laws, i.e. family law, in particular. This is due to the fact that the intertwining of legal systems takes place not only at global level but also within the 'nation state'.

Karl-Heinz Ladeur's chapter focuses on the problem of the 'democratic deficit' in the EC and in global institutions. He takes the view that, first of all, both at national and at transnational level, the autonomy of the legal system and its new 'relational rationality', which replaces top-down conceptions and practices of law, have to be taken seriously. Starting from this assumption, the democratic potential of the intertwining of the political and the legal system can, to a large extent, be

---

35   Cf. Habermas, *supra* n. 28, pp. 5-26.

mobilized also at global level if one avoids the overestimation of democratic legitimation processes in democratic societies. Apart from this, NGOs might play a major role in the creation of transparency of spontaneous and institutionalized processes.

Jean-Jacques Rosa warns us not to believe in the rationality of anything such as the 'world state'. He stresses the necessity to establish a competitive order among states in order to constrain them to fulfil a productive function in the sense of producing more flexibility within the EC system. He develops a conception of the optimal size of a state which should not be trespassed.

Pedro Teixeira tries to build a bridge between a legal theory of a procedural legal order which draws on both the evolutionary potential of rules and his practical experience as a member of the staff of the European Central Bank in the field of the regulation of financial markets. He stresses the link between public norms and private institutions which are set up for the search of 'best practices'.

Joel Trachtman explains the discontinuity between the domain of WTO dispute resolution and the body of general public international law. He tries to develop a conception for the relationship between judges and legislators at international level.

Martin van Creveld has a look at the origin of the state in the 'Westphalian System' and emphasizes that this is only an intermediate step in a much longer ambivalent story. Globalization has transformed war into a phenomenon, which is regarded as legitimate more or less exclusively for the UN and the Security Council in particular. In a way, this means that the process which ended in the 'Westphalian System' is being reversed. The most recent evolution (the war in Afghanistan) highlights another aspect of this evolution: namely, that more and more 'public-private partnerships' in wars are coming to the fore, a phenomenon which transforms war far beyond the limits which were hitherto set by the partisan war.

Gunther Teubner emphasizes in his chapter the requirements of global society's 'self-created laws' as being based on the self-organized response to needs for stability of expectations and solution of conflicts. The idea of this chapter consists in the assumption of a 'multiplicity of sub-constitutions – linkages of global law to other global sub-systems' that have escaped from 'constitutional governance dominated by politics'. The dominant sources of law are now to be found at the 'periphery of law', which compete with the traditional 'centres of law-making', such as parliaments, etc. This assumption may shed new light on the relationship of law and politics (whose centre is the nation state). This is again a thesis which is opposed to the description of globalization as a process of mere economic 'imperialism' with respect to other legal systems including the legal system. The constitutional requirements, which are far from being made superfluous by the process of autonomization of global law, might then be transferred to the requirement of guarantees for the institutionalization of social autonomous sectors. Within the 'law beyond the state', new potentials for the re-politicization, re-regulation and re-institutionalization of norm-making processes would be expected to emerge. This hypothesis also draws on the mobilization of a heterarchical 'relational rationality' emerging from the autonomization of legal systems – so to speak bottom-up – and not being derived from a higher level in the hierarchy (of a new type of international order).

Charles Sabel and Joshua Cohen's chapter design the challenge of promoting deliberative democracy as a principle for the formation of a political consensus at European level. They develop the idea of a 'deliberative polyarchy' which focuses on the possibility of accepting autonomy for experiments with trial and error processes carried out within broadly defined areas of public policy. This means that, again, search processes are attributed a (procedural) rationality beyond derivative processes of legitimation which might lead towards an 'emergent form of democracy' linked to an experimental logic. Such logic would respond to the increased 'disembeddedness' with reference to hierarchical conceptions of democracy. It would draw on interdependence between private actors which generates a 'web of connections' creating a spillover effect of constructing a new pool of capabilities.

Anne-Marie Slaughter has developed the concept of the 'disaggregate state' in the sense that more and more agencies are deploying a co-operative approach to decision-making within the nation state, which is based on different versions of common inquiry, imposition of 'giving-reasons requirements' also *vis-à-vis* their peer agencies in other democratic states. The EC is in the process of developing this kind of transnational co-operation which can no longer use the traditional bottleneck of international co-operation with governments as the intermediaries. Her chapter raises the problem of holding such a co-operative network of agencies accountable. She demonstrates that different ways of opening up the veil of the state via mutual recognition of administrative acts, committee deliberation and 'positive conflict' allow countries to take the lead in the process of inaugurating new institutions.

Mark Van Hoecke draws our attention to the intertwining of legal systems and its theoretical consequences. In the past, we have known the 'collision rules' of international private law which, in fact, organize the mutual exclusivity of legal systems based on the legitimacy of the nation state, in spite of the fact that private persons may have a strong influence on the 'choice of law'. However, the rise of transnational legal and governmental networks – private and public – makes visible the reluctance to accept overlapping relationships of legal systems. In some way, states have to manage the unavoidable overlap of legal norms that stem from different legal origins. On the other hand, and as a consequence, this effect has to be re-introduced in the processes of decision-making and law-making. New types of horizontal linkages are necessary in order to allow for the emergence of a venture of mutual learning and adaptation.

PART I

TOWARDS A GENERAL THEORY OF GLOBALIZATION

Chapter 2

Frontiers: National and Transnational Order

Lawrence M. Friedman[*]

The letter inviting us to this conference begins by repeating an accusation that is often levelled against globalization. Globalization, it is said, is a process that 'undermines the hitherto established model of the nation state and the welfare state in particular'.

I would like to address this issue, at least obliquely, although I will not say very much about the welfare state. I think the issue is real enough; something new and important is going on in the contemporary world – processes and events that have significance for the legal order as well.

Before going any further, I have to ask, exactly what do we mean by globalization? Of course, there is and can be no hard and fast definition of the word. People use it to mean different things. And it means different things to different people. But the core meaning of the term refers to a change in *scale* and in *site*. When people talk about globalization, they are usually thinking of processes and events and movements that spill over and cross national borders. The term refers to movement, diffusion, expansion, from a local level and with local implications, to levels and implications that are worldwide, or at least region-wide. Exactly what is expanding and diffusing is something I want to deal with in this chapter. When people talk about globalization they also seem to assume that what is happening is either inevitable or unavoidable – at least for you and me. Globalization therefore means that no man, woman, or nation is an island, to misquote John Donne. As a result of the process of diffusion, everything seems to be connected with everything else. There are no longer any hermit kingdoms. There are no longer any desert islands. Tuvalu has now became a member of the United Nations, and will presumably send somebody to New York to represent that tiny island country. There are hardly any hermits of any sort, on any level, in this world of the 21st century.

Globalization, whatever else it may mean, is about movement – of images, goods, and ideas – across state borders; and, for that matter, across oceans and mountain barriers as well. Of course, there have always been trade relations between

*   Marion Rice Kirkwood, Professor of Law, Stanford University.

countries; spices and trinkets and gold and shells and pottery and implements of all sorts, even in the ancient world; Phoenician and Greek traders, and Lombard merchants, and Arab dealers in slaves and ivory. But the sheer scale is new, and also the share of the total world economy that is devoted to transnational trade. Similarly, people have always been on the move, and ideas, images, religions, cultures and diseases have always travelled across borders. Modern history, however, has been a process of opening up – of combining and recombining and making the world into one. There was, for example, the 'discovery' of the New World, which of course was not a discovery at all, but the meeting of two worlds, which had once been far apart. Then came the exploration (and conquest) of Africa, and the islands of the Pacific; and the opening of China and Korea and Japan to outside influences.

The modern diffusion of people and concepts is, as we shall see, a consequence of this opening up; and it is rather different from the older forms of *Völkerwanderung*. For one thing, it is far more *individual*; it is not a migration of peoples – not the Goths or the Tartars sweeping across great areas; or the crossing of the Bering Sea by the ancestors of the American tribes, slowly diffusing all the way down to Patagonia. It is not the movement of peoples but of people.[1] Millions of those who, in the 19th century, flocked to countries like the United States or Argentina, or, more recently, to Germany or France, have migrated as solitary movers, or in tiny family groups. In the 19th century, this was the case of the so-called 'immigration countries'; today, all the rich and developed country are targets of individual decisions of this sort. I will return to this theme.

What makes modern diffusion possible is the miraculous advance of technologies of movement and communication. These technologies are instruments or tools that make globalization possible. Without radio, TV, satellites, without cars, trains, and planes, nobody would be talking about globalization at all. The Internet is now adding yet another dimension to globalization. It is possible to send a message around the world in nano-seconds. It takes a lot longer than a nano-second to move physically from one country to another; but still, the time is drastically shorter than it was not very long ago. Jules Verne wrote 'Around the World in Eighty Days' in 1873; and this was almost science fiction; but any fool today can go around the world, if necessary, in one day or less. The satellites that spread news and entertainment do it in fact much quicker.

Globalization is about diffusion; but ideas and movements can diffuse even if people do not go anywhere at all; if they stay exactly where they are, and never get up from their couches and chairs. Globalization, as we will argue, is essentially a cultural phenomenon. Culture, however, does not require travel; it can be beamed directly into the human brain, so to speak. This is what happens to societies, when they acquire those modern miracles of radio, movies and TV. TV, in particular, has

---

1   To be sure, there are many examples of *mass* migrations still – particularly of the helpless and hapless refugees in places like Kosovo or in central Africa.

had and still has an immense cultural influence. It transports scenes, images, ideas – in short, the grammar and syntax of culture – at great speed across great distances. It insinuates itself into millions or even billions of homes. Movies and radio have had a similar impact, though probably on a smaller scale. Now, the Internet promises to make an even greater difference in the future; it has the potential to connect everybody with everybody else in the developed world; and it is already a storehouse of billions and billions of bits of information. It may be too early for us to grasp the significance of the Internet, or to know what this will mean in the long run to the global community. The potential impact is surely immense. It is already hard to remember what the world was like before e-mail. The world with e-mail is a world in which people can and do send messages to each other across every border, with an ease and a speed that 'snail mail' or the telephone could never achieve.

Suppose we ask *what* is it that the globalising process is globalizing – exactly what is it that gets shipped across borders? The most obvious answer is trade; globalization is economic; it is international business, international transactions, international buying and selling and deal-making. It is tankers of oil from Saudi Arabia and container ships of toys and television sets from Taiwan, shoes and blouses from Indonesia, wheat and walnuts from the United States. A second answer is that what has globalised is human capital – people, in other words, to use a less cold and unfriendly term. Human beings themselves have become global; they move rapidly in and out of their countries and across the world – ordinary people, business people, jet setters, tourists, refugees, in-migrants and out-migrants.

Both of these – trade and human capital – are at the core of globalization. But both in turn depend on the rise of something truly primary and basic: globalization is about *messages*; it is about ideas; it is about global *culture*. From this, everything else follows. That is, ideas, images, patterns of behaviour, thought processes that are, to an extent at least, shared all over the world – certainly all over the developed world, and, more and more, elsewhere as well. What emerges is a new and global culture. What is the nature of this culture? In the first place, it seems to hail primarily from the developed countries – it spreads from 'the West' to the east and the south. Bertrand defines globalization ('mondialisation') as 'the invasive influence of cultural, political, and economic models, which are born in the countries of the first world... and are progressively imposed on a great many other countries'.[2] There has been, of course, some traffic in the other direction – African art, Asian religions, foods from everywhere (think of the spread of sushi or pad thai); but the *cultural* aspects of globalization, in their actual origins, do have a heavy Western character.

Television is one of the obvious carriers of the global culture. It transmits its images all over the world, subtly and invisibly, and it seems to have a devastating

2   Marie-Andree Bernard, 'Le Droit Comme Instrument de Mondialisation', in Johannes Feest (ed.), *Globalization and Legal Cultures* (Onati Papers, n. 7, 1999), pp. 113-114.

effect on all the rival cultures that it touches. The television programmes that embody global culture, and which are beamed everywhere, are mostly entertainment programmes, comedies, game shows, talk shows, police and detective dramas, sports events, and the like, interrupted (at pretty frequent intervals) by commercials. Television also devotes a lot of time and attention to 'news', but it is getting less and less easy to tell the difference between news and entertainment. The popular programmes come in all shapes and sizes, but underlying them is a definite message– one might even call it an ideology. In truth, this underlying message is not much different from the message of the commercials. It is a message of consumerism, of individualism, of leisure and the ways to enjoy leisure. Television, generally speaking, describes a world of fun, thrill, mystery, adventure; it is a world of celebrities, of the rich and famous; or at least a world of the young and beautiful, of people who live exciting lives, sometimes tragic, but rarely humdrum, and rarely reflecting the grinding, daily struggle of most people on earth. Since most of these programmes come from the wealthy countries of the West, they show Western styles, dress and manners. There are, of course, popular programmes from other parts of the world – say, soap operas from Latin America – but they are not very different in kind from the programmes that come from the United States. My impression is that the rich crop of local programmes in such countries as India or Egypt share at least some themes and aspects with programming in the West. In any event, local or native programmes must compete with seductive rivals from the West.

Television is enormously popular and ubiquitous; there are some remote and underdeveloped places where television rarely penetrates, but this is perhaps the very definition of remote and underdeveloped. Some television programmes are amazingly popular almost everywhere. Apparently, the single most watched program, at one time at least, was Bay Watch – one of America's gifts to the world. The program featured some very good-looking young people, who ran around in bathing suits on a beautiful beach. There was a plot of sorts, but this hardly accounts for the program's popularity. The show had an obvious, though rather mild, appeal to human lust. Beyond this, it revealed or reflected an imaginary world of fun, leisure, sunshine, punctuated from time to time with some more or less serious problem that got resolved by the end of the programme. But the primary image was of slimness, youth, beauty, free time, fun, and a healthy dash of sex.

These TV images have tremendous power. According to an article in the newspaper, girls in Fiji – where once upon a time fat was considered beautiful – have now morphed into bulimics, because of the images they see on foreign television programmes (where fat is definitely *not* beautiful).[3] It would be impossible to tell how many people dye their hair, change their style of dress, do

3   Erica Goode, 'Study Finds TV Trims Fiji Girls' Body Image and Eating Habits', *New York Times*, National edition (20 May 1999), p. A13.

workouts at a gym, or take up some new habit, because of these images. The programmes arouse, all over the world, a culture of envy and desire.

Movies are another key medium of popular culture. Movies are also an American success story; in much of the world, the films that make the most money and attract the biggest audiences are American. In country after country, American movies have almost driven the local product to extinction. Americans seem to be the world masters at seductive cinematic junk. Germans, Finns, Japanese, Guatemalans, all swarm into theatres to see the latest Clint Eastwood or Bruce Willis movie. The top grossing film in Argentina in 1991 was *Terminator 2*; in Egypt it was *Dances with Wolves*; in Sweden, it was *Pretty Woman*.[4] A few years later it was reported that the United States 'commands a staggering 85 per cent of the world's film market, and 90 per cent of the European film market'; 88 of the top 100 movies in 1993 were American.[5] There have been attempts at national protectionism, of the cultural sort – in Canada, for example, and in the European Union. Some countries – the French very notably – make more or less serious attempts to protect their culture from the invasion of what they call the Anglo-Saxons.[6] But this is an age of satellites and the Internet, so that it is getting harder and harder to protect these cultural borders – harder than the physical borders.[7] And the underlying problem, of course, is that French audiences *like* American movies, American music, American TV. It is not entirely clear why this should be the case; but perhaps the Americans are simply very good at this job.[8] American entertainment companies have a magic touch, a wonderful way of sensing what sorts of cultural junk-food people enjoy, just as the French seem to have a better grasp of *haute cuisine* and perfume, and the Italians turn out what people consider the world's most beautiful shoes.

---

4 Benjamin R. Barber, *Jihad v. McWorld* (1995), pp. 299-300.

5 Judith Beth Prowda, 'United States Dominance in the "Marketplace of Culture" and the French "Cultural Exception"', New York U. J. Int'l Law and Politics 29:193, 200 (1996).

6 Ibid, n. 3.

7 Lawrence M. Friedman, *The Horizontal Society* (New Haven, Conn.: Yale University Press, 1999), p. 51.

8 There may be other reasons for this dominance. A French report to the Council of Europe in 1986 claimed that American visual productions can gain easy access to the European market 'as they have already made a profit on the American market. They can thus be offered very cheaply for distribution in Europe'. An hour of 'fiction' bought from abroad costs far less, then, than a French production.

There may be something to this, but the question is: why doesn't it also work the other way? After all, a French production could be 'dumped' in America, after making money in France. Indeed, the French report admitted that American productions were 'universalistic' and 'accessible to a maximum audience'. Council of Europe, *European Ministerial Conference on Mass Media Policy* (Vienna, 1986), pp. 35-36.

In short, there are no longer any real barriers to the diffusion of culture (in all senses of this word). The only real obstacle is language, which is unimportant in music, and is only a slight hindrance with regard to TV and the movies, since they can always be dubbed or provided with subtitles (in many movies, the dialogue is almost irrelevant, anyway, compared to the 'action' and the 'special effects'). It is not easy to measure the impact of this invasion of images on the culture of various societies. One suspects the impact is enormous.

Science and technology have transformed the world in even more basic ways. They have revolutionized the making and selling and transporting of goods, and this has been in turn the engine for the creation of enormous wealth in the developed world. To be sure, the distribution in many countries is highly unequal – a rich elite on top of a mass of relatively poor people; and disparities *between* countries are even more extreme. Millions of people, even billions, live in poverty and misery; these people have no access to the Internet, to jet travel, or even to television; their daily lives are a struggle for a piece of bread or a bowl of rice, and a roof to shelter them from the rain and the wind. But in the developed countries of Europe and North America, in Australia, in Japan, Korea, Hong Kong and Singapore, and in Israel, there is a huge middle class; other countries, though perhaps less well off in general, also have a growing middle class – imagine the size of the middle class in India, where even ten per cent of the population adds up to an awful lot of people. Thus enormous numbers of people do have a certain measure of affluence and leisure – they no longer live on the razor's edge of subsistence. They have a bit of extra money jingling in their pockets; and what is even more important, they have some extra time, after work, on Sunday, on holidays, during vacations, in which to spend that money. Their time and their leisure makes them into massive consumers; they do in fact buy goods of all sorts, and millions of them also have an insatiable appetite for sports, entertainment, hobbies; they are, in short, active consumers of fun.

Fun is, of course, a commodity; movies and CDs are just as much a commercial product as pig iron or automobiles or bananas. The emphasis on entertainment strengthens the point that globalization is, among other things, an economic development. What is crucially different from the past is the sheer scale of international trade. All national economies today are interlocked; many small countries have economies that are completely dependent on international trade; and no country is so large, and has such a huge domestic market, that it can ignore the flow of international trade. Different countries buy and sell different products – oil flows from Saudi Arabia to countries that have no oil of their own; some countries mine coal or copper or cut down trees, and ship raw materials to countries that process them; some countries specialize in making computers or computer chips, others in shoes and shirts and sealing wax. Whatever the product or products, the fact of international trade takes on more and more importance.

Today's trade is unlike trade in the days when the West exploited its colonies, and bought silk and spices from the East. One difference is the development of multi-national corporations, companies that are everywhere and nowhere; another, related phenomenon is the 'geographic dispersal of firms' factories, offices, service outlets, and markets and 'the global assembly line in manufacturing'. In the early 1990s, American firms had more than 18,000 'affiliates overseas'; and German firms 'had even more'.[9] An official of Coca-Cola, speaking at Stanford Law School, claimed (somewhat pompously) that Coca-Cola was not really an American company. It was, he said, an international company. And indeed it operates in more than 100 countries.

But what makes international trade today so different from past international trade is again a cultural factor: the commonality of commodities and desires. There is a worldwide hunger for American blue jeans, or for Nike shoes, or for slices of pizza. If Coca-Cola is sold everywhere, it is because there are people in Albania and Honduras and Mauritius who like the taste and want to buy it. In the 'global marketplace', the Japanese 'eat poultry fattened in Thailand with American corn'; consumers 'on both sides of the Atlantic wear clothes assembled in Saipan with Chinese labour, drink orange juice from concentrate made with Brazilian oranges, and decorate their homes with flowers from Colombia'.[10] The surface point of the quote is about the globalization of production; but implicit is the globalization of consumption: the idea that consumers *want* the same things, or much the same things, everywhere in the world.

Of course, this is not strictly true; countries do differ in their syndromes of consumer desire. There are goods that sell like hot cakes in one country, and die on the market in another. Still, compared to any past era, the similarities are much more striking than the differences. Influences and fashions flow on the whole from West to East, but not exclusively. You can eat sushi in Berlin or Miami as well as in Tokyo. It strikes Americans as weird to see a Pizza Hut in Beijing, but pizza is not American, it is Italian. And it is not really Italian, it is Neapolitan, and probably originally as exotic in Milan as it is in Bangkok. Blue jeans are an American gift to the world, but they were originally designed for gold miners in California. The fact that they appeared eventually in New York as a fashion statement is as much an example of cultural diffusion as is the fact that blue jeans have also invaded Moscow or Jakarta. It is the hunger for the *same* sorts of goods that fuels modern international trade; this hunger creates the converging culture of the global village – indeed it *is* that culture.

9   Saskia Sassen, *Losing Control? Sovereignty in an Age of Globalization* (New York: Columbia University Press, 1996), pp. 7, 9-10.

10   Philip McMichael, *Development and Social Change: A Global Perspective* (Thousand Oaks: Pine Forge P., 1996), p. 1.

No modern phenomenon, perhaps, is as important as this one – that is, the globalization of patterns of consumption. Since so many of the products, ideas, images and patterns are definitely American, it is tempting to talk about American imperialism or cultural hegemony. But this is somewhat misleading. 'Americanization' turns out to be fairly selective. Many aspects of American culture do not travel well at all. Coca-Cola has swept the world; but nobody drinks root beer, an old, established American drink, outside of the United States of America. The same point can be made about other Western countries. Italian food is popular in dozens of countries where nobody would dream of going to a German restaurant. It happens that the United States, for whatever reason, is very good at satisfying the hungers and tastes of masses of people who inhabit the middle class. Perhaps this is no accident. America was the first middle class society – the first society in which broad masses of people (with glaring exceptions, of course), owned a piece of land, had a bit of money, the right to vote, and in other ways *mattered* in society. America might be able to draw on long experience in understanding what middle class masses want; it is expert in catering to these tastes and desires.

'America', to be sure, has become more than a place; it has become a symbol of much of what is alluring about modern life; American products and fashions may thus come to stand for America itself, and for the good life in general. In many ways, American culture has elements that are unusually attractive to the emerging middle classes of other countries. America is (formally, at least) classless; it is full of rich people, to be sure, and millions try to copy, as best they can, the lifestyle of the rich and famous. Yet that life-style itself borrows from the lifestyle of the poor and obscure. Blue jeans, for example, are both chic and classless at the same time. The music and dress habits of the urban ghettos filter up into the most unlikely places. And the very image of the rich is, in a sense, torn free from the moorings of class. The most obvious of the rich are rock stars, movie stars and sports heroes; in the world of business and finance, the most obvious of the rich are either young or self-made (like Microsoft's Bill Gates). This lends to wealth the glitter of the ordinary. Becoming rich seems, in a way, like winning the lottery; and the lottery itself is a symbol of real but accidental wealth and all that wealth brings with it.

What the sources and impulses, the global culture of consumption is a fact: the common property of every middle class. It is a powerful instrument of convergence. Of course, it is a much-debated question whether the global culture is anything more than skin-deep. Take, for example, the case of Japan. The Japanese have cars, computers, skyscrapers, air conditioners and antibiotics; they dress in the 'Western' style; and hordes of young Japanese in Tokyo chomp down hamburgers from McDonald's. Arguably, then the Japanese middle class is much the same as the Swedish or Australian middle class. But is this the case? Some argue that 'Westernisation' is a veneer, a gloss – underneath the Western clothing is a Japanese core, a Japanese heart and soul, that is and remains fundamentally constant, fundamentally different from the heart and soul of the West.

Which of these views is correct? There is no yes or no; the question is, in part, an empirical one (though a very difficult question); in part it is a matter of subjective interpretation. Human beings are essentially the same as chimpanzees from one viewpoint – the DNA of these two species is *almost* (but not entirely) identical. If we compare people *and* chimpanzees to an earthworm, or a clam, or a pine tree, the resemblance of man and ape seems positively overwhelming. But the differences between people and chimpanzees, I hardly need say, are also extremely significant. The differences between the Japanese middle class and the Finnish middle class are also significant– though they are also, in my view, rather small.

My own opinion – and it is only a guess – is that culture is more fluid and malleable than most people think. If you dress modern, eat modern, use modern tools, then you *become* modern. Your thought processes are, inevitably, altered.[11] Nobody would say Japan in the late 20th century has become exactly like France in the late 20th century. Anybody who spends even a day in either place is bound to be struck by what seem to be crucial differences in habits, manners, even the looks of the place. But the question is: is the Japan of today more like the France of today, than it is like old, feudal Japan, the Japan of Lady Murasaki or the Kyoto court? The answer, I think, is yes. And the France of today, in turn, is more like the Japan of today than it is like the France of Charles Martel or Jacques Villon.

I.   Globalization of Law

If there is a globalized world, if business and trade are globalized, and if there is a globalized culture of production and consumption, then it follows that there must also be a globalized sector of law. In the modern world, or at least in the developed world, legal systems have increased in scale and scope in recent decades. The legal order has become, more than ever, dense, ubiquitous and pervasive.[12] What, then, can we say about the impact of globalization on the legal order? What can we say about the transnational sector of the legal world? If there is a global legal order, what does it consist of?

There is so much talk about globalization (including the globalization of law) that we have to be careful to avoid exaggeration. Most lawyers remain firmly rooted in their own legal habits and traditions, even if they work for transnational corporations. They deal mostly with the local problems and concerns of these corporations, and they live in a world of local, domestic, legal culture. This is true as well of the thousands of lawyers who spend their days working on small real estate

---

11   See Alex Inkeles, *Exploring Individual Modernity* (New York: Columbia University Press, 1983); Alex Inkeles and David H. Smith, *Becoming Modern: Individual Change in Six Developing Countries* (London: Heinemann, 1974).

12   Lawrence M. Friedman, 'Is There a Modern Legal Culture?' Ratio Juris 7:117 (1994).

deals, drawing up wills, helping couples get a divorce, defending criminals, coping with contract disputes between small and medium companies, arguments over driveways and boundaries, tax audits, land-use planning, and similar issues. In some ways, then, the legal world may be one of the more primitive sectors of modern life – a sector much less globalized than business, the economy and the culture in general.

Of course, there *is* an international legal sector; there *are* lawyers with international practices, and it seems pretty obvious that this part of the legal domain is growing rapidly. One symptom is the rise of the transnational law firm. Many large American firms have one, two, or even many branches overseas. In 1995, the Wall Street law firm of Sullivan and Cromwell, a famous old firm, besides branches in other American cities, had offices in London, Paris, Hong Kong, Melbourne, Tokyo and Frankfurt. Other large American firms also broadened their practice in this way; and law firms in other countries have more and more internationalized as well. A leading firm of solicitors in London has European branches from Brussels to Moscow as well as offices in Singapore, Bangkok, Hanoi and Beijing. A Hamburg firm has offices in Bratislava, Budapest, New York, Hong Kong and other places; and an Italian firm adds Dubai and Tirana to the list.[13] The leading law firm in Taipei, I have been told, does half of its legal business in the English language.

In a way, then, the legal world has a form of diglossia – a fancy word borrowed from linguistics. The term refers to a 'situation where two very different varieties of a language co-occur throughout a speech community'. These two varieties are usually divided into a 'high' and a 'low' version. People use the low version at home and on the street; it is also used in popular literature and soap operas; the high version is found in speeches, newspaper articles, and in formal literature.[14] Diglossia is common in many language areas; and a mild form of it is almost universal among languages that have a written as well as a spoken form. In the legal world, there is a kind of internationalized law, or globalized law, which exists side by side of, or on top of, the national or local sector. It may well represent a minority – even a small minority – of the total work that lawyers do in any particular country. But it is a significant, and growing, sector.

And it is a sector that has not been, as yet, studied at all adequately. There are, so far, serious gaps in the literature. What there is runs heavily to doctrine, expositions of the texts of various treaties and the like, manifestos, general essays (this one included), without much in the way of serious rigorous, empirical research of the actual work that the lawyers do in the global sector. There are dozens of articles and treatises on 'private international law' (conflict of laws). But the sociology of transnational law lags seriously behind.

---

13   Source: Martindale-Hubbel's International Law Directory, Vol. 1, 1998.
14   David Crystal, *An Encyclopedic Dictionary of Language and Languages* (Oxford: Blackwell, 1992), p. 104.

One point is clear: to the extent that there is a globalized legal order, it generates (of necessity) a kind of *lingua franca*. The *formal lingua franca* is (increasingly) English. A huge proportion of the world's international business is conducted in English. There is probably also another, more subtle, but even more important inner *lingua franca*: a commonality of habits of thought and practices, including legal practices, that develops among the players in the game of international lawyering and international deal-making.

It is worth imagining the situation of one of the world's many small nations – Slovenia, for example. In today's world, the Slovenians may dress internationally, and eat international food, they may be eager to join NATO, the European Union, the United States, and any international organization they can get their hands on; but they still speak Slovenian, at least at home, and they treasure their linguistic heritage. There are less than two million Slovenians. As they enter the world of international trade, or try to, they cannot expect to find dealmakers from abroad who are comfortable speaking Slovenian. Business cannot be conducted through grunts or sign language. It is possible to do business through interpreters, and this is certainly done often enough; but it is a clumsy business at best.[15] As a matter of sheer necessity, the parties to a deal will have to fall back on the *lingua franca*. The major candidate, it turns out, is English, for historical reasons. Regionally, there are rivals – Slovenians will certainly need to know German, because of their geography; and they might well find Russian or French quite useful. But English is more and more the international standard; and it seems likely that it will dominate in transnational lawyering, for a long time to come. In a prominent law firm in Warsaw, Poland, for example, of 29 lawyers, 26 claimed fluency in English. This was the claim, too, of virtually all of the 150 lawyers in the largest law firm in Korea.[16] The use of English as a super-language is, naturally, a wonderful gift to those of us who learned it as our mother tongue; and a problem for almost everybody else. But there is, basically, no other way. The dominance of English may also mean that American ways of writing contracts and thinking about law are likely to have more influence than they otherwise would. In some fields of law, American institutions have been powerful models.[17] Perhaps (as in the case of Coca-Cola), what we have here is not really an instance of American power, or American economic and political imperialism, but simply the fact that Americans, for

---

15 For small languages, it is not even practical to use interpreters. A Slovenian business that wants to deal with a company from Thailand is not likely to find somebody who can shuttle between these two particular languages with ease. Almost certainly both parties will do their business with each other in English.

16 The source of this information is Martindale-Hubbell's International Law Directory (Vol 1, 1988).

17 See Wolfgang Wiegand, 'Reception of American Law in Europe', AM. J. COMPARATIVE LAW 39:229 (1991).

whatever reasons, were ahead of the game in developing institutions and ways of behaving that seem to fit modern legal needs. There are, however, complaints about American legalism, about a certain fussiness and over attention to legal detail. In any event, it is obviously quite valuable, in raw money terms, to win the game of international business; hence I do not want to rule out the role of power and coercion in tactics and strategies.

II.   Substance and Style

What does the globalized sector of the legal order consist of? There is, to begin with, a body of hard law: that is, treaties, conventions, GATT and GATT-like arrangements, regional pacts like NAFTA and Mercosur, and the European Union. Some of these are truly international; others are confined to some region of the world; but they all, at any rate, are intended to have impact across national borders. Some of this 'hard law' has also generated the beginnings of what we might call hard institutions – organizations that have the right or the duty to enforce the norms and conventions; the European Union has a number of such institutions.

Then there may be what we might call a body of soft law – international customs, practices and behaviours. There is some dispute about this rather elusive body of norms. Some scholars have described it as a kind of *lex mercatoria*. The original *lex mercatoria* grew out of the custom of merchants, especially the Lombard merchants, who formed a kind of transnational business class in the Middle Ages. Many rules and practices of banking and commercial law can be traced back to this *lex mercatoria*. The idea is that today's transnational lawyers have their own customs, norms and patterns of behaviour, so that a new law merchant is emerging, without benefit of legislation, or any recognition of any sort.

Very likely there is less here than meets the eye. There are, to be sure, transnational customs and practices. Some aspects of international business law have been formalized – standard contract forms, provided by international trade groups, and such devices as the INCOTERMS, which the International Chamber of Commerce puts out. These 'contractual provisions with legal or quasi-legal (customary) character' are supplemented by 'codes of conduct with more or less sanctioning power', which are part of the international 'normative order'. All this is supposed to constitute, in Gessner's words, 'autonomous norm creation within the international economy'.[18] But in the end all such customs and practices cannot exist in the air, so to speak; they have to be validated somehow by national courts applying what they consider to be national law; or, at any rate, applying some body of law that the parties to a contract may have stipulated.

18   Volkmar Gessner, 'Global Legal Interaction and Legal Cultures', RATIO JURIS 7:132, 137-138 (1994).

Those who have written about the *lex mercatoria* associate it, in particular, with the growing field of international arbitration.[19] A recent and significant study by Dezalay and Garth has described this area of legal concentration.[20] The world of commercial arbitration is 'global' in the sense that it is not closely tied to any particular system of local law. It comes into play when two parties to a contract or deal agree in advance that they will take any problems or disagreements to arbitration. This way, they avoid the courts (of every country), at least initially; they avoid whatever peculiarities there might be in this or that local legal system; and they turn their problems over to a group of skilled and prestigious international practitioners. Most of these arbitrators are lawyers. But the solutions they reach are at times not at all 'legalistic'. Not that these solutions are necessarily contrary to whatever national law the courts would apply in the end; but they are supposed to flow from social customs, norms and understandings that are common to business people all over the world. Litigation always lurks in the background; but as a last resort. Many business people prefer arbitration, which seems less disruptive than litigation. It seems easier to keep up a business relationship while arbitrators are trying to settle some controversy than if the two sides are at each other's throats in a courtroom.

Lex mercatoria is a fairly fancy phrase, and surely conveys something of a wrong impression. Wrong in two ways: first, in suggesting that the norms followed are precise, hard-edged, known, and that they contradict or sidestep the institutions of the great commercial nations. Second, in suggesting that jet-set dealmakers are fundamentally or radically different in thought and habit from national or local dealmakers. After all, commercial arbitration is certainly common enough in domestic systems of law. Business people everywhere prefer to settle their affairs peaceably, if they can, and especially if they are doing business with each other, in a kind of continuing relationship; they also tend to ignore or sidestep the 'legalism' of the formal law, and follow their own set of norms, which one can call customary norms if one likes.[21]

Of course, without further research, there is not much that can be said about the norms, habits and practices of the international dealmakers, just as it is hard to say much about the norms and customs of business people in the living law of their

---

19   See the essays in Thomas E. Carbonneau (ed.), *Lex Mercatoria and Arbitration: a Discussion Of The New Law Merchant* (revised ed., The Hague: Kluwer Law International, 1998).

20   Yves Dezalay and Bryant G. Garth, *Dealing in Virtue: International Commercial Arbitration and the Construction of a Transnational Legal Order* (Chicago: Chicago University Press, 1996).

21   This is the message of the classic study by Stewart Macaulay, 'Non-Contractual Relations in Business: A Preliminary Study', AMERICAN SOCIOLOGICAL REV. 28:55 (1963).

home community. The research is simply too thin. Is there really a kind of culture of global legal practice, which differs dramatically from local business law practice, normatively speaking? I suspect that deals at any level have some traits in common. This is because of the pervasive influence of unplanned convergence – the process that pulls systems of living law closer together in the modern world. There is nothing mysterious about the process. Systems come to resemble each other more, because they share problems and solutions and are part of the global culture; they all share in a transnational commonality of products and desires.[22]

Such commonalities, on the international level, are perhaps an extension of a process that began earlier, and operated at the level of the nation. We hear a lot about the gradual disappearance of borders – of how borders come to mean less and less in our times. [23] We hear about the erosion or withering away of the nation state. But the nation state itself is in most senses a fairly recent creation. 'Nations' grew up and defined themselves by wiping out or uniting all sorts of sub-regions and diversities, *inside* their borders. There is nothing inevitable or natural about the emergence of any particular 'nation'. In fact, all modern nations are in a way fictions, constructions: they are 'imagined communities', in Benedict Anderson's trenchant phrase.[24] They were all painfully and slowly put together. To create a 'France' or a 'Spain' was a long and deliberate process, which, in the course of its meanderings, wiped out, or tried to wipe out, or marginalize, local languages, dialects, customs and ways of life.[25] The nation-building process also tends to divide as well as to unite. The 'nation' gets a standard language, history, ideology – and this then claims some kind of political and cultural monopoly. The process creates majorities and minorities, nations and sub-nations, each one of which becomes its own 'imagined community', through a similar development. The end result can be a volatile and explosive mixture – it can be ethnic or religious conflict.

Is it possible that something analogous to nation-building is going to take place *across* traditional borders? Is the European Union an example of what the future is going to bring? Will there emerge a new 'imagined community', that is, Europe, which absorbs and obliterates its constituent parts? This hardly seems likely – right now. Still: in the age of the Internet, in the age of transnational corporations, in the age of international arbitration, borders do come to mean less and less, culturally speaking.

22	Friedman, 'Is There a Modern Legal Culture', *supra* n. 12.

23	See David Jacobson, *Rights Across Borders: Immigration and the Decline of Citizenship* (Baltimore : Johns Hopkins U P, 1996).

24	Benedict Anderson, *Imagined Communities: Reflections on the Origin and Spread of Nationalism* (Rev. Ed., London: Verso, 1990).

25	On France, see the fine study by Eugen Weber, *Peasants into Frenchmen: the Modernization of Rural France, 1870-1914* (London: Chatto & Windus, 1976).

On the other hand, in some other senses, almost paradoxically, *because* borders are so weak culturally and economically, they become much more important as sheer physical barriers. After all, in the past, most people tended to stay where they were; a Spaniard or a Romanian, let alone a Sri Lankan or Somali, was born and died at home, in the native village, or nearby; moving to Italy to wait on tables or sell trinkets on the street was unthinkable. Modern technology and the global culture have made a shambles of this kind of demographic fixity. Without stiff border controls, masses of people would move from places they do not want to be or cannot earn a living, to places that seem more attractive, places whose wealth and (apparent) masses of jobs make them magnets for a floating world population.

III.   Risks and Opportunities

I want to mention two more aspects of globalization, both of which have some importance for the legal order. First, is the globalization of risk and misfortune, the internationalization of problems? These are of all sorts, and I can do little more than offer a kind of checklist. First, there are the problems of what Ulrich Beck has called the 'risk society'.[26] His book, which attracted considerable attention, was stimulated by the Chernobyl disaster. A nuclear reactor in what was then the Soviet Union failed; and radioactive winds swept over neighbouring parts of Europe. These winds obviously had no respect for borders. The same is true for global warming, or the problems of the ozone layer, and so on. Technology nowadays is so powerful that it is easy to imagine destruction on a transnational scale. Humanity seems capable of causing greater and greater calamities. The vast Indonesian forest fires of 1997 poisoned the air over several countries.

Global problems are caused by global processes, even when they seem totally local. In a sense, the birth rate in Kenya is nobody's business but the Kenyans, and when we think about globalization, the sex lives and marriage patterns of people in Kenya do not immediately come to mind. But the soaring populations of African countries owe a lot to advances in medicine and technology. These advances spread from the 'advanced' countries, and cut back drastically the rate at which little babies die. Moreover, in many ways a population explosion in Africa or Brazil *does* affect the rest of the world. It creates pressure on resources. It leads to a hunger for migration.

Similarly, the ravenous Chinese appetite for turtle-meat or rhinoceros horns is arguably of no concern to anybody outside of China. But these tastes in the first place cannot be satisfied within the borders of China, since China has no rhinoceroses and too few turtles. But these Chinese desires, and the money incentives they engender, threaten to drive these poor creatures to the brink of

26   Ulrich Beck, *Risikogesellschaft* (Frankfurt: Suhrkamp, 1986).

extinction. There was a time when the rest of the world would have considered this fact of no particular interest; but the sense of interconnection, and the (thoroughly modern) environmental movement makes these into matters of global interest. All of the world's wild pandas live within the borders of the People's Republic of China; but their fate seems to attract the attention of millions of people who have only a mild or passing interest in, say, the fate of Tibet.

Rare animals can therefore be redefined and reconstructed as a global problem: basically aesthetical, but also political and cultural. Common animals are an even worse problem. In a global age, it is almost impossible to keep various maggots, beetles, weeds, and invasive pests from spreading all over the world; they come in cargo ships, but they also fly on the fastest jets. A plague of tree snakes on one island; mongoose populations on another; fruit flies bedevilling California: the list is long and depressing. And there is always the danger that some exotic virus will make the leap from an animal host to helpless human beings. Once it does so, there is the further danger that the virus will spread from its original focal point to the rest of the world. This is, apparently, the history of the AIDS virus. The spread of this disease is related, too, to another factor: a 'dramatic increase in multiple-partner sex around the world'.[27] Obviously, this 'dramatic increase' is one of the by-products of modernization, which everywhere attacks and often destroys traditional codes of morality. Other viruses, just as deadly as the AIDS virus, might be lurking in the tropics or waiting for the right moment to make a murderous mutation.

The globalization of risk is an obvious problem for the international order. It generates a demand for, and a need for, actions that are as universal as possible. Voluntary behaviour, treaties, conventions and the like, will probably not do the trick: countries, for political and economic reasons, will always be tempted to break the rules, unless there is some way to control, monitor and discipline them. The whole world needs clean air and water, and it wants (and perhaps needs) the rainforests and the steppes and the prairies and the coral reefs. Yet most of these habitats and resources are located, legally speaking, within national borders, and a giant, invisible fence, called 'national sovereignty', keeps foreigners, for the most part, out. Still, for more and more people, *laissez faire* on a global scale here seems intolerable. This suggests a need for hard law, and enforceable law: but where would this come from, and how? The 'force of world opinion' sometimes makes a difference; but when 'vital national interests'[28] are at stake, countries feel free to ignore what outsiders think.

---

27   David P. Fidler, 'The Globalization of Public Health: Emerging Infections Diseases and International Relations', INDIANA J. OF GLOBAL LEGAL STUDIES 5:11, 19 (1997).

28   See, for example, the discussion in Ruth L. Gana, 'Has Creativity Died in the Third World? Some Implications of the Internationalization of Intellectual Property', DENVER J. OF INTERNATIONAL LAW AND POLICY 24:109 (1995).

Outside interference is, of course, not always benign. Historically, it was rarely benign; it was colonialism. Colonialism is, perhaps, not dead, in a variety of senses. Is it a form of neo-colonialism to try to save the whales, if saving whales meaning starving out some Inuit villagers? If we impose international norms of 'intellectual property' on native art, medicines, processes, customs and the like, are we imposing a norm on indigenous people that will, in fact, help to destroy them?

IV. Reflections in a Mirror: Global Law at Home

The world of the international arbitrators and the jet-set dealmakers is obviously 'global'. But globalization also has an enormous impact on strictly local law and the work of strictly local courts. Indeed, global law, in general, depends on the work of local lawyers, courts and judges. The great treaties and conventions would be merely words on paper if this were not the case, if they were not enforceable locally. There are, after all, no strong, international institutions to enforce international norms. Even international arbitration depends, in the last resort, on the goodwill of national courts.

In a broader sense, domestic law, even in mundane, local fields, reflects the influence, as it must, of a world that every country is connected to every other one. Take, for example, the law of child custody. This is a branch of family law; and we think of this branch of law as the most intensely local, the most 'cultural', the most resistant to change. (In fact, family law is not at all resistant to change; and few fields of law have undergone a more thorough revolution.) In any event, family law more and more has global implications. This is because of migration, and because, as a result of migration, more and more countries are ethnically diverse. This is a world in which a Pakistani can move to London and marry an English woman, or an Eritrean woman can bear a child fathered by an Italian man in Rome. Not all these romances and unions last. Then there can be squabbles over custody; and these may have a strong international dimension. What happens when one parent whisks the children off to his or her 'motherland'? There are treaties, conventions and legal tools to deal with the issue; but there is no fully satisfying way to resolve the problems that come from the underlying clash of cultures, or to prevent bias on the part of local courts.[29]

---

29 See June, 'The Global Battlefield: Culture and International Child Custody Disputes at Century's End', ARIZ. J. INT'L & COMP. LAW 15:791 (1998); on the bias of local courts (in this case German courts), see *New York Times*, (2 August 1999). See also Pierre Guibentif, 'Cross-border Legal Issues Arising from International Migrations: the Case of Portugal', in Volkmar Gessner and Ali Cem Budak (eds.), *Emerging Legal Certainty*: *Empirical Studies on the Globalization of Law* (Aldershot; Brookfield, USA: Ashgate, 1998), p. 241.

Our times are restless times; thousands of men and woman are migrating, legally or otherwise, from one country to another; or trying to. The pressure of this migration puts a lot of colour and spice into the street scenes of rich countries. It improves the restaurant situation enormously. But it also gives the rich, developed countries an ethnic and racial diversity that many of the older inhabitants may not particularly want. Some of these countries – Norway, for example – were once fairly monotone, demographically speaking; but no longer. The thousands and thousands of people banging on the doors of rich countries put pressure on the laws of immigration and citizenship. Immigration, asylum, citizenship rights were not high on the legal and political agendas of Germany and France in the 19th century; now they most definitely are.

The so-called 'immigration' countries (the United States or Australia, for example) are not immune to the discontents of global mass movement – far from it. It is often said that the United States had no restrictions on immigration during most of the 19th century. At the end of the century, laws were passed to keep out the Chinese who were flocking to the West Coast, particularly California.[30] Well into the 20th century, most European countries were exporters of bodies, not importers; Swedes and Poles and Greeks and Italians left for the United States or Canada or Chile or Australia. The immigration countries were eager to get these workers – as farmers, miners and labourers. They even advertised for souls in foreign countries. But the assumption always was that the right sort of people would come. Nobody expected thousands of Chinese peasants or impoverished Tongans or Hindus to knock on the door.[31] In the 20th century, however, the *cultural* barriers to immigration have broken down. Television and the movies spread the word to remote places; traditional societies are undergoing rapid change, and in some places population explosions put a strain on resources; the land in the villages can no longer feed all the hungry mouths. There is a tremendous pool of surplus labour: high unemployment (in rich countries as well as poor ones); as many as 80,000,000 'expatriate labourers' are working all over the world;[32] and tens of millions more would gladly join their ranks. Moreover, once there are even small colonies of fellow countrymen in London or Rome or Sydney or New York, people who speak your language, serve your food, and practise your religion, it becomes easier and

---

30 There is of course a very large literature on American immigration history; see, for example, Elliott Robert Barkan, *And Still They Come: Immigrants and American Society 1920 to the 1990s* (Wheeling, Ill: H. Davidson, 1996); on the Chinese immigration issue, see Bill Ong Hing, *Making and Remaking Asian America through Immigration Policy, 1850-1990* (Stanford: Stanford University Press, 1993).

31 In the United States, Protestant immigrants from northern Europe were the most welcome; and the influx from southern and eastern Europe – Catholic, Jewish, and Orthodox – led eventually to the passage of a restrictive immigration law in 1924.

32 McMichael, *supra* n. 10, p. 187.

less alienating to leave your village or your country, and move to the foreign city. The rich countries frantically try to build fences around themselves, literally and legally. Anti-immigration politics is on the rise in Europe. Whether the rich countries can and will protect themselves remains an open question. The source of their problem (if it is a problem) is the globalized society, a society in which cultural barriers against immigration have largely if not entirely broken down.

Mexico is the largest source of illegal aliens for the United States. It would surprise many people to learn that there were no restrictions at all on Mexican immigration before the middle of the 20th century. The story of legal and social control over Mexican immigration is, in fact, quite complicated; but in essence what protected the borders of the United States for most of its history was culture and poverty, not barbed-wire fences and immigration laws. There was no border patrol at all before the 1920s. Most Mexicans did not live near the border; they lived on the central plateau. Before there was a railroad network linking the two countries, it was too expensive for most poor peasants and slum-dwellers to travel to the glittering world of El Norte. Raging population pressure, and the breakdown of traditional society, removed the other, invisible barriers. Moreover, there were American agri-businessmen who welcomed cheap Mexican stoop labour. And since there were already substantial colonies of Mexicans in the American south-west, it was no trick to find a cousin or a neighbour who could lend you a cot, and a friend from the village who could get you a job picking lettuce or washing dishes in Los Angeles.[33] In Europe, the end of colonialism weakened one set of controls over in-migration, and the fall of the Iron Curtain weakened another set of controls. This produced what has become a politically volatile and controversial immigration 'problem' in country after country.

Moreover, in the balmy days of economic growth after the World War II, countries like Germany and the Netherlands suffered from a severe labour shortage; to solve this problem, they invited in millions of foreign workers – Italians, Spaniards and Turks. The children and grandchildren of these workers are still there, but the labour shortage is gone, replaced by high unemployment. The 'guest-workers' are at least partially assimilated. In any event, they show no great passion to go 'home'. For most of them, home is where they are right now. Yet some European countries – Germany in particular – have been strikingly reluctant to admit these 'foreigners' to citizenship.[34]

The foreigners, and their children, and their children's children, are objects of suspicion in part because they seem to threaten the essence of (say) German identity and culture (whatever that might mean). But whether they get a passport and

---

33 On Mexican immigration, see Friedman, *The Horizontal Society, supra* n. 7, pp. 196-197; Kitty Calavita, *Inside the State: The Bracero Program, Immigration, and the I.N.S.* (New York: Routledge, 1992).

34 Friedman, *The Horizontal Society, supra* n. 7, pp. 157-159.

citizenship papers or not, they have changed German society simply by *being* there; they have made Germany into a multi-cultural society. The state itself – and a large part of the public – may not want to recognize this fact; but it is nonetheless true.

Immigration is a good example of how the globalization of wishes and desires sets forces in motion that lead to dramatic changes in the behaviour of masses of people; and these changes in turn put enormous pressures on the legal and political systems. In response, one sees a kind of backlash, which takes the form of barriers against the free flow of goods or people or ideas, or all of these. Earlier we mentioned one example: attempts to keep out, or control, the plague of American movies and TV shows. These and other laws of self-defence would not be necessary if cultural boundaries were not so weak and spineless. Physical boundaries are stronger than the cultural boundaries – but only relatively. The United States spends billions on border control – much of it, apparently, is money thrown away. Millions of illegal aliens in fact live in the United States; and at times there almost seems to be a traffic jam of illegals at night on the Mexican border. Still, without the system of border controls there might be millions more.

Trade boundaries are less visible than barbed-wire fences. But they are also increasingly feeble. They are crumbling in an age which is ideologically committed to free trade, and in which economies are so interdependent that many countries do not dare restrict trade, because they are afraid of retaliation and revenge.

But free trade has consequences; and it makes winners and losers. Most countries in the developed world feel threatened by cheap imports and the cheap labour of immigrants. In Europe, North America and Japan, much of the manufacturing base has simply rotted away. The factories have moved to countries where labour costs a lot less. It is not just jobs that are lost. Labour standards are also eroded. Sometimes the only recourse is to try to block goods made under conditions that violate local law. Does the free trade ideology mean that a country is helpless to prevent a flood of sweaters and blouses and shoes made under revolting conditions, or rugs woven by eight year olds? Of course, a country is entitled to keep out products that are harmful or unhealthy; and many do. This right, on the other hand, can easily degenerate into a form of protectionism. It is not easy to tell the difference. If American farmers pump hormones into cows, does this make the meat unfit to eat, or is this only an excuse for Europeans to keep American meat products out? As Martin Shapiro has pointed out, the problem of local standards has plagued the European Union too. 'Differing national product standards and rules on advertising and marketing' can become 'very effective barriers to... trade'. Hence the push, in Europe, toward harmonization of standards.[35] Hence the push to make 'free trade' an international, and enforceable norm.

---

35 Martin Shapiro, 'The Problems of Independent Agencies in the United States and the European Union', JOURNAL OF EUROPEAN PUBLIC POLICY 4, n. 2 (1997), 276-277.

Globalization of trade threatens wage rates in the West, and Western labour standards; but this is not all. The price of Western goods includes costs of environmental controls and worker safety. Third World countries pay (on the whole) no attention to these; and the multi-national corporations often seem to be beyond anybody's control. Shell Oil can pollute the Niger delta in Nigeria – and does – without much fear that the Nigerian government, or *any* government, will do a thing about it. The imperial countries are, in some ways, just as much prisoners of the great multi-national corporations as the imperialized countries at the bottom of the heap.

V. Globalization of Human Rights

In the period since World War II, there has been an important movement to globalize human rights, that is, to develop, proclaim, publicize and (hopefully) enforce standards of human rights. These rights are said to be universal. There are all sorts of charters, treaties, and pronouncements about human rights; and there are organizations (such as Amnesty International) that work on a worldwide basis trying to make these rights a reality.

There is an obvious conflict between any concept of universal human rights and that sacred cow, national sovereignty. Each independent country is supposed to be free to run its own show; and other countries are not allowed to meddle in 'internal affairs'. Needless to say, this 'right' is frequently violated. Big powerful countries can get away with a great deal of bullying and interference. We also hear a lot of talk about the erosion of the 'concept of nationality'; supposedly, this is replaced by 'a concept emphasizing that the state is accountable to all its residents on the basis of international human rights law'.[36] Of course, there is at present no way to enforce 'international human rights law'; and for the most part, the dozens of satraps, dictators and petty tyrants who are in power all over the world do what they please with their subjects. World opinion counts the least with those despots who need it the most. On the other hand, when NATO bombed Serbia over the Kosovo crisis, in 1999, and later sent troops into the area, this was done at least partly in order to uphold standards of human rights. The NATO allies never denied that Kosovo 'belonged' to the Serbs and that Kosovo had no right to be an independent state.

What *are* these human rights, which are supposedly universal? There seems to be general agreement about a certain common core of rights and wrong. Nobody nowadays would argue that a state should have the right to kill and torture its citizens for no good reason. There are plenty of regimes *practising* these black arts; but even these regimes feel the need to lie about it. And, moreover, nobody claims that this norm is contingent and culture-bound (although it is). But beyond a certain

36   Sassen, *supra* n. 9, p. 97.

basic list, there is the question of whether notions of human rights are truly universal. One argument, which ones hears frequently from such places as Singapore, is that some of the conventional list of rights are not universal at all, but are essentially tied to Western culture. Thus, they do not fit societies in other parts of the world – Asia, very notably.[37]

It is certainly easy to make a case for the cultural relativity of rights. Slavery and torture were in fact once features of Western life. China and (say) France have very different traditions with regard to human rights (among other things). There is a lively discussion about whether it is right to export (if one could) the Western brand of feminism; and even whether female circumcision is a violation of women's rights or a precious cultural tradition.[38] In the modern world, concepts of human rights show real signs of convergence. No doubt, Western concepts of freedom and rights are not neutral, timeless and inherent; and no doubt they found early and eloquent expression in Western ethical and political philosophy. But these concepts are, in fact, not really 'Western'. Rather, they are *modern*. They developed first in the West, because the West was the first to modernize. Thus they are, as one author put it, 'historically but not culturally relative'.[39] Globalization is really an extension of the process of modernization; and the spread of the idea of (say) free speech is just as much part of the process as the spread of electricity or Coca-Cola. Free speech is, to be sure, alien to the traditions of Cambodia or Japan; but it was just as alien to Russia or to Germany until quite recently; and how long has it been the norm in Sweden or the Netherlands? The demand for human rights is part of modern legal *culture*, part of global legal culture; and it therefore cannot be brushed off with arguments that it is alien to this or that part of the world.

The culture of human rights, if we analyze it carefully, is really a culture of individualism. It is a culture that locates a cluster of rights within individuals, not families, clans, tribes or groups. The engines that produced and produce modernity foster this culture. The mass media play an extremely important role. They spread the gospel of a world of individual consumers. They are propaganda engines, consciously or unconsciously, for this gospel. Modern culture, as I have argued, is a culture of leisure and consumption. Such a culture is necessarily focused on the individual, who sees, wants, buys, entertains and consumes.

---

37   See, for example, Tommy T. B. Koh, *The United States and East Asia: Conflict and Co-operation* (Singapore: Institute of Policy Studies, Times Academic Press, 1995), pp. 100-101.

38   See Leslye A. Obiora, 'Bridges and Barricades: Rethinking Polemics and Intransigence in the Campaign against Female Circumcision', CASE WESTERN RESERVE LAW REVIEW 47:275 (1997).

39   Rainer Bauböck, *Transnational Citizenship: Membership and Rights in International Migration* (Brookfield, Vt.: E. Elgar, 1994), p. 239.

Modern politics, to be sure, in many countries, is preoccupied with issues that at least seem focused on the group, rather than the individual. This seems to be true of racial politics in countries as disparate as the United States, Malaysia, Fiji or Guatemala. Feminist movements, the gay rights movement, the various 'liberation' or separatist movements of ethnic minorities: all these seem to be flying a banner of group identity, group empowerment, and the like. But, paradoxically, group identity and group empowerment, when you dig beneath the surface, turn out to be aspects of individualism. Empowering women means giving women the right, as individuals, to choose their way of life – the right to be whatever they choose to be; the right not to be judged in terms of gender stereotypes; the right not to be relegated to some narrow, specific social role. If a woman wants to bake cookies and raise children, that should be her choice; but if she wants to be prime minister or mine coal or play soccer, that should also be her choice. In the same way, a submerged individualism lies at the base of all the other 'liberation' movements, racial and otherwise. Group rights are only a path toward individual fulfilment.[40]

VII. Is the Nation-State Withering Away?

As we have seen, globalization erodes the meaning of borders, at least to a degree; it also sets processes in motion that lead countries to try to *strengthen* their borders, in defence against some of the consequences of globalization. The process is one of action and reaction. The extreme cases are countries like Iran or Saudi Arabia (and, to a degree, China) – countries trying desperately to keep at least some aspects of the modern world at bay. Some societies still try to keep the doors closed: still try to remain self-contained, traditional and free from the seductions of global culture.

Most Westerners feel convinced that this is, in the end, a losing battle. They may also feel that 'the state' in its classical sense is everywhere losing some of its vigour and autonomy. In the legal and economic senses, true 'sovereignty' seems impossible for most states. For most countries and surely all small countries, economic independence is not attainable. It is even a question whether the giants can survive on their own in so interconnected a world. Of course, to a degree, small and weak countries have always been economic vassals – how much true independence did a banana republic enjoy, even when it was nominally 'sovereign'? Colonialism made vassals out of half the globe. The old empires have all crumbled into dust; but a good many 'independent' nations are still tied to the apron strings of their former colonial masters.

United Fruit once dominated the banana republics. Today, the great multi-national corporations are stronger than most small, weak countries; and in the aggregate, their power rivals even that of some large, rich countries. And in many

40 Friedman, *The Horizontal Society, supra* n. 7.

regards, they seem to be beyond the reach of the state. Only some kind of world federalism could tame them. Technology, too, seems to conspire to undermine the nation state. It fosters a global culture that threatens to overwhelm individual, national cultures. The latest toy of technology, the Internet, is as difficult to control as the winds. As we have seen, modern transport (allied with socio-culture change) poses threats to national borders that were unimaginable a century ago.

Weakness in the nation state is not necessarily a bad thing. As far as economic conservatives are concerned and free market ideologues, the less the state does, the better they like it. Almost everybody would agree that many states are not weak enough – that they have too much ability to do radical harm to the people living inside their borders. There are plenty of dictatorial regimes that badly need inside or outside control.

The rich industrial countries seem in the mood to shrink the (economic) role of central governments; they are anxious to sell off their banks, railroads, telephone companies and general businesses; they are also cutting back on the welfare state, at least to a degree, because the programs have become too expensive. Socialist ideology is certainly at a very low ebb. Most ordinary people and most scholars, think that bureaucracy needs a higher standard of accountability; that the bureaucrats need to have their wings clipped, once and for all.

The idea of the 'rule of law' is an idea about limits on the state. The phrase is seductive everywhere, even in China, which by and large lacks it, but which seems eager to give it at least lip service. Of course, there are many definitions of the 'rule of law', but they have certain traits in common. They all imply a body of rules, more or less definite and knowable, which monitor and limit state power; these rules can and should apply to everybody, including powerful people in the government and their minions and favourites. The definitions also imply that some body or institution can enforce the rules against everybody. This is taken to mean, in many countries, a strong, honest and independent judiciary.

Some definitions of the 'rule of law' seem to equate the concept with legal formalism – for example, Kermit Hall's statement that the phrase refers to 'a body of rules and procedures... that have an autonomy and logic of their own'.[41] Law and society scholars, quite properly, are sceptical about definitions that lean too much on the idea of 'autonomy'. Much of the sociology of law is devoted to debunking the idea of strict legal autonomy and neutrality. The logic of the legal order is a cultural logic, not a formal, deductive logic; the legal system is always messy and complicated; it cannot be turned into a free-standing machine-like operation, that runs entirely by itself and in which power, wealth, social influence and prevailing norms do not count for much. No such system exists or can exist.

---

41   Kermit Hall, *The Magic Mirror: Law in American History* (New York: Oxford University Press, 1989), pp. 6-7.

Nonetheless, there is obviously a big difference between a country that purports to be a *Rechtsstaat* and the various autocracies, dictatorships, one-party states and police states. The legal system may not be 'autonomous'; but it can be and often is *independent*, that is, judges and civil servants do their job, free from the power of a regime to reward and punish and interfere. A state with the 'rule of law' has its hands tied in some important regards; a strong judiciary is often part of the working system. Nowadays, many people would add to the definition of the *Rechtsstaat* some degree of commitment to free markets. Not so long ago, this would not have figured very prominently in European discussions of the rule of law. Whether the rule of law in fact depends on free-market economics, or some variant, is an open question.[42]

Each country tends to define *its* version of the rule of law as the one true faith. But whatever the definition, the rule of law implies a strong sense of right and of *rights*; and some force (a court, an ombudsman) to translate the rights into reality. Courts and ombudsmen, however, are passive in the sense that they do not, as a rule, initiate complaints; they sit, rather, waiting for customers, like spiders in their webs.[43] Formal rights, then, also depend on a culture of rights: on a willingness, or eagerness to make use of institutions with power to decide when rights have been infringed on or broken. Rights-consciousness is supposed to be very variable, culturally – Americans, for example, are supposed to be addicted to rights, entitlements, litigation;[44] the Japanese, on the other hand, are supposed to be litigation-shy and weak in the rights-consciousness department.[45] Undoubtedly there are important cultural, historical, traditional and institutional differences between societies and these affect litigation, rights-consciousness and the working reality of the 'rule of law'. But the argument of this essay would suggest at least some degree of convergence, in all developed countries, including the United States and Japan. The ideology of the rule of law did not come out of nowhere. It is historically contingent. It is obviously connected to the decline of traditional, hierarchical societies and the growth of a strong sense of individualism and individual rights. It

---

42 See the interesting remarks on this point by Boaventura de Sousa Santos, 'The GATT of Law and Democracy: (Mis) Trusting the Global Reform of Courts', in Feest (ed.), *Globalization and Legal Cultures* (Onati Papers, No. 7, 1999), p. 49.

43 A partial exception might be the active investigative judges of, say, Italy and Spain.

44 See Robert A. Kagan, 'American Lawyers, Legal Cultures, and Adversarial Legalism', in Lawrence M. Friedman and Harry N. Scheiber (eds.), *Legal Culture and the Legal Profession* (Boulder, Colo: Westview Press, 1996), p. 7.

45 Whether this is so or not is a matter of dispute. See, for example, Robert L. Kidder and Setsuo Miyazawa, 'Long-Term Strategies in Japanese Environmental Litigation', LAW AND SOCIAL INQUIRY 18:605 (1993); Takao Tanase, 'The Management of Disputes: Automobile Accident Compensation in Japan', LAW AND SOCIETY REVIEW 24:651 (1990).

is, therefore, at least in an implicit way, a message carried into millions of homes each day by the mass media. It is, in short, a global ideology in a global age.

Chapter 3

De-Nationalized State Agendas and Privatized Norm-Making

Saskia Sassen*

States today confront a new geography of power.[1] The changed condition of the state is often explained in terms of a decrease in regulatory capacities resulting from some of the basic policies associated with economic globalization: deregulation of a broad range of markets, economic sectors and national borders and privatization of public sector firms.

But in my reading of the evidence, this new geography of power confronting states entails a far more differentiated process than notions of an overall decline in the significance of the state suggest. We are seeing a repositioning of the state in a broader field of power and a reconfiguring of the work of states. This broader field

---

*   Ralph Lewis Professor of Sociology, University of Chicago and Centennial Visiting Professor, London School of Economics. This is based on the author's larger project 'De-nationalization: Territory, Authority, and Rights in a Global Age' (Princeton: Princeton University Press, 2003).

1   Many scholars coming at the subject from a variety of angles would agree, even as they might use other vocabularies. See, e.g. Eric Hobsbawm, *On the Edge of the New Century / Eric Hobsbawm; in conversation with Antonio Polito*, translated from the Italian by Allan Cameron (London: Little, Brown, 2000); Charles Tilly, 'Globalization Threatens labour Rights', INTERNATIONAL LABOUR AND WORKING CLASS HISTORY JOURNAL, (1995) 47: 1-23; Robert Jessop, 'Reflections on Globalization and its Illogics', pp. 19-38 in Kris Olds, et al. (ed) *Globalization and the Asian Pacific: Contested Territories* (London: Routeledge, 1999); Michael Hardt and Antonio Negri, *Empire* (Cambridge, MA: Harvard University Press, 2000). See also various chapters in each of the following collections to get a cross-section of perspectives: James Mittelman (ed.), *Globalization: critical reflections*, Vol. 9 (Boulder, Co: Lynne Rienner Publishers, 1996); Kris Olds, Peter Dicken, Philip F. Kelly, Lilly Kong, Henry Wai-Chung Yeung (ed). *Globalization and the Asian Pacific: Contested Territories* (London: Routledge, 1999); David Smith – D. Solinger and S. Topik (eds.), *States and Sovereignty in the Global Economy* (London: Routledge, 1999) and Calabrese and Burgelman (eds.), *Communication, Citizenship and Social Policy: Re-thinking the Limits of the Welfare State* (Lanham, MD: Rowman & Littlefield, 1999) just to cite English language literature.

of power is constituted partly through the formation of a new private institutional order linked to the global economy and partly through the growing importance of a variety of institutional orders engaged with various aspects of the common good broadly understood, such as the international network of NGOs and the international human rights regime. This new geography of power also entails a more transformative process of the state than the notion of a simple loss of power suggests. The work of states or *raison d'état* – the substantive rationality of the state – has had many incarnations over the centuries. Each of these transformations has had significant consequences. Today the conditionalities for and the content of specific components of the work of states have changed significantly compared to the immediately preceding period of the post-World War II decades. Some of these changes are typically captured with the image of the current neo-liberal or competitive state as compared with the welfare state of the post-war era.

In this chapter I develop three arguments.[2] First, I posit that the marking features of this new, mostly but not exclusively, private institutional order in formation are its capacity to privatize what was heretofore public and to de-nationalize what were once national authorities and policy agendas. This capacity to privatize and de-nationalize entails specific transformations of the national state, more precisely of some of its components. Further, I posit that this new institutional order also has normative authority – a new normativity that is not embedded in what has been and to some extent remains the master normativity of modern times, *raison d'état*. This new normativity comes from the world of private power yet installs itself in the public realm and in so doing contributes to de-nationalize what had historically been constructed as national state agendas.[3] Finally, I posit that particular institutional components of the national state begin to function as the institutional home for the operation of powerful dynamics constitutive of what we could describe as 'global capital' and 'global capital markets'. In so doing, these state institutions contribute to reorient their particular policy work or, more broadly, state agendas towards the requirements of the global economy. This then raises a question about what is

2   Inevitably much will have to be left unaddressed. For a full treatment of these issues as well as a whole set of other governance questions linked to the sphere of human rights, citizenship and immigration, please refer to Sassen's project 'De-nationalization: Territory, Authority, and Rights in a Global Age'.

3   I have developed this at greater length in Saskia Sassen, *The 1995 Columbia University Leonard Hastings Schoff Memorial Lectures* published as *Losing Control? Sovereignty in an Age of Globalization* (New York: Columbia University Press, 1996); Saskia Sassen, 'Servicing the Global Economy: Reconfigured States and Private Agents' in Olds et al. (eds.), *supra* n. 1, pp.149-162. I should clarify that when I first developed the construct 'de-nationalization' in the 1995 Memorial Schoff Lectures (1996) I intended it to denote a specific dynamic – discussed later in this chapter. I did *not* intend it as some general notion that can be used interchangeably with post-national, global, or other such terms. In this regard see the debate in Indiana Journal of Global Legal Studies (2000), and the Special Millennium Issue on Globalization of Public Culture (2000).

'national' in these institutional components of states linked to the implementation and regulation of economic globalization.

Geared toward governing key aspects of the global economy, both the particular transformations inside the state and the new emergent privatized institutional order are partial and incipient but strategic. Both have the capacity to alter possibly crucial conditions for liberal democracy and for the organizational architecture for international law, its scope and its exclusivity. In this sense both have the capacity to alter the scope of state authority and the inter-state system, the crucial institutional domains through which the 'rule of law' is implemented. We are not seeing the end of states but, rather, that states are not the only or the most important strategic agents in this new institutional order and, secondly, that states, including dominant states, have undergone profound transformations in some of their key institutional components.

Both of these trends are likely to add to the democratic deficit and to further strengthen the 'legitimacy' of certain types of claims and norms.

I.   The State and Globalization

One of the roles of the state *vis-a-vis* economic internationalization has been to negotiate the intersection of national law and the activities of foreign economic actors – whether firms, markets or supra-national organizations – in its territory as well as the activities of national economic actors overseas. This is not a new role, but it is a transformed and expanded one. In the case of the US, the government has passed legislative measures, executive orders, court decisions that have enabled foreign firms to operate in the US and markets to become international. Are there particular conditions that make execution of this role in the current phase distinctive and unlike what it may have been in earlier phases of the world economy?

While this is in many ways a question of interpretation, I will argue that there is indeed something distinctive about the current period. We have, on the one hand, the existence of an enormously elaborate body of law developed in good measure over the last hundred years which secures the exclusive territorial authority of national states to an extent not seen in earlier centuries, and, on the other, the considerable instutionalizing, especially in the 1990s, of the 'rights' of non-national firms, the deregulation of cross-border transactions and the growing influence/power of some of the supra-national organizations. If securing these rights, options and powers entailed an even partial relinquishing of components of state authority as constructed over the last century, then we can posit that this sets up the conditions for a transformation in the role of the state. It also signals a necessary engagement by national states in the process of globalization.

The next question, then, would concern the nature of this engagement and how it will vary for different types of state.[4] Is the role of the state simply one of reducing its authority (e.g. as suggested with terms such as deregulation and privatization and generally 'less government') or does it also require the production of new types of regulations, legislative items, court decisions, in brief, the production of a whole series of new 'legalities'?[5]

Further, if it is in fact some states, i.e. the US and the UK, which are producing the design for these new legalities, i.e. particular aspects derived from Anglo-American commercial law and accounting standards and are hence imposing these on other states given the interdependencies at the heart of the current phase of globalization, then this creates and imposes a set of specific constraints on participating states.[6] Legislative items, executive orders, adherence to new technical standards and so on, will have to be produced through the particular institutional and political structures of each of these states.[7]

The accommodation of the interests of foreign firms and investors under conditions where most of a country's institutional domains have been constructed as 'national' entails a negotiation.[8] The mode of this negotiation in the current phase

4   Even as I confine this discussion to what are described as states effectively functioning under the rule of law, we must allow for considerable differences in the power of these states. As has been said many times, the government of the US can aim at imposing conditions on the global markets and on participating states that the government of Argentina, for instance, cannot.

5   I use this term to distinguish this production from 'law' or 'jurisprudence'. (Saskia Sassen, *The 1995 Columbia University Leonard Hastings Schoff Memorial Lectures*, *supra* n. 3, chapter 1.)

6   This dominance assumes many forms and does not only affect poorer and weaker countries. France, for instance, ranks among the top providers of information services and industrial engineering services in Europe and has a strong though not outstanding position in financial and insurance services. But it has found itself at an increasing disadvantage in legal and accounting services because Anglo-American law and standards dominate in international transactions. Anglo-American firms with offices in Paris do the servicing of the legal needs of firms, whether French or foreign, operating out of France. Similarly, Anglo-American law is increasingly dominant in international commercial arbitration, an institution grounded in continental traditions of jurisprudence, particularly French and Swiss.

7   While it is well known, it is worth remembering that this guarantee of the rights of capital is embedded in a certain type of state, a certain conception of the rights of capital, and a certain type of international legal regime: it is largely embedded in the state of the most developed and most powerful countries in the world, in Western notions of contract and property rights, and in new legal regimes aimed at furthering economic globalization, e.g. the push to get countries to support copyright law.

8   In terms of research and theorization this is a vast uncharted terrain: it would mean examining how that production takes place and gets legitimated. This signals the

has tended in a direction that I describe as a de-nationalizing of several highly specialized national institutional components.[9] My hypothesis here is that some components of national institutions, even though formally national, are not national in the sense in which state practice has constructed the meaning of that term since the emergence of the so-called regulatory state particularly in the West. Though imperfectly implemented and often excluding national minorities, Keynesian policies aimed at strengthening the 'national' economy, 'national' consumption capacity, raising the educational level of 'national' workforces, are a good illustration of this meaning of the 'national'. There are, clearly, enormous variations among countries, both in terms of the extent to which such a national policy project existed and the actual period of time of its implementation.

Crucial to my analysis here is the fact that the emergent, often imposed, consensus in the community of states to further globalization is not merely a political decision: it entails specific types of *work* by a large number of distinct institutions in each of these countries. In this sense, that consensus partly shapes the actual work of states rather than being just a decision. Furthermore, this work of states has an ironic outcome insofar as it has the effect of destabilizing some aspects of state power. Thus the US government as the hegemonic power of this period has led/forced other states to adopt these obligations towards global capital, and, in so doing, has contributed to strengthen the forces that can challenge or destabilize what have historically been constructed as state powers.[10] In my reading this holds both for the US and for other countries. One of the ways in which this becomes evident is in the fact that while the state continues to play a crucial, though no longer exclusive, role in the production of legality around new forms of economic activity, at least some of this production of legalities is increasingly feeding the power of a new emerging structure marked by de-nationalization in some of its components and by privatization in other of its components.

possibility of cross-national variations (which then would need to be established, measured, interpreted).

9   The question for research becomes: What is actually 'national' (as in national state, not as in national people) in some of the institutional components of states linked to the implementation and regulation of economic globalization. The social sciences are not well equipped for this task given a strong state-centric approach to theory and research. (For a critical examination of the state-centric bent in the social sciences see, e.g. Peter J. Taylor, 'World Cities and Territorial States under Conditions of Contemporary Globalization'. POLITICAL GEOGRAPHY 19 (5): 5-32; Hardt and Negri, *supra* n. 1; see also Janet Abu-Lughod, *Towards 21st Century Sociology* (Chicago: Chicago University Press, 1999).

10 See, i.e. the argument by Giovanni Arrighi, The Long Twentieth Century: Money, Power and the Origins of our Times (London: Verso, 1994); see also the debate in Diane E. Davis (ed), 'Chaos and Governance', POLITICAL POWER AND SOCIAL THEORY Vol. 13, Part IV: Scholarly Controversy. Stamford, CT: JAI Press (1999) Vol. 13 (Annual). Debates Section.

In this case the state can be seen as incorporating the global project of its own shrinking role in regulating economic transactions. The state here can be conceived of as representing a technical administrative capacity that cannot be replicated at this time by any other institutional arrangement; furthermore, this is a capacity backed by military power, with global power in the case of some states. Seen from the perspective of firms operating transnationally, the objective is to ensure the functions traditionally exercised by the state in the national realm of the economy, notably guaranteeing property rights and contracts. How this gets done may involve a range of options. To some extent this work of guaranteeing is becoming privatized, as is signalled for instance by the growth of international commercial arbitration and by key elements of the new privatised institutional order.[11] I turn to this in the following sections.

II.   De-nationalized State Agendas

We generally use terms such as 'deregulation', financial and trade liberalization and privatisation, to describe the changed authority of the state when it comes to the economy. The problem with such terms is that they only capture the withdrawal of the state from regulating its economy. They do not register all the ways in which the state participates in setting up the new frameworks through which globalization is furthered, nor do they capture the associated transformations inside the state – precisely my two concerns in this lecture.

Let me illustrate. Central banks are national institutions that address national matters. Yet over the last decade they have become the institutional home within the national state for monetary policies that are necessary to further the development of a global capital market and indeed, more generally, a global economic system. The new conditionality of the global economic system – the requirements that need to be met for a country to become integrated into the global capital market – contains as one key element the autonomy of central banks.[12] This facilitates the task of instituting a certain kind of monetary policy, e.g. one privileging low inflation over

---

11   See Yves Dezalay and Bryant Garth, *Dealing in Virtue* (Chicago: The University of Chicago Press, 1996) on international commercial arbitration; Claire A. Cutler, Virginia Haufler and Tony Porter (eds). *Private Authority in International Affairs* (Sarasota Springs, NY: SUNY Press, 1999), and Thomas J. Biersteker, Rodney Bruce Hall and Craig N. Murphy (eds.), *Private Authority and Global Governance* (Cambridge: Cambridge University Press, 2002), on private authority.

12   While we take this autonomy for granted in the US or in most EU countries (though not all! Thus France's central bank, before the formation of the European Central Bank, was not considered as quite autonomous from the executive), in many countries the executive or local oligarchies have long had undue influence on central banks – incidentally not necessarily always to the disadvantage of the disadvantaged.

job growth even when a president may have preferred it the other way around particularly at re-election time. While securing central bank autonomy certainly cleaned up a lot of corruption, it has also been the vehicle for one set of accommodations on the part of national states to the requirements of the global capital market. A parallel analysis can be made of ministries of finance (or the Treasury in the US) that have had to impose certain kinds of fiscal policies as part of the new conditionalities of economic globalization.

At the level of theorization, it means capturing/conceptualising a specific set of operations that take place within national institutional settings but are geared to non-national or transnational agendas where once they were geared to national agendas. I conceptualize this as de-nationalization, more precisely, the incipient and partial de-nationalisation of specific, typically highly specialized, state institutional orders and of state agendas.[13] From the perspective of research I have argued that this entails the need to decode what is 'national' (as historically constructed) about the particular set of activities and authorities of central banks or ministries of finance briefly described above.

There is a set of strategic dynamics and institutional transformations at work here. They may incorporate a small number of state agencies and units within departments, a small number of legislative initiatives and of executive orders and yet have the power to institute a new normativity at the heart of the state; this is especially so because these strategic sectors are operating in complex interactions with private, transnational, powerful, actors. Much of the institutional apparatus of the state remains basically unchanged. (The inertia of bureaucratic organizations, which creates its own version of path dependence, makes an enormous contribution to continuity.)

In my current research on the US, I am extricating from what has been constructed as 'US legislative history' a whole series of legislative items and executive orders that can be read as accommodations on the part of the national state and as its active participation in producing the conditions for economic globalization. This is a history of micro-interventions, often-minute transformations in our regulatory or legal frameworks that facilitated the extension of cross-border operations of US firms. This is clearly not a new history, not for the US nor for other Western former imperial powers (e.g. the 'concessions' to trading companies under British, Dutch and other colonial regimes). Yet, I argue, we can identify a new phase, one that has very specific instantiations of this broader feature.[14]

Among the first of these new measures and perhaps among the best known, are the tariff items passed to facilitate the internationalization of manufacturing, which exempted firms from import duties on the value added of reimported components

---

13   See also *supra* n. 3.
14   The effort here is also to distinguish current forms from older notions of the state as a tool for capital, comprador bourgeoisies, or neo-colonialism.

assembled or manufactured in offshore plants. I date the beginning of this micro history of legislative and executive interventions to the late 1960s, with a full crystallization of various measures facilitating the global operations of US firms and the globalization of markets in the 1980s and work continuing vigorously in the 1990s. The Foreign Investment Act of 1976, the implementation of International Banking Facilities in 1981, the various deregulations and liberalizations of the financial sector in the 1980s and so on, are but the best known landmarks in this micro history.

Further, the new types of cross-border collaborations among specialized government agencies concerned with a growing range of issues emerging from the globalization of capital markets and the new trade order, are yet another aspect of this participation by the state in the implementation of a global economic system. A good example is the heightened interaction in the last three or four years among antitrust regulators from a large number of countries.[15] This is a period of reinvigorated antitrust activities because economic globalization puts pressure on governments to work towards convergence in antitrust regulations in a situation where countries tend to have often very diverse competition laws or enforcement practices.[16] This convergence around specific antitrust issues frequently exists in an ocean of enormous differences among these countries in all kinds of laws and regulations about components of the economy that do not intersect with globalization. It is then a very partial and specialized type of convergence among regulators of different countries who often begin to share more with each other than they do with colleagues back home in the larger bureaucracies within which they work.

There are multiple other instances of this highly specialized type of convergence: regulatory issues concerning telecommunications, finance, the Internet, etc. In some of these sectors there has long been an often-elementary convergence, or at least co-ordination of standards. What we see today is a sharp increase in the work of establishing convergence. For instance, we see an intensification in transactions among central bankers, necessary in the context of the global capital market. While central bankers have long interacted with each other across borders, we can clearly identify a new phase in the last ten years. The world of cross-border trade has brought with it a sharpened need for convergence in standards, as is evident in the vast proliferation of ISO items. I would think that

---

15 Known as competition policy in most of the world.

16 For a detailed study of these developments, especially the intensification of cross-border interactions among competition policy regulators see Brian Portnoy, *Constructing Competition: The Political Foundations of Alliance Capitalism*, Ph.D. dissertation, Department of Political Science, University of Chicago (1999).

another example would be the institutional and legal framework necessary for the operation of the cross-border commodity chains identified by Gereffi (1995).[17]

One outcome of these various trends is the emergence of a strategic field of operations that represents a partial disembedding of specific state operations from the broader institutional world of the state geared exclusively to national agendas. It is a fairly rarefied field of cross-border transactions among government agencies and business sectors aimed at addressing the new conditions produced and demanded by economic globalization.

In positing this I am rejecting the prevalent notion in much of the literature on globalization that the realm of the national and the realm of the global are two mutually exclusive zones.[18] My argument is rather that globalization is partly endogenous to the national and is in this regard produced through a dynamic of de-nationalizing what had been constructed as the national. And it is partly embedded in the national, e.g. global cities and in this regard requires that the state re-regulate specific aspects of its role in the national.[19]

17   See also generally the work by Slaughter on transgovernmental networks; Max Castro (ed.), *Free Markets, Open Societies, Closed Borders?* (Berkeley, Ca: University of California Press, 2000).

18   For a discussion of this issue see Saskia Sassen, *The Global City* (2nd edition - Princeton, N.J.: Princeton University Press, 2001), chapters 5 and 7.

19   An important point for me, typically disregarded in much general commentary about the global economy, is that a firm can participate in the latter even if it operates inside a single country: the key is whether it participates in a market or a transaction that is part of the global 'system'. My concern in this regard has been to show that there is considerable institutional development of that which we call the global economy – it is not simply a matter of goods or money crossing borders. For a firm's operations to be part of the global economy they need to be encased in this institutional framework. If they are not, they may be an informal cross-border transaction or part of the new transnational criminal economy. A simplified illustration of the point that the distinctiveness of participating in the global economy does not necessarily lie in the fact of crossing borders would be, for example, a US based firm (whether US or non-US) that invests in a non-US firm listed on the NY stock market. The point here is that there is a regime – a set of conditions and legalities – that governs the listing of foreign firms on a stock market that has been incorporated in the global system and that governs the conditions under which the investor can acquire stock in that firm. The key, determining issue for me is whether the firms and investors involved are operating under the umbrella of this regime. This umbrella is partly constituted through national institutions and partly, perhaps increasingly so, through the new privatized institutional framework I discuss later. What comes together in this example in my reading are some of the specifications I summarize in the global city model and in the notion of de-nationalization. On the other hand, the following would not be an instance of firms operating in the global economic system, even though it entails actual physical crossing of borders: two individuals residing in different countries making a deal informally for one of them to bring items, also informally – without following regulations, including

It is a field of particular types of transactions: they are strategic, cut across borders and entail specific interactions with private actors. They do not entail the state as such, as in international treaties, but rather consist of the operations and policies of specific sub-components of the state – for instance, legislative initiatives, specialized technical regulatory agencies, or some of the agendas pursued by central banks, e.g. setting what are called adequate capital ratios for banks. These are transactions that cut across borders in that they concern the standards and regulations imposed on firms and markets operating globally and hence produce a certain convergence at the level of national regulations and law in the creation of the requisite conditions for globalization.

By saying that they entail specific interactions with private actors I mean that it is not simply about interstate transactions, or a sub-field of the interstate system. On the contrary it is a field of transactions partly embedded in the inter-state system and partly in a new, increasingly institutionalized cross-border space of private agents/actors.

It is in this fairly rarefied field of transactions, partly disembedded from the broader institutional world of the state, that de-nationalized state agendas get defined and enacted. This field of transactions represents then an unbundling of whatever the condition of state bundling preceding the current period, i.e. the decades immediately following the end of World War II. The current period can be considered to be fully in swing for the case of the US by the mid 1980s. This unbundling is also one element in the broader dynamic of a changed relation between sovereignty and national territory – a subject I began to work on in my book *Losing Control?*

But for all of this to happen, it took a broader normative transformation in matters concerning the substantive rationality of the state, matters concerning *raison d'etat*. In good part this normative transformation is enacted outside the state and originates outside the inter-state system. Further, there is a multiplicity of private agents, some minor, some not so minor, that ensure and execute this new normative order. This transformation has to do with the normative weight gained by the logic of the global capital market in setting criteria for key national economic policies. Here I will only touch on this briefly since it is the focus of my second lecture.

WTO regulations – for the second individual to sell in the second country, with both individuals using informal accounting and trust systems to guarantee enforcement of the conditions of the agreement. This is an extreme contrast; there are many cases that are more ambiguous.

III. The Global Capital Market: Power and Norm-Making

In the multiple negotiations between national states and global economic actors we can see a new normativity that attaches to the *operational logic* of the capital market and that is succeeding in imposing itself on important aspects of national economic policy-making, though, as has been said often, some states are more sovereign than others in these matters. Some of the more familiar elements are the new importance attached to the autonomy of central banks, anti-inflation policies, exchange rate parity and the variety of items usually referred to as 'IMF conditionality'.[20] In this new normative order, certain claims emerge as legitimate. But that is not all: other types of claims are delegitimated – generally matters concerned with the well-being of people at large now often interpreted as making states 'less competitive' in a normative context where states are expected to become more so.

I try to capture this normative transformation in the notion of a privatizing of certain capacities for making norms that we have associated with the state, at least in our recent history. This brings with it strengthened possibilities of norm-making in the interests of the few rather than the majority – which in itself is not novel, except in its formalization and in its sharper restricting of who might benefit. It also brings with it an absence of accountability in domains of norm-making which when in the public sector were, at least in principle, subject to public scrutiny. Again, while in practice this might not spell much of a difference, it is the formalizing of this withdrawal from the sphere of public accountability that concerns me here.[21]

What I want to emphasize here is that the formation of a global capital market represents a concentration of power that is capable of influencing national government economic policy and by extension other policies. A key issue here has to do with questions of normativity – the fact that the global financial markets are not only capable of deploying raw power but also have produced a logic that now is seen as setting the criteria for 'proper' economic policy. IMF conditionality has some of these features.[22] These markets can now exercise the accountability functions associated with citizenship: they can vote governments' economic policies down or in; they can force governments to take certain measures and not others.

---

20 Since the South East Asian financial crisis there has been a revision of some of the specifics of these standards. For instance, exchange rate parity is now evaluated in less strict terms.

21 Again, to repeat, I am concerned here with a privatizing of types of norm-making which in the recent history of states under the rule of law were in the public domain. Thus, the Catholic Church has long had what in some ways could be described as private norm-making capacities. These kinds of cases do not concern me here.

22 There is an emerging literature on this. I have discussed this issue and some of the literature in *Losing Control? Sovereignty in an Age of Globalization, supra* n. 3, chapter 2.

How does this massive growth of financial flows and assets and the fact of an integrated global capital market affect states in their economic policy-making. Conceivably a global capital market could just be a vast pool of money for investors to shop in without conferring power over governments. The fact that it can discipline governmental economic policy making is a distinct power, one that is not *ipso facto* inherent in the existence of a large global capital market.

These conditions raise a number of questions concerning the impact of this concentration of capital in markets that ensure high degrees of circulation in and out of countries. How does this affect national economies and government policies? Does it alter the functioning of democratic governments? Does this kind of concentration of capital reshape the accountability relation that has operated through electoral politics between governments and their people? In brief, does it affect national sovereignty?[23]

Here I want to make just two observations. One is that national states have participated in the formation and implementation of some of these conditions and rules. It could be said that there is a consensus, even if imposed in some cases, among states to further the interests of this type of economic globalization.[24] This raises some rather specific questions about the absence of accountability one can detect in some of this work of the state geared towards producing instruments necessary for globalization; for instance, it is not clear to what extent the work done by some of the technical agencies regarding deregulation of the financial and of the telecommunications sector has been subjected to public scrutiny and debate.[25]

The second observation concerns what have been called the implicit ground rules of our legal system – matter that has not been formalized into rules of prohibition or permission and constitutes a *de facto* set of rules of permission.[26] The ground rules on which economic globalization is proceeding contain far more

23 See *Losing Control?*, *supra* n. 3 (chapter 2) where I examine some of the mechanisms through which the global capital market actually exercises its disciplining function on national governments and pressures them to become accountable to the logic of these markets.

24 Though many states are beginning to signal resistance and recognition that globalization will not bring the promised benefits. See in this regard the rapidity with which half of the ministers of trade attending the WTO meeting in Seattle were ready to forego signing. See also the finding by UNCTAD that the number of deeply indebted poor countries has gone up from 25 in 1985 to 41 today.

25 This is a crucial issue in my current research project (see supra n. 1 above).

26 To clarify what I mean, see Duncan Kennedy, 'The Stakes of Law, or Hale and Foucault!' in *Sexy Dressing Etc.: Essays on the Power and Politics of Cultural Identities* (Cambridge: Harvard University Press, 1993), pp. 83-125, on the argument that these ground rules in the case of the US contain rules of permission that strengthen the power of employers over workers, or that allow for a level in the concentration of wealth under the aegis of the protection of property rights that is beyond what is needed to ensure the protection of property rights.

permissions than have been formalized in explicit rules of permission and prohibition. Private firms in international finance, accounting and law, the new private standards for international accounting and financial reporting and supra-national organizations such as WTO, all play strategic non-government centred governance functions. This is the subject of the next section.

IV. A New Institutional Zone of Private Agents

While central, the role of the state in producing the legal encasements for economic operations is no longer what it was in earlier periods. Economic globalization has been accompanied by the creation of new legal regimes and legal practices and the expansion and renovation of some older forms that bypass national legal systems. This is evident in the rising importance of international commercial arbitration and the variety of institutions that fulfil rating and advisory functions that have become essential for the operation of the global economy.[27]

One aspect of this question concerns the particular forms of legal innovation that have been produced and within which much of globalization is encased and framed; and, further, how these innovations interact with the state, or more specifically, with the sovereignty of the state. The emerging privatized institutional framework to govern the global economy has possibly major implications for the exclusive authority of the modern national state over its territory, that is, its exclusive territoriality. There is a new set of intermediary strategic agents that contribute to the management and co-ordination of the global economy. They are largely, though not exclusively, private. And they have absorbed some of the international functions carried out by states in the recent past, for instance in the predominantly protectionist regimes of the post-World War II decades through which governments governed international trade.

Private firms in international finance, accounting and law, the new private standards for international accounting and financial reporting financial governance functions. The events following the Mexico crisis provide us with some interesting insights about these firms' role in changing the conditions for financial operation, about the ways in which national states participated and the formation of a new institutionalized intermediary space.

---

27   Dezalay and Garth, *supra* n. 11; Salacuse, *Making Global Deals: What Every Executive Should Know About Negotiating* (New York: Times Books, 1992); Timothy J. Sinclair, 'Passing Judgement: Credit Rating Processes as Regulatory Mechanisms of Governance in the Emerging World Order' 1: 1 (Spring 1994) 133-159; Sylvia Maxfield, *Gatekeepers of Growth* (Princeton: Princeton University Press, 1997); Sol Picciotto and Ruth Mayne, *Regulating International Business: Beyond Liberalization* (London: Macmillan, in association with OXFAM, 1999).

J.P. Morgan worked with Goldman Sachs and Chemical Bank to develop several innovative deals that brought back investors to Mexico's markets.[28] Further, in July 1996, an enormous US$ 6 billion-five year deal that offered investors a Mexican floating rate note or syndicated loan – backed by oil receivables from the state oil monopoly PEMEX – was twice oversubscribed. It became somewhat of a model for asset-backed deals from Latin America, especially oil-rich Venezuela and Ecuador. Key to the high demand was that the structure had been designed to capture investment grade ratings from S&P and Moody's (it got BBB- and Baa3). This was the first Mexican deal with an investment grade. The intermediaries worked with the Mexican government, but on their terms – this was not a government-to-government deal. This secured acceptability in the new institutionalized privatized intermediary space for cross-border transactions – evidenced by the high level of oversubscription and the high ratings. And it allowed the financial markets to grow on what had been a crisis.

After the Mexico crisis and before the first signs of the Asian crisis, we see a large number of very innovative deals that contribute to further expand the volumes in the financial markets and to incorporate new sources of profit, that is, debts for sale.[29] Typically these deals involved novel concepts of how to sell debt and what could be a saleable debt. Often the financial services firms structuring these deals also implemented minor changes in depository systems to bring them more in line with international standards. The aggressive innovating and selling on the world market of what had hitherto been thought to be too illiquid and too risky for such a sale further contributed to expand and strengthen the institutionalization of this intermediary space for cross-border transactions operating partly outside the inter-state system. The new intermediaries have done the strategic work, a kind of 'activism' towards ensuring growth in their industry and to overcome the potentially devastating effects of financial crises on the industry as a whole and on the whole notion of integrated global financial markets.

---

28 The US$ 40 billion emergency loan package from the IMF and the US government and the hiring of Wall Street's top firms to refurbish its image and find ways to bring it back into the market, helped Mexico 'solve' its financial crisis. With J.P. Morgan as its financial advisor the Mexican government worked with Goldman Sachs and Chemical Bank to come up with several innovative deals. Goldman organized a US$1.75 billion Mexican sovereign deal in which the firm was able to persuade investors in May 1996 to swap Mexican Brady bonds collateralized with US Treasury bonds (Mexican Bradys were a component of almost any emerging market portfolio until the 1994 crisis) for a 30-year naked Mexican risk. This is in my reading quite a testimony to the aggressive innovations that characterize the financial markets and to the importance of a whole new subculture in international finance that facilitates the circulation, i.e. sale, of these instruments.

29 For a more detailed account of these deals see Sassen, *The Global City, supra* n. 18.

Finally, the growing importance and formalization of what is now generally referred to as private authority is yet another component of the new privatized institutional order through which the global economy is governed and organized.[30] One important component of this development is the emergence of self-regulation in economic sectors dominated by a limited number of firms. It indicates the extent to which the global economic system needs governance and regulation, though of a different sort from that associated with the older normativity of the Keynesian state.

These and other such transnational institutions and regimes do raise important and difficult questions about the relation between the state and economic globalization. As Rosenau has noted, because so many processes are transnational, governments increasingly are not competent to address some of the major issues confronting our societies; this is not the end of sovereignty, but rather an alteration in the 'exclusivity and scope' of the competence of governments.[31]

V. Conclusion

A central effort in this chapter was to recover the ways in which the state participates in governing the global economy. The context is one increasingly dominated by deregulation, privatization and the growing authority of non-state actors, with some of these assuming new normative roles. In many of these new dynamics and conditions, the state continues to play an important role, often as the provider of the institutional home for the enactment of the new policy regimes we associate with globalization.

30 See, e.g. Thomas J. Biersteker, Rodney Bruce Hall and Craig N. Murphy (eds.), *Private Authority and Global Governance supra* n. 11; Claire A. Cutler, Virginia Haufler and Tony Porter (eds). *Private Authority in International Affairs, supra* n. 11; Rodney Bruce Hall, *Private Authority in the Changing Structure of Global Governance*. Presented at the workshop on 'Private Authority and International Order'. Thomas J. Watson Institute for International Studies, Brown University, (12-13 February 1999) among others.

31 There is a wider systemic process here that needs to be distinguished from the effects of globalization. There is a worldwide and apparently growing distrust of governments and bureaucracies. Martin Shapiro, 'The Globalization of Law', INDIANA JOURNAL OF GLOBAL LEGAL STUDIES 1 (Fall): 37-64, finds that this has contributed to the emergence of certain commonalities in law, notably the growing importance of constitutional individual rights that protect the individual from the state and other organizations. The particular hallmark of American constitutionalism is constitutional judicial review, which now has also emerged endogeneously in Germany and Italy, and to some extent even in France (where there is now an active constitutional court and a constitutional bill of rights). The Court of Justice of the EU has evolved into a constitutional court with human rights jurisdiction (which entailed that constitutions and rights had to come about in Europe), Saskia Sassen, *The 1995 Columbia University Leonard Hastings Schoff Memorial Lectures, supra* n. 3, chapter 1.

My concern with unpacking this particular issue stems in good part from the fact of the embeddedness of much of globalization in national territory under conditions where national territory has been encased in an elaborate set of national laws and administrative capacities. The new geography of global economic processes and the strategic spaces for economic globalization, had to be produced, both in terms of the practices of corporate actors and the requisite technical and institutional infrastructure (i.e. global cities), as well as in terms of the work of the state in producing or legitimating new legal regimes. This signals a necessary participation by the state, including in the regulation of its own withdrawal. The question then becomes one of understanding the specific type of authority/power this participation gives to the state, or attaches to various institutions of the state, as might be the case with some of the increasingly specialized technical regulatory agencies.

The mode in which this participation by the state has evolved has been towards strengthening the power and legitimacy of privatized and de-nationalized state authorities. The outcome is an emergent new spatio-temporal order that has considerable governance capabilities and structural power. This institutional order contributes to strengthen the advantages of certain types of economic and political actors and to weaken those of others. It is extremely partial rather than universal, but strategic in that it has undue influence over wide areas of the broader institutional world and the world of lived experience yet is not fully accountable to formal democratic political systems. While partially embedded in national institutional settings it is distinct from these. Insofar as it is partly installed in national settings, its identification requires a decoding of what is national in what has historically been constructed as the national.

These developments have consequences for certain features of the state and the inter-state system and in this regard inevitably perhaps for liberal democracy as well as for international law and the modes of accountability therein contained. Firstly, the fact of a growth in cross-border activities and global actors operating outside the formal inter-state system, affects the competence and scope of states and of international law as these have been constituted historically. Secondly, the fact that this domain is increasingly being institutionalized and subjected to the development of private governance mechanisms, affects the exclusivity of state authority and the (albeit always partial) exclusivity of international law. Thirdly, the fact of growing normative powers in this private domain affects the normative power of international law. Fourthly, the state's participation in the re-regulation of its role in the economy and the incipient de-nationalization of particular institutional components of the state necessary to accommodate some of the new policies linked to globalization, transform key aspects of the state and in so doing alter the organizational architecture for democratic accountability inside states and they alter the organizational architecture for the inter-state system and for international law.

My emphasis on the multiple ways, including very minor ones, in which the new regime for the implementation of the global economy is constituted in good part through the work of states, aims at understanding the possibilities for constructing new forms of state authority under the current conditions. This would include forms of state authority that would not be confined to furthering economic globalization but rather aim at greater equity and accountability. In this regard then, my position is not comfortably subsumed under the proposition that nothing much has changed in terms of state power. Nor can it be subsumed under the proposition of the declining significance of the state. It aims rather at mapping an intermediate zone marked by great possibilities for changing current alignments. It is then a possibly highly dynamic intermediate zone with different outcomes depending on the types of political work that gets done.

PART II

THE TRANSFORMATION OF THE RELATIONSHIP BETWEEN PUBLIC AND PRIVATE IN A GLOBALIZING SOCIETY

Chapter 4

Global Private Regimes: Neo-Spontaneous Law and Dual Constitution of Autonomous Sectors?

Gunther Teubner[*]

I. Standard Theses and Counter Theses on Globalization

In the current globalization debate the law appears to be dependent upon economic and political developments that move into a new dimension of de-politicization, de-centralization and de-individualization. For all the correct observations in detail, though, this debate is bringing about a drastic (polit) economic reduction of the role of law that I wish to challenge in this chapter. Here one has to take on Wallerstein's misconception of 'worldwide economies' according to which the formation of the global society is seen as a basically economic process.[1] Autonomous globalization processes in other social spheres running parallel to economic globalization need to be taken seriously. In protest against such (polit) economic reductionism several strands of the debate, among them the neo-institutionalist theory of 'global culture', post-modern concepts of global legal pluralism, ideas of differentiation of global society and various versions of 'global civil society' have shaped the idea of a polycentric globalization.[2] From these angles the remarkable multiplicity of a global

*   I would like to thank Sean Smith for his helpful comments on this chapter.
1   Immanuel Wallerstein, *The Capitalist World Economy* (Cambridge: Cambridge University Press, 1979).
2   'Global Culture': Alexander Meyer, 'World Society and the Nation State', 103 AMERICAN JOURNAL OF SOCIOLOGY, 144 (1997); 'global legal pluralism': Boaventura d. S. Santos, *Toward a New Common Sense: Law, Science and Politics in the Paradigmatic Transition* (New York: Routledge, 1995); Lawrence M., 'Borders: On the Emerging Sociology of Transnational Law', 32 STANFORD JOURNAL OF INTERNATIONAL LAW 65 (1996); 'global society': Niklas Luhmann, 'Der Staat des politischen Systems: Geschichte und Stellung in der Weltgesellschaft'. in U. Beck (ed.) *Perspektiven der Weltgesellschaft* (Frankfurt: Suhrkamp, 1998), 345-380 at 373ff.;

society, in which tendencies to re-politicization, re-rationalization and re-individualization are becoming visible at the same time, becomes evident.[3] I shall contrast two standard theses on the globalization of law with two less current counter-theses:

- *First standard thesis*: globalization is relevant for law since emerging global markets undermine the control potential of national policy and therefore also the chances of legal regulation.
- *First counter-thesis*: globalization produces a set of problems intrinsic to law itself, consisting of a self-deconstruction of the dominant law-making processes.
- *Second standard thesis*: globalization means that law's role is to institutionalize the worldwide shift in power from governmental actors to economic actors.
- *Second counter-thesis*: globalization means that the law has a chance of contributing to a dual constitution of autonomous sectors of world society.

II.   Global Private Regimes as Sources of Law without the State

The narrow view sees above all a crisis of law sparked off by the globalization of the economy: world markets are taking the control instruments away from national politics, entailing an evaporation of expectations of control through law too, which is seen as only an instrument for the political regulation of society.[4] The corresponding hopes are concentrated on political responses to the de-nationalization of politics, energetic pushes toward political unification processes at European and global levels and on concepts of cosmopolitan democracy, strengthening the democratic potential of supra-national political processes systematically, *inter alia* by making extensive use of legal norms.[5]

'global civil society': Martin Shaw, 'Die Repräsentation ferner Konflikte und die globale Zivilgesellschaft' in U. Beck (ed.) *Perspektiven der Weltgesellschaft* (Frankfurt: Suhrkamp, 1998), 221-255.

3   Gili S. Drori, 'Science, Democracy and Governability: On the Political Consequences of Science Globalization' in G.S. Drori, Th*e National Science Agenda as a Ritual of Modern Nation-Statehood: The Consequences of National Science for Development Projects* (G. S. Drori ed., 2001).

4   E.g. Ralf Dahrendorf, 'Anmerkungen zur Globalisierung' in U. Beck (ed.) *Perspektiven der Weltgesellschaft* (Frankfurt: Suhrkamp, 1998), 31-54 at 42 ff.

5   Most clearly in David Held, *Democracy and the Global Order: From the Modern State to Cosmopolitan Governance* (Cambridge: Polity Press, 1995); David Held, 'Rethinking Democracy: Globalization and Democratic Theory' in W. Streeck (ed.) *Internationale Wirtschaft, nationale Demokratie: Herausforderungen für die Demokratietheorie* (Frankfurt: Campus, 1998), 59-78.

In Streeck's cold critique of such 'concrete utopias',[6] this view hopelessly over-estimates not just the democratic potential of global politics, but also the control capacity of transnational law and the guarantees of individual action through fundamental rights. At the same time, however, the inherent range of problems for law itself in globalization are overlooked.[7] For the deconstruction to which global law is exposed comes not just from outside, from the shrinking control potential of politics *vis-à-vis* the economy, but also and especially from within, from an erosion of fundamental validity claims of law itself. Globalization of law itself is taking place in relative distance from political globalization and in it the traditional forms of law are deconstructed through its norm-producing routines themselves.[8]

For the source of the new global law is no longer only institutionalized politics which is still not really global but only international politics, but also and especially other social systems that in the race to globalization have long overtaken politics.[9] The economy, not just the economy but other social sectors such as science, technology, the mass media, medicine, education or transport are, on their specific path to globalization, developing a massive requirement for norms that is met not by governmental and intergovernmental institutions but by themselves in direct action upon the law. Increasingly, global private regimes are producing substantive law without the state, without national legislation or international treaties.[10] Everywhere the cancerous spread of private regulation, agreements and dispute resolution is growing; in short, law-making is happening 'alongside the state'.[11] The requirements of global societies' self-created laws are then not at all primarily

---

6   Wolfgang Streeck, 'Einleitung: Internationale Wirtschaft, nationale Demokratie?' in W. Streeck (ed.) *Internationale Wirtschaft, nationale Demokratie: Herausforderungen für die Demokratietheorie* (Frankfurt: Campus, 1998), 11-58 at 17.

7   Martin Shapiro, 'The Globalization of Law', 1 INDIANA JOURNAL OF GLOBAL LEGAL STUDIES 37 (1993); Lawrence M. Friedman, supra n. 2; Gunther Teubner, 'Global Bukowina: Legal Pluralism in the World-Society', in Gunther Teubner (Hg.) *Global Law Without A State* (Dartsmouth: London, 1996), 3-28; Gunther Teubner, 'The King's Many Bodies: The Self-Deconstruction of Law's Hierarchy', 31 LAW AND SOCIETY REVIEW 763 (1997); Mathias Albert, 'A Global Law Field: What Makes Law Law in World Society'. Paper for 1999 World Congress for Legal and Social Philosophy (IVR-99), (New York, 1999a); Mathias Albert, 'Globalisierung und Entgrenzung des Rechts'. in R. Voigt (ed.) *Globalisierung des Recht*. (Baden-Baden: Nomos, 1999) 115-137.

8   For more on this see Gunther Teubner, 'The King's Many Bodies: The Self-Deconstruction of Law's Hierarchy', supra n. 7; Gunther Teubner, 'Breaking Frames: The Global Interplay of Legal and Social Systems', 45 THE AMERICAN JOURNAL OF COMPARATIVE LAW 149 (1997).

9   For references see supra n. 2.

10 Oran Young, *International Governance. Protecting the Environment in a Stateless Society* (Ithaca: Cornell University Press, 1994).

11 Volker Ronge, *Am Staat vorbei* (Frankfurt: Campus, 1980).

political control of social processes, but derive from original needs for security of expectations and solution of conflicts.

In this dynamic, the most dramatic changes are as it were taking place at the edges of law, in the structural linkages of law with other social subsystems.

A political constitution, formed in the history of the nation states as a linkage between politics and law and at the same time claiming to govern law's relations to other social sectors, is not present at global level.[12] Instead, as it were there naturally emerges a multiplicity of subconstitutions – linkages of global law to other global subsystems – that to date have escaped constitutional governance dominated by politics. It is no wonder, since the structural linkage to politics happens at global level now only through the cumbersome and not very efficient institutions of international public law.

The focus in law-making is shifting to private regimes, that is, to binding agreements among global players, to private market regulation through multinational enterprises, internal rule-making within international organizations, inter-organizational negotiating systems, and worldwide standardization processes.[13] The dominant sources of law are now to be found at the peripheries of law, at the boundaries with other sectors of world society that are successfully engaging in regional competition with the existing centres of law-making – national parliaments, global legislative institutions and intergovernmental agreements.

Justice in the narrower sense, the national and international courts, is seeing counterparts develop in quasi-private bodies for resolving conflicts in society.[14] International organizations, courts of arbitration, mediation bodies, ethical committees and treaty systems are developing into courts of private justice, acting as an organized subsystem of world law, but getting along without prior governmental infrastructural provision.[15] Autonomous global law is increasingly basing itself on its own resources. International organizations, multinational enterprises, global law

12   Niklas Luhmann, *Das Recht der Gesellschaft* (Frankfurt: Suhrkamp, 1993), 571ff.

13   Peter Muchlinski, "Global Bukowina" Examined: Viewing the Multinational Enterprise as a Transnational Law-Making Community' in G. Teubner (ed.) *Global Law Without A State, supra* n. 7, 79-108; Jean-Philippe Robé, 'Multinational Enterprises: The Constitution of a Pluralistic Legal Order', in G. Teubner (ed.), *Global Law Without A State, supra* n. 7; Andrea Bianchi, 'Globalization of Human Rights: The Role of Non State Actors', in G. Teubner (ed.) *Global Law Without A State*, op. cit., 179-212.

14   Rosalyn Higgins, 'The Reformation in International Law' in R. Rawlings (ed.) *Law, Society and Economy* (Oxford: Oxford University Press: 1997), 207-224 at 216 ff.

15   Cf. e.g. for contractual systems, Jean G. Belley, *Le contrat entre droit, économie et société* (Cowansville: Yvon Blais, 1998) at 155ff; for associational systems, James R. Nafziger, 'International Sports Law as a Process for Resolving Disputes', INTERNATIONAL AND COMPARATIVE LAW QUARTERLY (1996), 130-149. A detailed case study of global law-making in one specialized private regime is in Jens Kellerhoff, *Oil and Money* (Firenze: European University Institute, 1998).

firms, global funds, global associations, global arbitration courts, are legal institutions that are pushing forward the global law-making process.[16]

All in all, in globalization dominant law-making is shifting from the centres of law that had been politically institutionalized in the nation state (legislature and judiciary) to the peripheries of law, to the boundaries between the law and other globalized social sectors. The new world law is primarily peripheral and spontaneous. Private government, private regulation and private justice are becoming central sources of law[17] – phenomena intrinsically legal that within the nation state had been successfully shoved off into the grey areas of non-legal factuality only because they were caught up in and disciplined by a comprehensive set of rules in national law. On a world scale, however, legal regulation of social activities by private actors is effectively escaping from the thoroughly institutionalized framework conditions of the nation state without comparable framework conditions growing up, or even being within sight. In the global private regimes an effective self-deconstruction of law is coming about that is quite simply setting essential basic principles of national law out of force: the derivation of validity of legal norms in a hierarchy of sources of law, the legitimation of law through a political constitution, the making of law by parliamentary bodies, the rule of law based on institutions, procedures and principles, and the guarantee of individual freedoms through basic rights that have been fought for politically.

III. What makes the Difference between Customary and Neo-Spontaneous Law?

Ought this sort of 'spontaneous' global law to be seen as a hypermodern variant of traditional customary law? There are indeed attempts to equip this honourable, but false, category with new respectability, particularly in international public law.[18]

---

16 Yves Dezalay and Bryant Garth, 'Merchants of Law as Moral Entrepreneurs', 29 LAW & SOCIETY REVIEW 12 (1995); John Flood and Eleni Skordaki, 'Normative Bricolage: Informal Rule-Making by Accountants and Lawyers' in G. Teubner (ed.) *Global Law Without A State* (Aldershot: Dartmouth Gower, 1997), 109-131; David M.Trubek, Jim Mosher and Jeffrey S. Rothstein, 'Transnationalism in the Regulation of labour Relations: International Regimes and Transnational Adcocacy Networks', 11 JOURNAL OF LAW AND SOCIAL INQUIRY 1 (1999).

17 Stuart Henry, *Private Justice* (Boston: Routledge and Kegan Paul, 1983); Oliver Gerstenberg, 'Law's Polyarchy: A Comment on Cohen and Sabel'. 3 EUROPEAN LAW JOURNAL 343 (1997).

18 Cf. Stephen Zamora, 'Is There Customary International Economic Law?' 32 GERMAN YEARBOOK OF INTERNATIONAL LAW 9 (1989); Bruce L. Benson, 'Customary Law as a Social Contract: International Commercial Law', 3 CONSTITUTIONAL POLITICAL ECONOMY 1 (1992); David P. Fidler, 'Challenging the Classical Concept

What is there in the law-making decisions of private governance regimes that can be seen as corresponding to the *consuetudo longa* of states as subjects of international law? Where is the *opinio iuris doctorum*?

Admittedly, old customary law and the new private regimes do have something in common. Both bodies of rules have a social origin, and did not emerge from positive law-making by a national sovereign; indeed the sovereign is no longer even centrally involved in their legal recognition. And they have no central body to allocate validity. But the differences weigh much more. True customary law grows out of long-term processes of diffuse communication and recursive interaction that particularly in traditional societies constitute a dominant type of law-making. Social norms owed to silently operating forces of informal co-ordination of conduct are in certain circumstances taken over into the legal system as customary law.[19] By comparison with such diffuse communication processes the new private regimes are a typical product of social differentiation. They are highly specialized forms of explicit norm-making within functional subsystems in the modern world. They emerge not on the basis of informal co-ordination of conduct in a gradual process of repeated interactions, but through positive law-making in organized decision-making processes in specialized formal organizations.[20] That is why they cannot be celebrated as new 'spontaneous rules' *à la* Hayek,[21] able to stand up against the constructivist excesses of the nation states on a world scale.[22] For against Hayek's artificial separation of constructivist and spontaneous law-making and his unrestrained overestimation of habits and customs, the specificity of the neo-spontaneous law lies only in the fact that it is based not on governmental decision but on more or less thoroughly organized social processes that – and here is the problem for legal policies – each bring about a very specific selectivity of the norm-making.

of Custom: Perspectives on the Future Customary International Law', 39 GERMAN YEARBOOK OF INTERNATIONAL LAW 198 (1996).

19   The best analyses are still Theodor Geiger, *Vorstudien zu einer Soziologie des Rechts* (Neuwied: Luchterhand, 1987), (Berlin: Duncker & Humblot, 1964); on this see Thomas Raiser, DAS LEBENDE RECHT (Baden-Baden: Nomos, 1995) at 138 ff; 142 ff; cf. also Hans O. Freitag, GEWOHNHEITSRECHT UND RECHTSSYSTEM (Berlin: Duncker und Humblot, 1976).

20   Stuart Henry, *Private Justice*, supra n. 17; Stuart Henry, 'The Construction and Deconstruction of Social Control: Thoughts on the Discursive Production of State Law and Private Justice' in J. Lowmann, R. Menzies and T. Palys (ed.) *Transcarceration: Essays in the Sociology of Social Control* (Aldershot: Gower: 1987), 89-108.

21   Friedrich A. Hayek, Law, Legislation and Liberty. Volume 1: Rules and Order, (London: Routledge & Paul, 1973).

22   This is just what was said in a symposium on Hayek's legal thinking: Robert D. Cooter, 'Decentralized Law for a Complex Economy'. 23 SOUTHWESTERN UNIVERSITY LAW REVIEW 443 (1994).

How then are the new qualities to be understood, if not as resembling customary law? Calling them 'spontaneous' law-making without further ado is certainly a false romanticism, in view of the 'constructivism' in planning and implementing decisions in the private regimes, in ISO standards, in standard business contracts, in thoroughly codified sets of rules in multinational enterprises, and international specialized associations. Obviously, though, what we are looking at is a new and peculiar mixture of spontaneous and organized processes. Its special feature seems to be that by contrast with traditional customary law there has been a reversal of the relationship between spontaneous and organized norm-making we have known till now. Increasing formality, organization and positivity of social norms versus increasing spontaneity, fragmentation and chaos of their juridification – is this supposed to be the characteristic feature of neo-spontaneous law? An orderly world society *vis-à-vis* a disorderly world law?

Traditionally, while spontaneous rule-making (usages, social norms) was concentrated in society, on the periphery of the legal system, organized rule making took place at the centre of law (courts, legislation). This prefigured a strict conceptual and institutionalized separation of normativity and validity. The substantive constitution of norms in society was clearly separated from their validity-allocating transformation into law. Relative indeterminacy, diffuseness and vagueness of long-term norming processes in society were counterposed to clearly outlined procedures of validity allocation, organizational hierarchies of law-making bodies, a system of precedents and a thorough textualization of law. To this there corresponded a clear trend to minimize customary law in modern societies.[23] Legal doctrine tends to downplay it into a 'possible inspiration' for official law-making.[24] Jurists usually look only at the legal validity allocation of the social norms in question by courts and legislators, but do not bother particularly about their social origin. It is only the (legislative or judicial) validity allocation that was of interest. But that means losing sight of one feature essential to legal decision-making: how ought the law to respond to the differing selectivity of diverse social norm-setting processes that distort the 'justice' of social norms?

The category of customary law ended up by losing its shape entirely. As the act of judicial decision increasingly took centre stage and social processes came to be regarded as merely sociological facts and therefore juridically irrelevant, lawyers began more or less to equate judge-made law and customary law.[25] Thus today in private law heterogeneous institutions, i.e. typical social norming of economic transaction on the one hand, and on the other such typical judicial innovations

23   John W. Salmond, *Salmond on Jurisprudence* (London: Sweet & Maxwell, 1966) at 66 ff.

24   Klaus Adomeit, *Rechtsquellenfragen im Arbeitsrecht* (München : Beck, 1969), 57.

25   Josef Esser, 'Richterrecht, Gerichtsgebrauch und Gewohnheitsrecht' in *Festschrift für Fritz von Hippel* (Tübingen : Mohr & Siebeck, 1967), 95-130.

inspired by legal scholarship are equally treated as modern forms of customary law.[26] In this way customary law and judge-made law, two equally questionable ways of making law in the light of the official legislative monopoly on law-making, were able to support and legitimate each other. But at the same time there was a loss of the sense that the legal transformation of social norms has to be subject to quite different procedures and criteria than the constitution of norms through the judicial dispute-settling process itself.

By contrast today in the process of globalization one can note a reversal of the relationship between the spontaneous and the organized. Since there is no global political body to underpin the institutionalization of an organized sphere of decision in law politically, the genuinely legal norm-setting process becomes fragmented in the wide-open spaces of the Brave New World, unco-ordinatedly and uncontrollably. To that extent this justifies the talk of the 'New Middle Ages' in global post-modernity.[27] So does the observation that 'the world legal system looks more like the types of order in tribal societies, meaning that it has to renounce organized sanctioning power and authentic definition of infringements of law on the basis of known rules'.[28] On the other hand, however, the thorough rationalization of social subspheres on a world scale has the consequence that social norms are based increasingly less on spontaneous co-ordination of conduct but are increasingly positivised, i.e. brought into validity on the basis of highly organized 'private' decision-making processes. Both together amount to the tendency to have organized norm-making in social subspheres at the periphery of law and spontaneous norm-making at the centre of law.

This changes the relationship between normativity and validity. Since at global level clear-cut fully institutionalized procedures and centralized decision-making bodies are lacking, the validity criteria for law are extremely diffuse. This is connected with one typical feature of global society, for which 'heterarchical, connectionistic, network-type linkage of communications at the level of organizations and professions'[29] is typical. In view of the unco-ordinated multiplicity of decentrally organized legal deciding bodies, the question of what legal rule actually applies can be answered unambiguously now only for the individual case which has been decided. Establishing the validity of a rule in world law that extends temporally and spatially is, however paradoxical it may sound, extremely difficult if not impossible. For on a world scale there is no decision-

---

26 Klaus F. Röhl, *Allgemeine Rechtslehre* (Köln: Heymanns, 1995) at 555.
27 Hedley Bull, *The Anarchical Society: A Study of Order in World Politics* (London : Macmillan, 1977).
28 Niklas Luhmann, 'Das Paradox der Menschenrechte und drei Formen seiner Entfaltung' in N. Luhmann, *Soziologische Aufklärung 6: Die Soziologie und der Mensch* (Opladen : Westdeutscher Verlag, 1995), 229-236 at 234.
29 Niklas Luhmann, 'Der Staat des politischen Systems: Geschichte und Stellung in der Weltgesellschaft', *supra* n. 2 at 375.

making hierarchy, no established body of precedents, but only heterarchical, spontaneous co-ordination among various law-making bodies.[30] This explains the phenomenon, extremely irritating to jurists trained in national law, of the only weak identification of norms. Hence the remarkably old-fashioned appeal to diffuse 'customary law' (but without *consuetudo* and without *opinio juris*), the rather unrealistic recourse to such corporatist legal forms as the *lex mercatoria*, the natural-law invocation of generally valid legal principles of the international legal community, the relying on the harmonizing of national systems, the exaggerated hopes for convergence in comparative law, the reliance on legal scholarship and the secret but legally authoritative negotiating processes at international conferences of experts.

At the same time, however, it also becomes remarkably indefinite where the locus of the positivization of law, the locus where binding decisions on normativity and validity are taken, is to be found. Wherever you look, the relevant validity decision appears always to be being taken somewhere else. In the global private regimes where the typical combination of organized social norm-making and spontaneous processes of law-making occurs, the norm production is decentralized to a multiplicity of political and private actors without it being possible to make out any clear decision-taking centre. Law-making is at the same time remarkably circular: the actors constantly appeal to legal norms the basis for the validity of which is however questionable. And just this ongoing practice of pretension to be law – or even swearing by legal myths – and not, say, a decision, influenced by a lobby of private actors, of a central law-making body is what brings the new law into validity.[31] A striking example is the *lex mercatoria*, so reproached for its phantom nature.[32] It is on the same mechanism that standardization is based, coming about silently in a sequence of very wordy international expert conferences. And a current example of such 'neo-spontaneous' law-making in non-economic fields is the law of humanitarian intervention, where the persuasive role of the media in the 'emerging international law' cannot possibly be overestimated. It is not the breach of law that makes the scandal, but the scandal that makes the new law. Another example are such NGOs as Greenpeace or Amnesty International, which appeal continually to the validity of human rights although these have not in any way been made positive through treaties or court judgements. A whole range of really non-legitimated private actors is involved in this peculiar invocation of law: media,

---

30 Ursula Stein, *Lex mercatoria: Realität und Theorie* (Frankfurt: Klostermann, 1995), 164 ff.
31 Luhmann, *supra* n. 12, 579 ff.
32 Ursula Stein, *supra* n. 30; Yves Dezalay and Bryant Garth, *supra* n. 16.

professional associations, non-governmental organizations and multinational enterprises.[33]

Ultimately, the selectivity of rule-making changes by comparison with the traditional political positivization of law. This is a challenge for legal policies to develop criteria and procedures that would compensate for this selectivity. It is no longer enough for the law to become sensitive to the selectivity of genuinely political institutions further and set up more or less openly compensatory procedures and criteria within the law for cases of 'failure of politics'. Here, in the specific selectivity of neo-spontaneous global law, there lies the challenge for the theory of sources of law. For the law of the nation state disposed in relation to 'private' normings of a range of political and administrative corrective mechanisms (judicial review of standard contracts, regulatory bodies, corporatist negotiations with decisive involvement of the state). But these are all largely absent on a world scale. If the theory of sources of law is not just to classify by origins of norms but to analyse according to social legitimation and legal monitoring different types of law-making, then it has to distinguish the global norm-making processes strictly according to the various social rationalities involved and their various specific selectivities, in order to be able to develop differing procedures and criteria for their legal review.

In the relationship between law and politics the nation state tradition has set a model that still has to be developed in the relationship of law to other social sectors in analogous fashion. In what respect does the law have to adapt to the rationality of the other system, and in what respect clearly distance itself from it? In national legal systems typical techniques of distancing from institutionalized politics are developed: depoliticization and neutralization of party political decisions, reconstruction of result-oriented 'policies' as universal legal principles, modified incorporation of political decisions in legal doctrine according to legal criteria of consistency, and most massively, of course, the constitutional review of legislative acts. But legal review of political legislation is, as the example of party financing shows, all the more present the less the political process is structurally capable of adopting regulations adequate to the matter. On the other side, however, there has also – and this is often overlooked – been a far-reaching adaptation of modern law to the logic of politics, in which the programmes of law, not just the contents of norms but also the methodological programmes, were drastically 'politicized': from teleological interpretation via policy orientation and interest balancing up to impact assessment and consequentialist orientation.

But where is the analogous policy-mix of distance and adaptation that global law would have to develop *vis-à-vis* non-political sectors if the latter are now increasingly responsible for non-legislative law-making? Global technological

---

33   Andrea Bianchi, 'Globalization of Human Rights: The Role of Non State Actors', *supra* n. 13 at 185 ff.

standards require different procedures and criteria of legal review than do international standard contracts or global codes of conduct of international professional associations.

Global standardization processes, coming about partly through market forces, partly through being laid down internally in international organizations, partly through negotiations between private and public actors, are among the most important sources of global law.[34] If scientific, technical or medical cognitive standards are normed and ultimately juridified, then here too the law has developed an adequate mixture of distance and adaptation *vis-à-vis* science and technology. The depoliticization of legislative decisions corresponds to a 'descientification' of standards. The borderline between lawful and unlawful is (necessarily) fixed 'arbitrarily' without adequate scientific foundation. At the same time it is charged with political, moral and economic aspects. In this way standards turn into 'trans-scientific issues'.[35] Procedures and criteria for this transformation are still largely *desiderata* that would go far beyond the usual call to involve the participation of interest groups concerned. On the other hand a scientification of law comparable to the politicization of legal methodology is coming about. Irrespective of whether the law makes exact threshold values positive or makes reference to the 'state of knowledge', it still makes itself dependent on scientific and technological development. Here too, procedures and criteria are available only in rudimentary fashion, and as the debate on 'science courts' is showing have not yet got beyond legal policy approaches.

Rule-making within international organizations is a further source of global law. Routines and hierarchical law-making within these organizations are rendered positive internally, and then juridified in conflict situations through relatively informal procedures.[36] Here, too, the law still has to find an adequate mixture of distance from and adjustment to the formal organization. Legal norms marked as valid must be separated clearly from the micro-politics of the organization, even if they have their origin there. On the other hand, law-making remains dependent on the processes in international organizations. General clauses of 'the interest of the organization' are suitable for legally combining aspects within the organization and outside.

Mutatis mutandis the same applies to the role of law in relation to rule-making by international negotiating systems, organizational agreements and contractual agreements of various private actors, but also to standard contracts of multinational

---

34 Christian Joerges, Karl-Heinz Ladeur, and Ellen Vos, (Hrsg.) *The Integration of Scientific Expertise into Standard-Setting* (Baden-Baden: Nomos, 1997).

35 Giandomenico Majone, 'Science and Trans-Science in Standard-Setting', 9 SCIENCE, TECHNOLOGY & HUMAN VALUES 15 (1984).

36 Jean-Philippe Robé, 'Multinational Enterprises: The Constitution of a Pluralistic Legal Order', *supra* n. 13 at 45-77.

enterprises. If the law incorporates private regulation of markets by collective actors, then here too the point is a combination of de-economization of transaction expectations with a continuing dependence of law on economic processes.

Accordingly, instead of talking of a unitary 'customary law' at global level, various types of social law linking up with various global sectors and typified by differing internal organization of norm production have to be distinguished, and differing requirements as to the law's distance and adjustment have to be correspondingly clearly developed.

IV. Global Civil Society and the Rise of a Dual Constitution

The standard repertoire of the globalization debate includes a second thesis: the law's role in globalization is essentially only to formalize the new shift of power between governmental and economic actors in legal terms. The law is seen as recording the global primacy of the economy, and developing the appropriate concepts, norms and principles. Here again I should like to criticize the (polit) economic narrowing of the focus in the legal debate and raise a counter-thesis: globalization simultaneously opens the chance for law to institutionalize a dual constitution in sectors of global society.

Ought one in this connection to speak of a global civil society able to oppose the steering mechanisms of globalized markets and political arenas with a third aspect, a civil and democratic one? In fact, hopes for global potential for democracy are, along with a renewal of the political system, concentrating on the emergence of a civil society on a global scale, opening up new chances for re-politicization and re-individualization.[37]

> Finally new international systems have also arisen that are able more or less to escape the grip of the State: think only of the regulatory systems for international financial markets, the Internet, the networks of non-governmental organizations, the decision-making structures of transnational groups, but also, on the downside, of organized, globally organized, crime ... yet they also constitute a global potential for democratization.[38]

What are the catalysts of a global civil society that might be able to oppose the economic and political dynamic with a credible dynamic of its own? Alongside politics and the economy other social phenomena are pursuing a globalization path of their own, but it seems difficult to identify the new subjects of global society.

37 Martin Shaw, *supra* n. 2 at 238 ff.
38 Ulrich Menzel, *Globalisierung versus Fragmentierung* (Frankfurt: Suhrkamp, 1998), 258.

Proposals for identification oscillate between the idealization of social movements and concentration on formal bureaucratic organizations.

In view of spectacular success recently, protest movements are the natural candidates for a democratic potential at world level.[39] Yet as a countervailing power to globalized economies and politics, they would no doubt be hopelessly out of their depth. Admittedly they are indispensable in their provocative focusing on social problems that no specialized social institution is taking up. And these provocations ought to become steadily more important with the relative loss of power by national political institutions. Yet their activities are only irritations: they themselves have little potential to solve the problems they raise. Protest movements are at bottom parasitic. They presuppose specialized institutions with high problem-solving potential, which they accuse of over-specialized tunnel vision and can provoke into innovations.

Ought one then to identify the global civil society with interest groups on a world scale? Similarly to the interest group pluralism in nation states, they are able to politicize civil-society problems and exercise political pressure upon globally acting political institutions.[40] Yet this view suffers from its narrowing down to politics, something that given the glaring weakness of genuinely political institutions in world society has particularly fatal outcomes.

If not protest movements or lobby groups, then at least NGOs! The non-governmental organizations have been seen as the new successful type of global actor, between states and the multinationals.[41] The astonishing success of Greenpeace, Amnesty International, environment groups and human rights organizations seems to support a certain view that sees the crystallization point of a global civil society here. For by contrast with the diffuse protest movements, they have at their disposal the punch and chances for rationalization of a formal bureaucratic organization that make them able to communicate with government organizations and multinational groups. Yet this organizational strength of theirs is at the same time their weakness in civil society. The false starting point lies in their

---

39 Markus S. Schulz, 'Collective Action Across Borders: Opportunity Structures, Network Capacities, and Communicative Practice in the Age of Advanced Globalization', 41 SOCIOLOGICAL PERSPECTIVES 587 (1998); Richard Falk, 'Die Weltordnung innerhalb der Grenzen von zwischenstaatlichem Recht und dem Recht der Menschheit: Die Rolle der zivilgesellschaftlichen Institutionen' in M. Lutz-Bachmann und J. Bohman (eds.) *Frieden durch Recht: Kants Friedensidee und das Problem einer neuen Weltordnung.* (Frankfurt: Suhrkamp, 1996), 170-186.

40 Wolfgang Streeck and Philippe Schmitter, Private Interest Government: *Beyond Market and State* (London: Sage, 1985); W. Streeck and Ph. Schmitter, 'From National Corporatism to Transnational Pluralism: Organized Interests in the Single European Market', 19 *Politics and Society* 133 (1991).

41 Richard Falk, *supra* n. 39.

formal organization. Formal organization is no substitute for a social dynamic that might be comparable with globalized markets and politics.

The only realistic candidate for a dynamic civil society is a pluralism of autonomous global social subsystems. This is the point where theories on 'global culture' and on global civil society, drawing attention to a plurality of global institutions between the economy and politics, converge with systems-theory analyses of the polycontextural world society.[42] Only here can one find a social dynamic that has a chance of autonomy *vis-à-vis* world markets and global political arenas. Social subsystems pursuing a globalization path of their own in their autonomous rationality are what in the first place forms the social basis relatively independent of political and economic processes, starting from which interest groups, non-governmental organizations and private governance regimes on the one hand and social movements on the other can develop their activities. The point is therefore a combination of social spheres of autonomy and corresponding formal organizations, if we wish to speak at all realistically of civil society elements in global society.

Here chances are now becoming apparent for globalization that remain hidden from a political and economic view. The dynamic of globalization makes the peculiar relationship between a spontaneous and a formally organized sphere visible within the various social subsystems. Globalization means that many social sectors have the chance to free themselves from the restrictions that nation state politics had imposed on them. In the relationship of the subsystems to each other, the cards are being re-dealt. Research, education, the health system, the media, arts – for these social sectors the globalization process is opening a chance not just to assert the autonomy of their activities but also to establish an autonomous regime.[43] For law there accordingly arises a new role of institutionalizing a dual constitution in the various sectors.

In the nation states, autonomous spheres of civil society were not able to develop any autonomous regimes worth mentioning. Research, education, medicine, art, and media – these social activities were located either in private markets or in public hierarchies. Why were these autonomous activities always colonized by political and economic regimes? After all, it is obvious that their intrinsic rationality and

---

42   Alexander Meyer, ,World Society and the Nation State', *supra* n. 2; Niklas Luhmann, 'Der Staat des politischen Systems: Geschichte und Stellung in der Weltgesellschaft', *supra* n. 2 at 373 ff; Martin Shaw, 'Die Repräsentation ferner Konflikte und die globale Zivilgesellschaft', *supra* n. 2.

43   For the distinction between activities and regimes, see Roger Friedland and Robert Alford, 'Bringing Society Back In: W. Powell and P. di Maggio (eds.), Symbols, Practices, and Institutional Contradictions in The New Institutionalism' (Chicago: Chicago University Press, 1992); Gunther Teubner, 'After Privatisation? Invoking Discourse Rights in Private Governance Regimes', 51 CURRENT LEGAL PROBLEMS 393 (1998).

their intrinsic normativity cannot fully develop either under political dominance or under the profit principle of the market.

The answer is that in none of these areas has it to date been possible to achieve a dualism of formally organized rationality and informal spontaneity as a dynamic interplay without institutionalizing the primacy of the one or the other. If spheres of civil society did conquer a certain autonomy *vis-à-vis* political hierarchies and economic markets, then they tended to lose it again by seeking a corporatist constitution. Attempting to institutionalize the whole social activity sector as a formal organization at large, they stifled in their own guild structures. They were, to be sure, able to establish a regime autonomous from politics and the economy, but built it up only as a formally organized sphere of bureaucratic decisions that had no adequate counterpart in a correspondingly dynamic spontaneous sphere.

By contrast a dual social constitution, that is, the internal differentiation of a social subsystem into a spontaneous sector and an organized sector, has to date historically been at all partially successful only in the economy (enterprises/market) and politics (government/public opinion), even though their potential too is not yet remotely exhausted. In the economy, the relation between a market-constituted spontaneous sector and an organized sector of enterprises is firmly established globally too. Though highly organized economic enterprises can enormously enhance technical expertise, organizational capacities and financing techniques, the 'corporate sector' has not succeeded in subjecting the economic sphere as a whole to its control. Globalization itself has exposed the largest corporate groups to a dynamic of world markets that is uncontrollable for them, and will not be removed even by the most recent mega-mergers. In similar fashion, in politics the organized sector of political parties and state administration are counterposed to the spontaneous area of the electorate, lobbying and public opinion. And here too globalization has enormously strengthened the spontaneous sector of politics. In both systems, accordingly, a highly rationalized decision sector is exposed to a chaotic challenge that it is unable to dominate and control. The organized decision sector perceives hardly any unambiguous signals from the spontaneous sector. It is, as it were, condemned to freedom. But once the critical decisions are taken, the specific responsibility mechanisms of democracy and the market are triggered. This spontaneous/organized counterposition seems to be one of the secrets of the success of liberal democracies. At the same time, though, its democratic deficit is the target of critique and point of crystallization for political reform movements. The need will always be to keep adjusting the precarious balance between spontaneous sector and organized sector. And the classical democratic institutions – participation, deliberation and election mechanisms – can serve to enhance the potential for democracy if they build up on mutual controls by the spontaneous sector and the organized sector.

This dualism of spontaneous sector and organized sector as a principle of 'successful' social differentiation is seldom looked at in its aspects of democratic theory. Democracy, understood as an organizing principle that goes beyond institutionalized politics, can work only if in different social fields on the one hand decision potentials are highly specialized, organized and rationalized, on the other hand, however, do not take over total control of their social sector, but are in turn exposed to a control process through a decentralized multiplicity of spontaneous communication processes.

Usually, theories of social differentiation see only the autonomy into which sectors of politics, the economy, law and religion develop since the late Middle Ages in various thrusts. The critical difference between spontaneous sector and organized sector within a subsystem is less well theorized. It emerged in the economic system for the first time in Britain in the Industrial Revolution. The economy was constituted neither as an atomistic market among individual actors nor yet as a sum of formal organizations, but as a complex interplay of formal organizations and spontaneously organized markets. The corresponding political difference was constituted in the American and French Revolutions as spontaneity of democracy and fundamental rights against the formal organization of the highly rationalized state organization. In other subspheres, in contrast, there are only weak approaches to this sort of internal differentiation of spontaneous and organized sector. Perhaps closest, in the classical German academic world there was an institutionalized interplay of highly organized rationality in the universities and a spontaneous educated civic society.[44] Today's descendant of this is perhaps best found in the US university system, which has by contrast with the bureaucratized and politicized European universities succeeded in combining organized and spontaneous activities in a regime that is relatively autonomous *vis-à-vis* politics and the economy.

Accordingly, the thesis of globalization as a mere power shift from political to economic actors is going in the wrong direction. Also at stake are different social sectors and their autonomy. The stifling of social activities in political hierarchies and administrative bureaucracies is, to be sure, obvious. While the shift to the economy opens up the dynamic interplay of spontaneous market and organized enterprises, control through profit blocks the intrinsic rationality of civil society areas no less than does control through political power. Their development becomes possible only once they manage to establish an autonomous regime of organized decisions and spontaneous control processes identical neither with the profit-controlled market nor with power-controlled political processes.[45]

---

44 For thorough historical analyses in this perspective, Rudolf Stichweh, 'Self-Organization and Autopoiesis in Development of Modern Science', 14 SOCIOLOGY OF THE SCIENCES, 1990; Rudolf Stichweh, *Wissenschaft, Universität, Professionen* (Frankfurt: Suhrkamp, 1994).

45 On this see Gunther Teubner, 'After Privatisation? Invoking Discourse Rights in Private Governance Regimes', *supra* n.43.

Can constitutions for civil liberties in the globalization processes be identified as social structural opportunities, or indeed legally institutionalized? Worldwide research, to the extent it does not get caught up entirely in the wake of economic market processes, seems to show certain tendencies towards the development of a global spontaneous area. The issues are: depoliticization, debureaucratization, forms of non-economic competition, pluralization of research financing, and competition among research promotion institutions. Similar trends can be discerned in the education sector, where the worldwide competition of universities is driving them out of political and bureaucratic tutelage and increasingly exposing them to the control dynamic of their own spontaneous sector.

Globalization as opportunity for the law would, then, mean institutionalising constitutions for global villages of social autonomous sectors, in relative distance from politics and the economy. Within the autonomous sectors there would be potentials for re-politicization, re-regionalization and re-individualization of norm-making processes. And the main attention of global law would then have to be directed towards underpinning the duality of social autonomy in the subsystems, i.e. a mutual control dynamic of spontaneous sector and organized sector.

Chapter 5

Globalization and the Conversion of Democracy to Polycentric Networks: Can Democracy Survive the End of the Nation State?

Karl-Heinz Ladeur[*]

I. Is Globalization Destroying the State and Democracy?

1. Are the State and Civil Society Endangered by Globalization?

The critical view of the 'manic logic of global capitalism'[1] is determined by the fear that the global expansion of the market economy will dissolve – or at least considerably weaken – the legal, political and cultural ties of the economic systems. This problematic development is thought to be caused by an economic trend whereby firms progressively transfer investments to countries offering favourable institutional infrastructures that allow them to reduce wage costs.[2] This is associated with a fear that states might 'race to the bottom', resulting in lower wages but also the demolition of social security systems. The race might even transcend economic policy and undermine state democracy. The policy decisions of nation states are increasingly dependent on global economic development lines over which they have increasingly diminishing influence. On this view, various types of law – especially labour and social law, but also environmental and planning law, and the

---

* Translated by Ian L. Fraser.

1 William Greider, *One World – Rready or Not: The Manic Logic of Global Capitalism* (New York: Simon & Schuster, 1997); Noreena Hertz, *The Silent Takeover: Global Capitalism and the Death of Democracy* (London: Heinemann, 2001); Viviane Forrester, *The Economic Horror* (Cambridge: Polity Press, 1999); Margret Levi/David Olson, '*The Battle over Seattle*', POLITICS & SOCIETY 28, 309-329 (2000).

2 Dani Rodrik, *Has Globalization Gone Too Far?* (Washington: Institute for International Economics, 1997).

development of transport systems and education (to mention just a few examples) – become 'location factors' whose value and importance are determined on the global market. Democratic policy and decision-making at the nation state level have only a limited influence over such location factors. Firms that operate globally are thought to be able to escape involvement in political deliberation at nation state level. By removing firms from the economic and labour jurisdictions of any particular nation state, they are also perceived to be able to evade democratic, parliamentary decisions.

Protection of the labour force and social security in case of unemployment, illness, etc. might thus transform into a system of social *in*security, and state protection can become a competitive disadvantage that leads to unemployment because the 'protected' labour power is too expensive and therefore not in demand. Less productive employees are particularly threatened under these conditions. If the very object of democratic decision-making is increasingly de-territorialized, the very substance of the democratic nation states will ultimately be affected.[3] This is because it will either become the victim of competitive cost calculations when decisions are being made about where to locate a business (as in the case of environmental protection regulations), or because tax revenue in the long-term erodes as a consequence of globalization, making the financial basis even for not directly economy-related policies disappear. This has severe effects on popular participation in the network of charitable organizations, neighbourhood assistance, political parties and their informational infrastructure, newspapers and other media (local and transregional), that nourishes the democratic life of 'civil societies'. A division arises between those people whose careers and incomes are increasingly determined by global decision-making processes (and who have some influence over these) and those working in areas under greater economic control of the state or directly dependent on its social benefits. This is observable even in societies with economies that are largely centrally controlled. This leads to divergent economic and political development. The political orientation of economic organizations is the development of global arenas of the de-territorialized economic order, so they are less involved in the networks of civil society within the nation state, less dependent on nation state decisions, and contribute less to maintaining the civil society infrastructure of the nation states in which they are based. This endangers the non-economic 'social capital'[4] on which maintenance of modern – non-traditional – societies depends. This phenomenon can be seen particularly in the threshold

---

3   Jean-Marie Guéhenno, *The End of the Nation State* (Michigan University Press: Minneapolis/London, 1995); *id.*, 'Demokratie am Wendepunkt', INTERNATIONALE POLITIK 4, 13-20 (1998); Andrew Moravcsik, *The Choice for Europe: Social Purpose and State Power from Messina to Maastricht* (Ithaca: Cornell University Press, 1998).

4   Robert D. Putnam, *Bowling Alone: The Collapse and Revival of American Community* (New York: Simon & Schuster, 2000); Karl-Heinz Ladeur, *Negative Freiheitsrechte und gesellschaftliche Selbstorganization* (Tübingen: Mohr, 2000).

countries of the Third World. For example, Castaneda has described the rise of a Mexican social stratum that is actively involved in the economic integration of Mexico and the US through NAFTA.[5] The lives of these people are determined far more by American than Mexican politics. Yet they are not citizens of the US and cannot participate in US politics, and they are legal participants in Mexican politics, even though the latter is of only slight importance to them.

This development is also evident in the economically dominant countries, though it is less dramatic than in the threshold countries. The differences result chiefly from the fact that the governments of economically strong countries compensate for their declining domestic decision-making powers by obtaining rights of involvement at supra-national and international levels (such as the EU and WTO).[6] In this way they secure legitimacy for the national neo-liberal policy they pursue partly from conviction and partly due to transnational constraints.

The recent literature also displays an attempt to explain the formation of Third World associations between the state and organized crime as a manifestation of globalization. In many countries, local elites' dependence on the leading economic regions has grown into an import economy in which there is a reluctance to export globally marketable goods. Instead they favour the emergence of a heterogeneous social capital comprising social mobility, an inclination towards individuality and enterprise among local elites.[7] This development is disadvantageous to the inclusion of the population in the economy, politics and culture, and leads – especially with the devaluation of anti-communist loyalty as a tradable commodity on the political world market – to links between the state and organized crime.[8]

This description of the effects of globalization on nation state politics accords with the neo-liberal position that has been winning influence in the economic and social sciences, though it offers a more positive evaluation of the erosion of the state's decision-making capacity. The state's assumption of responsibility for decision-making in a multitude of areas that go beyond the classical liberal functions of protecting negative freedoms can be criticised.[9] It does not enhance the inclusive effect of democracy by producing *de facto* positive freedom for all citizens, but is instead an illegitimate way of restricting individual autonomy and responsibility. It has negative effects on market dynamism and the 'discovery procedure' (v.Hayek),

5   Jorge G. Castaneda, 'Mexico's Circle of Misery', 75 FOREIGN AFFAIRS, 92-135 (1996).

6   Moravcsik, *supra* n. 1; Joseph H. H. Weiler (ed.), *The EU, the WTO and the NAFTA. Towards a Common Law of International Trade* (Oxford: Oxford University Press, 2000).

7   Jean-Francois Bayart, *The Criminalization of the State in Africa* (London: James Currey Publications, 1999).

8   See Hernando de Soto, *The Mystery of Capital. Why Capitalism Triumphs in the West and Fails Everywhere Else* (London: Bantam Press, 2000) for general doubts concerning the viability of a capitalist economic system for non-Western countries.

9   Jean-Jacques Rosa, *Le second XXe siecle* (Paris: Grasset, 2000); Ladeur, *supra* n. 4.

which institutionalizes the search for innovations or for the efficient satisfaction of existing preferences. It also saps the 'social capital' of post-modern society. The expectation of state aid removes individuals' incentives to adapt to and learn from a rapidly changing environment. By contrast, the alleged loss of the embeddedness of democracy in civil society[10] is either ignored or disputed, while the performance of the family and public education, and the 'docility' ('adaptability') and therefore flexibility they produce, is stressed as a pre-condition for the maintenance of market society.[11]

Alongside the possibility that big transnational undertakings can go 'forum shopping' (which concerns their individual choice of law decisions and state decisions about regulatory systems), there has recently also been a self-production of norms or functionally equivalent standards in the practice of transnational legal transactions. The *lex mercatoria* of the Middle Ages was an early form of transnational legal practice beyond the state and was associated with personal trust between merchants. A post-modern variant of this sort of law is increasingly developing.[12] Its conditions go beyond the personal relationships of those involved and require longer-term ties. They have become specified through experience of the interchangeability of roles (e.g. buyer and seller, producer and recipient of services, etc.) and the development of atypical relational (incomplete) co-operation agreements. A new decision-making perspective is developing in the bigger firms, not least because of increasing mutual dependency (beyond the bounds of earlier practical exchange relationships). This is oriented towards the *institutional* reduction of uncertainty and the creation of co-operation on the basis of common interests. The rise of knowledge as an important resource is particularly enabling complex ties among contractual parties. It is oriented towards co-ordinated and structured invention and towards allowing an overlapping of perspectives because it is thought to be important to maintain a productive basis of legal constraints and possibilities to associate, as well as the reliability of contractual relationships in the face of uncertainty. Whether the self-organized production of binding effects is to be seen as 'law' in the traditional sense, or as mere *de facto* coercion, is a question of mainly

---

10 Mark Granovetter, 'Economic Action and Social Structure: The Problem of Embeddedness', in Mary Zey (ed.), *Decision-Making. Alternatives to Rational Choice Models* (Newbury Park: Sage, 1992), p. 304; Philip Pettit, 'Reworking Sandel's Republicanism', JOURNAL OF PHILOSOPHY, 73-96 (1998).

11 Herbert A. Simon, *Reason in Human Affairs* (Stanford: Stanford University Press, 1983).

12 Gunther Teubner, *Global Law without a State* (Aldershot: Brookfield, 1997); generally see James G. March and Jan P. Olsen, *Democratic Governance* (New York: Free Press, 1995), p. 115, 158; *id.*, 'The Institutional Dynamics of International Political Orders', in Peter J. Katzenstein, Robert O. Keohane and Stephen D. Krasner (eds.), *Exploration and Contestation in the Study of World Politics* (Cambridge, MA: MIT Press, 1999), p.303-330.

theoretical importance.[13] The functional equivalent compels an affirmative answer (particularly because it is only then that productive questions about co-operation and relations between self-created company law and national law can be asked). We shall return to this in more detail; at this point, the goal is to describe the phenomena of globalization. At any rate, the future of the economic system (including its organizational and institutional varieties) is far less obvious than many critics of globalization seem to assume.[14] It is involved in a process of self-transformation but this evolution is multifaceted and cannot be reduced to the dominance of a handful of multinational firms.

The neo-liberal anti-critique sees the 'competition of institutions'[15] as an important prerequisite for rational regulation-making. It is also important in the context of legitimate state action. The movement of firms between different systems, or even the development of a state-free regulatory system on the basis of non-personal trust and the capacity to develop longer-term perspectives for action in transnational legal transactions, is as a sort of 'second-order' discovery procedure. It not only produces criteria for individual decisions but enables – through the competing patterns of social institutions, including the alternative between public and private rules – the optimization of social norm systems. The criterion of market-defined efficiency is introduced as an argument in political decision-making procedures at national level ('law and economy'), but also as an object of practical options by market actors and of self-organization of regulatory patterns that spontaneously form on this basis.

2. New Institutional Forms of Globalization

The institutional forms of globalization, whether organized on a public- or private-law basis, similarly arouse mistrust in the public debate: the WTO rules and procedures are perceived to have a strong free-trade orientation and to be too closed to considerations of conflicting goods and interests (environment, social interests, and so on). At the same time, its intergovernmental component is dominated by the national executives. It thus evades the Parliaments,[16] while the supra-national

---

13   Harold H. Koh, 'Why Do Nations Obey International Law?', 166 YALE LAW JOURNAL, 2599-2659 (1997); see also Kenneth W. Abbott, Robert O. Keohane, Andrew Moravcsik, Anne-Marie Slaughter and Duncan Snidal, 'The Concept of Legalization', 54 INTERNATIONAL ORGANIZATION 457, 401-419 (2000).

14   Hertz, *supra* n. 1; *The Economist*, 22nd December 2001, European edition, p.76.

15   Rainer Eichenberger and Bruno S. Frey, 'Demokratische Regierungsform für eine globalisierte Welt', 81 SCHWEIZERISCHE MONATSHEFTE 3, 12-16 (2001).

16   Danilo Zolo, *Cosmopolis. Perspectives for the World Government* (New York: Polity Press, 1997); Robert Housman, 'Democratizing International Trade Decision-Making', 27 CORNELL INTERNATIONAL LAW JOURNAL, 699-747 (1994); Marco C. Bronckers, 'Better Rules for a New Millennium: A Warning against Undemocratic Developments in

approaches to the development of a dispute settlement procedure (WTO) that is oriented to continual application and review of the rules have – as in the EU (ECJ) – a judicial constitution and are thus similarly largely institutionally guaranteed by democratic policy-making organized through nation states. They are perhaps even more adjusted to it than is the case at the national level, because the recruitment processes also run only through the national executives. In relation to the development of international commercial law through the WTO – and especially the 'judicial' component,[17] – it seems difficult to develop a conception of the unity of the legal system following the traditional nation state model, and to, for example, formulate general principles that correspond to national general administrative or private law, or even to the corresponding written or unwritten procedural rules of national legal systems. This problem is already evident at the EU level, which is similarly dependent, for the implementation of specific legal norms, on underpinning through the (diverse!) infrastructure of national legal systems. Here the question arises as to how far a supra-nationally organized unification of global legal relations, founded on the basis of a world free-trade system, can intervene in national legal systems. The WTO admittedly allows reservations in favour of national regulations – as does EU law, though only to a limited extent – but the prerequisites and scope for them remain unclear. There are, in particular, no systematic rules that link transnational WTO law and national regulations, such as criteria focusing on policy formation in the individual nation states themselves, according to which the two potentially conflicting aspects could be harmonized with each other.[18] Here again the question arises as to how far national cultural, social and political peculiarities can be brought to bear legally, and how far a supra-national or transnational standard of general principles and procedural rules can and should be presumed.

Another manifestation of globalization that democratic theory perceives to be problematic lies in the formation of international financial markets.[19] These are

the WTO', 2 JOURNAL OF INTERNATIONAL ECONOMIC LAW 4, 547-566 (1999); Jan A. Scholte, 'Global Capitalism and the State', 73 INTERNATIONAL AFFAIRS, 427-452 (1997).

17 *See* Meinhard Hilf, 'Power, Rules and Principles – Which Orientation for WTO/GATT Law?', JOURNAL OF INTERNATIONAL ECONOMIC LAW, 111-130 (2001); for the ECJ see Joseph H. H. Weiler, 'The European Court of Justice: 'Beyond Doctrine' or 'The Legitimacy Crisis of European Constitutionalism', in Anne-Marie Slaughter, Alec Stone Sweet and Joseph H. H. Weiler (eds.), *The European Court and National Courts – Doctrine and Jurisprudence* (Oxford: Hart 1998), pp. 365-391.

18 Joel P. Trachtman, 'The Domain of WTO Dispute Settlements', 40 HARVARD INTERNATIONAL LAW JOURNAL, 333-377 (1999); John O. McGinnis and Mark L. Movsesian, 'The World Trade Constitution', 114 HARVARD LAW REVIEW, 511-605 (2000).

19 Geoffrey R. D. Underhill, '*Keeping Governments out of Politics: Transnational Securities Market Regulatory Co-operation and Political Legitimacy*', 21 REVIEW OF INTERNATIONAL STUDIES, 251-278 (1995); Robert Jackson, '*Sovereignty in World*

thought, above all, to worsen, or spark off, regional economic crises: the extreme volatility, particularly of some highly speculative financial instruments and especially in view of the speed and ease of worldwide data transfer and the accumulation of small disruptions of equilibrium into crisis-type collapses, is seen as a risk for the stability of world markets in general and individual regional markets in particular.

The internationally institutionalized organizations for dealing with crises – the IMF and the World Bank – are seen to be politically inadequate because of their allegedly one-sided orientation to market criteria. They are also thought to be economically inefficient, as their limited capacity to act is at least in part already discounted by states with unstable economies (that is, the need to help risky developments that are about to fail is already factored in). This not only allows irrational government policies, but systematically redistributes their consequences to economically weak groups.[20] In addition, the private self-regulatory institutions that set 'best practice' standards in risk limitation on financial markets (notably through 'accounting rules' for creating transparency in evaluating firms, and their development risks), are seen by democratic theorists to be questionable because they delegate quasi-legal norm-setting functions to private economic institutions.[21]

The alternative to the development of various private independent international and supra-national or self-organized forms of global economic institution is a legal strategy to limit the freedom of transnational economic relations 'beyond the State'.[22] This is to be implemented partly by the EU and partly by the nation states, especially in various schemes of national economic protectionism. The 'institutional competition' among the states can also be limited by setting various minimum standards. In established transnational economic areas with strong legal systems, like the EU, these could include common tax rates, social security principles and similar regulations with binding effect for the national legislatures, in order to limit competition over 'location factors'. The aim is to underpin 'negative' integration (by removing of quota rules and similar anti-market restrictions) with an eye to creating a common market through a strategy of positive integration.[23] In relation to products standards, this policy has been replaced by the 'new approach' of mutual

---

Politics: A Glance at the Conceptual and Historical Landscape', POLITICAL STUDIES XLVII, 431-456 (1999); Saul Picciotto, 'Introduction: What Rules for the World Economy?', in Saul Picciotto and Ruth Mayne (eds.), *Regulating International Business* (Oxford: St.Martin's Press, 1999), pp.1-25; Paul Hirst, 'The Global Economy - Myths and Realities', *International Affairs*, 409-425 (1997).

20 McGinnis and Movsesian, *supra* n. 18.

21 Picciotto, *supra* n. 19; Koh, *supra* n. 13.

22 McGinnis and Movsesian, *supra* n. 18.

23 Fritz Scharpf, 'Positive und negative Koordination in Verhandlungssystemen', in Adrienne Héritier (ed.), *Policy-Analyse – Kritik und Neuordnung* (PVS-Sonderheft 24, 1993), pp. 57-83.

recognition of national standards on the basis of common normative quality requirements.[24] The EC Commission has now proposed a policy of harmonizing essential fiscal, labour-law and social-law conditions. It is therefore doubtful whether Member States will want to be so extensively bound. It is noteworthy that at the (failed) negotiations for the development of the WTO system, the new EC Commissioner for free trade, Pascal Lamy, wished to be guided by the idea that 'freeing trade should be controlled, steered and managed according to the concerns of EU countries'.[25] It is accordingly to be expected that the problem will not actually be dealt with within the EU, but will instead be shifted in a different form and with other matters by EU Member States to the WTO level. Thus, the EU wants to emphasize greater consideration for the 'precautionary principle' at the WTO context, particularly to avoid conflicts about genetically modified products, use of hormones in meat production, and so on.[26] This would expand the area of discretion for social regulations.

One theoretically ambitious answer by critics of globalization lies in the – utopian-sounding – project for a democratic world government with a democratically constituted world public as its counterpart.[27] This would be based on large supra-national systems like the EU, and would be able to generate legitimacy from deliberative processes rooted in civil societies. With a strong shift in emphasis towards a 'polyarchy' of the post-modern variant of democracy in a globalized society, Gerstenberg and Sabel[28] also stress the possibility of establishing legitimacy through public deliberative processes. Christian Joerges[29] has classified the

24 Christian Joerges, 'Good Governance through Comitology?', in Christian Joerges and Ellen Vos (eds.), *EU Committees: Social Regulation, Law and Politics* (Oxford: Hart, 1999), pp. 311-338.

25 *The Economist*, 27th November 1999, Eurean edition, p. 13.

26 For environmental policy see Trachtman, *supra* n. 18; Ronnie D. Lipschutz, '*From Place to Planet: Local Knowledge and Global Environmental Governance*', 3 GLOBAL GOVERNANCE, 83-102 (1997).

27 Jurgen Habermas, '*Remarks on Dieter Grimm's: Does Europe need a Constitution*', EUROPEAN LAW JOURNAL, 303-315 (1995); *id., 'Kants Ideen zum Ewigen Frieden aus dem historischen Abstand von 200 Jahren'*, KRITISCHE JUSTIZ, 293-319 (1995).

28 Oliver Gerstenberg and Charles F. Sabel, '*Directly Deliberative Polyarchy*', EUROPEAN LAW JOURNAL, 343-358 (1997); for a critique see Nancy L. Rosenblum, '*Democratic Character and Community - The Logic of Congruence*', 2 JOURNAL OF POLITICAL PHILOSOPHY, 67-97 (1994); Ian Shapiro, 'Enough of Deliberation - Politics is about Interests and Power', in Stephen Macedo and Amy Gutmann (eds.), *Deliberative Politics. Essays on Democracy and Disagreement* (New York: Oxford University Press, 1999), pp. 28-38.

29 Joerges, *supra* n. 24; for the international level Thomas Risse, *"Let's Argue!": Communicative Action in World Politics'*, 54 INTERNATIONAL ORGANIZATION, 1-40 (2000); Michael Zürn and Dieter Wolf, '*European Law and International Regimes - The Features of Law beyond the Nation State*', 5 EUROPEAN LAW JOURNAL, 272-292 (1999).

European 'comitology' as a form of transnational deliberation that makes the states amenable to promoting a pluralized public interest beyond their own frontiers, and that can compensate for the deficiency of hierarchical democratic strands of legitimacy. Criticism of this seems justified in so far as there is, as yet, only a diluted relationship between civil society and its discussion venues. Instead, more effort should be made concerning the 'managerial' aspect of building transnational co-operation networks,[30] which are coming to typify globalized law 'inside Europe too'. To that extent the comitology might very well be regarded as a network of overlapping networks that is typical of the globalization of law, it is able to supply a functional equivalent for national standardization and – through the distribution of heterarchical participation relationships – the national hierarchical legitimacy structures.

The critical movement against the present forms and institutions of globalization bases itself either on an association between territorial sovereignty and democracy (at least in practice, coming to terms in this variant with the political objectives of protectionist movements), or aims to extend a 'civil society on a world scale' following the classical democratic model of the State.[31] That is, it promotes a world-embracing network of public-interest movements, citizens' initiatives, associations, and a corresponding informational discussion infrastructure modelled on its classical state-centred predecessors. In part, the worldwide Internet-organized (and not ineffective) protests against the 1999 WTO meeting in Seattle,[32] and NGOs acting at an international level, are seen as a core around which a global civil society can crystallize.

3.   Interim Summary

In a first intermediate stage, it should first be stated that fears that globalization endangers social security, the state democratic institutions and social coherence cannot be rejected outright. However, economists correctly note that the inevitability of such a development is implausible. It can hardly be proven that wage levels have a decisive influence on companies' investment decisions.[33] If they did, far more undertakings would have established themselves in Eastern Europe and the

---

30   Stephen D. Krasner, *Sovereignty - Organized Hypocrisy* (Princeton: Princeton University Press, 1999), p. 12; Koh, *supra* n. 13; Karl-Heinz Ladeur, 'Toward a Legal Concept of the Network in European Standard-Setting', in Joerges/Vos (eds.), *supra* n.24 , 151-170 (1999); see also Gunther Teubner, 'Polykorporatismus: Der Staat als 'Netzwerk' öffentlicher und privater Kollektivakteure', in Hauke Brunkhorst (ed.), *Das Recht der Republik* (Frankfurt/M.: Suhrkamp, 1999), p. 346.

31   Habermas, *Kants Ideen zum Ewigen Frieden aus dem historischen Abstand von 200 Jahren*, *supra* n. 27.

32   *The Economist*, 27th November 1999, European edition, p.13.

33   Paul R. Krugman, *Pop Internationalism* (Cambridge: MIT Press, 1996).

Third World. Economists rightly note the compensatory effect of productivity rises, which is ultimately decisive for decision based on the cost of production. Nevertheless, the market position of less-qualified workers is at serious risk in the leading economic nations, as more and more unskilled work is being shifted to less-developed areas. But, in a view oriented to the development prospects of the world economy, this is not *a priori* negative. Furthermore, it can be seen that political stability and the reliability of political and legal framework conditions are also important location factors, as are workers' skills. On these criteria, the industrialized countries retain an important advantage over the poorer regions, which almost always have worse-functioning civil institutions (administration, legal system, and so on). Moreover, the rise of information and knowledge as decisive production resources – a point we return to – similarly speaks against the likelihood of a major shift of investment to the Third World. A large number of transfers of investment outside the EU are associated with the globalization of markets, which compels companies to be present in the various economic areas at more than a commercial level.

Paul Krugman has rightly pointed out that globalization's effects on the modern economy have not 'yet' been exaggerated.[34] The pressure for change under which the political and legal institutions of post-modern societies are emerging is not produced primarily by globalization processes, but is instead connected with the basic transformation of the economy into the 'knowledge society'.[35] This generally makes the economy flexible and also favours globalization processes as *one* of its manifestations. Pressure on the welfare State, the rise of neo-liberal policies, and similar manifestations of the weakening of the democratic welfare state, have additional causes. These are found inside the various social and political systems, and particularly in those related to the new organizational forms accompanying the transition to the 'knowledge society', which are making the boundaries between inside and outside, market and company, public and private, increasingly permeable.[36] This development has consequences for the maintenance of the normal employment relationship, or the legal forms of 'corporate governance': the permeability of company boundaries also allows new hybrid legal relationships to emerge. These can be found between an employee's position and entrepreneurial independence, or between traditional exchange relationships or work contracts and the social integration of production in firms that allows flexible linkages between productive processes (for example, through quality management contracts).

---

34 *Ibid.*
35 Carl Shapiro and Hal R. Varian, *Information Rules* (Cambridge: Harvard Business School Press, 1999).
36 Georg von Krogk and Ikujiro Nonaka, *Enabling Knowledge Creation* (Oxford: OUP, 2000).

Accordingly, globalization has an undeniable effect on the transformation processes that are breaking the bounds of traditional legal institutions in postmodern society.[37] We shall therefore start by trying to identify the prerequisites and bases for the institutionalization of democracy and its association with the nation state. The question has to be asked so that the adaptability of democracy to the changed conditions of the global flexible forms of the economy and of labour and their association with political institutions can be re-thought. The conception of democracy presupposed by globalization's critics may very well turn out to be too narrowly associated with a concept of sovereignty oriented to a single will.[38] In conditions of globalization, such a will is *de facto* difficult to maintain because it has lost discriminatory capacity. In the same sense, the 'knowledge society' contains linkages between changing social economic forms, and it is necessary to inquire about the possibilities of developing political and legal institutions that count as a functional equivalent of liberal democratic statehood. The critique of globalization and its effects on state and democracy assumes that only state-centred democracy can be defended against globalization – specifically against the danger of protectionism – unless a global state has to reproduce the classical ordering forms of the nation state on a worldwide scale. A third possibility, that might lie in strengthening non-state, de-territorialized, self-organized networks and their co-operation with heterarchical plural public institutions beyond the hierarchical model of the state, is thereby ruled out. It can be deduced from this approach that the possibility of a combination of various transnational public forms of guaranteeing learning capacity and the enabling and enhancing of self-observation and observation of others within a global 'network of networks', adapted to the self-organizing and self-transforming de-territorialized networks of relationships, is here thought to be plausible.[39] One may start from achievements of democracy still seen in earlier variants of theory, while the close association with state sovereignty has instead pushed the unitary-will component to the fore.

37   Mark W. Zacher, 'The Decaying Pillars of the Westphalian Temple: Implications for International Order and Governance', in James N. Rosenau and Ernst-Otto Czempiel (eds.), *Governance without Government. Order and Change in World Politics* (Cambridge: Cambridge University Press, 1992), pp.58-101.

38   Tracy B. Strong, *Rousseau: The Politics of the Ordinary* (Thousand Oaks: Sage, 1994); Rosenblum, *supra* n. 28; id., *Bentham's Theory of the Modern State* (Cambridge, MA: Harvard University Press, 1978); see also James Bohman (ed.), *Deliberative Democracy. Essays on Reason and Politics*, Cambridge: MIT Press (1997).

39   Guéhenno, *Demokratie am Wendepunkt, supra* n. 3.

II.   Democratic Theory and the Challenge of Globalization

1.   Democracy – Sovereignty – Volonté Générale

The neo-liberal anti-critique of the objections to globalization sketched above has the merit of drawing attention to the question of the limits of democracy as a form of unitary state-centred policy formation. Liberalism has always stressed the order-creating achievement of negative freedoms,[40] and also dimensioned its concept of the democratic state and of the general interest to be formulated by it, particularly the general law, on this basis. This does not rule out the fact that liberal freedoms must themselves have democratic legitimacy in the constitution: this is chiefly because democracy has to break with the heteronymous will of the sovereign monarch and thus ultimately a God-willed order. While it makes use of the old form of unity formation in the concept of 'popular sovereignty', it in practice stresses the facts of tradition by shifting the emphasis onto 'will as a creative force of order'.[41] The link was possible because monarchical sovereignty too was construed as that of *all*, thereby making everyone author of the sovereign act and thus committing them to subjection.[42] In Rousseau, this form takes on a fictitious character: the legal order must be understood 'as if' it was produced by all. This means a break with the *de facto* link with tradition.

However, in Rousseau, democracy is not fixed on bringing about the institutionalization of unity in the state as bearer of the '*volonté générale*': it has its root in the free will of all and thus also refers to the 'Other' I can find in myself through others.[43] In the pre-modern period, the transcendental Other imposed on the individual from outside was decisive for the conception of the state and for the individual's self-perception. The concept of '*volonté générale*' may in part be seen as creating a quasi-totalitarian link between individuals and the people. But, more correctly, one may – with T. B. Strong[44] – bring against this that the generality of the will paradoxically presupposes a 'multiple, decentred self'. Since the God-willed – that is, heteronomous – definition of 'humanness' is no longer available, only a new openness of the distributed 'small general wills', with the common freedom of all as condition for the freedom of the individual, is conceivable. And it is only through the non-closure of the 'multiple or divided self' that the capacity arises to

---

40   Ladeur, *supra* n. 4.

41   Rosenblum, *supra* n. 28, p. 82; Scholte, *supra* n. 16; Jan A. Scholte, Robert O'Brien and Marc Williams, '*The WTO and Civil Society*', 33 JOURNAL OF WORLD TRADE, 107-123 (1999), p. 107; Martin van Creveld, *Aufstieg und Untergang des Staates* (München: Gerling Akademie Verlag, 1999), p. 220.

42   Yves-Charles Zarka, *Philosophie et politique à l'âge classique* (Paris: PUF, 1998), p. 129.

43   van Creveld, *supra* n. 41, p. 220.

44   Strong, *supra* n. 38, p. 83.

produce collective social orders under the changed conditions. The '*volonté générale*' then becomes that which 'resists deconstruction of the self into the immediacy of power relations in modern society'. This becomes possible only by 'the will of the common self' opposing actual circumstances.[45] The previous (traditional) form of personality was based on incorporating collective norms, but not in the form of interiorization (which assumes a link with the individuals' own selves). This means the person in the traditional pre-modern order must identify with the totality of society, and acquires self-determination only within a symbolically pre-given fixed regulatory framework. In the modern sense, the human being is thus not yet an individual. The symbolic order constitutes the person directly. Even in the early modern period, the 'precedence' of the collective is explicitly recognized; at the same time, in the interest of enabling individuals' freedom of choice, it is oriented towards an interiorizing appropriation. The individual obtains the 'right to criticize'[46] and is no longer bound by the factuality of relations; binding by legal rules replaces binding by traditional customs. The collective norms need to be individually appropriated, and allow for variation but also for production of novelty. But the symbolic order does not develop its organizing and structuring power directly in the consciousness, which passes few alternatives for individualization, as all of the individuals bear the collective order within themselves. Thus the modern conception of a collective order based on the 'general will' makes a decisive break: the will becomes a creative force and shakes off the weight of tradition.

The '*volonté générale*' is one way of denoting the paradox thus produced, that the will keeps the relationship between individual and collective in suspense. The general will refers to the individual will. This can in turn only confirm itself through recognition of the other (equal) wills. The modern individual is required to have the capacity to look at society from the viewpoint of others; these others are no longer the pre-determined transcendental Other, so this relationship of interiorization of the Other must take on an abstract, generalizing form that, at the same time, contains a fictional aspect of 'as if'. The form of justification of the state and the collective order points to the self-justification of the language of *law* rendered autonomous, which can hold the relationships of will together.[47]

Juergen Habermas[48] has recently started again from this construction, in seeing the democratic *process* as the source of the law's legitimacy, in so far as it must

---

45 *Ibid.*, p. 84.
46 Marcel Gauchet, 'Essai de psychologie contemporaine', *Le Débat No. 99*, 169-182 (1998), p. 176.
47 Zarka, *supra* n. 42, p. 240.
48 Jurgen Habermas, *Between Facts and Norms* (Cambridge: MIT Press, 1996).

understand itself as a rational procedure of formulating the general will.[49] Its rationality follows from the fact that the process follows the rules of an inter-subjective 'communicative reason'. But here one might join V. Descombes in asking what sort of universalism it is that can be based on nothing but a consideration about the conditions of rational discussion (as Habermas derives from it the concept of a world civil society, we shall return to this below). This 'deliberative' re-formulation of the democracy concept is only conceivable on the basis of an already existing unity, but it cannot itself establish this. In this way, Habermas wishes to transcend the law's tie to religion, but ultimately the law's link with social reality is also abandoned. However, the law – as an autonomous thing emerging from the connection between morality and religion – consists of nothing other than the emergence of ties and linkage patterns that make the uncertainty of the new modern order bearable and enable the formation of expectations under conditions of partial knowledge. Law functions on the basis of the capacity and willingness of the individuals (and organizations) to internalize the self-organizing constraints and operate with the possibilities contained in them.[50]

2.   Democracy and the Change in Forms of Subjectivity

The differing emphases on collective decision (democracy) and on individual freedom (liberalism) point to the two strands of a dilemma. A modern democracy can no longer have common interest as a basis; this is a problem that is supposed to be coped with through the circular proceduralization of democracy. Conversely, liberalism tends to narrow the scope of collective political decisions in favour of spontaneous discovery procedures that are institutionalized through the liberal freedoms, thereby insisting on the limits of democracy. This dilemma can be resolved because of the objective historical process that has taken the place of breakdown of the unity of the 'Other' of the symbolic order;[51] (which implied, above all, the priority of religion) into differing rationalities of law, morality, and so on. On the view adopted here, this is perceived as a manifestation of the autonomisation of law. The dissolution of the transcendental 'Other' in modern legal society is reflected in the breakdown of the distinction between the 'universal and the particular' that constitutes the modern concept of 'subject': the subject is characterized by its share in humanity in general. Here the autonomization flows

---

49   Vincent Descombes, *'Le contrat social der Jürgen Habermas'*, Le Debat *No. 99*, 169-181 (1999), p. 35, 46; Karl-Heinz Ladeur, *'Discursive Ethics as Constitutional Theory?'*, 13 Ratio Juris, 95-116 (2000).

50   Descombes, *supra* n. 49, p. 48.

51   Daniel Sibony, *Le groupe inconscient* (Paris: Bourgois, 1980); Adam B. Seligman, 'Towards a Reinterpretation of Modernity in an Age of Postmodernity', in Bryan S. Turner (ed.), *Theories of Modernity and Postmodernity* (Special Number of 'Theory, Culture and Society', 1990), pp. 118-133.

from conditions that are created by the 'pre-individual' formation of the order, because the individual still has to develop a perspective on the totality of the collective order – an important distinction from the post-modern evolution of the collective – while the collective patterns of order lose their substance (determined by ties to factuality) and admit subjectivity and a general will open to the Other henceforth only in a distributed, split form. The stable boundary between the universal and the particular gets lost.[52] The universal and the particular coincide, bringing the conception of the society as a product of universal subjects (that is, of a general will) that no longer has its reference point outside the individuals in the transcendental 'Other' but is oriented towards the discovery of the 'common self' in the other. This makes order conceivable only through the mediation of a medium oriented towards self-transformation. This medium is the law, which replaces the structuring function of tradition and the binding effect of the divine (heteronomous) will.

These problems can be overlooked if, like Habermas, one equates the question of the law's functions with that of the legitimacy of statutes.[53] The notion of replacing the transcendental foundation of law by a discussion procedure is related to the fact that, in contrast with pre-modern society, there are no longer any common values (which could be identified with the transcendental 'Other') that must be replaced by the self-justifying reflective activity of joint debate. But this still presupposes the necessity and possibility of a foundation for law in an overreaching order which, though it has lost its content (substance), continues its claim, which can be redeemed through a discussion procedure. However, if modern society has lost its transcendental foundation and the law has come out of its link with religious and moral values, the question that must first be asked is one about the function of an autonomous legal system, and it cannot be answered by exchanging moral foundation values for ethic-discursive argumentation procedures. If the law acquires autonomy[54] by differentiating its own function out of the example of the primarily religiously integrated tie to tradition and the associated stock of values, then the question of the foundation of law itself loses its basis. This does not mean the question of the legitimacy of statutes has no meaning – quite the contrary – but the autonomization of law brings a shift in perspective that first accentuates the function of law, thereby raising the question of the possibilities and the ties (with no moral, religious or quasi-transcendental foundation) and becoming able to form and uphold stable expectations.

Democracy needs a multiplicity of viewpoints to determine the effect of statute on the legal system; this makes deliberation an important element in social self-

---

52   Seligman, *supra* n. 51, p. 125.
53   Descombes, *supra* n. 49, p. 48.
54   See generally Niklas Luhmann, *Das Recht der Gesellschaft* (Frankfurt: Suhrkamp, 1993).

observation, but the law cannot have the foundational effect ascribed to it by Habermas. That would mean neglecting the functions of the other components of law – court practice, contract law, standards, social practice and other rules of experience – that constitute a component of law. The acts of the democratic legislator must not only meet constitutional norms and requirements of public debate; they are above all dependent on the 'embeddedness' of autonomous law in a network of possibilities and constraints for linkage, as well as relations of social norms and expectations that are not absorbed into rules of discourse but are tied to a practice of law. This also pre-structures the problems ('issues') that have to be dealt with and that the Act's operation must be linked to, if it is not to fail. The democratic argumentation procedure cannot replace this productive and practical network of possibilities.[55] It is only through the practical formation of this sort of network of relations among individuals, storing up linkage patterns and rules among the individuals, that the paradox of the self-construction of society from the relations between the wills of open subjects no longer tied to something pre-given can be resolved. According to Habermas, individuals can ultimately attain freedom only in the publicly constituted space. This space is fixed to the finding of explicit consensus mediated through discourse, and around which also the *part* of civil society that, for Habermas, constitutes the *whole* of it (that is, the circles, movements, groups) that reason about problems of the public interest abstractly from purposes, is centred.[56]

3. System-theory and Democracy

On a system-theory conception, by contrast, democracy can be seen as a 'mechanism' for coupling the political system with other functional systems of society, including the law.[57] Democracy is thus built into a polycontextural conception that calls the possibility of hierarchical foundations for social regulatory systems through democratic procedures into question, and instead operates with a heterarchical model of the mutual overlapping of differing functional systems arising from the breakdown of the traditional pre-individual hierarchical order. Niklas Luhmann calls this mutual overlapping of self-observation and observation of others by systems a form of 'communication' that uses the adoption of others' perspectives as an experimental irritation through which novelty can emerge through the overlapping of differing rationalities. But this would, itself, be a form of 'relational rationality' that rules out the unity of foundational reason.

---

55   Pettit, *supra* n. 10, p. 201, 245.

56   Axel Honneth, '*Democracy, Not So Ancient and Not So Modern – Democracy as Reflexive Cooperation*', 26 POLITICAL THEORY, 763-783 (1998), p. 763, 768.

57   Niklas Luhmann, *Die Gesellschaft der Gesellschaft* (Frankfurt: Suhrkamp, 1997), p. 845; Udo Di Fabio, *Das Recht offener Staaten* (Tubingen: Mohr Siebeck, 1999), p. 45.

From another viewpoint, Alexis de Tocqueville[58] earlier emphasized the indirect effects of democracy he believed he saw, not so much in politically institutionalized decisions or public debate (in this connection democratic legislation is diagnosed as pretty 'mediocre'), as in the dynamization of society: the enlivening of all sorts of activities. Tocqueville critically establishes the lacking capacity of the democratic form of government precisely in those areas that are directly the object of political decisions and therefore of public debate. By contrast, the main advantage of democracy – particularly of representative government – is identified by Tocqueville in the spread of willingness for co-operative conduct and for the development of new forms of practical actions. The replacement of the order-creating power of the transcendental 'Other' produces the feeling that the citizens have something 'in common'. This self-perception of dependency on the 'Others', but also the insight it conveys into one's own abilities and the possibilities of co-operation among equals, is transferred especially to the private areas of creativity and general social vitality. This is a practical manifestation of the breakdown of the incorporation of tradition into the identity of the self, which makes the multiple, split individual capable of flexible co-operation with other equally 'incomplete' individuals.

This could very well be interpreted in systems theory terms as an effect of 'irritation', of production of indirect effects through structural coupling between politics, the economy and the individual consciousness: citizens' participation in politics has its indirect effect in the mobilization of private co-operation and the enabling of the permeability of persons boundaries to mutual influences. And if many of the activated citizens deciding their own destiny are interested in politics, politics will not move away from concord with the citizens. This effect of polycentric 'dispersion' of power over society with the formation of overlapping purposes and networks of relationships is also stressed by Madison in the Federalist Papers.[59] He sees the positive effect of avoiding a one-sided orientation of politics. In this interpretation of democracy, the importance of democratic 'consent' in political decision-making is de-emphasized, and the point is instead to distribute both private and public power in society.[60] Accordingly, the importance of the self-creation of a network of 'civil norms and trust' for extending the citizen's horizon is

58 Stephen Holmes, 'Tocqueville and Democracy', in David Held, John B. Thompson and John E. Roemer (eds.), *The Idea of Democracy* (Cambridge: Cambridge University Press, 1993), p. 23, 28, 34; Pierre Manent, *Tocqueville and the Nature of Democracy* (Lanham: Rowman & Littlefield, 1996); Marcel Gauchet, *Tocqueville e noi: Sulla genesi delle Società democratica* (Milano: Donzelli, 1996).

59 Richard Boyd, *'The Unsteady and Precarious Constitution of Individuals'*, 61 REVIEW OF POLITICS, 465-491 (1999), p. 465, 487.

60 *See* Mary Ann Glendon, *'Philosphical Foundations of the Fedelist Papers: Nature of Man and Nature of Law'*, HARVARD JOURNAL OF LAW AND PUBLIC POLICY 16, 23-32 (1993).

accentuated: through the systems' permeability to reciprocal influences it creates democratic social capital, which enables decisions to be viable in the longer term.[61]

In theories of deliberative democracy,[62] this infrastructure of social norms, networks of relationships and the trust based on them is narrowed down to the non-economic forms of mutual communication, assistance, social commitment to public goals, and so on. These become a reservoir of possibilities for democratic policy-making and decision within institutionalized statehood. However, democracy is fed not just by these parts of the civil society, but from all the living combinations of relations in individuals' self-transcendence, and the networks of relations between them. This is also how John Dewey is to be understood when he postulates a multiplicity of 'shared undertakings' and experiences as the prerequisite and consequence of democracy.[63] The 'general will' thus has a substrata in the totality of 'shared ideas' rooted in the 'collective life' of society. This view of democracy emphasizes the bounds of collective action in view of the spontaneous relations between the wills of the market subjects, not because it mistrusts the possibilities of forming an institutionalized collective will, but because it believes it can – through the indirect collective effects of the formation of flexible practical networks of relations, the production of experience within a universally acceptable 'pool of variety' and the possibility of developing trust[64] – secure an enormously more important organizational and ordering effect than is conceivable through public debate and politically institutionalized decisions. This form of association between politics and (economic) society is based on emergent order formation: as long as a society develops sufficient variety and dynamism – as democracy allows – it is possible to rely on the production of spontaneous patterns of order emerging from the self-organization of relations of will between individuals and organizations and displaying a 'common knowledge' produced and continually renewed by the distributed 'society of enquirers' (Dewey). Those taking part are guided by the constraints and linkage possibilities that can be utilized in productive co-operation. Here it is the capacity to vary experience and practical rules, and thus to learn and to

---

61   Adam B. Seligman, *The Problem of Trust* (Princeton: Princeton University Press, 1997); Philip Pettit, *Republicanism. A Theory of Freedom and Government*, (Oxford: Clarendon, 1997), p. 201, 247.

62   James Bohman (ed.), *Deliberative Democracy. Essays on Reason and Politics*, *supra* n. 38; Gerstenberg and Sabel, *supra* n. 28 and in this volume; Joshua Cohen and Joel Rogers, '*Secondary Assessments and Democratic Governance*', 20 POLITICS AND SOCIETY, 392-472 (1992); Amy Gutmann and Dennis Thompson, *Democracy and Disagreement* (Cambridge: The Belknap Press of Harvard, 1996); Rainer Schmalz-Bruns, *Reflexive Demokratie: Die demokratische Transformation moderner Politik* (Baden-Baden: Nomos, 1995).

63   John Dewey, *Democracy and Education* (New York: Macmillan, 1916), p. 74.

64   George Klosko, '*Rawls's Political Philosophy and American Democracy*', AMERICAN POLITICAL SCIENCE REVIEW 87, 348-364 (1993).

contribute to the creation of new knowledge, over and above explicit debate, that is regarded as decisive.[65]

This is a shift in emphasis from the mere assumption of the search for efficient rules determined by the constraints of the economic system. Instead, it is the very mobilization of productive effort that is stressed, arising from the differences between individuals enabled only by modern society, democracy and the autonomy of law; and the self-transcendence of the given society is seen as being fed from disturbance in the overlapping networks of relations.

In complex social systems of spontaneously generated macrostructures, the will relationships of individuals enable and delimit, and define, available knowledge; each separate individual or organized actor is in co-evolution with the patterns of order arising from relations with others, which characterize the infrastructure of society and the scope of their alternatives for action.[66] The autonomy of law, which cannot be reduced to the legitimacy of democratic statute, enables this self-organization of social patterns of order generated and varied as a transcendent effect from the artificial construction and design of ties over and above tradition between actors. This theoretical intermediate consideration opens up a changed perspective on democracy under conditions of globalization. For what follows from the interpretation of democracies sketched out is that it is not so much a consensus on democratic values that explicitly constitutes the collective order (even in Rawls's sense of an 'overlapping consensus', the core of which is fed from varying political considerations) that is needed. Instead, the concept of democracy can – following the considerations set out above – be reformulated more to the effect not of consenting to a basic stock of rules and principles. It is instead the practical, heterarchical, distributed social network of networks among citizens producing 'overlapping consensus', in the sense that the citizens are in practice involved in differing networks in different roles, and a heterarchical organized stock of linkages and co-ordinations arises from their overlapping and permeability to each other, that enables a 'polycontexturally' distributed self-observation and observation of others by the various patterns of actions produced, continually feeding the associated 'pool of knowledge' with novelty.[67]

This is also the basis for trust in the political system: its permeability to incorporation of multiple social interests, its capacity to observe the social networks for potential self-blockings that may well need interventions. This means that the 'democratic consensus' has its reference framework in the example of the practical linkages of the political system in other networks, and not in shared principles. The citizens observe a distributed allocation of power and legal possibilities of action,

---

65   Peter M. Allen, '*Modelling Complex Economic Evolution*', 3 SELBSTORGANIZATION, 47-65 (1998), p. 47, 62.

66   *Ibid.*

67   Klosko, *supra* n. 64, p. 356.

reflected in overlapping networks. This is the basis for a practical 'consensus', not tied to 'principles' (Klosko).

4.   Subject – Democracy – Post-modernity

A further interim consideration, following M. Gauchet,[68] is that we have to focus on a new model of creation of individuality in post-modernity: this is a form of individuality marked by a further weakening of the incorporation of the collective into consciousness. Following the considerations so far, this could be specified by saying that the self-transformation of the network of networks of relations between individuals and their associated linkage patterns speeds up, notably through change in the organizations which, after the end of the epoch of (stable) organizations oriented to producing quantity advantages, produce ever more possibilities. In this a centric, fragmentary context, the individual has difficulties – with both the symbolic basic structure and in cognitive respects – in recognizing the underlying patterns of order of the collective and building up a corresponding internal structure of consciousness. This also changes the position of the public and the media, which can scarcely claim to focus generalizable interests in the individual systems any longer, but which can take up and change their themes autonomously according to an economy of attention.[69] There is no reason for culturally pessimistic lamentations because of the emergence of the 'internally fragmented individual'.[70] And the scope of this development (and the correctness of the diagnosis) certainly still needs testing. For our purposes, it is enough to state that, in the change of subjectivity from modern to post-modern society, the *'univers des réseaux'*[71] in which individuals act and by which they are stamped becomes further autonomized, excluding any form of general subjectivity or ideal observer standpoint detached from it, from which society can be seen as a whole.

In cognitive respects, this is reflected in the fact that increasingly specialized knowledge is produced in the rapidly changing networks that transcend traditional distinctions and boundaries, which it is increasingly hard to subsume under general structural principles and rules. In the state and administration, this transformation of society is reflected in the fact that even the notion of mediating between general and particular interests and the interiorization of a universal knowledge necessary for this is possible only within narrow limits.[72] The state itself becomes (at best) a

---

68   Gauchet, *supra* n. 46, p. 176.

69   Georg Franck, *Die Ökonomie der Aufmerksamkeit* (Munich/Vienna: Hanser, 1998).

70   A formulation that is, of course, a simplification. Panajotis Kondylis, *Der Niedergang der bürgerlichen Denk- und Lebensform* (Weinheim: VCH, 1991), p. 83.

71   Jean-Marie Guéhenno, *L'avenir de la liberté* (Paris: Flammarion, 1999), p. 111.

72   Guéhenno, *The End of the Nation State*, *supra* n. 3, p. 30.

'manager',[73] seeking to cope indirectly in co-operation with various private organizations, using specialized knowledge (bypassing the forms of 'universalizing' institutionalization of law) with limited, situationally defined problems. Accordingly, we may join J. M. Guéhenno in saying: 'Nothing is more foreign to our age than the idea of a subject that could exist in and out of itself'.[74] It is instead constituted by the networks of relations themselves, in which it operates with the situational possibilities generated by them,[75] thereby transcending itself.

III.   The Compatibility of Democracy and Globalization

1.   Towards a 'Conception of Polycentric Control' of Law

These long prior considerations on the concept of a model of democracy not fixated on state and public is of importance for discussing the questions arising here, to the extent that one can draw the conclusion that the development of globalization cannot be seen as a process coming about primarily from the outside as large transnational actors break out of the territorial housing of the nation state. Moreover, the conception of democracy must also be kept open for historically varied forms of life, not least because the concept of subjectivity inevitably changes with time. Correspondingly, the institutional solutions focusing either defensively on the state (and excluding it off externally), or utopically on a world state, are entirely inappropriate. The order of the classical liberal democratic state is coming under pressure from both outside and inside because the traditional distinctions between a general interest (and universal knowledge and institutionalized stocks of rules) and the concrete particular applications of law that do not call its regulatory character into question are being undermined. This also calls into question the traditional concept of 'public decision' and the notion of a subject equipped with its own will and a defined circle of possibilities of action.[76] The acceleration in societies' self-transformation is reflected, above all, in the increasing importance of information and knowledge. This is becoming flexible and making permeable distinctions and boundaries that were previously assumed to be stable. This is ultimately enabling the de-territorialization of the economy, and therefore also of law.

Against the background of the considerations presented so far, the development towards globalization and the emergence of a complex 'global public (private governance)' can be seen in more differentiated fashions. First, a note on the

---

73   Guéhenno, *L'avenir de la liberté, supra* n. 71, p. 61; Paul E. Gottfried, *After Liberalism: Mass Democracy in the Managerial State* (Princeton: Princeton University Press, 1999).

74   Guéhenno, *The End of the Nation State, supra* n. 3, p. 93.

75   Guéhenno, *L'avenir de la liberté, supra* n. 71, p. 111.

76   Strong, *supra* n. 38; Rosenblum, *supra* n. 28.

concept of 'global governance' is appropriate to explain the terms. R. A. W. Rhodes has rightly termed the concept 'governance', 'imprecise but popular'.[77] The term in fact has several meanings. However, it primarily denotes (by contrast with the classical concept of a politically and legally describable sphere of 'government'), a no longer precisely legally definable area of responsibility for decisions, the binding effect of which cannot be described in traditional categories of unilateral sovereign disposal either. Instead, 'governance' follows a 'networked logic'[78] in which the separation between public and private, between universal and particular interest, between general norm and its application in the specific case and the hierarchically graded deciding organization (Ministry) can henceforth act to create order only to a limited extent. This de-territorialized heterarchical linkage of differing public organizations (state, international organizations with different structures), from multinational treaty systems up to supra-national institutions like the EU, cannot (after what has been said earlier) be seen without reference to the fundamentally changed relations between state and individual, and between public and private. The position of states can no longer reasonably be described using the concept of 'sovereignty';[79] many legal forms are unusable, and the hitherto incompatible has become interchangeable. For instance, regulations can be made through private standards or public law-norms without having to distinguish clearly between their importance, because the concept of state sovereignty as a whole has lost distinguishability from private action within the heterarchical overlapping network.[80] Patterns of linkage among relations between private persons do not only emerge spontaneously, but may be conceived strategically, as both private and public organizations now produce knowledge rather than merely using spontaneously generated experience. Not only do 'public powers' (in the plural) emerge because sovereignty has decayed, but the state can no longer claim to regulate the 'universal' and undertake lasting gradations in the superordination and subordination of interests. The aspect of creation, of experimenting with new forms of law, of producing new knowledge which does not just fit into the continuity of

---

77   R.A.W. Rhodes, '*The New Governance: Governing without Government*', POLITICAL STUDIES XLIV, 652- 667 (1996); *see also* Stuart Hoffman, '*A New World and its Troubles*', 69 FOREIGN AFFAIRS, 115 (1990); James N. Rosenau, 'Governance, Order and Change in World Politics', in James N. Rosenau and Ernst-Otto Czempiel (eds.), *Governance without Government: Order and Change in World Politics*, (Cambridge: Cambridge University Press, 1992), pp. 1-29; Oran Young, *International Governance* (New York: Cornell University Press, 1994); Anne-Marie Slaughter, 'The Real New World Order', 76 FOREIGN AFFAIRS, 183-197 (1997).

78   Guéhenno, *Demokratie am Wendepunkt, supra* n. 3.

79   Krasner, *supra* n. 30, p. 12; Scholte, *supra* n. 16, p. 427; Michael Reisman*, Designing and Managing the Future of the State*, EUROPEAN JOURNAL OF INTERNATIONAL LAW 8, 409-420 (1998).

80   Di Fabio, *supra* n. 57, p. 133, 142.

experience, and the importance of information as a decisive resource, are the most important features of a de-territorialized economy that admits of legal norms only with the close participation of private persons, or supports their self-organization, merely observed publicly.

The very production of new possibilities beyond experience is a reason for the rise of self-organized private-, or only imperfectly publicly established legal-, binding: this also applies to legal phenomena such as the *lex mercatoria*.[81] Especially when the stress is placed on the rise of information in the economy and the formation of new ways of producing and organizing the development of new stocks of knowledge tied to practical networks, the hierarchically graded state order (in the traditional sense) can no longer be a reference framework for thinking about 'public governance' (whether as the classical sovereign state or the utopian world state, conceived essentially on the same pattern, only extended worldwide). In this sense, J. A. Scholte rightly says that the bounds of the state are not being crossed (nonetheless ultimately observed) but 'transcended' (the territorial reference is being evaded overall through the rise of information and the formation of new hybrid forms of economic organization and the importance of financial markets).[82] This makes 'parallel governments' – international, supra-national and national – emerge, which no longer have the various separate competences of the past, but bring into being 'associations' (networks whose reference no longer lies in a geographically described competence). This leads to 'overlapping regulatory systems', among which it is necessary to use a form of co-ordination that no longer follows the traditional model of stable (federal state) or vertical (intergovernmental) demarcations.[83] It must instead follow a logic of its own of linkages ('relational rationality'), and a search for rules of 'intersystematicity'[84] of co-operative harmonization between regulatory systems. By contrast, traditional international legal transactions were characterized more by one-off state-mediated contacts that did not change the structure of national law as a whole.

This does not mean – as has been claimed in the literature[85] – the end of the state or of national law: instead the state is being transformed, itself inevitably taking up

---

81 Teubner, *supra* n. 12.

82 Jan A. Scholte, '*Global Capitalism and the State*', 73 INTERNATIONAL AFFAIRS, 427-452 (1997), p. 427.

83 See Jody Freeman, '*The Private Role in Public Governance*', 75 NEW YORK UNIVERSITY LAW REVIEW, 543-575 (2000); Peter L. Lindseth, '*Democratic Legitimacy and the Administrative Character of Supra-nationalism*', 99 COLUMBIA LAW REVIEW, 628-738 (1999).

84 Mark Harrington and Mark van Hoecke, '*Legal Cultures, Legal Paradigms And Legal Doctrine: Towards a New Model for Comparative Law*', 47 INTERNATIONAL AND COMPARATIVE LAW QUATERLY, 495-536 (1998).

85 Kenichi Ohmae, *The End of the Nation State. The Rise of Regional Economies* (New York: Free Press, 1995).

elements of transnational de-territorialized self-organization of variable networks, and orienting itself, for instance, border-crossing transnationally variable interests rather than just to national clienteles. In this way, the state's territorial unity becomes permeable both from the inside and from the outside for the pursuit of changed interests, calling for new procedural forms for upholding them. In this sense, the WTO and its forms of dispute settlement can also be seen as a form of emergence of a new co-operative law, the logic of which no longer follows classical international law but in the long term requires a process of variable linkage and compatibilization of differing legal norms and principles and creation of global procedural rules and principles developed in practice case by case, but not accessible to any general fixation.

The network of legal regulations, of partly governmental, partly transnationally private, partly international origin is typified by its incompleteness and openness to situational experimental linkages and specifications. But even at the national level, this is not essentially different as the development towards regulation is no longer primarily a movement of de-juridification but more towards a co-operative private-public strategy of situational legal ties processed through a combination of varying competences, legal forms and involvements. The state has, in turn, become a 'network of public and private collective actors';[86] this facilitates its further de-centralization, also through the transnational co-operative networks. Creating these follows the transnationalization of markets, which produces a dense network of legal relationships beyond national frontiers that can no longer be translated into the traditional system of nationally channelled 'external trade relationships'. This development has considerable repercussions for the overlapping between domestic and transnational law. Taking this into account, the conception of 'legalization' of international relations recently formulated by Abbott et al. seems too narrow: they stress, above all, the advantage of law lying in its binding effect owing to its 'precision' of rules.[87] But this very thing is tending to be of decreasing importance within domestic legal relations. The specifically legal aspect of the new domestic and transnational relations in conditions of complexity lies more in the fact that those involved enter into a network of various co-operative relationships that process ties through association constraints and possibilities going beyond current interests and will relationships. This peculiarity is marked chiefly by the search, utilizing the law's autonomy to stabilize emergent linkage patterns produced through practice that cannot be reduced to *ex ante* harmonization of mutual interests (because these, specifically, must bind uncertainty and enable learning, and thereby offer advantages even where short-term interests are frustrated). However, the possibility of utilizing the network of legal possibilities of relation offers, on the whole, a considerable institutional advantage just because the calculation of interests

---

86   Teubner, *supra* n. 30, p. 346.
87   Abbott et al., *supra* n. 13.

in conditions of complexity is often not readily possible. In particular, the need for experimental production of new operating possibilities is given only on the basis of the possibility of forming and institutionally underpinning expectations through law. Accordingly, one cannot reduce the law to a stock of rules. The network continues to function primarily by operating with the legal possibilities of linkage and binding. 'Precision' is therefore not some pronounced feature of post-modern law, but the productive operation with ties that produce more possibilities of experimental action on the basis of partial knowledge.[88]

As an interim consideration we should state that the manifestations of globalization cannot be established solely by the quantity and multiplicity of the crossings of the nation state's boundaries alone; instead, a qualitatively new process of self-transformation of economy, state and law is emerging, covering all social institutions and calling for new descriptions.

2. Prospects of Democracy in Times of Globalization

The considerations so far about a less state-fixated form of democracy and the importance of forming new institutional modes of globalization allow some consequences to be drawn for reformulating the democracy principle in conditions of post-modernity: if democracy were necessarily bound up with the classical hierarchical concept of the state and popular sovereignty, globalization would not really be compatible with the maintenance of democracy, especially as a world state is not conceivable (for various reasons, but not least because a global state would not really be compatible with the maintenance of a hierarchical order).

This link is however – as we have shown – not necessary: indeed, it cannot be reconciled with the transformation of the forms of individuality in post-modern society. A non-hierarchical variant of democracy would focus less on common decision through sovereign organized unity of will than on producing a distributed self-observation and observation of others made possible by a 'network of networks' and the associated productive association possibilities and constraints, which are so openly dimensioned that far-reaching inclusion of citizens is guaranteed. This makes democracy conceivable even in conditions of a heterarchical social self-organization that escapes the conceptual grip of the traditional categories.[89]

As shown earlier, the conception of classical liberal democracy and of citizens' consensus to its basis must also be reformulated more openly if consensus is associated less with the concept of a common substance of values and procedures than with mutual control through overlapping networks of relations that also

---

88   Karl-Heinz Ladeur, '*Postmodern Constitutional Theory*', 60 MODERN LAW REVIEW, 617-629 (1997).

89   Ohmae, *supra* n. 85.

correspond with the transformed conception of a form of 'networked variable acentric individuality' in post-modern society. On this basis, the concept of participation rights can also be productively reformulated. The specific network method of distributing such rights (possible, for instance, also through NGOs) could contribute to mutual monitoring through self-observation and observation of others among the various networks. Under such conditions, participation is not a manifestation of direct democracy (which would in turn be unity-related) but an adjusted variant of the linkage among various networks taking on the inclusion of all citizens in altered shape. If participation is separated from the idea of direct democracy, then perspectives open for a model of 'control through transparency'[90] and 'learning through mutual observation',[91] which could be systematically improved through procedures and adapted to new challenges through linkage rules. In this way, learning processes might be established and maintained through the mutual irritation of systems and networks. The state would then have a decentralized function: the maintenance of the productivity and innovative capacity of the networks and supplying them with diversity and observing the results.[92] Against this background, participation and transparency would have more the function of enabling the mutual irritation of the networks of relations, than of aggregating a general will in unitary fashion.

One of the most important ways of linking up networks and mutual openness might lie in the introduction of nationally organized 'accountancy rules', or rules formulated through social standardization bodies, establishing a constraint to improved self-observation and flexibilization of the networks of relations (such as rules for finance markets, but also collective wage negotiations, and so on), that would correspond to the aspect of drafting and experimenting through systematic incorporation of self-observation procedures. In view of the growing acceleration of self-transcendence of the social 'network of networks', the point would be to organize systematic constraints to produce knowledge, as it would no longer be possible to rely on the spontaneous production of knowledge. Especially at transnational level, there would be a need to institutionalize transparency and accountancy to cope with global problems (like environmental protection) and other complex issues. One might also think of establishing agencies that are largely screened off from political influences and that could create the necessary knowledge basis for decisions.

If the form of self-transformation of post-modern societies thus described is taken into account, a new perspective on the crisis of the welfare state also opens

90 Lindseth, *supra* n. 83; Adrienne Héritier, '*Composite Democratic Legitimation in Europe*', *MPPG* preprint 2001/6 (2001).

91 March and Olsen, *Democratic Governance, supra* n. 12, p. 105, 158.

92 Idem, p. 225; March and Olsen, *The Institutional Dynamics of International Political Order, supra* n. 12; Guéhenno, *Demokratie am Wendepunkt, supra* n. 3, p. 18.

up: social security adapted to the changed conditions of the global economy is not only not incompatible with the requirements of a knowledge society, but is incompatible with it because social security is the very thing that makes it possible and acceptable to take risks. As labour power is largely territorially bound, there would be a need to strengthen the state's possibilities within the global network of public actors in the area of social security, but simultaneously to dimension security systems in a way that would facilitate adjustment to the changed constraints, but that would not offer the possibility of evading adjustment. The theme taken here allows no more than these hints; at any rate, it follows that, at least for the moment, the possibility of conveying responsibility for social security to transnational systems seems very limited. When analysing the specific role of the nation state and the transformation it is undergoing in the process of globalization, one has first of all to lay open a certain idea of its origin and function. This remains implicit in many critical approaches. Many critics of the globalization process presuppose a concept of the nation state as a model that we must focus on when considering the establishment of a new international order.

This idea refers to a one-sided construction of the modern state. Its role, which in fact allows for abstract legal relationships beyond the traditional order, was always based on the necessity to make order possible under conditions of change that destroy a sense of continuity.[93] The state will also be able to fulfil this role under new conditions in the future (that is, the organization of solidarity in the form of transferring knowledge to new generations, guaranteeing safety, and protecting order from basic social risks). But the importance of a 'symbolic intensification' (Habermas) of political order, as opposed to the structuring of economic and social order through efficient rules, should not be overestimated. The liberal collective order is not abstract, but consists of a universalized economic practice that abstracts from traditional relationships.

However, economic orders in the future will be increasingly characterized by legal models that are no longer based on abstract rules (as it was the case on the European continent) structured by hierarchical order. This is because law and legal practice will be much more intertwined.[94] All the fundamental separations and distinctions that lie at the basis of legal order are questioned. Market and organization are no longer kept separate, hybrid models of co-ordination are spreading, and they no longer differentiate clearly between internal and external (exchange) relations ('relational contracts' for long-term relationships), markets are re-established within the organization ('profit-centres'), co-operation and

---

93   Manus I. Midlarsky, *The Evolution of Inequality* (Stanford: Stanford University Press, 2000), p. 36, 50; Stephen E. Toulmin, *The Return to Reason* (Cambridge, MA: Harvard University Press, 2001), p. 158.

94   Karl-Heinz Ladeur, *Die rechtswissenschaftliche Methodendiskussion und die Bewältigung des gesellschaftlichen Wandels*, RABELS ZEITSCHRIFT 64, 60-103 (2000).

competition overlap ('joint ventures' in high technology). This tendency demands flexible new forms of legal regime that do not allow for stable legal and administrative hierarchical order but that are part of a heterarchy of overlapping public and private rules, practices, standards.

This tendency, which can now only be referred to in a sketchy way, has almost nothing to do with globalization; it is due to the rise of information and knowledge as the main economic resource. Globalization is just one phenomenon, which is also made possible by this transformation of the economic order. The major part of the recent problems of government cannot be attributed to a tendency of globalized economic conglomerates to shift production from one country to another as they please. They stem 'from within'. Abstract rules of law and hierarchical decision-making no longer work – even when mediated by big 'representative' organizations (trade unions, employers' associations, and so on) – because society is undergoing a rapid process of transformation towards network-like self-organized types of co-ordination. Society creates flexible patterns of co-ordination with overlapping and heterogeneous models, instead of opting for clear-cut alternatives. This evolution creates trouble for a state whose basis had been a model of universal and abstract order which were exempt from processes of change.

In the new 'society of networks',[95] the state does not find stability in the realm of intermediary organizations that stem from the welfare state and had produced practical organizational knowledge for public decision-making. This evolution has changed the welfare state, but it will not make the state itself obsolete. It is the welfare state, in particular, which is based on the assumption that only the citizens of a specific state profit from its redistributional activities;[96] this notion is valid not only for social assistance and social security, but also for economic intervention (such as the protection of declining industries). In this respect, the state loses its hold on the economy and this lack of efficiency of public activities raises some doubt as to whether this development should be deplored.

Globalization is only one phenomenon of transformation of the state, and it is hitherto not very important. But whereas 'protectionism' has a bad image, the contrary is true for 'democracy'. All the interests that claimed protection form economic change in the past, prefer to invoke 'democracy' when they protest against globalization. This might be understandable inasmuch as new forms of public governance (a term whose openness reflects the evolution of forms of public order beyond the state) have yet to be found both at the level of the nation state and at the global level, which might be adapted to network-like organizations and the rise of the 'knowledge society'. These forms have to be based on co-operation,

95   Manuel Castells, *The Information Age: The Rise of the Network Society – Vol.1* (Cambridge: Blackwell, 2000).

96   Robert Gilpin, *Global Political Economy. Understanding the International Economic Order* (Princeton: Princeton University Press, 2001), p. 366.

proceduralization (instead of substantive goals), and flexible adaptation to uncertainty. This is valid for all levels of public order, from the nation state to global order.

The reproduction of the state model at the European-, or even at the global-, level would be a step in the wrong direction. This model is not obsolete, but it cannot meet the requirements for flexibility that are created by the knowledge society and the new global order.

This is why the acentric structure of the EC might turn out to be a functional hybrid organization that, beyond the rhetoric of the 'Europe of nations' or 'the Member States as the masters of the treaty', should not de transformed into a state-like organization with a constitution as a 'foundational act' of its own. There are also theoretical reasons for this. The new, hybrid types of organizations do not have a hierarchical structure, and the new problems of public order cannot be managed by reproducing the old state model at a more abstract level. The predominance of the intergovernmental element in the European model – as opposed to the supra-national element (which serves an element of stabilization and continuation of order) – might do justice to the social processes generating international, transnational and domestic networks of overlapping heterarchical networks in a much more flexible and adaptive way than would a superstate. This open construction would also be able to better integrate the problems of the Member States themselves, which used to be kept separate from questions of European institution building.

The Prime Minister of Luxembourg, J. C. Juncker, recently proposed abandoning the idea of a European constitution altogether. He instead suggested thought about how to introduce elements of European integration and transnational governance into the constitution of Member States. This might be a productive idea as it allows for much more openness for the phenomenon of overlapping levels of order. This normative concept comes close to the empirical approach of 'intergovernmentalists' to the European integration process. A. Moravcsik rightly argues that the European integration process can easily be interpreted as the outcome of a 'post modern, multicultural experiment',[97] which has been 'accepted by overlapping cultural and political groups' in Member States. With reference to the overestimation of the 'democratic deficit', he points out that within the nation state there is a habit of insulating certain interests from processes of balancing countervailing interests (competition, monetary policy, and so on). In spite of the rhetoric of democratic decision-making, political processes in Member States are increasingly characterized by a dominance of special interest groups. This is due to the fact that the integrative function of representative 'encompassing' groups (Olson) is breaking down, whereas constraints of reciprocity and compliance may

---

97 Andrew Moravcsik, *'Despotism in Brussels? (Review of Siedentop)'*, 80 FOREIGN AFFAIRS, 114-123 (2001), p. 118.

exclude narrow short-term interests at the European level. The same might be valid for the international level. In many cases, we can observe the discrepancy between democratic rhetoric and the narrow mindedness of political groups, especially in Third World countries, abusing political power for the preservation of interest structures that are far from productive for the population as a whole.

International law could also profit if it could be mobilized for breaking up the traditional core of state sovereignty and deploying the internal dynamic of states.

In the long run, responsibility will be concentrated neither at the level of domestic governments nor at the supra-national level of international organization alone; it will instead rest with private-public networks of decision-makers and groups that overlap at national, transnational and international levels.[98] In the long run, democracy is characterized by its potential to adapt to new challenges, and to reinforce the dynamic of societies, not by strong states.

---

98   Wolfgang H. Reinicke, *Global Public Policy. Governing without Government?* (Washington: Brookings Institution Press, 1998); Gilpin, *supra* n. 96, p. 384.

PART III

THE CHANGE OF LAW AND THE STATE UNDER THE PRESSURE OF GLOBALIZATION

Chapter 6

Global Government Networks, Global Information Agencies, and Disaggregated Democracy

Anne-Marie Slaughter[*]

Can global governance be democratic? That is the question that animates this volume and many others, that brings protesters into the streets in Seattle and Prague and Washington, and that has national and international government officials working on a host of reforms to enhance 'transparency' and 'access' to their global deliberations. It has motivated a raft of efforts to define global governance and to distinguish it from government of various types. The next step, at least for many, is to redefine democracy.

Many of the contributions to this volume seek to elaborate a post-modern conception of democracy, one that can at least provide the foundation or the framework for democratic global governance. They proceed from the assumption that the old modern conception of democracy relies on an identifiable polity within defined boundaries that can be assumed to exercise a fictional unitary will to create a hierarchical body of law. Such a conception cannot be globalized without the creation of a world state, which is generally agreed to be both impossible and undesirable. Conversely, however, these analyses agree that globalization cannot be stopped or shut down. The alternative, at least intellectually, is to redefine the terms of the debate.

The post-modernists begin with a redefinition of the self, and proceed to a redefinition of democracy, the state, sovereignty, and law. There are almost as many variations on these themes as there are authors, but within this radically reconceptualized world, many new possibilities for self-government within a globalized economy and society emerge. These are fundamentally optimistic scenarios, fashioned by scholars unafraid to grapple with seismic shifts in human

* J. Sinclair Armstrong, Professor of International, Foreign and Comparative Law, Harvard Law School.

self-perception, technology, and mental geography. They are genuinely breaking the boundaries of political possibility.

The results are heady, exciting, and likely to be unintelligible to the vast majority of policymakers, activists, and citizens who seek to achieve specific goals in an age of globalization, information, and politicization. Reinterpreting Rousseau's theory of the general will, as compelling as it may prove to political philosophers, will not change the view of those who perceive themselves to be disenfranchised through globalization. These actors may in fact be making a post-modern world, but the purportedly outdated 'modern' ideas of democracy – electoral accountability, the control of the elite by the mass, a clear understanding of who is governing whom and by what means – remain remarkably potent.[1] Perceptions that international institutions, much less shadowy 'networks' of government officials, are fundamentally undemocratic are easy to promulgate and hard to erase.

The problem is not merely rhetorical. Proponents of global governance, particularly through multiple parallel networks of public and private actors, must offer at least a partial response to the problems of democracy as traditionally defined, before redefining it. After all, in true post-modern fashion, post-modernity cannot displace modernity, but only exist alongside it.

I propose in this chapter to ground the discussion in many of the other contributions to this volume by developing a typology of more concrete and prosaic accountability problems connected with a rapidly growing form of global governance – transgovernmental regulatory networks, or, more generally, 'government networks'.[2] These are networks of national government officials exchanging information, co-ordinating national policies, and working together to address common problems.[3] For some, they herald a new and attractive form of

1   Robert Dahl, who in a sense has devoted his life to defining democracy, nevertheless suggests for the purposes of one of his books that 'we can get along adequately with the notion of democracy as "rule by the people", or, to narrow down the idea a bit more, as rule by a demos, a citizen body consisting of members who are considered equals for purposes of arriving at governmental decisions'. Robert A. Dahl, *Democracy and Its Critics* (New Haven: Yale University Press, 1989), p. 83.

2   Various authors have various names for these networks; in my terminology they are a subset of the larger and growing phenomenon of 'government networks': networks of different types of government institutions from courts to legislatures. See Anne-Marie Slaughter, 'The Real New World Order', FOREIGN AFFAIRS, 76 (1997), 183-97; Anne-Marie Slaughter, 'Judicial Globalization', VIRGINIA JOURNAL OF INTERNATIONAL LAW, 40 (2000), 1103-24.

3   See, e.g. Sol Picciotto, *Networks in International Economic Integration: Fragmented States and the Dilemmas of Neo-Liberalism*, 17 NORTHWESTERN JOURNAL OF LAW & BUSINESS 1014 (1996-97); Sol Picciotto, *Fragmented States and International Rules of Law*, 6 SOCIAL & LEGAL STUDIES 259 (1997); Scott H. Jacobs, *Regulatory Co-Operation for an Interdependent World: Issues for Government*, in Organization for Economic Co-operation and Development, REGULATORY CO-OPERATION FOR AN INTERDEPENDENT

global governance, enhancing the ability of states to work together to address common problems without the centralized bureaucracy of formal international institutions.[4] For others, however, these networks portend a vast technocratic conspiracy, a shadowy world of regulators bent on 'de-politicizing' global issues in ways that will inevitably benefit the rich and powerful at the expense of the poor and weak.[5]

This chapter seeks to broaden our understanding of government networks by placing them in more historical context and by elaborating different types of government networks within and without traditional international institutions. After a brief overview of the literature on transgovernmentalism since the 1970s in Part I, Part II sets forth a typology of three different categories of government networks. Part III then seeks to pinpoint the specific accountability concerns associated with each type. Part IV offers one approach to answering some current accountability concerns by adapting the concept of 'information agencies' from the European Union to the global level. This analysis rests on a claim of similarity between global government networks and a number of EU governance structures, primarily the 'comitology' system and related transgovermental and public-private networks. Finally, building on the same premise, Part V briefly surveys some of the more

---

WORLD (1994), pp. 15-38; Anne-Marie Slaughter, 'Governing the Global Economy through Government Networks', in Michael Byers, (ed.), *The Role of Law in International Politics* (Oxford, New York: Oxford University Press, 1999); *id., The Real New World Order, supra* n. 2; Thomas Risse-Kappen, CO-OPERATION AMONG DEMOCRACIES 38 (1995) (defining 'transgovernmental coalitions' as 'transboundary networks among subunits of national governments forming in the absence of central and authoritative national decisions'). Risse-Kappen further defines 'transgovernmental networks' as those among state officials in sub-units of national governments, international organizations, and regimes frequently pursuing their own agenda, independently from and sometimes contrary to the declared policies of their national governments. Id. at 38-40. Finally, he insists that in a genuine transgovernmental regime, '[s]ub-units of national governments have to act on their own, in the absence of national decisions, not just on behalf of their heads of state implementing agreed-upon policies'. Id. at 9. When this occurs, '[t]ransgovernmental coalitions are then defined as networks of government officials which include at least one actor pursuing her own agenda independent of national decions'.

4 Slaughter, *Real NewWorld Order, supra* n. 2, p. 185; Slaughter, *Governing the Global Economy through Government Networks, supra* n. 3, pp. 179-80. I continue to argue the merits of this form of governance; however, I am increasingly aware of the actual and potential problems associated with these networks. Hence the importance of focusing on accountability.

5 See, e.g. Sol Picciotto, *Fragmented States, supra* n. 3, p. 273. (dispersal of politics into functional arenas 'appears to allow particular issues to be regulated in a depoliticized, technocratic manner, by managers or professionals who are directly accountable to their "customers".'); also Picciotto, *Networks in International Economic Integration, supra* n. 3, p. 1037.

fundamental reconceptualizations of democracy developed in this volume and elsewhere and distils various elements of these visions that could be useful in strengthening the democratic pedigree of government networks. It concludes with an appeal to add global legislative networks to the pluralist mix of global governance mechanisms.

I.   A Short and Selective History of Transgovernmentalism

Analysts have spent more time identifying and labelling government networks than distinguishing between them. They are typically identified as part of the larger phenomenon of 'transnationalism'. Philip Jessup introduced international lawyers to 'transnational law' in 1958, defining it as 'all law which regulates actions or events that transcend national frontiers. Both public and private international law are included, as are other rules which do not wholly fit into such standard categories'.[6] Henry Steiner and Detlev Vagts later translated this concept into a casebook, collecting materials designed to bridge the gap between the domestic and international legal world.[7]

Political scientists embraced transnational relations somewhat later, in the late 1960s and 1970s, acknowledging the plethora of non-traditional actors in the international system and trying to relate them both to states and international organizations. The theoretical debate initially focused on whether to define transnationalism in terms of the identity of the actors or the nature of the activity. In an influential edited volume, *Transnational Relations and World Politics*, Keohane and Nye defined transnational relations as, 'contacts, coalitions, and interactions across state boundaries that are not controlled by the central foreign policy organs of government'.[8] Samuel Huntington responded to this idea, arguing that the definition

6   Philip Jessup, Transnational Law 2 (1956). In footnote 3 of the first chapter, Jessup cites Joseph Johnson as one of the originators of the term in an address of 15th June 1955 to the Harvard Foundation.

7   Transnational Legal Problems xv-xvi (Henry J. Steiner and Detlev F. Vagts, eds., 2d ed. 1976). Steiner and Vagts built on Jessup's broad definition and focused on topics including aspects of national legal systems dealing with principles and procedures for decision-making that have been specifically developed to regulate problems with some foreign element. The relevant participants in transnational activity include private individuals or firms, national courts or legislators or treaty-makers, governmental instrumentalities, international officials, and regional and international organizations. *Id.* at xvii.

8   Joseph S. Nye, Jr. and Robert O. Keohane (eds.), Transnational Relations and World Politics xi (1972) (hereafter TRANSNATIONAL RELATIONS). They identify a separate subset of 'international interactions' as 'the movement of tangible or intangible items across state boundaries when at least one actor is not an agent of a government or an intergovernmental organization. *Id.* at xii.

of transnational relations should focus not on the actors involved in the process, but rather on the activity itself. He viewed transnationalism as a peculiarly American mode of expansion, based on 'freedom to operate' rather than 'power to control'.[9]

Several years later, Nye and Keohane explicitly distinguished 'transgovernmental' activity from the broader category of transnational activity, defining 'transgovernmental relations' as 'sets of direct interactions among sub-units of different governments that are not controlled or closely guided by the policies of the cabinets or chief executives of those governments'.[10] They quoted Francis Bator for the proposition that 'it is a central fact of foreign relations that business is carried on by the separate departments with their counterpart bureaucracies abroad, through a variety of informal as well as formal connections'.[11] Their principal interest in this article was to identify the various ways in which the existence of transgovernmental politics, as well as transnational politics, offered ways for international organizations to play an important role in world politics.[12] Nevertheless, they identified different types of transgovernmental activity – policy co-ordination and coalition-building, specified the conditions under which transgovernmental networks are most likely to form, and specified different types of interactions between international organizations and transgovernmental networks.

Prominent international relations theorists largely lost interest in transnational and transgovernmental relations during the 1980s and early 1990s, as interest focused on security studies and inter-state 'regimes'. Events over the course of the 1990s, however, cast a spotlight on a new generation of transgovernmental networks. As the bipolar state system of the Cold War disappeared and non-state, substate, and supra-national actors rode the tide of globalization, pundits and many scholars began heralding the era of complex, multi-level, global governance, tied together by networks.[13] Early on, Peter Haas explored the role and power of

9   *Id.* at 344.

10   Robert O. Keohane and Joseph S. Nye, *Transgovernmental Relations and International Organizations*, XXVII WORLD POLITICS 39, 43 (1974) (hereafter *Transgovernmental Relations*). They included in their definition the increased communication between governmental agencies and business carried on by separate departments with their counterpart bureaucracies abroad. *Id.* at 41-42. By contrast, a meeting of heads-of-state at which new initiatives are taken was still the paradigm of the state-centric (interstate) model. *Id.* at 43-44. Compare their earlier depiction traditional 'interstate' relations, in which 'actors are behaving in roles specified or reasonably implied by the formal foreign policy structure of the state'. TRANSNATIONAL RELATIONS at 383.

11   Testimony of Francis Bator before the Subcommittee on Foreign Economic Policy, Committee on Foreign Affairs, House of Representatives, 25th July 1972. *US Foreign Economic Policy: Implications for the Organization of the Executive Branch*, 110-11, quoted in Keohane and Nye, *Transgovernmental Relations*, p. 42.

12   *Ibid.*

13   See generally James N. Rosenau and Ernst-Otto Czempiel (eds.), *Governance without Government: Order and Change in World Politics* (Cambridge: Cambridge University

'epistemic communities', which he defined as networks 'of professionals with recognized expertise and competence in a particular domain and an authoritative claim to policy-relevant knowledge within that domain or issue-area'.[14] Later work absorbed the insights about the power of shared learning and knowledge production generated by the epistemic communities literature, but focused on more concrete and observable organizational forms. A number of convergent factors focused growing attention on the more specific phenomenon of transgovernmental regulatory networks.

First were observable changes in the organization and activities of national financial regulators. The Basle Committee on Banking Supervision was created in 1974 and is now composed of the representatives of thirteen central banks that regulate the world's largest banking markets.[15] Between 1975 and 1992 it issued the Basle Concordat, with several sets of subsequent amendments, to enhance co-operation between regulators of multinational banks by dividing specified tasks between home country and host country regulators. In 1988 the Basle Committee issued a set of capital adequacy standards to be adopted by all its members as the new regulatory standard within their countries, which had a sharp impact on the

---

Press, 1992); James Rosenau, *Along the Domestic-International Frontier: Exploring Governance in a Turbulent World* (Cambridge, England: Cambridge University Press, 1997); Thomas Friedman, *The Lexus and the Olive Tree: Understanding Globalization* (New York: Farrar, Straus and Giroux, 1999). For an excellent review of much of the governance literature, see Gerry Stoker, 'Governance as theory: five propositions', *International Social Science Journal,* vol. 155, pp. 17-28 (1998); For an influential discussion of multi-level governance within the EU, see Fritz W. Scharpf, *Community and Autonomy: Multi-Level Governance in the European Union*, 1:2 JOURNAL OF EUROPEAN PUBLIC POLICY 219 (1994); Fritz Scharpf, *Community Policy and Autonomy: Multilevel Policymaking in European Union*; Gary Marks, Lisbet Hooghe and Kermit Blank. *An Actor-Centered Approach to Multi-Level Governance*, 6 JOURNAL OF REGIONAL AND FEDERAL STUDIES 20 (1996); Marcus Horeth, 'The Trilemma of Legitimacy: Multilevel Governance in the EU and the Problem of Democracy' (Bonn: Zentrum für Europäische Integrationsforschung, Rheinische Friedrich-Wilhelms-Universitaet Bonn, 1998).

14　Peter M. Haas, '*Introduction: Epistemic Communities and International Policy Coordination*', 46 INTERNATIONAL ORGANIZATION 1, 3 (1992). *See also* Peter M. Haas (ed.), Knowledge, Power and International Policy Coordination, 46 INTERNATIONAL ORGANIZATION (Special Issue) (1992); *id., Saving the Mediterranean: The Politics of International Environmental Cooperation* (New York: Columbia University Press, 1990).

15　The members of the Basle Committee come from Belgium, Canada, France, Germany, Italy, Japan, Luxembourg, the Netherlands, Spain, Sweden, Switzerland, United Kingdom, and United States. See http://www.bis.org/bcbs/aboutbcbs.htm (last modified 19th April 2001).

availability of credit in the world's most important economies.[16] The International Organization of Securities Commissioners (IOSCO), emerged in 1984, followed in the 1990s by the creation of the International Association of Insurance Supervisors and a network of all three of these organizations and other national and international officials responsible for financial stability around the world called the Financial Stability Forum.[17] As a number of scholars point out, these 'organizations' do not fit the model of an organization held either by international lawyers or political scientists – they are not composed of states and constituted by treaty; they do not enjoy legal personality; they have no headquarters or stationery.[18] According to Sol Picciotto, however, they 'form part of a more general shift from "government" to "governance", involving the delegation or transfer of public functions to particularized bodies, operating on the basis of professional or scientific techniques'.[19]

A second major impetus for the study of transgovernmental networks has been the emergence of a new 'multi-layered regulatory system', concentrated among OECD countries.[20] These governments have had to respond to deepening economic and financial integration and increasing interdependence across a wide range of issues by developing strategies for regulatory co-operation and rapprochement. Transgovernmental networks have proliferated in response to these needs. However, as an OECD study concluded in 1994, the new forms of governance necessary to make regulatory co-operation work cannot simply follow function. They must instead be managed within a principled framework designed not only to improve

---

16   Tony Porter, *States, Markets and Regimes in Global Finance* (Basingstoke: Macmillan, 1993); see also David Zaring, *International Law by Other Means: The Twilight Existence of International Financial Regulatory Organization*, 33 TEXAS JOURNAL OF INTERNATIONAL LAW 281, 284 (1998)

17   The Financial Stability Forum was initiated by the finance ministers and central bank governors of the Group of Seven industrial countries in February 1999, following a report on international co-operation and co-ordination in the area of financial market supervision and surveillance by the President of the Deutsche Bundesbank. In addition to representatives from the Basle Committee, IOSCO, and IAIS, its members include senior representative from national authorities responsible for financial stability in significant international financial centres; international financial institutions such as the BIS, the IMF, the OECD, and the World Bank; and committees of central bank experts. See http://www.IMF.ORG/external/np/exr/facts/groups.htm#FSF. For a discussion of additional networks created by the Basle Committee, IOSCO, and the IAIS, such as the Joint Forum on Financial Conglomerates and the Year 2000 Network, *see* Slaughter, *Governing the Global Economy. supra* n. 3, pp. 186-88.

18   Zaring, *supra* n. 16. See also Porter, *supra* n. 16, at 4-5.

19   Picciotto, *Networks in International Economic Integration, supra* n. 3, at 1039.

20   Jacobs, *supra* n. 3, at 18.

their effectiveness and the quality of their output, but also to 'protect democratic processes'.[21]

Third, the most concentrated site for multilevel governance, and particularly transgovernmental regulatory interactions, is the EU itself. In the wake of the completion of the single market in 1992, the EU has emerged as a 'regulatory state', exercising power through rule making rather than taxing and spending.[22] In response to the challenges of trying to harmonize or at least reconcile the regulations of its diverse and growing members, the EU has developed a system of 'regulation by networks', located in the Council of Ministers and closely connected to the complex process of 'comitology' that surrounds Council decision-making.[23] The question now confronting a growing number of legal scholars and political theorists is how decision-making by networks of national regulators fits with varying national models of European democracy.[24]

Fourth is the emergence of a system of 'transatlantic governance' to help foster and manage the increasingly dense web of transatlantic economic cooperation.[25] Although transatlantic regulatory relations may seem only a subset of the larger multi-layered regulatory system just discussed, they take place within the framework of a number of specific initiatives launched by heads of state. As described by Mark Pollack and Gregory Shaffer, transatlantic governance involves co-operation at the inter-governmental level, the transgovernmental level, and the transnational level.[26] The evolution of transatlantic relations over the course of the 1990s has thus spawned questions concerning the inter-relationship and relative importance of these three levels.[27]

---

21   *Id.* at 20, 35.

22   Giandomenico Majone, *The European Community as a Regulatory State*, 5 COLLECTED COURSES OF THE ACADEMY OF EUROPEAN LAW 321-419 (1994).

23   Renaud Dehousse, *Regulation by Networks in the European Community: the Role of European Agencies*, 4 JOURNAL OF EUROPEAN PUBLIC POLICY 246-61, 254 (1997).

24   This question is the subject of many of the contributions to this volume. Previous work on this subject, often in the context of the European Union, includes Joshua Cohen and Charles Sabel, *Directly-Deliberative Polyarchy*, 3 EUROPEAN LAW JOURNAL 313 (1997); Christian Joerges and Juergen Neyer, 'From Intergovernmental Bargaining to Deliberative Political Processes: The Constitutionalisation of Comitology', 3 EUROPEAN LAW JOURNAL 273 (1997); Joseph H.H. Weiler, *The Constitution of Europe*, (Cambridge: Cambridge University Press, 1999). For an excellent range of arguments by many of the authors engaged in these debates through the 1990s, see the articles collected in Christian Joerges and Ellen Vos (eds.), *EU Committees: Social Regulation, Law and Politics*, (Oxford: Hart, 1999).

25   Mark A. Pollack and Gregory C. Shaffer (eds.), *Transatlantic Governance in the Global Economy*, (Lanham, Md.: Rowman & Littlefield, 2001).

26   *Id.*, Chapter I.

27   *Id.* These are the questions animating the case studies collected in this volume.

Finally, transgovernmental networks play an important role in several recent and still actively debated theories of compliance with international rules. Abram and Antonia Chayes and Harold Koh have emphasized the importance of regular interaction, dialogue, and 'jawboning' among networks of government officials at both the international and transnational levels.[28] Both theories penetrate the traditional black box of the state to focus on the activities of specific government institutions and officials.

II.   A Typology of Transgovernmental Networks

Based on this earlier work and current empirical observation, it is possible to identify three different types of transnational regulatory networks, based on the different contexts in which they arise and operate. First are those networks of national regulators that develop within the context of established international organizations. Second are networks of national regulators that develop under the umbrella of an overall agreement negotiated by heads of state. And third are the networks that have attracted the most attention over the past decade – networks of national regulators that develop outside any formal framework. These networks arise spontaneously from a need to work together to address common problems; in some cases members interact sufficiently autonomously to require the institutionalization of their activities in their own transgovernmental regulatory organizations.[29]

These three types are inter-linked in many ways; some may seem such a standard part of the international furniture as to be beneath notice; others compete directly with actual or possible international organizations. But for present purposes, each raises different accountability problems. Hence it is valuable to develop this typology as a first step toward pinpointing precisely what 'lack of accountability' means in this context and what specific steps might be taken to address it.

1.   *Government Networks within International Organizations*

What's new? National government officials have always networked within international organizations; once the heads of state have gone home, the task of actually getting on with the mission of a particular institution, however fragile and sketchy, falls to the national government officials in the issue area concerned.

---

28   See Harold H. Koh, '*Transnational Legal Process*' NEBRASKA LAW REVIEW_75 (1996); Abram Chayes and Antonia H. Chayes, *The New Sovereignty: Compliance with International Regulatory Agreements*, (Cambridge: Harvard University Press, 1995).

29   Zaring refers to these as international financial regulatory organizations. Zaring, *supra* n. 16.

Indeed, dependent on the issue area, they often play a role before the creation of the institution – US Treasury Secretary Harry Dexter White was certainly present at Bretton Woods.[30] But certainly once an institution has been established, whether to regulate international labour issues, environmental protection, health issues, international criminal activity, or the sprawling and increasingly untidy global markets, it will fall to the national ministries or agencies charged with the particular issue area in question to work with the nascent international secretariat officially charged to represent the organization's interests.

Keohane and Nye describe networks of government ministers within international organizations as emblematic of the 'club model' of international institutions.[31] Within a particular intergovernmental institution established by treaty, 'cabinet ministers or the equivalent, working in the same issue-area, initially from a relatively small number of relatively rich countries, got together to make rules. Trade ministers dominated GATT; finance ministers ran the IMF; defence and foreign ministers met at NATO; central bankers at the Bank for International Settlements (BIS)'.[32] This mode of operation was very efficient for participating governments, because the relatively small and like-minded number of ministers involved came to form a negotiating 'club' in which they reached agreements and then reported them to national legislatures and publics.[33]

The OECD is perhaps the quintessential example of transgovernmental regulatory networking within an established international institution. Its primary function, at least in recent decades, has been to convene government officials in specific issue areas for the purpose of addressing a common problem and making recommendations or promulgating a model code for its solution.[34] As discussed above, the EU Council of Ministers operates the same way, although Council members exercise actual decision-making power. Finally, in some cases, the secretariat of an international institution deliberately encourages the formation of a

---

30 Richard N. Gardner, *Sterling-Dollar Diplomacy: The Origins and Prospects of Our International Economic Order* (New York: Columbia University Press, 1980).

31 Robert O. Keohane and Joseph S. Nye, Jr., '*The Club Model of Multilateral Co-operation and Problems of Democratic Legitimacy*', Paper prepared for the American Political Science Convention, Washington, D.C., 31st August – 3rd September 2000, available at http:www.ksg.harvard.edu/cbg/trade/keohane.htm (last visited 28th March 2000).

32 *Id.* at 3.

33 *Id.* at 4.

34 For an excellent brief overview of the OECD's origins and current activities, see James Salzman, *Labour Rights, Globalization and Institutions: The Role and Influence of the Organization for Economic Co-operation and Development,* 21 MICHIGAN JOURNAL OF INTERNATIONAL LAW 769, 776-83 (2000). The OECD website is also a rich source of information. See, e.g. Organization for Economic Co-operation and Development, *What is OECD?,* at http://www.oecd.org/about/general/index.htm (last visited Mar. 20, 2000).

network of officials from specific governments to act as a negotiating vanguard in developing new rules ultimately designed to apply to all members.[35]

2. *Government Networks within the Framework of an Executive Agreement*

The second type of transgovernmental network is more striking as a form of governance, in that it emerges outside a formal international institution. Nevertheless, the members of these networks operate within a framework agreed on at least by the heads of their respective governments. A prime recent example is transatlantic transgovernmental interactions specifically authorized and encouraged by executive agreement. Pollack and Shaffer chronicle a series of executive agreements between the US President and the President of the EU Commission to foster increased co-operation, including the Transatlantic Declaration of 1990, the New Transatlantic Agenda of 1995 (with a Joint US-EU Action Plan attached), and the Transatlantic Economic Partnership agreement of 1998.[36] Each of these agreements spurred 'ad hoc meetings between lower-level officials', as well as among business enterprises, environmental, and consumer activist groups, 'on issues of common concern'. Many of these networks of lower level officials were emerging anyway, for functional reasons, but they undoubtedly received a boost from agreements at the top.

Another example is the web of transgovernmental networks among financial officials that have emerged as the pragmatic answer to calls for 'a new financial architecture for the 21st century' in the wake of the Russian and East Asian financial crises of 1997 and 1998.[37] Notwithstanding a wide range of proposals from

---

35   *See* Marney L. Cheek, *The Limits of Informal Regulatory Co-operation in International Affairs: A Review of the Global Intellectual Property Rights Regime*, 33 GEORGE WASHINGTON INTERNATIONAL LAW REVIEW 277 (2001) (describing deliberate creation of a negotiating network of the intellectual property officials of selected countries). See also Keohane and Nye, *supra* n. 10 (1974 article), at. 54 (describing the ways in which international organizations 'facilitate face-to-face meetings among officials in "domestic" agencies of different governments; suggesting that "strategically minded secretariats" of international organizations could plan meetings with an eye to encouraging such contacts; and identifying several networks involving both transgovernmental and transnational contacts specifically created by international organizations'.

36   Mark A. Pollack and Gregory C. Shaffer, *'Introduction: Transatlantic Governance in Historical and Theoretical Perspective'*, in Pollack and Shaffer, *supra* n. 25, pp. 3-42, pp. 14-17.

37   Speech by President Clinton to the Council on Foreign Relations, 14th September 1998, Federal News Service, 1998. Clinton was echoing calls by British Prime Minister Tony Blair to build a 'new Bretton Woods for the next millennium'. 'Global finance. Don't wait up', The Economist, 3rd October 1998, US edition, p. 83.

academics and policymakers, including one for a global central bank,[38] what actually emerged was a set of financial reform proposals from the G-22 that were subsequently endorsed by the G-7 (now the G-8).[39] The United States pushed for the formation of the G-22 in 1997 to create a transgovernmental network of officials from both developed and developing countries, largely to counter the Eurocentric bias of the G-7, the Basle Committee, and the IMF's 'interim committee', which is itself a group of finance ministers.[40] The East Asian countries most affected were happy to leave the details of financial reform to the G-22, in lieu of any grander vision.[41] And a number of the more sweeping reform proposals advanced suggested the formation of still other networks – a G-16 or a G-15.[42]

The actual work done within these networks – policy recommendations, new sets of standards, model codes – is done by finance ministers, securities regulators, central bankers, and other officials responsible for different aspects of national economic policy. But they are again convened and approved by heads of state, often simply through informal agreement or joint communiqué. In fact, when the G-7 issued a statement on global economic reform in October 1998, the statement itself was issued by finance ministers and central bank governors, accompanied by a parallel statement from heads of government.[43]

---

38   Jeffrey Garten, *Needed: A Fed for the World*, *N.Y. TIMES*, 23rd September 1998, at A29. Two British economists, John Eatwell and Lance Taylor, also proposed a World Financial Authority. 'Global finance. Don't wait up', The Economist, 3rd October 1998, US edition, p. 83.

39   Robert Chote, Economics Notebook, '*A World in the Woods*', *The Financial Times*, 2nd November 1998, p. 20.

40   'Global finance. Don't wait up', *The Economist*, 3rd October 1998, US edition, p. 83. President Clinton and other leaders of the Asia-Pacific Economic Forum (APEC) announced the creation of the Group of 22, on a temporary basis, at their meeting in Vancouver in November 1997. It was to be a group of finance ministers and central bank governors to advance reform of the architecture of global financial reform. Its original members included finance ministers and central bank governors from the G-7 countries plus 15 emerging market countries (Argentina, Australia, Brazil, Canada, China, France, Germany, Hong Kong SAR, India, Indonesia, Italy, Japan, Korea, Malaysia, Mexico, Poland, Russia, Singapore, South Africa, Thailand, the United Kingdom, and the United States). It subsequently evolved into the G-33 and then the G-20. http://www.imf.org/external/npl/exr/facts/groups.htm.

41   APEC's Family Feud, *The Economist* (London), 21st – 27th November 1998, at 41.

42   Jeffrey Sachs proposed the creation of a G-16, composed of the G-8 plus 'eight counterparts from the developing world'. The group would 'not seek to dictate to the world, but to establish the parameters from a renewed and honest dialogue'. Jeffrey Sachs, 'Making it work', *The Economist*, 12th September 1998, US edition, p. 23 (I don't have pages of actual quotes'.) Jeffrey Garten proposed a G-15 (the G-8 plus 7) to monitor the actions of a new global central bank. Garten, *supra* n. 38.

43   Chote, *supra* n. 39, p. 20.

3. *Spontaneous Government Networks – Agencies on the Loose?*

In 1974, Keohane and Nye wondered 'whether the common interests of central bankers in a stable currency system have been implemented as fully by transgovernmental contacts as they might have been'.[44] In 2001, the complaint is the opposite. The transgovernmental regulatory networks that have spurred the greatest concern are those that have emerged outside formal intergovernmental agreements, whether treaties or executive agreements. The Basle Committee is the leading suspect. The image of national regulators coming together of their own volition and regularizing their interactions either as a network or a networked organization raises the spectre of agencies on the loose.

These spontaneous networks themselves divide into two further categories. First are the networks that institutionalize themselves as transgovernmental regulatory organizations. The founding and designated members of these organizations are domestic agencies, or even sub-national agencies such as provincial or state regulators. The organizations themselves tend to operate with a minimum or physical and legal infrastructure. Most lack a foundational treaty, and operate under only a few agreed-upon objectives or by-laws. Nothing they do purports to be legally binding on the members, and typically there are few or no mechanisms for formal enforcement or implementation. Rather, these functions are left to the members themselves.[45]

The second category comprises agreements between domestic regulatory agencies of two or more nations. The last few decades have witnessed the emergence of a vast network of such agreements effectively institutionalizing channels of regulatory co-operation between specific countries. These agreements embrace principles that can be implemented by the regulators themselves; they do not need further approval by national legislators. Widespread use of Memoranda of Understanding (MOUs) and even less formal initiatives has sped the growth of transgovernmental interaction exponentially, in contrast to the lethargic pace at which traditional treaty negotiations proceed. Further, while these agreements are most commonly bilateral arrangements, they may also evolve into plurilateral arrangements, offering greater scope but less formality than traditional transgovernmental organizations.

III. Pinpointing Accountability Concerns

Transgovernmental interactions within each of these three categories raise distinct, if often inter-related, accountability concerns. Accountability itself is such a complex concept, with many different definitions in different contexts and

44 Keohane and Nye, *Transgovernmental Relations, supra* n. 10, at 51.
45 Zaring, *supra* n. 16, at 287.

according to different political theories, that it makes little sense to address it apart from specific factual situations. It can stand for democracy, legitimacy, control, responsiveness, and many other attributes of an ideal government or governance structure.

Nevertheless, the umbrella of 'accountability' captures a core central point. Keohane and Nye put it sharply: 'Even in democratic societies, the borderline between legitimate transgovernmental behaviour and treason may be unclear'.[46] Can voters be sure that their government officials are in fact advancing their interests versus the interests of citizens of other polities? Or are their interests perhaps best advanced if the officials of their government charged with responsibility for a specific issue area make common cause with their counterparts abroad? This section will try to identify specific accountability concerns as precisely as possible within each category. It will focus on responses to these concerns primarily in the third category of transgovernmental networks outside the framework of a treaty or an executive agreement.

1. The Accountability of Transgovernmental Interaction within International Organizations

The traditional working assumption about international organizations has been that if they are duly established by treaty, with the attendant national ratification procedures, then they exercise only delegated powers from the Member States and do not raise any formal accountability concerns. That is not to say that they do not arouse suspicion – often intense suspicion – among certain domestic constituencies in Member States. Within the United States, for instance, the UN has been accused of mounting a fleet of 'black helicopters' to threaten loyal US citizens.[47] But both the executive and the legislatures of participating states have had to approve the organization's activities and can at least theoretically withdraw this approval by restricting funding or even withdrawing from the treaty.

In practice, of course, as Keohane and Nye again pointed out in 1974, international organizations can be vital sites for different government officials, including heads of state, to form policy coalitions with their foreign counterparts to strengthen their hand in domestic bureaucratic struggles.[48] The impact of the international organization is to 'transform potential or tacit coalitions into explicit ones', as well as to form alliances between an organization's secretariat and relevant national officials.[49] They argued that the existence of the international organization

---

46 Keohane and Nye, *Transgovernmental Relations*, *supra* n. 10, at 49.
47 John M. Goshko, 'U.N. Becomes Lightning Rod for Rightist Fears', *Washington Post*, 23rd September 1996, at A1.
48 Keohane and Nye, *Transgovernmental Relations*, *supra* n. 10, at 50-55.
49 *Id.* at 52.

itself symbolized member governments' recognition of the need for co-operation and joint decision-making in a particular area and hence helped to legitimize transgovernmental activity.[50]

By 2000, public doubts and suspicion about the activities of at least certain international organizations had increased sharply, often due precisely to the perception of elite transgovernmental interactions taking place within them. The 'club model' had broken down, due to a combination of factors including the increasing intensity and changing nature of interdependence, the expansion of clubs to include a wide range of developing countries, and the rise of non-state actors in global politics.[51] In response, organizations from the WTO to the UN to the OECD have instituted a raft of 'outreach efforts' to global civil society, enhancing transparency, hosting NGO meetings, and acknowledging and promoting 'global policy networks'.[52] Thus far, these efforts have not been enough – the organizations themselves may simply prove too tempting a target for their detractors. But in these cases the transgovernmental activity within these organizations and the activity of the organization itself seem indistinguishable; hence the issue is much larger than can be addressed here.[53]

2. *Transgovernmental Activity within the Framework of Executive Agreements*

Transgovernmental activity within the framework of executive agreements is often less visible than transgovernmental networks within established institutions. Further, the very fact of their creation by executive agreement rather than treaty means that they have not been approved by the legislature, even prospectively. And the legitimacy provided by head of state approval may be negated if heads of state themselves are engaging in 'transgovernmental collusion'.

John Peterson finds evidence of exactly such collusion in his study of US-EU efforts to implement a New Transatlantic Agenda in the 1990s.[54] He argues that American and European chiefs of government (COGs) have colluded with one another to reward some domestic interest groups over others.[55] Further, 'a central

---

50   *Id.* at 50.

51   Keohane and Nye, *The Club Model of Multilateral Cooperation, supra* n. 31, at 7-8.

52   These efforts are clearly evident with the advent of special NGO offerings on organization websites. See, e.g. http://www.wto.org/english/forums_e/ngo_e/intro_e. htm, http://www.oecd.org. UN Secretary General Kofi Annan devoted a section of Millennium Report to the emergence of global policy networks. See http://www.un.org/millennium/sg/report.

53   Roberto Unger, ADD cite to Unger contribution to edited volume arguing against the 'supra-national technocracy' of the IMF and the World Bank.

54   John Peterson, 'Get Away from Me Closer, You're Near Me Too Far: Europe and America after the Uruguay Round', in Pollack and Shaffer, *supra* n. 25, pp. 45-72.

55   *Id.* at 46.

ambition of the New Transatlantic Agenda . . . is to manufacture the same sort of complicity between administrations and societies, as distinct from intergovernmental elites, through new transgovernmental and transnational exchanges'.[56] Pollack and Shaffer agree, noting that the entire set of transatlantic initiatives can be understood as a joint effort between the US administration and the EU Commission to 'institutionalise their joint preference' for more transatlantic and global trade liberalization, as well as to strengthen key domestic constituencies.[57]

Such accounts can legitimately raise fear and concern among disfavoured domestic constituencies, in this case consumers, environmentalists, and labour. When the head of state throws his or her power behind some kinds of transgovernmental (and transnational) contacts but not others, without legislative input, it can seriously tilt the domestic political playing field. Observers could draw a similar conclusion from the practice, noted above, of accompanying a statement by finance ministers and central bankers with a parallel statement by heads of government. These interactions by heads of state and the transgovernmental relations resulting from them are analogous, at least for the US and the EU Commission, to the domestic innovation of 'presidential administration', whereby the head of state controls the political agenda by executive decree rather than collaborative legislation.[58] The response to the resulting accountability concerns is likely to be legislative, prodded by the disaffection of outmanoeuvred domestic constituencies.

3. *Spontaneous Transgovernmental Networks*

Transgovernmental networks that arise outside the framework of international organizations and executive agreements are most likely to spawn fears of runaway technocracy. That a regulatory agency would reach out on its own account to its foreign counterparts, even in an effort to solve common problems, raises not only the possibilities of policy collusion, whereby transgovernmental support can be marshalled against domestic bureaucratic opponents, but also of the removal of issues from the domestic political sphere through deliberate technocratic de-politicization.[59]

---

56   *Ibid.*
57   Mark A. Pollack and Gregory C. Shaffer, '*Who Governs?*', in Pollack and Shaffer, *supra* n. 25, p. 295.
58   Elena Kagan, *Presidential Administration*, 104 HARVARD LAW REVIEW (forthcoming 2001).
59   See Picciotto, *Networks in International Economic Integration, supra* n. 3, at 1037. On the other hand, it is also possible that spontaneous networks can be less threatening due to their very flexibility and ability to incorporate only like-minded members. Networks within the framework of treaty-based international organizations and executive agreements necessarily incorporate officials from all the governments party to the treaty

A wide range of possible measures can combat these perceptions and enhance public awareness of and even participation in spontaneous networks. Creating well-serviced websites can make a network real by making it virtual.[60] The following two sections propose additional steps toward enhanced transparency and popular accountability – creating the global equivalent of EU 'information agencies' and encouraging the formation of legislative networks – perhaps of representatives of key legislative committees – to share information and co-ordinate efforts to pass parallel domestic legislation.[61] Alternatively, as is already happening in many cases, transgovernmental networks can be folded into larger 'mixed networks' of governmental and private actors.[62]

Another quite different response to accountability concerns regarding spontaneous networks is the claim that they do not exercise actual power; they are merely 'talking shop'. With a few exceptions such as the Basle Committee, participants in these networks cannot actually make rules or adopt policies. They can only disseminate information and bring back recommendations and even proposals for consideration through the normal domestic legislative or agency rule-making process.

This view of transgovernmental networks is short-sighted. It misses a key dimension of the exercise of power in the Information Age. The 'talking shops' generate compilations of best practices, codes of conduct, and templates for everything from a Memorandum of Understanding to an environmental assessment review. As a senior official from the World Bank has recently noted, the dissemination of information has played a far greater role in triggering policy convergence in various issue areas than more deliberate and coercive attempts.[63]

---

or the agreement, whether or not their interests converge on any set of specific issues. Spontaneous networks, by contrast, should arise where the government officials involved, at least, immediately perceive a benefit in developing closer ties with foreign counterparts who share their views or face common problems. The question still remains, however, whether the officials in question are not simply seeking foreign reinforcements for domestic bureaucratic battles in ways that skew outcomes away from the preferences of the median domestic voter. That is a very hard empirical question to address; it remains unanswered.

60 Anne-Marie Slaughter, 'Virtual Visibility', FOREIGN POLICY, Nov/Dec 2000, 84-85.
61 See Slaughter, *Governing the Global Economy Through Government Networks, supra* n. 3, at 197 (describing existing legislative networks). For a more general discussion of all these mechanisms aimed at enhancing accountability, see Slaughter, '*Agencies on the Loose? Holding Government Networks Accountable*', in George A. Bermann, Matthias Herdegen and Peter Lindseth, (eds.), *Transatlantic Regulatory Co-operation* (Oxford: Oxford University Press, 2000).
62 Mark A. Pollack and Gregory C. Shaffer, '*Who Governs?*', *supra* n. 25, pp. 301-05.
63 Andres Rigo, *Law Harmonization Resulting From the Policies of International Financial Institutions: The Case of the World Bank*, paper presented at a conference on

This result is not surprising. In a world awash with information, credible and authoritative information is at a premium.[64] Even more valuable is a distillation and evaluation of information from many different sources. Recommended rules and practices compiled by a global body of securities regulators or environmental officials offer a focal point for convergence. Equally important, it offers a kind of safe harbour for officials the world over looking for guidance and besieged with consultants.

Yet should government officials be held accountable for either disseminating or using information? As new forms of global governance emerge wielding informational power, and probably engaging in new forms of informational politics, the very concept of accountability – even accepting its current complexity – must grow and change. These are questions not only for lawyers and public policymakers, but also for political theorists.

IV. Global Information Agencies

At this juncture, the EU offers a deceptively simple source of analogies and potential institutional solutions to the general problem of enhancing the accountability of government networks. Lawyers and political scientists studying the EU have spent much of the past decade grappling with the growing phenomenon of 'comitology' – the extraordinarily complex web of committees that play advisory, management, and regulatory functions in between the European Commission and the Council of Ministers.[65] Although the leading scholars in these debates have different positive understandings and normative evaluations of comitology, they all agree that it is a critical and distinctive dimension of EU governance that must be addressed in any effort to promote constitutionalism and democracy within the EU as an institution and/or an emerging polity.

The next section explores some of the larger implications of debates over comitology for arguments over the accountability of global government networks. To understand the relevance of these debates, however, it is first necessary to delve a bit deeper into the distinctions between different types of EU institutions and government networks as defined here. The European Community (EC), one of the pillars of the EU, has a number of different types of committees – scientific

'The Evolution of Legal Systems, Bijuralism and International Trade', University of Ottawa Law School, 2000.

64   Robert O. Keohane and Joseph S. Nye, Jr., *Power and Interdependence in the Information Age*, FOREIGN AFFAIRS, vol. 77, no. 5, pp. 81-94 (1998).

65   For an excellent overview of the complexities of comitology, see Ellen Vos, *EU Committees: the Evolution of Unforeseen Institutional Actors in European Product Regulation*, in Joerges and Vos, *supra* n. 24, pp. 19-47.

committees, interest committees, and policy-making/implementation committees.[66] Many of these committees must be consulted as part of the Community legislative process. The policy-making/implementation committees are the most powerful of these committees; they are composed of representatives of the Member States from the different issue-areas under consideration – agriculture, transport, health, etc.[67] In terms of membership and structure, these committees most resemble networks of national government officials charged with responsibility for a particular issue-area. However, as the semantic distinction between 'committee' and 'network' suggests, the committees are more tightly structured and have a specific charge and function within a larger governance structure – specifically, mediating between a supra-national entity, the Commission, and an intergovernmental one, the Council. They are theoretically responsible for ensuring that the views of the different EC Member States are fully and powerfully represented in the legislative process.[68]

The EC also has agencies and more informal networks of both public and private actors. Agencies are entities with legal personalities and their own administrative structures.[69] Networks, as used in EC parlance, typically describe the looser and more informal interactions between national government officials that are increasingly necessary to implement EC policies.[70] According to two prominent EU scholars, Giandomenico Majone and Renaud Dehousse, the relationship between these two types of governance structures is the wave of the future in the EC. Together they are best poised to exploit the potential of 'regulation by information'. This conception of both the substance and form of governance within the EU parallels many of the perceptions and insights that animate the description of government networks as an emerging form of global governance. Indeed, closer examination of this line of scholarship yields a European proposal that can be transposed fairly easily to the global context: the creation of global information agencies.

Majone, who pioneered the concept of the EU as a 'regulatory state',[71] distinguishes regulation by information from direct regulation, which relies on a variety of 'command and control techniques' such as orders and prohibitions.[72] Regulation by information operates instead by attempting 'to change behaviour

---

66   *Id.*, pp. 21-22.

67   *Id.*, p. 22.

68   *Ibid.*

69   *Id.*, p. 32.

70   Renaud Dehousse, '*Regulation by networks in the European Community: the role of European agencies*', JOURNAL OF EUROPEAN PUBLIC POLICY 4 (June 1997), pp. 246-261.

71   Giandomenico Majone, *From the Positive to the Regulatory State: Causes and Consequences of Changes in the Mode of Governance*, 17 JOURNAL OF PUBLIC POLICY 139-167 (1997).

72   Giandomenico Majone, *The New European Agencies: Regulation by Information*, 4 JOURNAL OF EUROPEAN PUBLIC POLICY 261-75, 265 (1997).

indirectly, either by changing the structure of incentives of the different policy actors, or by supplying the same actors with suitable information'.[73] Simply having access to credible information can change the calculations and choices that different actors make.

Dehousse links the concept of regulation by information to the EU phenomenon of 'regulation by networks'.[74] He sees regulation by networks as the response to a basic paradox in EU governance: 'On the one hand, increased uniformity is certainly needed; on the other hand, greater centralization is politically inconceivable, and probably undesirable'.[75] The effort to harmonize national laws within the European Community (EC) involves the passage of regulations at the Community level but depends on national authorities for their implementation.[76] This process is slow, cumbersome, and invariably spotty. It also leaves enormous power and discretion in the hands of the national regulatory authorities.[77] The resulting regulatory gaps must be addressed, but how?

The EU alternative is the 'transnational option' – the use of an organized network of national officials to ensure 'that the actors in charge of the implementation of Community policies behave in a similar manner'.[78] Such spontaneous convergence requires that they agree on the definition of a common problem and the range of possible responses, which in turn depends on their access to comparable data and expert opinions.[79] In short, they need to proceed on a base of mutual information.

These same officials meet together within the framework of comitology. Yet Dehousse has a larger phenomenon in mind – the functional need for mid-level officials from national ministries in different issue-areas to exchange information with one another and with both Commission officials and private actors. Dehousse describes these networks in far more benign terms than do many of his fellow EU observers. Even for him, however,

> *ad hoc* meetings of national officials, no matter how frequent, are not enough to bring about a true 'community of views', let alone a 'community of action'. Partnership must be structured by common rules, which lay down the rights and duties of all members. Equally important, the network itself must be given some

---

73 *Ibid.*
74 Renaud Dehousse, '*Regulation by networks in the European Community*', *supra* n. 70.
75 *Ibid.*, p. 259.
76 *Ibid.*, p. 248.
77 *Ibid.*, pp. 249-51.
78 *Ibid.*, p. 254.
79 *Ibid.*

stability, which generally implies the setting-up of a structure which will manage the interaction among network members.[80]

European regulatory agencies fulfil this function. Eight new agencies were created at European level between 1990 and 1997 as a way of facilitating further harmonization. Four of these – the European Environmental Agency, the Lisbon Drug Monitoring Centre, the European Agency for Health and Safety at Work, and the European Agency for the Evaluation of Medicinal Products – are best described as 'information agencies'.[81] Their job is to collect, co-ordinate, and disseminate information needed by policymakers. They lack decision-making authority, much less coercive enforcement power.

Both Majone and Dehousse describe these agencies as easy to underestimate but actually likely to play an important and powerful role. Majone sees them as the quintessential example of regulation by information. Their power will lie not in their coercive apparatus but in their ability to exercise influence through 'knowledge and persuasion'.[82] He notes a general disenchantment with the 'efficacy of [command-and-control] policy instruments', undermined by factors from increasingly porous national borders to the growing complexity of public policy.[83] 'Modes of regulation based on information and persuasion' are perceived to be more flexible, responsive, and effective.[84] To be successful in this environment, an information agency needs to establish its credibility and professional reputation.[85]

Dehousse also sees the European information agencies as network creators and co-ordinators.[86] 'Their primary aim is to run networks of national administrations which come into play in the implementation of Community policies'.[87] They

---

80   Dehousse, *supra* n. 70, p. 254.
81   Majone, *supra*, n. 72, pp. 262-63; Dehousse, *supra* n. 70, pp. 256-57. Dehousse quotes the regulation establishing the Lisbon Drug Monitoring Centre as specifying that: 'The Centre may not take any measure which in any way goes beyond the sphere of information and the processing thereof.' Article 1) 4 of Council Regulation EEC 302/93, OJ No. L 36/1, 12th February 1993, quoted in *id.* Similarly, Council Regulation No. 1210/90, 7th May 1990, sets forth the task of the European Environmental Agency as follows: 'to provide the Member States and the Community with information; to collect, record and assess data on the state of the environment; to encourage harmonization of the methods of measurement; to promote the incorporation of European environmental information into international monitoring programmes; to ensure data dissemination; to co-operate with other Community bodies and international institutions'. Majone, *supra* n. 72, p. 263.
82   *Id.*, p. 264.
83   *Id.*, pp. 267-268.
84   *Ibidem.*
85   *Ibidem.*
86   Dehousse, *supra* n. 70, p. 255.
87   *Ibidem.*

accomplish this function by setting up a 'permanent technical and administrative secretariat', which tries not only to collect and disseminate necessary information but also to encourage 'horizontal cross-fertilization' among counterpart national officials.[88] From a more dynamic perspective, it appears that the emergence of transgovernmental networks through the process of comitology has given rise to the need for a central node, which in turn helps spur more co-ordinated and effective transgovernmental action.

Another important virtue of these regulatory agencies, understood as convenors and co-ordinators, derives from their projected impact on the democratic legitimacy of EU regulatory processes. First, they enhance transparency. 'Several agencies are explicitly required to make accessible to the public the data they collect. Moreover, the provision of information has generally been broadly construed; it often encompasses policy analysis and the preparation of measures and legislation in their field of activity ... '.[89] Second, and equally important, they are often able to expand the transgovernmental network to include private actors in a particular policy area.[90] This activity need not be merely inviting comment from NGOs of various types as well as regulated entities, but can also include bringing together all relevant actors and inviting them to pool information.

The Commission on Environmental Co-operation (CEC), established under the North American Agreement on Environmental Co-operation (NAAEC), takes regulation by information one step farther.[91] The CEC is specifically charged with mobilizing public participation in environmental policy-making by disseminating information. The NAAEC is a side agreement to the North American Free Trade Agreement.[92] Under its terms, Canada, the United States and Mexico granted private parties, including NGOs, the power to bring a complaint before the CEC against one of the three states for failure to enforce its environmental laws.[93] The Secretariat of the CEC decides whether the complaint is sufficiently credible to warrant the preparation of a 'factual record'; if it decides in the affirmative, the Council of the CEC, composed of the environmental ministers of all three states, must vote whether to go forward.[94]

In the event that the Council votes to authorize preparation of a factual record, the Secretariat has considerable latitude not only to solicit information from both the plaintiffs and the state party defendant concerning the charges, but also to develop

---

88   *Ibidem.*
89   *Ibidem.*
90   *Id.*, p. 256.
91   North American Agreements on Environmental Cooperation, 14 September 1993, US-Can.-Mex., 32 INTERNATIONAL LEGAL MATERIALS 1480 (1993).
92   North American Free Trade Agreement, opened for signature 8 December 1992, US-Can.-Mex., 32 INTERNATIONAL LEGAL MATERIALS 296 (1993).
93   NAAEC, Arts. 14 and 15.
94   *Id.*, Arts. 15(1) and (2).

information from outside experts that is relevant to understanding the strength and nature of the allegations.[95] Neither the Secretariat nor the Council of the CEC can actually reach a legal conclusion as to whether the state party in question is failing to enforce its environmental laws; however, the Council of the CEC must vote whether to accept the factual record and make it public.[96] Making it public invites increased public participation in the enforcement process; the factual record and supporting documents become strong weapons for NGOs to use in mobilizing domestic public opinion in favour of stronger domestic enforcement measures.[97]

Why not create global information agencies? In many ways, the secretariats or technical committees of existing transgovernmental regulatory organizations such as the Basle Committee or IOSCO perform some of the same functions. But these are essentially ad hoc, organic entities, created and empowered by networks of national officials to serve various needs as they arise. Suppose national governments were to come together to create a global securities agency, or a global environmental agency, but with the express charge not of arrogating power from national officials, but rather of providing information to such officials and helping to co-ordinate relations among them. Further, these agencies would service not only transgovernmental networks, but also transnational networks within their issue areas, working to bring together both private and public actors in a particular policy sector.

Equating a 'global agency', of any kind, with enhancing the democratic legitimacy of global regulatory processes may seem oxymoronic. 'Agency' conjures automatic images of bureaucratic technocrats and technocratic bureaucrats. Beyond the stereotypes, however, the proposal has a number of potential advantages.

First, convening heads of state to establish an international institution, even one with only informational powers, would highlight the existence and importance of current transgovernmental networks, helping to legitimate them by acknowledging them as key elements of a system of global governance. The purpose of the agency would be to facilitate the functioning of these networks and to expand them both to other governments and to private actors as necessary. Notice and approval by heads of state would also help allay charges of transgovernmental policy collusion to strengthen the hands of particular national officials in domestic bureaucratic infighting.

Second, and perhaps paradoxically, the creation of a *global* entity would emphasize the *national* identity of network participants. The existence of even a small group of international bureaucrats to meet the needs of national officials can only emphasize the location of actual decision-making power in national hands.

---

95 *Id.*, Art. 15(4).

96 *Id.*, Art. 15(7).

97 See David L. Markell, '*The Commission for Environmental Cooperation's Citizen Submission Process*', 12 GEORGETOWN INTERNATIONAL LAW REVIEW 545, 571 (2000).

Even if those national officials are networking with one another to plug growing gaps in national jurisdiction and to solve common problems, they remain national officials answerable only to national legislatures and chief executives. In this regard, it is interesting to note that the European information agencies have actually resisted an increase in their power over national officials, perhaps because 'instilling a degree of (vertical) hierarchical control in structures created to promote (horizontal) co-operation among peers may result in the undermining of the basis of consensus, which is indispensable for the smooth and efficient operation of the network'.[98]

Third, the appellation 'information agency' would focus attention on whether the collection and cross-fertilization of information is in fact problematic. How could it be wrong or even worrisome to know more about what other countries are doing? For many, however, even to pose the question this way, however, betrays an academic or even technocratic bias. If, as many critical scholars maintain, 'technical' decisions are but a convenient way of depoliticizing political decisions with distributional implications, then models and ideas borrowed helter-skelter from different political contexts are likely to prove at best useless and at worst dangerous.[99] On the other side of the political spectrum, as Justice Scalia has argued vehemently with regard to the question of whether the US Supreme Court should take account of ideas and decisions from foreign courts, foreign transplants contravene basic notions of local democracy.[100]

In the increasingly borderless 'information age', where citizens of many countries have access to a literal worldwide web of information, this debate seems archaic and almost preposterous. But it should be had – openly and directly. If the objections are real and resonate with a wider public, then existing government networks are on much weaker ground than previously imagined. But even well short of such a scenario of wilful ignorance, questions of how the information collected from foreign counterparts is used and disseminated are not only legitimate but also necessary. As Michael Dorf and Charles Sabel point out, regulation by information comes in many different models.[101]

Fourth, as in the European context, the existence of an information agency charged with convening and supporting networks of national officials immediately invites expansion of the network to a host of private actors. UN Secretary General Kofi Annan has recognized the importance of this function by positioning the UN as the convener of 'global policy networks', designed precisely to bring together all

---

98   Dehousse, *supra* n. 70, p. 260.

99   Picciotto, *Networks in International Economic Integration*, *supra* n. 3, p. 1037.

100 Justice Scalia has engaged in an open debate with some of his fellow justices concerning the propriety of looking to foreign decisions, even on an entirely persuasive basis. For an account of this debate, *see* Anne-Marie Slaughter, 'Judicial Globalization', *Virginia Journal of International Law*, vol. 40, no. 4, pp. 1103-24, p. 1118.

101 Michael C. Dorf and Charles F. Sabel, *A Constitution of Democratic Experimentalism*, COLUMBIA LAW REVIEW, vol. 98, no. 2, pp. 267-473, pp. 286-87.

public and private actors on issues critical to the global public interest.[102] Transgovernmental and transnational networks currently parallel each other in many cases and intersect in all sorts of ways, such as the NGO conferences held together with major intergovernmental conferences on issues ranging from the environment to women's rights. Nevertheless, the process is haphazard and in some cases chaotic. Information agencies could provide focus and a minimum degree of organization.

Beyond these minimal functions, it is imaginable that information agencies could become the focal points for dispute-resolution processes designed to disseminate information and mobilize public participation to check and correct government performance, as with the CEC. If the basic paradigm for global regulatory processes is the promulgation of performance standards, codes of best practices, and other aspirational models based on compiled comparative information, together with national legislation taking account of global practice but tailored to individual national circumstance, then why should citizens not have some means of shaming their governments into complying with their own rules? The entity charged with hearing the dispute would have the power only to issue some kind of informational record – backed by its legitimacy and credibility. It would be up to national and transnational citizen groups to do the rest.

These may seem fanciful visions. But the European Union has in fact pioneered the paradigm of transgovernmental networks as governance structures within a community of states that have come together for a set of specific purposes. It has also run aground on the questions of the democratic legitimacy of these structures. To the extent that European information agencies offer at least a partial solution to these problems, they merit examination on a global scale.

V. Disaggregated Democracy

Adding another type and even layer of institutions to the existing patchwork of intergovernmental, transgovernmental, and transnational global governance structures still seems a rather patchwork approach to addressing a fundamental democracy deficit above the level of the nation state. As Keohane and Nye observe, it cannot address the more fundamental democratic problem, which they identify as a lack of intermediating politicians directly responsive to the electorate.[103] It is possible to do better, but only in the context of a rethinking of the elements of democratic legitimacy. Here it is helpful to return to the broader frameworks for

---

102 Kofi A. Annan, *Millennium Report of the United Nations Secretary-General: We the Peoples: The Role of the United Nations in the 21st Century* 7, UN Doc DPI/2103 (2000).

103 Keohane and Nye, *The Club Model of Multilateral Cooperation, supra* n. 31.

democratic governance set forth by other contributors to this volume, as well as by other scholars pondering the conundrum of the EU democratic deficit.

These scholars include Giandomenico Majone, Karl-Heinz Ladeur, Christian Joerges, Juergen Neyer, Charles Sabel, Joshua Cohen, Oliver Gerstenberg, Fritz Scharpf, Renaud Dehousse, Gunther Teubner, Joseph Weiler and many of their co-contributors and critics in various collective research projects designed to identify and reimagine the structures of EU governance over the past decade. The debates to date have proceeded more or less dialectically, with different individuals or teams of scholars attacking each other and proffering an alternative vision as the only or at least the best account of democratic legitimation. For the purposes of the project in this essay, it is particularly important to understand that some of the strongest claims of a democratic deficit in the EU focus precisely on the phenomenon of comitology.

Joseph Weiler points out that although the self-appointed guardians of European democracy have long focused on the supra-national features of the EU – chiefly the Commission and the Court – it is now 'time to worry about infranationalism – a complex network of middle-level national administrators, Community administrators, and an array of private bodies with unequal and unfair access to a process with huge social and economic consequences to everyday life'.[104] To dramatize the point, he adds: 'Consider that it is even impossible to get from any of the Community institutions an authoritative and mutually agreed statement of the mere number of committees that inhabit that world of comitology'.[105] Along similar lines, Beate Kohler-Koch reacted with incredulity to a claim by Christian Joerges and Juergen Neyer that the deliberative processes of comitology in fact enhance democracy within the Community. She retorted: 'None other than comitology, that notorious system of inter-bureaucratic negotiation-diplomacy that even parliamentarians wish to abolish in the interest of democracy, is supposed to bring an element of democratically-legitimated politics into the Community?'[106]

The networks that comprise comitology differ from the global government networks described here in many ways, not least that they operate within a self-consciously integrating community of nations that has delegated a substantial degree of sovereignty to a set of intergovernmental and supra-national institutions. Nevertheless, it is also possible to identify many similarities, beginning with the desire to achieve co-operative outcomes at the international level without

---

104 Joseph H.H. Weiler, 'To Be a European Citizen – Eros and Civilization', JOURNAL OF EUROPEAN PUBLIC POLICY, vol. 4, no. 4, pp. 495-519, p. 512.

105 *Ibidem.*

106 Beate Kohler-Koch, '*Die Europaeisierung nationaler Demokratien. Verschleiß eines eruopäischen Kulturerbes*', in M. Th. Greven, ed., *Demokratie – eine Kultur des Westens?* (Opladen 1998), pp. 263-88, p. 277.

committing either power or personnel to an autonomous international institution.[107] Most important, the debate about comitology as either a source of or a solution to the democracy deficit in the EU not only prompts proposals for specific measures that could be taken on a European or global scale, it also creates a catalyst for rethinking more fundamental ideas of democracy in the face of problems and institutions whose scope and scale seem to defy popular participation or control.

This section offers a brief and sharply simplified overview of some of the most important positions staked out in the European debate.[108] A longer-term effort to develop a framework within which to understand and justify the distinctive contribution of global transgovernmental networks to global governance is likely to be most successful if it can synthesize a number of different arguments about the relationship between government networks and democratic values. As a first step, it is possible to isolate some of the most important legitimating arguments about transgovernmentalism (or infra-nationalism, in Weiler's parlance) in the EU, including arguments about delegation to independent agencies, the possibilities of deliberative supra-nationalism, a reimagination of the essential possibilities of individual self-governance in a heterarchical society, and democratic experiment-talism.

At a very deep level, these different arguments proceed from different conceptions of democracy. Arguments about delegation to non-majoritarian institutions and deliberative supra-nationalism, although often at loggerheads with one another, nevertheless all proceed from a fairly traditional conception of vertical representative government, in which the principal question is how to design state institutions 'above' the citizens they represent, to represent them as well as possible. 'Post-modern' arguments about individuals with multiple selves operating in multiple parallel forums to advance their interests and develop their identities rest on a more horizontal conception of democracy, a challenging yet empirically grounded vision of the ways in which self-government can take place in settings that are neither public nor private and that exist in a space between hierarchy and anarchy.

In a world in which the basic unit of operation is not a unitary state but a disaggregated state, meaning that the elements of both government within the state and governance between and above states are different government institutions, both conceptions are important. No amount of post-modern theorizing and prostration

---

107 John A. E. Vervaele, *Shared Governance and Enforcement of European Law: From Comitology to a Multi-level Agency Structure?*, in Joerges and Vos, *supra* n. 24, pp. 129-49, p. 137.

108 For a somewhat different typology that nevertheless draws the same basic distinctions between non-majoritarian views, deliberative supra-nationalism, and post-modern market regulation, see Michelle Everson's account of three 'constitutional' models of the internal model polity. Michelle Everson, 'The Constitutionalisation of European Administrative Law: Legal Oversight of a Stateless Internal Market', in Joerges and Vos, *supra* n. 24, pp. 281-309, 298-305.

before the gods of technology is likely to displace the very basic concept of electoral accountability on as small a scale as possible consistent with a minimum level of government effectiveness. On the other hand, the impossibility of fully 'reaggregating' the state in a tidy democratic package will ultimately require a much more sophisticated understanding of networks and the interaction of nodes in a network with each other – whether individual or institutional. A successful synthesis of these two approaches – at least for the purposes of reconciling many of the functional and ideational needs of global governance – will be a vision of disaggregated democracy.

1. Vertical Democracy

A first and familiar effort to legitimate transgovernmental networks is through an appeal to the desirability of de-politicization. In this view, politics means rent-seeking and deal-making, messy processes that prevent adoption of the 'optimal' policy. Insulating specific policy areas by delegation to independent technical experts will produce much better outcomes for the society as a whole, reflecting the supposed choices of a hypothetical median voter.[109] In addition to this democratic justification, Majone also advances an argument from effectiveness, suggesting that 'today the main reason for delegating powers is the need to make credible policy commitments'.[110]

A second alternative is an updated model of deliberative democracy, in Habermasian more than Madisonian terms. Christian Joerges and Juergen Neyer originally advanced the concept of 'deliberative supra-nationalism' as both a normative and a positive paradigm of EU governance, based on extensive research

---

109 Gerstenberg and Sabel attribute this view to Majone, highlighting his assumption that independence (insulation from ordinary politics) and public accountability are mutually reinforcing. They question this assumption, as well as the more general presupposition of 'the possibility of a clear separation between efficiency-oriented and re-distributive politics'. See Sabel and Gernstenberg in this book. Implicit in Majone's mode of argument is the assumption of a 'right answer' that the public trusts experts to adopt. Andrew Moravcsik offers an alternative argument from equality, claiming not that independent agencies will produce correct policies, but rather policies that are closer to the desires of the median voter or a broad social consensus in favour of equity. Andrew Moravcsik, *'European Federalism: Rhetoric and Reality'*, in Robert Howse and Kalypso Nicolaïdis, (eds.), *The Federal Vision: Legitimacy and Levels of Governance in the US and the EU* (Oxford: Oxford University Press, May 2001); *id., 'Europe's Integration at Century's End'*, in Moravcsik, ed. *Centralization or Fragmentation? Europe Facing the Challenges of Deepening, Diversity, and Democracy* (New York: Council on Foreign Relations, 1998), p. 51.
110 Majone, *supra* n. 72, p. 270.

into the formation of European foodstuffs policy.[111] Empirically, they found that government representatives on the various foodstuffs committees do not bargain on the basis of national positions. Rather, they 'not only learn to reduce differences between national legal provisions but also to develop converging definitions of problems and philosophies for their solution. They slowly proceed from being representatives from national interests to being representatives of a Europeanised inter-administrative discourse characterized by mutual learning and an understanding of each other's difficulties in the implementation of specific solutions'.[112] Normatively, Joerges and Neyer argued that the EU committee system 'must be based upon, and controlled by, constitutional provisions favouring a "deliberative" style of problem solving'.[113] The result will be a 'vision of a law of transnational governance which would avoid both the pitfalls of intergovernmentalism and of building up a centralized technocratic governance structure'.[114]

Two years later, after responding to many attacks along the lines of those quoted from Weiler and Kohler-Koch above, Joerges tempered his original optimism but nevertheless continued to insist on at least the possibility of 'good governance through comitology'.[115] Here he offers deliberative supra-nationalism as a 'normative yardstick' by which to evaluate the legitimacy of the EU as a multi-level governance system. Although he recognizes many problems with the existing comitology system, he nevertheless insists on the *possibility* of designing rules and procedures to establish deliberative politics within transgovernmental networks. The architects of such a system should seek to structure '*national* decision-making processes by the imposition of supra-national standards', particularly designed to check 'parochial interests' and ensure that 'foreign concerns' be given equal consideration.[116] They should also seek to establish transnational 'regimes' that

111 Joerges and Neyer, '*The Constitutionalization of Comitology*', *supra* n. 24; Joerges and Neyer, '*Transforming Strategic Interaction into Deliberative Problem-solving: European Comitology in the Foodstuffs Sector*', JOURNAL OF EUROPEAN PUBLIC POLICY, vol. 4, pp. 609-25 (1997).

112 Joerges and Neyer, '*European Comitology in the Foodstuffs Sector*', *supra* n. 111, p. 620. In a later article, Joerges described the research questions he and Neyer posed to determine the deliberative quality of comitology decision-making as follows: 'Do those involved start from fixed positions which they try as far as possible to push through in the committee meetings, or are they ready to take critical objections to their views seriously and be persuaded by argument?'; and 'Do the discussants recognize standards of argument able to promote the reaching of a basic consensus, shared by all, on the "common weal"?' Joerges, '*Good Governance' Through Comitology*', in Joerges and Vos, *supra* n. 24, pp. p. 319.

113 Joerges and Neyer, '*The Constitutionalization of Comitology*', *supra* n. 24, p. 282.

114 *Id.*, p. 287.

115 Joerges, '*Good Governance' Through Comitology?*, *supra* n. 24, p. 329-38.

116 *Id.*, p. 315.

would be structured to encourage 'deliberative problem-solving procedures' instead of intergovernmental bargaining.[117]

Joseph Weiler, among others, remains unconvinced. He recognizes the force of Joerges and Neyer's data as supporting a major paradigm shift, forcing students of EU decision-making to wrestle with infra-nationalism as well as supra-nationalism and intergovernmentalism.[118] He accepts that infra-national decision-making has its own particular characteristics, including a remarkable degree of autonomy, polycentricity, administrative and managerial orientation rather than constitutional and diplomatic, and 'a *modus operandi* which is less by negotiation and more by deliberation'.[119] But in his view, it is definitely not democratic. It 'is a microcosm of the problems of democracy, not a microcosm of the solution'.[120] It is fatally flawed by the inevitably elitist identity of the participants in these networks, their corresponding biases in making vitally important public decisions and their unawareness of these biases, and the impossibility of creating equal access to these networks without destroying the very conditions that make them work as deliberative bodies.[121]

Note that Joerges never claims that transgovernmental deliberation is 'apolitical' in any way. On the contrary, he rejects the idea of delegation to 'technical' experts on both empirical and theoretical grounds, noting that 'no national constitutional state has ever given *carte blanche* to expert committees' and denying the possibility of a 'dichotomy between a-political social regulation and political distributive politics'.[122] Unlike Majone, he does not champion comitology networks as insulated from redistributors or rent-seekers, but rather as places where genuine persuasion is possible on the basis of a wider consideration of interests than purely national ones – a critical element, he argues, for democracy in a multinational space.

Further, Joerges insists that comitology is not separate from supra-nationalism, but rather an unavoidable part of it. It flows ineluctably from the dependency of the hierarchical elements of the EU system on de-centralized implementation systems. The participants in these systems must come together in networks to co-ordinate, co-operate, and solve common problems. Without a 'supra-national central implementation machinery headed by the Commission', national governments in the

---

117 *Ibidem.*

118 Joseph H.H. Weiler, '*Epilogue: Comitology as Revolution – Infranationalism, Constitutionalism and Democracy*', in Joerges and Vos, *supra* n. 24, pp. 337-50. Weiler describes this 'third paradigm' as addressing 'a meso-level reality which operates below the public macro and above the individual micro [and] is not a reflection of the State-Community paradigm', p. 342.

119 *Id.*, pp. 342-343.

120 *Id.*, p. 349.

121 *Id.*, pp. 348-49.

122 Christian Joerges, '*Bureaucratic Nightmare, Technocratic Regime and the Dream of Good Transnational Governance*', in Joerges and Vos, *supra* n. 24, pp. 3-17, 6.

EU are forced into a 'co-operative venture'.[123] Thus deliberation within transgovernmental networks is the flipside of a decision not to displace national officials with a layer of bureaucracy one step further away from the individuals they regulate.

This last point makes it easier to see how, notwithstanding their differences, both Joerges and Majone, as well as Dehousse and others in a more intermediate position, all assume a basic vertical relationship between the governors and the governed, the regulators and the regulated entities. The European level of governance still exists 'above' the national level in some conceptual space; the national level in turn exists 'above' individuals and groups in domestic and transnational society. The result is a two-tiered representative system in which the fundamental mechanism of self-government is the election or selection of officials who formulate and adopt rules that are then transposed back down a level in their application to the 'people'.[124]

2. Horizontal Democracy

A sharply contrasting and much more radical vision is an emerging horizontal conception of democracy, which imagines self-government as the product of a much richer set of interactions among individuals and groups in both private and public fora. It begins from the empirical fact of mushrooming 'private governance regimes' in which individuals, groups, and corporate entities in domestic and transnational society generate the rules, norms and principles they are prepared to live by.[125] It also takes account of important innovations in national and international administrative regulation, in which the elaboration of formal rules is increasingly giving way to 'rolling best practices rule-making'.[126] The challenge is to integrate these regimes into a revised understanding of public governance. Many different scholars are elaborating this vision in different ways and are engaged in a lively

---

123 Joerges and Neyer, '*The Constitutionalization of Comitology*', *supra* n. 24, p. 276.

124 Joerges emphasizes the impossibility of establishing a genuine governmental hierarchy in the EU, but nevertheless identifies '"hierarchical" elements' of the Europeanization process in conjunction with a necessary reliance on de-centralized and horizontal institutions and structures for problem-solving and implementation of EU regulations. Joerges, '*Good Governance through Comitology?*', p. 313.

125 See Sabel and Gernstenberg in this book, where they say: 'instead of disciplining the transnational PGR through a re-centralizing act of delegation, both the alternative views aim to reconcile heterarchy/legal pluralism with the substantive presuppositions of democracy through a horizontalization of the constitution which would take into consideration that private governments are public governments', citing Teubner, *Breaking Frames*, pp. 149 ff.

126 Dorf and Sabel, *supra* n. 101, p. 352.

debate with one another.[127] At this juncture, however, it is possible to identify three more or less distinct elements of this type of analysis.

First is a different conception of individual identity, premised not on a single self but on plural selves, defined in multiple ways through differentiation from others in many different contexts. Karl-Heinz Ladeur works through this conception in his contribution to this volume.[128] He identifies a 'multiple, decentred self' or a 'multiple or divided self', which cannot be presumed to achieve autonomy by merging with a fictional general will. Instead, individuals confirm their identity and their particular will through interaction with other equal wills in 'overlapping networks of relations'.[129] Similarly, Gerstenberg and Sabel distinguish between 'weak ties to be created by the continuous exploration of difference' over 'the strong ties imposed by a society imagined as a goal-oriented subject writ large'.[130]

The second essential element is a conception of how in fact individuals organize themselves to flourish and solve problems both as autonomous beings and as members of society. The labels here proliferate – heterarchy, polyarchy, polycontexturality – but the fundamental idea is the same. Individuals are able to organize themselves in multiple networks or even communities that are 'disembedded' from traditional state structures but that are nevertheless 'communicatively interdependent' in the sense of being able to compile and cumulate knowledge, problem-solving capacity, and normative frameworks. They are self-organizing, self-transforming, and de-territorialized.[131] A fundamental dimension of this vision is the perception that the traditional separation between the formulation and application of rules is being dissolved by technology, a development that is in turn undermining 'a shared common knowledge basis of practical experience'.[132] Instead, public and private actors are coming together to develop new ways of 'decision-making under conditions of complexity'.[133]

---

127 See Sabel and Gernstenberg in this book.

128 See Ladeur in this book. Ladeur seeks to 'reformulat[e] the democracy principle in conditions of post-modernity', a reformulation that begins with a different concept of the self and an exploration of the ways in which individuals flourish and grow and engage with others in 'the knowledge society'. Ladeur advances the concept of 'variable acentric individuality' (p 34), which means a 'multiple, decentred self', (quoting T.B. Strong [p. 15]) or the 'multiple or divided self' (p. 16). Since there is no unitary general will, but only a multiplicity of individual wills, then the individual can 'only confirm itself through recognition of the other (equal) wills. The modern individual is required to have the capacity to look at society from the viewpoint of others'. (17).

129 See Ladeur in this book.

130 See Sabel and Gernstenberg in this book.

131 See Ladeur, Sabel, Gernstenberg and Teubner in this book.

132 Karl-Heinz Ladeur, '*Towards a Legal Concept of the Network in European Standard-Setting*', in Joerges and Vos, *supra* n. 24, pp. 151-70, p. 157.

133 *Id.*, p. 161.

The third element is a revised conception of the state. Participants in these multiple, parallel networks, both domestic and transnational, face a continuous stream of problems and require a continuous stream of knowledge both about each other and about their counterparts in other networks. They are in 'permanent, polyarchic dis-equilibrium', which they are continually overcoming through problem – solving and information – pooling.[134] The state's function is not to regulate directly, but rather to manage these processes.[135] It must help empower individuals to solve their own problems within their own structures, to facilitate and enrich direct deliberation while also helping ensure 'mutual irritation between the networks'.[136] It must also devise norms and enforcement mechanisms for assuring the widest possible participation within each network, consistent with its effectiveness.[137] To complicate matters even further, states themselves should be viewed 'as co-operative networks of networks and not as sovereign units'.[138]

These ideas, even as compressed and over-simplified as they are here, are all valuable in helping to explain, justify and amplify the functions of global transgovernmental regulatory networks. They also provide a much richer context for introducing the idea of global information agencies. The ultimate task is to integrate ideas of delegation, transgovernmental deliberation, and horizontal democracy in ways that recognize the continuing existence of the territorial state and designated 'public' officials but that takes full and central account of the possibilities and actuality of 'private' self-organization.

3.   Legislative Networks

Even assuming a completely integrated concept of post-modern democracy, however, a key element would be missing. Elected representatives are surely not obsolete. Popular perceptions of democracy are likely to remain relatively impervious to theoretical redefinition. Dahl's very simple concept of democracy – the control of the elite by the mass – will still resonate. Government by elected representatives will still approximate this ideal in important ways.

Thus in a global governance system in which networks of appointed officials, from regulators to judges, operating both within and without inter-governmental

---

134 See Sabel and Gernstenberg in this book. This combination of direct participation in problem – solving combined with constant, structured information – pooling and benchmarking lies at the heart of Dorf and Sabel's vision of democratic experimentalism. Dorf and Sabel, *supra* n. 101.

135 Ladeur in this book; Sabel and Gerstenberg in this book ('different forms of localized and particularized experience from the so-called private sector have to be coordinated in the public').

136 *Ibid.*

137 Sabel and Gernstenberg in this book; *see also* Cohen and Sabel, *supra* n. 24, pp. 332-33.

138 Ladeur, '*Towards a Legal Concept of a Network*', *supra* n. 132, at 166.

institutions and agreements, play a critical role, it is vital to add legislative networks. Many worthy organizations exist designed to bring together the world's parliamentarians. A number of intergovernmental institutions, from the OSCE to NATO, have parliamentary assemblies composed of national legislators, many of which play a more important role than is often realized. Nevertheless, with all the summits of heads of government, central bankers, finance ministers, justice ministers, environmental ministers, and even judges, the absence of meetings among powerful national legislators is striking.

Senator Jesse Helms, chair of the US Foreign Relations Committee, finally went to the UN to meet the assembled ambassadors. He did not go, however, to meet his counterparts in control of foreign relations committees in legislatures around the world. With the advent of President Vincente Fox in Mexico, however, Senator Helms has agreed on a meeting between his committee members and their counterparts in the Mexican legislature.[139] Groups of legislators from around the world have also met to share ideas and initiatives on legislation in specific issue areas, such as human rights and the environment. But before entertaining any more ideas for a global parliament,[140] national policymakers should focus on creating global or at least regional legislative networks.[141]

VI. Conclusion

Global governance is taking place through global networks of national government officials. These networks can exist within international institutions, within the framework of intergovernmental agreements of various kinds, and on their own as spontaneous responses to the need to interact to co-ordinate policy and address common problems. This typology is hardly the only way to identify and categorize different types of transgovernmental networks; it would be equally possible and probably useful to distinguish them in terms of the different functions they perform, such as rule-making versus enforcement, or in terms of the different degrees and even types of power they can exercise.[142]

This particular typology, however, helps illuminate different types of accountability concerns. It appears to reflect varying degrees of democratic input

---

139 William Safire, 'Fox, Bush and Helms', *New York Times*, 2nd April 2001, sec. A, p. 15, col. 5.

140 See Richard Falk and Andrew Strauss, 'Toward Global Parliament', *Foreign Affairs*, vol. 80, no. 1 (2001), pp. 212-220.

141 Shirley Williams, '*Sovereignty and Accountability in the European Union*', in Robert Keohane and Stanley Hoffmann, (eds.), *The New European Community* (Boulder, Colo: Westview Press, 1991).

142 Vervaele, for instance, distinguishes enforcement networks from other types of networks. Vervaele, *supra* n. 107, p. 135.

and control, depending on the extent to which the elected representatives of the people were ever consulted as to the desirability of establishing such networks, much less their actual operation. It also allows us to see international institutions as just another framework for the operation of transgovernmental networks, at least in many cases. Genuine supra-national bureaucracies certainly exist, but they are far smaller than might be supposed.

Here also is the parallel to the EU. The networks of national government officials who comprise the comitology system exhibit many of the same characteristics of transgovernmental networks more generally, including perceptions of their lack of legitimacy. It is thus possible to borrow specific solutions from the EU context, such as the creation of global information agencies.

In the final analysis, however, disaggregated decision-making by national government officials who have a loyalty both to their national constituents and to the need to solve a larger problem in the interests of people beyond national borders requires a more sophisticated concept of disaggregated democracy. Developing such a concept is likely to require a synthesis of anti-majoritarian rationales, deliberative politics, and self-actualization through networks of every kind. The task ahead is to develop such a synthesis in such a way that it can be both operationalized and actually communicated to the people it is supposed to serve.

Chapter 7

Sovereignty and Solidarity: EU and US

Joshua Cohen and Charles F. Sabel

I. Some Stylized Facts About the EU's Democratic Vocation

In a world that still venerates democracy's principles but regularly despairs of its practice, the nascent political order of the European Union (EU) is a crucial test case. Can the ideal of self-government be extended to this new setting, with its welter of problem-solving committees, processes, and reflection groups that appear to lie beyond the reach of popular direction and accountability? What does the prospect of this extension tell us about the possibilities of popular sovereignty and redistributive solidarity when politics extends beyond current national political boundaries? And what does it tell us about the possibilities of democracy itself?

To address these questions, we begin with a stylized description of the EU. Although the elements of the description are not completely uncontentious, they command sufficient agreement that they must be respected by any theoretical characterization of what the EU is and what it might become.

Judged simply by its ability to survive, the EU is a success. 'Unity impossible, collapse improbable', is the grudging acknowledgment of a British observer inclined to euro-scepticism.[1] In a dynamic environment, where the basic terms of collaboration remain uncertain but paralysis would soon lead to breakdown, existence itself is an achievement. In particular the EU is managing to reconcile two tasks, each of which is extremely demanding even without the constraints imposed by pursuit of the other. Thus it is achieving an integrated market by eliminating obstacles to internal trade – in particular by mutual recognition of norms of commercial exchange (as urged by the European Court of Justice),[2] and by their harmonization through other means – while also protecting public health and safety,

---

1   Garton, Ash T., The European Orchestra, New York Review of Books, 48/8, 2001, pp. 60-7.

2   Case 120/78 Rewe-Zentrale AG v Bundesmonopolverwaltung für Branntwein (Cassis de Dijon) (1979) ECR 649; Case C-212/97 Centros Ltd. v Erhvervs-og Selskabssttryrelsen (1999) ECR I-1459.

avoiding regulatory races to the bottom and possibly initiating some races to the top. To be sure, outcomes differ by policy area, with greater harmonization, and at a higher level, in safety devices for machines than in highway or railroad transport, and more in transport than in taxation. But areas that seemed intractable ten years ago – such as transport, education, immigration and asylum – are no longer so. And areas such as taxation – that seemed indissolubly linked to the traditions and practices of individual Member States, and natural instruments of competitive conflict – now seem at least in principle possible arenas of harmonization.[3] Whatever the precise extent of regulation, dark predictions of a new laissez-faire order, established beyond the reach of existing national regulatory regimes, have been overturned by events.

Moving from policy to process, the EU is producing the regulatory setting for the integrated market through new forms of rule-making issuing in open-ended rules. One well-studied example is *comitology*. This system of expert committees, appointed by the Member States, works with the Commission and drafts regulatory proposals for areas such as telecommunications equipment, foodstuffs, cosmetics, or pressure vessels. In principle decision-making in these committees is by qualified majority vote. In practice they operate through deliberation – (self-) reflective debate by which participants reason about proposals and are open to changing their own initial preferences – aimed at consensus. Committee deliberations are driven by the comparison of differences among current regulatory systems in the Member States. Such comparisons permit identification of best practices that serve as the starting point for a detailed, harmonized regime. Because the Commission is formally implementing decisions of the Council, and the committees are formally assisting the Commission, comitology preserves, though just barely, the appearance that a sovereign lawgiver – the EU in the guise of the Commission and the Council – is setting the rules.[4]

A more recent and encompassing version of this kind of regulatory device – a decentralized specification of standards, disciplined by systematic comparison – is the Open Method of Co-ordination (OMC). In the OMC, Member States agree to

---

3   For an overview and references to detailed studies of developments in these policy areas see Héritier, A., *Policy Making and Diversity in Europe: Escaping Deadlock*, (Cambridge: Cambridge University Press, 1999).

4   Joerges, C., Ladeur, K.H. and Vos, E. (eds.), Integrating Scientific Expertise into Regulatory Decision-Making: National Traditions and European Innovations, Schriftenreihe des Zentrums für Europäische Rechtspolitik an der Universität Bremen (ZERP), Bd. 23 (Baden-Baden: Nomos, 1997); Joerges, C. and Vos, E. (eds.), EU Committees: Social Regulation, Law and Politics (Oxford: Hart Publishing, 1999); Van Schendelen, M. P. C. M. (ed.), EU Committees as Influential Policymakers (Aldershot: Ashgate, 1998); Christiansen, T. and Kirchner, E. (eds.), Committee Governance in the European Union (Manchester: Manchester University Press, 2000).

formulate national action plans to further, say, employment promotion. These plans integrate, and adjust their policies in related, but typically distinct areas such as training, the operation of the labour market, taxation, and aspects of social security. The plans are periodically criticized by a panel of expert officials from other Member States in light of other plans, and each country's performance is judged against its own goals, the performance of the others, and its response to earlier rounds of criticism. The exact mechanisms by which the OMC is applied differ between policy areas, especially with regard to the thoroughness of peer review and the sanctions for lax response by Member States. These (sometimes significant) differences aside, the goal here too is mutual correction, not uniformity, and here too peak-level consultation among experts grows out of and reflects back upon a broader process of consultation. The extent to which that consultation ramifies into the larger society – the extent to which deliberation by policymakers is connected to broader democratic debate and practice – is an open question.[5]

The OMC formalizes and makes manifest a form of policy-making that the EU has applied to encourage an integrated approach to economic development regionally and to social inclusion – as a response to grinding poverty – locally. With regard to social inclusion, for example, the EU typically funds at the municipal level a public-private partnership whose members are drawn from NGOs and the relevant statutory authorities (the welfare department, the training service, and so on). Organized as a not-for-profit corporation, this partnership solicits proposals to combat social exclusion from local groups, which may themselves be public-private partnerships organized as non-profits. The most promising proposals are selected and reviewed periodically in the light of their ability to achieve their goals, and the achievements of other projects in the parent company's jurisdiction. In addition to monies provided by the EU, funding for projects often includes resources formally allocated to the statutory agencies and placed at the disposition of the local partnership by board members with the approval of their home department. The performance of the parent company is, ideally, evaluated by comparison of its projects to those of its peers nationally and within the EU. But practice and ideal typically have only a nodding acquaintance in this regard. As in the case of the OMC, integrated programmes that reflect the peculiarities of their contexts emerge through iterated, critical comparison of local initiative[6]

The European Court of Justice (ECJ) has tolerated these innovations in regulatory process, despite their tenuous connection to the constitutional structure, such as it is, of the EU (or any other advanced democracy, for that matter). In

---

5   See the introduction and the chapters by Trubek and Mosher and Goetschy in this volume.

6   Sabel, C. F., *Local Partnerships and Social Innovation: Ireland* (Paris: OECD, 1996); Geddes, M. and Benington, J. (eds.), *Local Partnerships and Social Exclusion in the European Union* (London: Routledge, 2001).

particular, the ECJ has not substantially limited the cascading delegation of authority by the EU or Member States to experts or to public-private partnerships, and from them to actors in civil society. Instead, the ECJ has from time to time sought to regularize, if not 'constitutionalise' them. Thus the ECJ requires that comitological deliberations be generally transparent to the public, respect the full range of reasonable argument, and strictly apply certain other rules of procedure.[7] The ECJ has arguably itself encouraged a roughly analogous form of rule making by occasionally using its case law jurisprudence to articulate frameworks within which the parties, after extensive collaboration with affected interests, must construct concrete solutions. Is this *de facto* collaboration between the ECJ and the Commission a marriage of convenience, an expression of judicial deference or defeat, or an intimation of an emerging (if imperfectly grasped) understanding of a new form of democratic constitutionalism?[8]

So the EU is having some success in reconciling market integration and protection of public health and safety, creating integrative actors regionally and locally, and fostering deliberative policy-making in the regulatory surround of the single market. Moreover, the Commission and the ECJ (a *de facto* constitutional court) are amicably cohabitating. Nevertheless, the EU manifestly suffers from a 'democratic deficit'.

Most notably, it has failed to engage the attention of a European electorate. Turnout for elections to the European Parliament has declined steadily from some 60 per cent of the eligible voters a decade ago to some 50 per cent today, and would decline further still were it not for compulsory voting laws. Neither has it fomented, beyond the formalities of elections, the creation of an engaged European public sphere or a European demos, debating the future of a European polity.

Indeed, the EU has failed to give its political institutions even the gross outward trappings of constitutionality. It is unclear, for example, whether the EU legislature is the Council, comprising representatives of the Member States, or the European Parliament, with its represented deputies. More exactly, it is clear that whenever the co-decision procedure applies – and it is the most common option – Council and Parliament are co-equal in the legislative process (see article 251 EC). A further complication arises from the Commission's agenda-setting powers. Is it an administrative or executive organ of government? It is commonly and correctly

---

7   Case T-188/97 Rothmans International BV v Commission [1999] ECR II-02463; see for a more recent and ambitious effort to 'constitutionalize' EU regulatory processes, the opinion of Advocate General Jacobs C-50/00P, Union de Pequeños Agricoltores v. Council of the European Union, delivered 21st March 2002.

8   For an excellent anthology of current research on the ECJ, see de Búrca, G. and Weiler, J. H. H. (eds.), The European Court of Justice (Oxford: Oxford University Press, 2001).

remarked that the EU would not admit itself to membership, because it lacks the conventional features of representative democracy required of applicant countries.[9]

But – and now the stylization gets more complicated and for that reason more interesting – while the EU faces a democratic deficit, it is not entirely unaccountable, and not only because national level accountability is inherited at the EU level. In the 1990s the Member States have convened themselves in a nearly continuous series of 'intergovernmental' conferences (IGCs) and semi-annual European Council sessions, supplemented by the periodic formation of high-level reflection groups. These overlapping meetings would be called an extended constitutional convention if the result – or aim? – had been to establish a document with the foundational character of a constitution.[10] Instead the main results have been, by traditional standards, meta-constitutional on the one hand and sub-constitutional, verging on the operational, on the other. Meta-constitutionally the IGCs and their offspring have explicitly authorized the EU to extend its competence to areas such as health, education and protection against discrimination not contemplated in the treaties establishing the EU. Through the (non-binding) Charter of Fundamental Rights they have taken a step towards eventually founding or conditioning the law of the EU treaties and the ECJ on a jurisprudence of human rights, including such of these as begin to give substance to the idea of 'social Europe'. Sub-constitutionally, or, if you like, extra-constitutionally, they have produced innovations such as the OMC.[11] Is it political blockage or insight into the limits of the traditional notions of the separation of powers that hinders efforts at the intermediate level? Why the continuing oversight of the Member States has not issued in constitutionally conventional (re)form is, in any case, another open question.

The traditional social partners – labour unions and employers associations – can also be said to be actively acquiescing in, and in some measure validating, the new EU order. This claim seems of course absurd from the vantage point of German, British or French experience. In these large countries the EU, and globalization more generally, is seen as shaking the foundations of the labour movement. But in the small countries, such as Ireland, Portugal, the Netherlands or Denmark, labour participates in various social pacts that make it, with capital, a partner in national

9 On the complexity of the institutional relations see, for example the review of literature by Scully, R., The European Parliament as a Non-Legislative Actor, The Journal of European Public Policy, 8/1, 2001, pp. 162-9 and Tsebelis, G. and Garrett, G., The Institutional Foundations of Intergovernmentalism and Supra-nationalism in the European Union, International Organization, 55/2, 2001, pp. 357-390.

10 See Smith, B., Constitution Building in the European Union: The Process of Treaty Reforms, The Hague, Kluwer, 2002.

11 Craig, P. and de Búrca, G. (eds) The Evolution of EU Law. 1st ed.1999; revised ed. forthcoming 2003. Oxford: Oxford University Press.

adjustment to the new, EU context. Whether these pacts are durable, and whether they create 'new actors' in the sense of the EU regions and localities noted above, or rejuvenate traditional, neo-corporatist arrangements, are also open questions.[12]

These limits on the size of the democratic deficit notwithstanding, EU governance in general, and the success of its innovative rule-making in particular, depend on the participation of experts who are not accountable by the familiar methods of legislative oversight or judicial review. Technical experts are crucial to the committees of comitology, and to the OMC. But these technical experts play a novel role. Efforts to integrate discrete solutions in new regional and local institutions and in the OMC explicitly obligate participating experts to revisit their assumptions in the light of the experience of peers in related disciplines. Comitology teaches a similar lesson about the ambiguity and insufficiency of disciplinary knowledge by exposing experts to disparate solutions that an apparently homogeneous body of professional knowledge – their home field – warrants. Whether this opening by experts to outsiders in processes of practical deliberation extends to inclusion of laypersons – even as knowledgeable 'clients' or 'expert users' – in the circle of decision making is an open question. Whether such inclusion, assuming it exists, is extensive enough to influence our understanding of democratic participation and accountability is more open still.

Despairing of the see-saw character and sheer opacity of the debate about the EU's democratic accountability, moved by concern for popular control, or simply anxious to forestall 'populist' rejection of globalization in one region, the EU's elites have, finally, convened a constitutional convention in Brussels. Its current focus of attention on conventional proposals and its compulsive sideways glances at the EU's own unconventional practices together capture the yearning for normalcy and the thrall of experimentation that grips the Union today.

For now debate in the convention focuses on normalizing the EU by endowing it with the two classic elements of democratic constitutions dating to the French and American Revolutions: a statement of inalienable rights (enumerated recently in the Charter of Fundamental Rights of the European Union) and a *Kompetenzkatalog* delimiting the powers and privileges of the various branches and levels of government. The most salient such catalogue is the German proposal to restructure the EU on the model of the Bundesrepublik, with a bicameral legislature consisting

---

12 For an account emphasizing the influence of monetary constraints on bargaining structures see Iversen, T., Pontusson, J. and Soskice, D. (2000). Unions, Employers, and Central Banks: Macroeconomic Coordination and Institutional Change in Social Market Economies. New York: Cambridge University Press. For explanations focusing on new roles for the social actors as agents of welfare state reform see Green-Pedersen, C., van Kersbergen, K. and Hemerijck, A., Neo-Liberalism, the 'Third Way' or What? Recent Social Democratic Welfare Policies in Denmark and the Netherlands, Journal of European Public Policy, 8/2 (2001), pp. 307-25.

of a Parliament of Euro deputies elected by direct vote of the citizens and a Senate with members appointed by the governments of the Member States.[13]

But offstage there is acknowledgement and discussion of the two *de facto* abnormal efforts at constitutional reform noted above: the IGC and the OMCs. Both are constitutional insofar as they plainly allow the Member States, as masters of the EU's founding treaties, to extend the competence and transform the decision-making processes of the EU in ways not currently authorized by treaty provisions. Both, but most especially the OMCs, are constitutionally anomalous in that they foster integration across levels of government and between branches of government: they connect what the *Kompetenzkatalog* would sunder. More worrisome still, from the traditional perspective, the OMCs might come to shape the more detailed understanding of rights, rather than merely 'implementing' them: subject to international treaty provisions, the right to asylum in the EU could be shaped as much by the interpretation of practice through the OMC as by decisions of the EJC.

The connections between the traditional debate and consideration of the abnormal constitutional projects are more intimate than appears. The experienced politicians attending the convention are well aware that even cosmetic democratization of the formal relations among EU institutions could easily limit the effectiveness of current methods of decision-making. Allowing the European Parliament to enhance its control of the Commission by electing some proportion of Commissioners, for example, would likely set off strategic games in both institutions that could undermine the Commission's crucial role as a convening 'neutral' in comitological and other regulatory processes. More generally, and unintended or higher-order consequences aside, political operatives know that cosmetic solutions face a deep problem. A fundamental constitutional defect of the EU, from the traditional point of view, is the delegation or dispersion of state authority from formal organs of government to non-state actors. Reforms of gross constitutional framework that leave this 'defect' untouched will change only appearances. But the 'defect' also appears to be the source of regulatory success. So really eliminating it – by turning current regulatory arrangements into the administrative agencies of a newly constitutionalized Eurostate – may buy gains in conventional democracy at the cost of problem-solving efficacy.[14] In any case, given the dangers of inadvertently subverting problem-solving by cosmetic reform, and

---

13   The speech of the German foreign minister, Joschka Fischer, in Berlin on the 12th of May 2000, that opened the current constitutional debate, refers to the goal of a 'European Federation' in the first sentence.

14   A good statement of the mismatch between the innovative thrust of EU governance and efforts to democratize the EU on the model of classic administrative state is Dehousse R., Misfits: EU Law and the Transformation of European Governance, Jean Monnet Working Paper 2/2002. Available at:
http://www.jeanmonnetprogram.org/papers/02/020201.rtf.

the persistence of traditional differences regarding how to accomplish even the latter – the French are famously allergic to the word 'federalism' when sounded with a Germanic accent[15] – the convention is much more likely to produce constitutional rectification than a constitution.

So what is the EU? In a fuller discussion we would entertain four answers, each based on a reading of the stylized description considered thus far: the EU as technocracy,[16] as association of associations,[17] as Eurodemocracy founded on a transnational public sphere,[18] and as deliberative polyarchy.[19] Each of these readings links arenas of deliberative problem-solving and democratic possibilities. Each draws on a distinctive idea of sovereignty in relation to solidarity. This relation in turn suggests a characteristic understanding of regulation and redistribution and the connection between them. It pairs with a distinct concept of democracy. Finally, each reading of the EU also suggests a corresponding reading of US experience. Here we limit ourselves to the interpretation we favour: The EU as deliberative polyarchy. As you might expect, we think this interpretation respects the stylized facts better than competitors. But we are all too aware that many of our claims – and in particular, those regarding the democratic potential of deliberative polyarchy – are hostage to the eventual answers to the open questions.

II.   Europe as Deliberative Polyarchy

Consider a world in which sovereignty – legitimate political authorship – is neither unitary nor personified, and politics is about addressing practical problems and not simply about principles, much less performance or identity. In this world, the public is simply an open group of actors, nominally private or public, which constitutes itself as such in coming to address a common problem, and reconstitutes itself as

15   In replying to Fischer's speech before the Bundestag on 27th June 2001 the French President, Jacques Chirac uses the word 'federal' only in pronouncing the official title of one of his hosts, the Bundespräsident. For the texts of the speeches see Dehousse, R.(ed.), Une constitution pour l'Europe? (Paris: Presses Des Sciences Po., 2002).

16   Majone, G., The Credibility Crisis of Community Regulation, Journal of Common Market Studies, 38/2, 2000, pp. 273-302.

17   Schmitter, Ph. C., How to Democratize the European Union – and Why Bother? Governance in Europe (Lanham, MD: Rowman & Littlefield, 2000).

18   Habermas, J., Between Facts and Norms: Contributions to a Discourse Theory of Law and Democracy. Translated by W. Rehg. (Cambridge, Mass.: MIT Press, 1996). Id., On the Pragmatics of Social Interaction: Preliminary Studies in the Theory of Communicative Action. Translated by B. Fultner. (Cambridge, Mass.: MIT Press, 2001).

19   Cohen and Sabel, Directly-Deliberative Polyarchy, European Law Journal, 3 /4 1997, pp. 313-40.

efforts at problem-solving redefine the task at hand. The polity is the public formed of these publics: this encompassing public is not limited to a list of functional tasks (police powers) enumerated in advance, but understands its role as empowering members to address such issues as need their combined attention.

Solidarity here rests neither on a sentiment of identity nor on a complementarity rooted in the division of labor. Rather it is both moral and practical. Moral, in that individuals recognize one another as moral agents entitled to be treated as equals; practical, in that they are bound to each other by the recognition that each is better able to learn what he or she needs to master problems through collaboration with the others whose experiences, orientations and even most general goals differ from his or her own – a recognition that both expresses and reinforces a sense of human commonality that extends beyond existing solidarities. Such practical attachment is fostered by a pervasively uncertain world, where even the strongest have reason to favour a division of investigative labour to incurring the risks of choosing and executing a solution alone. In such a world the practical benefits that flow from constant testing and reexamination of assumptions and practices that defines a public provides a powerful motive to participate in collaborative problem-solving on equal terms. Conversely, the cultural homogeneity and intellectual closure of the demos and occupational group obstruct co-operation in this setting as much as they enabled it in more stable ones. Solidarity in the sense of mutual capacitating by equals cannot be placed on the spectrum reaching from selfish calculation to selfless abandon because actors' preferences and identities change in the course of their joint reasoning. And its deliberation is practical – about solving problems – rather than dispassionate, senatorial reflection on clashes among deep principles, as in the traditions of civic republicanism or the upper reaches of Madisonian democracy.

When sovereignty resides in a public that comprises practical publics and solidarity is capacitating, rule-making is open – the creation of frameworks within which actors are encouraged to experiment with local solutions, on condition they pool what they learn with others – and redistribution follows rule-making. If actors could devise precise rules, or even confidently delegate responsibility for doing so, they might well band with their likes or complements as the case might be and spare themselves the evident inconvenience of deliberating about difference. But the world is not with them. So the best they can do is authorize the search for best practices – promising solutions – by those in a position to judge their promise and domain of applicability, and periodically revise the general framework of investigation as results warrant.[20]

If rule-making is principally about empowering publics to explore and test solutions, so, too, is redistribution. The most promising way of avoiding

20 The following views are most ably developed by Fritz Scharpf. See for example Scharpf, F.W., *Governing in Europe: Effective and Democratic*, Oxford, New York: Oxford University Press, 1999.

unacceptable market outcomes is to explore collaboratively the sources of the risks and reduce them by re-ordering markets accordingly. This kind of risk reduction flows into regulation and becomes nearly indistinguishable from it when the latter is taken as market making subject to the protection of public health and safety broadly understood. The web of connections resulting from this kind of regulation might (indeed very probably does) redistribute resources from one group to another. But such redistribution would be the consequence of a solution adopted first and foremost to address common problems – above all, the problem of maintaining the ability to address together, as equals, unforeseen problems – not correct specific social or economic imbalances: standards requiring that citizens be provided with 'adequate' or 'current state of the art' environmental protection, employment policies, workplace health and safety, and education and vocational training – where the understanding of 'adequate' and 'current' is redefined in the light of experience in the respective areas – would have this result.

The OMC as applied to the development of a European Employment Strategy (EES) shows how the formation of a public relies on, but continuously perturbs and reshapes public entities and groups in civil society. It suggests as well the general architecture of the background institutions that make possible the generation of publics.

To see the relation between the activity of forming a public and the actors thus formed, consider the EES that has emerged from the Amsterdam Treaty and from the 'jobs summit' in Luxembourg in November 1997 as a flow chart. Initial employment guidelines are proposed by the Commission acting chiefly through the Employment Committee (EMCO), an advisory body composed of two officials from each Member State and two Commission officials. In formulating its proposals EMCO consults the European social partners – the peak associations of labour and capital – the European Parliament, the Economic and Social Committee, and the Committee of the Regions. The Commission then forwards the proposed guidelines to the Council, which must approve them by a qualified majority. Member States respond to the guidelines by elaborating annual National Action Plans on employment (NAPs). Ideally, these NAPs integrate and correct policies in such disparate areas as vocational training and continuing education, taxation, the collection of statistics, and so on. The Commission compares and reviews the NAPs, while the Member States, acting through EMCO subject their actual labour market performance to a peer review. A Joint Report on Employment, prepared by Commission and the Council, benchmarks the employment policies of the Member States and identifies best practices. The Council can, by qualified majority vote make recommendations that Member States that show badly in these comparisons conform their policies to the guidelines. The guidelines themselves are revised every year, and the process as a whole is reviewed every four to five years in light of experience.

One predictable outcome of the EES is attempts by the interests it threatens to manipulate the process itself. Member States and their ministers do not typically relish criticism by their peers, especially not when such criticism may provoke unrest among their domestic constituents and collaborators. A process as formal as the EES offers numerous occasions for self-protective interventions: the formulation of guidelines and the choice of peer reviewers are obvious opportunities. Early returns of reviews of the EES in action suggest that anxious members do sometimes seek shelter this way.

But another predictable outcome of the formulation of general guidelines and National Action Plans, and revision of each in the light of the other, is unpredictability: obligated to explain their choices and performance, and exposed to the justifications and achievements of others in like circumstances, the actors must expect to find their constitution – their relation to their key constituents, to each other, and to the policies they pursue – open to challenge from within and without. Some of these challenges will arise as routine response to EES questions: How do a Member State's continuing and vocational education programmes comport with its tax structure and pension system? What should be done about a mismatch? Some of the challenges will emerge as higher order effects of the process itself? How does participation in the formulation and revision of the NAP affect trade union federations at the national level and influence labour's understanding of the social welfare state? What are its effects on the strategies of trade unions at the local level, and their relation to the national federation?

It is next to certain that reactions will differ within and across nations. Try to imagine a mechanism that could ensure uniformity in the current, volatile environment. It is also likely that some of these reactions will cohere into alternatives to familiar models of social partnership and interest group representation. In the new Irish social pacts, for example, the central labour and employers' federations are less focused on questions of wages and hours than before. Instead they aim to provide information and services to local branches participating in the continuing reorganization of firms, helping members manage careers on local labour markets, or participating in local programmes of social inclusion – all of which entails new political combinations that potentially reshape the identity of 'labour'.[21]

The EES does not, of course, ensure this outcome or any other. But it makes it easier for those who want such changes to identify and learn from each other, and harder for those who oppose them for reasons that their current organization, rather than the public, finds plausible to succeed in their obstinacy. Or that at least is

---

21 See O'Donnell, R. and O'Reardon, C., Social Partnership in Ireland's Economic Transformation, in G. Fajertag and P. Pochet (eds.), Social Pacts in Europe – New Dynamics. Brussels: European Trade Union Institute/Observatoire Social Européen, 2000, pp. 237-56.

the result that will come to light if publics and public actors are forming on the lines suggested by this reading.

The EES depends in turn on an organizational infrastructure whose general architecture was anticipated above in the descriptions of comitology and social inclusion programs: local, or, more exactly, lower level actors (nation states or national peak organizations of various kinds within the EU; regions, provinces or sub-national associations within these, and so on down to whatever neighbourhood is relevant to the problem at hand) are given autonomy to experiment with their own solutions to broadly defined problems of public policy. In return they furnish higher-level units with rich information regarding their goals as well as the progress they are making towards achieving them. They agree as well to respect the framework rights of democratic procedure and substance as these are elaborated in the course of experimentation itself. The periodic pooling of results reveals the defects of parochial solutions, and allows the elaboration of standards for comparing local achievements, exposing poor performers to criticism from within and without, and making of good ones (temporary) models for emulation.

It is the pervasiveness of this new architecture in the EU, as well as its dependence on a centre – though a 'centre' that has nothing to do with the apex of a hierarchy – that causes us to speak of a directly deliberative polyarchy, rather than, say, a new form of anarchy. In anarchy the alignment of interests and incentives among the actors results in spontaneous co-ordination without the need for a centre to compel provision of information, to facilitate the pooling of the information provided or discipline those who abuse the grant of autonomy to victimize some within their own jurisdiction, or take advantage of outsiders acting in good faith. Traditional examples are the market of the neo-classical textbook or the Proudhonian federation, in which *'les industries sont sœurs'*.[22] Contemporary versions are found in the social law of George Gurvitch, which descends directly from Proudhon,[23] and certain versions of systems theory, in which the 'sub-systems' of law and economics mutually 'irritate' each other, causing an adjustment without need for mutual understanding between the adjusting parts.[24]

In deliberative polyarchy, problem-solving depends not on harmony and spontaneous co-ordination, but on the permanent disequilibrium of incentives and interests imperfectly aligned, and on the disciplined, collaborative exploration of the resulting differences. As both the exploration and the sanctioning depend on mutual checking by decentralized actors facilitated by the central provision of the relevant

22   Proudhon, P.-J., Du principe fédératif et de la nécessité de reconstituer le parti de la révolution. Paris : E. Dentu, 1863, p. 113.
23   Gurvitch, G., L'idée du droit social. Paris: Recueil Sirey, 1932.
24   Teubner, G., Contracting Autonomies: The Many Autonomies of Private Law, Social and Legal Studies, 9/3, 2000, pp. 399-418.

infrastructure – think of the process by which NAPs are criticized – we term the EU's practical deliberations polyarchic.

But what democracy, if any, might this be or become? Democracy is deliberative when collective decisions are founded not on a simple aggregation of interests, but on arguments from and to those governed by the decision, or their representatives. But deliberation, understood as reasoning about how best to address a practical problem, is not intrinsically democratic: it can be conducted within cloistered bodies that make fateful choices, but are inattentive to the views or the interests of large numbers of affected parties – without being connected to open public debate and practice. So deliberative polyarchy can be democratic only if the deliberation is democratized. But what might it be to democratize a deliberative polyarchy?

The question is hard to answer because so much conventional thinking about democracy – whether deliberative or aggregative, minimalist and electoralist or founded on more demanding idea of a public sphere – assumes a central authority that operates over a territory, monopolizes the legitimate use of force in that territory, and has a wide range of policy competences – employment, environment, health, product safety, domestic security, research/development, and so forth. In this setting, we have democracy when policy-makers are held accountable to citizens through regular competitive elections, against a background of basic liberties of speech and association, in which citizens debate issues and choose representatives, and representatives make policies and hold officials accountable for the articulation and implementation of those policies. The political architecture of deliberative polyarchy is different, and its democratization must take a correspondingly unconventional form.

Stepping back, then, from familiar forms of democratic polity, then, we have a democratic form of deliberative polyarchy when its dispersed and co-ordinated deliberative decision-making is subjected to what Frank Michelman calls the 'full blast' of diverse opinions and interests in society.[25] Meeting the full-blast condition requires open-ended, informed discussion about the decisions taken by separate units and the co-ordinating centre. But what makes for democracy is not simply the fact of discussion, but that those discussions shape subsequent decisions. To meet these full-blast requirements, then, a deliberative polyarchy must be located in surroundings that meet five conditions. Thus, full-blast political discussion requires assured protections of basic rights of speech, association and participation. Moreover, deliberation and decision must proceed under a norm of transparency that invites and informs wider public participation in policy argument. Furthermore, that public discussion must have the right content and focus, which means that it must be attentive to co-ordination across units as well as decisions by the separate units; in the case of OMC, this means EU level policy co-ordination, as well as national

---

25   Michelman, F. I., *Brennan and Democracy*, Princeton, N.J.: Princeton University Press, 1999.

policies. So the full-blast condition is not satisfied simply by the fact of separate discussions about national policy, together with administrative co-ordination across jurisdictions. In addition, the democratic form of deliberative polyarchy requires mechanisms of accountability that connect deliberative decisions in particular policy areas with wider public discussion about those areas. And, to ensure that such accountability respects the equality of those subject to the decisions, a democratic background of deliberative polyarchy includes an individual right to contest decisions.

A deliberative polyarchy that meets these full-blast conditions not only achieves the democratic ideal of accountability and responsiveness to those who are subject to its decisions. (Although we will not make the case here, it is also more plausibly an epistemic or learning democracy than principal-agent views [the citizens as the empowered 'shareholders' of the state], corporatist understandings [democracy as the bargaining forum for, and the outcome of bargains struck among, labour, capital, and other key groups], and notions about a Eurodemocracy based on a public sphere in which citizens deliberate about matters of high principle.) Recall that the defining feature of the EU on the deliberative, polyarchic reading is to transform diversity and difference from an obstacle to co-operative investigation of possibilities into a means for accelerating and widening such enquiry. Comparison of different projects by publics that are themselves diverse in their composition (peer evaluators, standard-setting bodies and so on, down to localities and neighbourhoods) makes it possible to examine each concept both in the mirror of the others and from the varying angles presented by differing points of view. This kind of examination has been shown in many settings to bring to light deep flaws in individual projects that remain long undetected when they are pursued in isolation, and to reveal novel possibilities that are missed when many projects are pursued simultaneously but in willful indifference to each other. Although deliberative polyarchy is not intrinsically democratic, when it is focused on practicality it seems tailor-made to encouraging the exploration of diversity in a way that exposes decision-makers to its 'full blast'.

Seen as a method of revising designs in the light of their realization, moreover, it is clear why deliberative polyarchy is especially well suited to this task. Assume that ends and means are mutually defining: that understanding the content of ends requires inquiring into means, and that understanding the content of means requires inquiring into ends. Deliberative polyarchy revises (sets of) ends in the light of (sets of) means and vice versa. It provides a general, and, judging by our two examples, broadly applicable and inclusive model for realizing the epistemic promise of deliberative democracy.

But how broad? How inclusive? Surely neither all-encompassing with respect to domain of application, nor all inclusive – fully engaging all potentially affected interests – within any domain. Deliberative democracy is often suspected, rightly, of being exclusive, or outright elitist: and when deliberation is the province of a professional problem-solving elite (of legislators, administrators, or judges) it is frankly exclusive. Distrust of deliberation is thus distrust of the exclusionary power of professionals, certified or not. It seems justified in that the very source of professional autonomy – the professional's ability to bring expertise to bear on complex, singular cases – does seem tied to an unaccountable aloofness from clients, let alone the public.

Thus in professions, as in crafts, learners acquire skill by applying familiar techniques to well understood problems under the supervision of accomplished masters. The real teaching of law or medicine is done not in the classroom, but in the clinic – the analogue to the apprentices' shop – or in the early years – as resident or associate – on the job. When the routine is second nature, the learner takes on novel problems, achieving mastery herself when these can be solved without supervision. The knowledge of problem-solving techniques acquired this way is tacit: professionals, like craftspersons, can make refined judgements about the quality of work, yet not be able to say with precision how it is done. Indeed, because professional dignity is tied to autonomy, and autonomy to freedom from supervision, inquiry into what a professional does can easily appear a veiled accusation of incompetence or worse. Thus the professional's autonomy – the ability to solve complex problems without the support, and free of the limits of hierarchy – goes hand in hand with distance from clients, other kinds of professionals, and even one's own colleagues.

Through the use of comparisons of performance and the formulation of various responses to the problems such comparisons reveal, deliberative polyarchy potentially transforms the professions: it reduces their technocratic pretence, and reveals the dependence of expert judgement on assessments of ends as well as means. By making tacit knowledge of problem-solving explicit, or explicable, in a way that disrupts the traditional hierarchy of skill within each, it may open the boundaries that separate it from the others and the larger public.

But this is, of course, speculative. The facts of the democratic vocation of deliberative polyarchy are inconclusive and equivocal, if not contradictory. One fundamental fact is that the extent to which deliberative polyarchy ramifies past the technical elite into civil society is an open question. Another is that the regulatory successes of the EU have gone hand in hand with the spread of parallel governments. So the democratization of deliberative polyarchy remains a project whose precise institutional commitments have not yet been fixed. To be so in the sense of the 'full-blast' conditions it must be broadly inclusive, both in the scope of its deliberations and in the arrangements of public accountability. It must also be officialized, openly acknowledged as part of the legitimate process by which a self-governing people make their laws.

A concomitant of – perhaps, indeed, a condition for – the democratization of deliberative polyarchy is an understanding of constitutionalism as the continuing activity of assessing a polity's practices in the light of its deep commitments, and vice versa. Constitutionalism in this sense begets not a constitution of enumerated powers and rights, but more activity like itself: constitutionalism. Indeed, insofar as this kind of constitutionalism respects the constraint of the joint determination of means and ends, it is by conventional standards anti-constitutional. Thus the separation of powers among the branches and levels of government and allocation of authority as between, say, the federal and state levels cannot be fixed in advance. Doing so would be to choose procedural means without attention to substantive ends. Neither can the content of the system of rights be fully fixed in advance. Doing so would fix ends without attention to the means for realizing them. Can this kind of constitutionalism possibly secure the accountability of government? The efficacy of rights?

The problem of accountability seems fairly tractable, at least in comparison to the task of making sense of experimentalist rights. Deliberative polyarchy makes official actors transparent and answerable to each other and the public in ways that severely limit unaccountability. Our Madisonian constitution takes the branches and levels of government to be natural units, and makes their rivalry for power the source of our protection against the self-aggrandizement of government. Deliberative, polyarchical constitutionalism might be called neo-Madisonian in that it uses the polyarchical competition of purpose-built and re-configurable problem-solving units to the same end.

If accountability is not an insurmountable problem, can polyarchic constitutionalism make assertion of constitutional values definite enough to bound behaviour, yet open enough to admit of re-elaboration by, literally, the means of practice? More generally, on the full-blast view, the exploration of democracy itself emerges from the elaboration of starting commitments under the pressure of the full blast of social diversity. So on that view it must be true that the particular rights, or clusters of these, that inform and define democracy as a whole are shaped the same way. In other words, the precise content of rights is, in the full-blast view, emergent: without free expression, there is no democracy; but the elaboration of the content of that right in light of alternative specifications is part of democracy's work.

Consider again the OMC. Think of this as constitutionalism without, or instead of a constitution. OMC-style re-elaborations of employment, welfare, and education and tax policies are what the EU's Member States are doing instead of creating a constitution on the French or American models. Taken together, these policies are at the heart of what a state does. Perhaps this benchmarking all the way up is a novel path to a constitution, or at least a way of making justiciable the elaborate charter of the rights-securing democracy. Or it may be that benchmarking all the way up just keeps going, and the forms of practical deliberation it engages become at one and the same time a form of problem-solving and new method of articulating constitutional values. This reading of EU constitutionalism is, if you like, not simply a theory about what has been happening, but an interpretation with a practical intent: it suggests the kinds of participation we ought to be looking for, where we might find it, and how to think about making participation officially accountable if and when it is found.

Finally, this reading calls attention to aspects of US experience that also link fluid problem-solving and new forms of accountability in strikingly similar ways. We presented deliberative polyarchy as a kind of construct, a way of reading the stylized facts that make sense of a pattern that confounds conventional interpretations even in raising troubling questions of its own. We might as well have said that it constitutes the accidental discovery of a promising response to a broad class of current situations in which inaction is unacceptable but omnibus solutions are plainly unworkable. There are many such situations in the US as well, and many responses that recall the essentials of the EU read as a deliberative polyarchy.

Consider developments in education first and foremost, but also the reorganization of police departments, social services and others besides: the areas at the core of the broad, now apparently humbled movement for general institutional reform that Chayes, three decades ago, called public law.[26]

The differences between public law and what we will call, mindful of a family resemblance, the new public law, parallel those between the familiar constitutionalism of the administrative state and the continuing constitutionalism of the OMC. Public-law courts aimed to establish the acceptable minimum standards of institutional performance – the wattage of bulbs in prison cells, to take an extreme but not exceptional case. New public law judges today declare their commitment to the vindication of broad, open-ended constitutional values or legislative mandates. Thus the Supreme Courts of Texas and Kentucky, referring to their respective state constitutions, insist that schools provide an 'adequate' education for all children, even if virtually every school, school district and the state department of education be restructured to meet the adequacy standard.[27] In cases of police abuse, courts, referring to recent federal legislation, make it the responsibility of police departments themselves to detect and correct a 'pattern or practice' of abusive behaviour.[28]

This commitment to open-ended, expansive values becomes an effective discipline for broad reform because it is accompanied by a shift in the responsibility for and the focus of the monitoring of institutional performance. In public law the

---

26 See Chayes, A., The Role of the Judge in Public Law Litigation, Harvard Law Review, 89/7, 1976, pp. 1281-316. Id., Public Law Litigation and the Burger Court, Harvard Law Review, 96/1, 1982, pp. 4-60.

27 See on the movement from 'equity' to 'adequacy' claims in school-reform litigation, and generally for the developments in Texas reported below, Liebman, J. and Sabel, C. F., A Public Laboratory Dewey Never Imagined, forthcoming in New York University Review of Law & Social Change, 2003.

28 For a review of the relevant literature see Garret, B., Remedying Racial Profiling, in Columbia Human Rights Law Review, 33/1, 2001, pp. 41-148.

court convened an *ad hoc* group, drawn from parties and outside experts, to monitor periodically the reforming institution. The monitors' report, addressed to the judge, comprehensively evaluated the institution's compliance with the minimal standards. Today monitoring is continuous, not episodic. This routine monitoring is a continuing responsibility of the reforming institution itself, not an exceptional engagement by the court and its adjuncts. The monitoring focuses on key indicators of the reforming institutions' overall performance, particularly with respect to constitutionally aggrieved groups, not on a comprehensive evaluation of the progress of reform. And the monitoring results are addressed at least as much to the staff and clients of the reforming institution, and often to the public at large, as to the judge.

For example, it is the responsibility of the Texas Education Agency (TEA) to report regularly on the performance of public school children in grades 3 to 10 on certain standardized tests of proficiency in reading and mathematics. Disaggregated by school and by ethnic and socio-economic groups within schools, and organized to permit comparisons of each school to the 39 others in the state that it most resembles on these dimensions, these results are reported publicly. In still more finely disaggregated form they are reported to school and district officials, and by the latter to teachers. Parents, administrators at the school, district and state levels can monitor the progress of individual schools and districts. The Supreme Court of Texas can as well determine whether the TEA, and beyond it the state legislature, are meeting their obligations both to monitor the performance of individual schools and to respond in case poorly performing ones fail to improve at an acceptable rate. (The No Child Left Behind Act, passed by Congress in 2001, requires states to adopt their own version of the Texas accountability system as a condition of receipt of federal subsides to schools serving poor children.)

Thus, despite their commitment to open-ended values and their disinclination to limit the scope of reform, the courts today are much less involved in the management of institutional reorganization than their public-law predecessors. Where public law invited courts to in effect create *ad hoc* public agencies to set standards and provide designs for meeting them, courts today leave the substantive elaboration of the constitutional standards, and the means for satisfying them, to the primary actors. In this sense the new reform movements, unlike public law, are not court-centric. In imposing on the primary actors a continuing obligation to monitor themselves, the courts induce novel forms of self-critical co-operation between these latter and other public and private parties. Designs for reform arise from this vigilant co-operation, and the courts' ability to evaluate it. It is this new division of labour among the branches of government and between them and civil society – a new separation of powers – that makes judicial affirmation of need-based claims to something so vague and so fundamental as an adequate education into an effective, justiciable right to disentrench current practices and seek, accountably, for better ones.

Or, put in a way that closes the circle of our argument, US courts are creating the equivalent of a constitutional OMC. Deliberative polyarchy as a serious possibility on both sides of the Atlantic? This reading, you may say, abuses the licence to speculate provided by the open questions. But then democracy, history shows, is a kind of collective licence to answer, by means that affirm our values and our obligations to each other, questions we never imagined being asked.

Chapter 8

Legal Orders Between Autonomy and Intertwinement

Mark Van Hoecke[*]

Unlike mathematical systems for example, legal systems are not independent from the society to which they apply and which they organize.

Each legal system forms part of a more general system of society. A legal system is a way of organizing social, economic, moral, and other patterns of behaviour. Thus, legal systems must fit with society. To a certain extent, legal systems are a form of translation of social structures and social relations. When analyzing the nature of law or when applying and interpreting law, one should take this functional nature of law into account.

This dependency of law raises questions of legitimacy. The problem of social, economic, moral, philosophical, etc. legitimation of law is directly linked to this lack of autonomy towards society. It also implies that some autolegitimation of legal systems is impossible, as long as one is talking about real legal systems.

Although embedded in society and strongly determined by it, modern legal systems are actually relatively autonomous systems. But, if law is intertwined to such an extent with society, with all different kinds of human interaction, how could law be 'autonomous'? To answer this question, we have to distinguish between 'formal' and 'substantive' autonomy of legal systems; between the autonomy 'as a system', on the one hand, and the autonomy in determining the content of the rules, on the other. First, we will discuss the formal autonomy of legal systems and afterwards their substantive autonomy as regards other legal and non-legal systems and data.

*   I would like to thank Sean Smith for his helpful comments on this chapter.

I.   Formal Autonomy

1. Circularity

According to traditional legal theory, following the approach of Hans Kelsen, legitimation is approached as a linear process, in which, step by step, a rule or a decision is based on a higher rule, until some 'basic norm' is reached, which has to be introduced in order to stop a *regressus ad infinitum*. This theoretical approach entails considerable problems, mainly related to the status of that 'basic norm'. Moreover, it does not fit very well with legal reality. Today, legal systems have more and more a circular structure, when it comes to legitimation.

'Circularity' means that the higher norms within the hierarchy of a legal system not only determine the lower ones, but also in turn are determined by these lower ones. An example, given by Günther Teubner, is the 'fiction theory of the legal person', 'according to which the state as a legal person must, like Münchhausen, pull itself up by its own bootstraps by reinventing itself'.[1] He, rightly, notes that this is not an error or a failure of the legal system. This circular paradox is an essential feature of law and of reality in general.[2] Including it in a theory of law is not only accceptable, but even a productive and heuristically valuable practice.[3]

Legal practice offers, indeed, more and more examples of circularity. A first one is the hierarchy of law within the European Union. Institutions of the European Union[4] have the power to impose rules and decisions on Member States, but the whole Union is based on the treaties agreed upon by these states and from which, in principle, they could withdraw at any time. Furthermore, these Member States participate directly in the creation of the European rules, with members of their respective governments constituting the European Council of Ministers, which is the main formal legislator in the EU Thus, European law determines state law, state law determines European law: a perfect circularity.

A second example is the balance of power between the legislature and the judiciary. According to the view in 19th century continental Europe, there was a clear hierarchy according to which the judiciary was completely subordinated to the legislature and should rightly be so. Today, we see an increasing emergence of courts exercising the power to repeal legislation and to force the legislature to change the law. The European Court of Human Rights, the European Court of Justice, together with the administrative and constitutional courts within most states,

---

1   Günther Teubner, *Law as an Autopoietic System* (Oxford: Blackwell, 1993), 5 and G. Teubner, '*Münchhausen Jurisprudence*', 5 RECHTSHISTORISCHES JOURNAL 1986 (350-356), 351. See also: M. Van de Kerchove and F. Ost, *Le système juridique entre ordre et désordre* (Paris: Presses Universitaires De France, 1988), 102-111.
2   Günther Teubner, *Law as an Autopoietic System, supra* n. 1, 10 and 11.
3   Ibid, 9.
4   European Commission, European Council of Ministers, European Court of Justice.

have the power to impose on legislatures their views on law and their interpretation of international treaties and national constitutions. The legislator determines the limits of judicial law-making, but in turn the judiciary determines the limits of legislative law-making: another perfect circularity.

In this circular way, legal systems partly (but only partly) legitimate themselves. For example, approval of an Act by a constitutional court legitimates the law created by the legislator, whereas this court derives its power, and thus the legitimacy of its decisions, from the (constitutional) legislator. This is not only a circular process, but also a communicative one. Legislation is submitted to courts for approval or disapproval, the reasons for such an approval or disapproval will in turn mainly be found in legislation. If court decisions bear the risk of endangering governmental policy, the government will react by changing legislation in order to prevent similar court decisions in the future. However, if this new legislation does not fit in every respect with the basic rules and principles (Constitution, European Convention on Human Rights) of the legal system, the court having the power to annul such legislation might do so. The importance of such phenomena is broader than conferring autonomy on the legal system through its circular closure, they also confer a certain degree of legitimation through the communicative action and argumentation they embody. Even if this legitimation would be considered to be only a *prima facie* one, it reinforces the legal systems autonomy by allowing it to function in daily practice without reference to non-legal sources, values or norms.

2.   Operative Closure and Cognitive Openness

Autopoietic theory has made the useful distinction between 'operative closure' and 'cognitive openness' of legal systems.[5]

The (legal) system, to a certain extent, determines its own elements (the content of the rules), but only to a certain extent. Social facts, values and norms are selected and translated into 'legal' facts, values and norms. Reality can only be described by selecting and structuring an immense flow of chaotic elements. For describing and ordering social reality, it is thus necessary for a legal system to select and to order social facts, values and norms. In a way there is nothing exceptional about this requirement, it is a necessary condition for a legal system to exist. But the basic or raw material comes to a very large extent from outside the legal system. As a completely closed system, a legal system simply could not exist. Legal systems are, thus, 'cognitively' open to the external world. However, they remain 'autonomous', because they are 'operatively' closed: external data are selected and adapted according to an internal logic of the legal system:

---

5   Günther Teubner, *Law as an Autopoietic System, supra* n. 1, 65.

Self-reproduction presupposes that the system is influenced by its environment. Both external and internal factors influence the way a system reproduces itself by extracting and constituting, as it were, new elements from the flow of events, which it then uses by linking them up selectively.[6]

As soon as legal commnications on the fundamental distinction between legal and illegal begin to be differentiated from general social communication, they inevitably become self-referential, and are forced to consider themselves in terms of legal categories .... The law is forced to describe its components using its own categories. It begins to establish norms for its own operations, structures, processes, boundaries and environments – indeed, for its own identity. When it actually uses these self-descriptions, it has begun to constitute its own components. This leads to the emergence of self-referential circles in relation to legal acts, legal norms, legal process, and legal dogmatics, with the result that the law becomes increasingly 'autonomous'. The law itself determines which presuppositions must be present before one can speak of a legally relevant event, a valid norm, and so forth. Law begins to reproduce itself in the strict sense of the word if its self-referentially organized components are linked in such a way that norms and legal acts produce each other reciprocally and process and dogmatics establish some relationship between these. It is only when the components of the cyclically organized system interact in this way that the legal hypercycle becomes possible.[7]

Legal autonomy thus refers not only to law's capacity to generate its own order, but also to the self-constitutions of legal actions, the regulation of processes, and the invention of new schemata in legal dogmatics.[8]

Teubner has laid emphasis on the essential role of human agents in the legal system and on the 'cognitive openness' of legal systems: their constant interaction and communication with the non-legal world. But, to what extent then can legal systems be said to be 'autonomous' if they cannot exist at all without human agents and without an external world 'feeding' them?

3.   Types of 'Autonomy'

In a very weak sense 'autonomy' merely means that a legal rule, or a legal system, can be identified as something that is different from morals, religion or other systems of rules and that it is not just a re-statement of any set of non-legal rules. Even if the legal system is to a large extent based on such a set, as for example, is Islamic law on

6   Ibid, 21.
7   Ibid, 33.
8   Ibid, 34.

the Koran, it changes and adapts these rules from some other perspective, more specifically to some inner logic. This minimal substantive autonomy is essential for a (legal) system simply to exist as an identifiable system.

The presence of secondary rules of change and adjudication guarantee the institutional autonomy of legal systems. This institutional autonomy has two aspects: a formal autonomy (own institutions) and a procedural autonomy (own procedures for law-making and for its adjudication).

In developed legal systems this institutional autonomy is strengthened by the professional autonomy of most people dealing with the creation or the application of the law.

This runs parallel to a methodological autonomy, which contains two aspects, namely:

- *Autonomy of language*: a technical legal language is developed, creating its own concepts and giving a specific meaning to words used in everyday language; it also encompasses an autonomy of style: statutes, judgements, contracts, and the like are drafted in a specific way;
- *Autonomy of argumentation*: the kinds of reasoning and argument accepted in law are different from those in other forms of discourse (e.g. economic, political or religious discourse).

An advanced professional and methodological autonomy leads to a doctrinal autonomy. The development of its own legal doctrine is an important element for the autonomy of legal systems towards other legal systems. International law and canon law are more autonomous because they have a legal doctrine of their own. Sub-state communities, like sports clubs, are less autonomous, partly because they lack any legal doctrine of their own.

A minimum degree of substantive and methodological autonomy, together with an institutional autonomy, is common to all legal systems. More advanced legal systems acquire a higher level of autonomy to the extent that they develop each of the elements contributing to their autonomy: content (legal rules derived from other legal rules and principles), language, argumentation, legal profession and legal doctrine.

In such a development, another type of autonomy is brought about: an autonomy as regards legitimation. The more sophisticated legal systems are, the more circular they become and the more legitimation of rules and of decisions is possible within the legal system, and the legal system as a whole may increasingly succeed in legitimizing itself. At least it offers *prima facie* legitimation, which will only be endangered if there are strong non-legal reasons for attacking it (e.g. the clearly immoral character of substantive parts of the Nazi legal system). Legitimation is more and more worded in legal terms and refers to legal sources and principles. It becomes more and more circular within a legal discourse. This circularity may limit itself to one and the same legal system, as in the example given above of legislature and judiciary legitimizing each other. But it is interesting to note that there is some circularity within the legal discourse across the borders of individual legal systems. Legal systems are legitimized by reference to other legal systems: international law by reference to national law, sub-state law by reference to state law and to international law (e.g. recognizing the rights of minorities), law of the Member-States of the EU by reference to the law of the European Union.

This conclusion leads to a fundamental question: is it the legal system, which can be considered 'autonomous', or is it rather the 'legal discourse'? Or to put it another way, what kind of 'system' has really started to live a life of its own, with relative independence from its human agents and the external world? Is it a mechanism of legal structures, procedures and rules, which, to a certain extent is living its own life, or is it a legal discourse, as developed within the legal structures and professions? As the autopoietic legal theorists allege, the components of all social systems, including legal systems, are communications, and not individual beings. Society is not a bio-system but a system of meaning, produced through communications.[9] As regards law, those communications obviously use a legal discourse. But this discourse is to a large extent common to all, or at least several, legal systems. Legal language, legal argumentation and legal doctrine are considerably similar for many legal systems. Moreover, legal systems happen to be intertwined, both at the level of rules and principles (e.g. the European Convention on Human Rights and its impact on European state legal systems) and at the level of institutions and procedures (members of national governments constituting together the European Council of Ministers, the European Court of Human Rights having the power to annul state legislation and the opportunity and obligation to ask preliminary opinions to the European Court of Justice within the frame of a purely domestic trial, etc.). In the end, it becomes very difficult to talk about 'autonomy' of legal systems towards each other. When legal systems are producing and maintaining each other, when they strongly influence and partly, or even sometimes completely, determine the content of each other's structures and procedures, where then is the autonomy? How could we speak of 'autopoietic', autonomous legal systems? Could we not see legal systems in the world today as being just dialects of one common legal language, variants of one common legal discourse? But, if this is correct, we have to analyse the autonomy of law in a way different to that of autopoietic theory.

For the purpose of argument, it is possible and it may be useful to distinguish form from content, i.e. to make a distinction between the formal structure of legal systems and the content of the rules they produce. But, if one may conceptually conceive of such a distinction, one should be aware of the fact that form and content are actually intertwined and not completely separated from each other. The question of the formal autonomy of legal systems cannot completely be answered without linking it to the question of their substantive autonomy.

9   Günther Teubner, ibid., 29-30, with reference to Niklas Luhmann.

II. Substantive Autonomy

1. *Which Kind of Autonomy?*

The content given to the rules in legislation, the interpretation of the law by civil officers, judges and individuals when applying it, or by legal doctrine when describing and structuring the law, are undoubtedly, to a (very) large extent determined by non-legal facts, values and norms. Legal systems are not autonomous in this sense. They get, and need, an input from outside the system. The substantive autonomy only lies in the fact that the legal system selects and 'translates' this external data. It is converted and assimilated in order to fit within the system of legal language and legal principles of the legal system concerned. In fact, this is a kind of formal autonomy, allowing only some marginal change as to content. The essence of the content of the law comes from outside the legal system.

Sometimes, officials who work within the legal system, having some power to decide on the application of the law, e.g. civil officers or judges, have a rather 'autopietic' view of law. They consider law to be cognitively closed from the external world, to be 'self-referring', 'self-regulating', 'self-reflexive', 'self-productive', in short, autopoietic, not in a Teubnerian sense, but in a literal one. This is the kind of Kafkaeasque bureaucracy which to a certain extent runs parallel to the development of advanced legal systems. Here, rules are indeed interpreted as if they would loosen their links with the non-legal world and start their own, new life within the legal system and only according to the mechanism of that system. In fact, legal systems could not function in a reasonable way if they would solely take from the 'outside world' that which they can use and assimilate acording to their own systemic rules. The relation of legal systems with the external world is one of constant communication, not of one-directional information. This communication appears most prominently in the interpretation of the law by courts, where the concrete facts of the case, its specific circumstances, sometimes changed societal views and other factors, may influence the outcome in a very decisive way. This communication is so intensive, this 'cognitive opennesss' is so prevalent, that any concept of 'self-production' of the law by the legal system is necessarily a very fragile one. The legal system 'producing' rules just means that the rules are technically adapted to fit into the legal system and so warrant the label 'legal'. But this is an extremely weak form of 'autonomy'.

In a way one could argue that advanced legal systems have acquired a higher degree of substantive autonomy in that they have produced 'legal values' which are not derived from non-legal values. A typical example is 'procedural' rights, as recognised in Article 6 of the European Convention on Human Rights.[10] These are

---

10   Article 6 of the European Convention on Human Rights:

human rights related to secondary rules of legal systems: minimum guarantees for a fair trial. They refer to values which make no sense except within legal systems. In this way, secondary rules do not only considerably strengthen the institutional autonomy of legal systems but even their substantive autonomy. But are these really 'internal values'? Procedural values may have a larger scope than the legal one. In Karl-Heinz Ladeur's proceduralist view on law, very general procedural values are emphasized: keeping open a variety of options; tolerating and making possible a variety of opinions; making a variety of language games mutually accessible and guaranteeing interchangeability among them by breaking up self-reinforcing discourses.[11] All those values have a broad scope, including the ideological and political fields. Thus, procedural values are not by definition 'internal' legal values. What is required is to put limits to the arbitrary use and Kafkaesque working of legal systems. It should prevent, on the one hand, the abuse of law as a legal facade for covering clearly immoral, unjust acts. On the other, it should prevent legal systems from becoming fully autopoietic, from running wild as a system, from losing contact with their societal reasons for existence and sense, from using human beings as simple means for the structural aims of the system. Can we say that the legal systems are to that extent 'autopoietic' that they 'spontaneously' limit

---

'1. In the determination of his civil rights and obligations or of any criminal charge against him, everyone is entitled to a fair and public hearing within a reasonable time by an independent and impartial tribunal established by law. Judgement shall be pronounced publicly but the press and public may be excluded from all or part of the trial in the interest of morals, public order or national security in a democratic society, where the interests of juveniles or the protection of the private life of the parties so require, or to the extent strictly necessary in the opinion of the court in special circumstances where publicity would prejudice the interests of justice.

2. Everyone charged with a criminal offence shall be presumed innocent until proved guilty according to law.

3. Everyone charged with a criminal offence has the following minimum rights:

   (a) to be informed promptly, in a language which he understands and in detail, of the nature and cause of the accusation against him;

   (b) to have adequate time and facilities for the preparation of his defence;

   (c) to defend himself in person or through legal assistance of his own choosing or, if he has not sufficient means to pay for legal assistance, to be given it free when the interests of justice so require;

   (d) to examine or have examined witnesses against him and to obtain the attendance and examination of witnesses on his behalf under the same conditions as witnesses against him;

   (e) to have the free assistance of an interpreter if he cannot understand or speak the language used in court'.

11 Karl-Heinz, Ladeur, '*Prozedurale Rationalität - Steigerung der Legitimationsfähigkeit oder der Leistungsfähigkeit des Rechtssystems?*', 7 ZEITSCHRIFT FÜR RECHTSSOZIOLOGIE (1986), 265-274 at 273.

themselves? Of course, from the point of view of the autopoietic theory we can. But what does this mean?

We could compare this situation to one of a slave, who, as an autopoietic being, is able to adapt to the environment, who is able to remain autonomous in that he or she takes and assimilates a limited number of elements from the chaotic flow of inputs from the external world. As such, the slave takes 'autonomously' the decision to behave as a slave and to comply, as a rule, with all the commands of his master, even if they are unpleasant, humiliating, unjust or unreasonable. It will not be possible to use a young child as a slave, because it cannot understand the commands and it cannot decide 'autonomously' to abide by them. If one shouts at a baby in an attempt to make it stop crying, it will cry even harder. The same will happen if one beats the child. Threats will have no influence at all. In a way, the child is the 'master' and the person responsible for caring for it at any given moment will be its 'slave'. However, as a system, it will be much more difficult for the baby to survive autonomously than it is for an average adult. Unlike autopoietic systems, it lacks 'self-observation', 'self-reference', 'self-description', 'self-reflexivity' and it is rather closed to the external world, with which only very limited comunication is possible for it. The adult, however, is able to communicate much better with the outside world and to act 'independently' in accordance with the results of all communications assimilated by him or her. Exactly because (s)he is a full autopoietic system, (s)he can be a slave. It is because (s)he is 'autonomous', that (s)he may have, to a large extent, no autonomy at all. If we can word our conclusion in this paradoxical form, it proves that we are talking about different types of 'autonomy'. The 'autonomy' of human beings or legal systems as autopoietic systems does not refer to the kind of autonomy we have in mind when talking about 'autonomous individuals' or 'autonomous legal systems'.

It is somewhat awkward to say that the autonomy of a human being enables him to be a slave or that the autonomy of a legal system allows it to be dependent on morals or any other ideology. Systemic 'autonomy' just refers to the identity of the system as such, to its ability to communicate with the external world and to assimilate the information received from it. A high level of communication implies a large influence from outside. The lower the systemic 'autonomy', the higher the autonomy as to content: the rules of a card game or of chess are not at all influenced by morals; as regards the content of their rules, these games are much more autonomous than legal systems are. The higher the systemic autonomy, the lower the autonomy as to content. This is the apparent paradox of autopoietic autonomy : the more legal systems are developed and autonomous in a systemic way, the less their autonomy for determining their content.

2. Degree of Autonomy

In order to analyse the degree of substantive autonomy of legal systems, we have to distinguish between different situations. On the one hand, the link between legal systems differs from their links with all other types of societal system. On the other, the influence from the external world may go deeper than just the level of the primary levels of conduct, and may also partly determine the secondary rules.

a) Autonomy vis-à-vis other legal systems

As we have argued above, there is a circularity, not only within legal systems, but also amongst legal systems mutually: e.g. international law is based on state law, but in some cases, state law is derived from supra-national law (e.g. The European Union or The European Convention on Human Rights). This circularity makes legal systems dependent upon each other. The 'collective' gain of autonomy *vis-à-vis* the economic, political, or other systems and discourses is at the price of a loss of autonomy towards each other. Here, one could also state that the decrease of autonomy *vis-à-vis* other legal systems increases the autonomy towards the non-legal systems. The primitive legal system of some isolated tribe will be completely autonomous towards all other legal systems, but it will have a very limited autonomy *vis-à-vis* other societal systems such as morals, religion, the economy, etc. Modern legal systems have gained more autonomy in this regard, but lost a great deal of autonomy towards each other. Even at the high point for relatively isolated, centralized nation states in the 19th century, there was a mutual level of legal interdependency. State legal systems cannot exist without at least some official recognition by other states.[12] They need each other to make, to develop and to enforce international law. Even if international private law has, until recently, always been exclusively national law, it contains rules of reference to other legal systems, thus incorporating 'by delegation' the private law of, in principle, all other state legal systems into the domestic legal system.

Non-state legal systems, like national or international sports associations, generally employ some state law to acquire the status of a 'legal person' under this state law. When drafting their constitution and rules, they borrow legal concepts from a legal doctrine which is linked to state law. As a corollary, they will also have to take account of fundamental rules and principles of the state legal system(s) in the territory in which they operate, and they will have to comply with basic rights as

---

12 The legal position as non-state of the South-African 'thuisland' – 'states', under the Apartheid regime is a good example; being officially recognised by the white South-African government only, these 'states' failed to function as a state. They actually remained some decentralized regions within the South African state, but were not real state legal systems on their own.

laid down in international treaties, such as the European Convention on Human Rights, which are enforceable within that same territory.

There is not only an inter-relationship between legal systems as regards their very existence and content, but a community of legal language, style, argumentation, in short of legal discourse, runs parallel with the development of legal doctrine and of the communication amongst legal systems and amongst lawyers in general. This, sometimes very strong community, as, for example with continental European state legal systems, in its turn weakens the autonomy of legal systems towards each other. Language, style and argumentation are not just a matter of form, they hide concepts and world views. For example, distinguishing between '*dominium*', '*possessio*' and '*detentio*' creates another kind of legal reality as regards ownership than when other concepts are used.[13] The kinds of arguments accepted in legal reasoning partly determine the outcome. Based on the same legal rules, the interpretation, and thus the application, of the law may be completely different depending on the acceptability of, for example a reference to legislative materials, to societal needs, to changed views in society, to a presumed rationality of the legislator, etc. In comparative law, it appears that related legal systems sometimes have different rules but similar judicial decisions when the rules are applied to concrete cases. In the first place, this shows to what extent the content of the law is determined through interpretation. Secondly, it proves the importance of a common ideology, based on similar societal circumstances, which, almost imperceptibly, penetrates into law through a common language, style and argumentation. Again, 'legal discourse' is the most appropriate term for denoting the whole of legal language and reasoning as embedded in its broad non-legal context. A common legal discourse thus has a decisive influence on the content of the law, on the meaning given to the law in its adjudication.

If we take, for instance, the civil law discourses in Belgium, France, Italy and Spain, they will have much more in common with each other, than they have with for example labour law, penal law or tax law within their own legal systems. This does not only show the important degree of communality of legal discourses amongst legal systems, it also points to another element which is important for our analysis: the rather limited unity of legal systems. This will not as such be discussed here. It will suffice to state that different branches of the law should probably be considered to be 'autopoietic systems' on their own, or at least, relatively autonomous 'auto-productive' systems. It is obvious, that there is more 'autonomy' of, for example environmental law *vis-à-vis* commercial law within one individual

---

13   An example of the importance of common language for the content of the law is offered by a few legal concepts, such as e.g. 'rechtsverwerking' (a specific kind of forfeiture right), developed in Dutch legal doctrine and taken on board by doctrine and by courts in the Dutch speaking part of Belgium. In the French speaking part of this country, this new concept has not been successful, because it proved not to have an appropriate translation in French.

legal system than there is between these branches of law within their own legal systems, on one hand, and the same branches in related legal systems, or in Europe where these fields are subject to regulation by the European Union, on the other. Where then lies the 'operative closure' of legal systems?

Ultimately, very little is left of the autonomy of legal systems towards each other: They have a circular interdependence; they have a common legal language, style and argumentation; they borrow rules and concepts from each other. They need to do this in order to strengthen their autonomy towards, for example moral, political or economic discourse (or systems). But, in so doing , they have to rely on each other and they lose their autonomy towards other legal systems. As a conclusion, we have to state that legal systems are not autonomous *vis-à-vis* each other. They may maintain autonomy towards some legal systems with which they do not have any links at all, but they will never be autonomous towards all, or even a majority of legal systems.[14]

b) Autonomy vis-à-vis other societal systems

In jurisprudence, the autonomy of legal systems with respect to other societal systems has mainly been discussed with regard to the relation between law and morals. But the influence exerted on law is much broader than that. Some societal systems are normative systems, notably morals, religion, etiquette, customs, usages, ideology. The important social norms will, in every community, be institutionalized through law. In a way, law is an institutionalized manifestation of all kinds of social norms. The law is used to give greater strength, greater authority and greater efficacy to such social norms.

Other societal systems, such as the economy, politics, the arts, sports, information (media), etc., are not normative. However, they offer factual elements which, often in relation with other social norms, lead to social and, eventually, legal norms. Economical data and insights may, together with principles of justice and equality, lead to the development of rules of labour law and social security law. To a certain extent, these non-legal discourses generate their own basic norms: e.g. the efficacy rule in economic discourse, the 'right of information' in media discourse, the majority rule in political discourse, etc. Such implicit or explicit normative positions inevitably influence the content of law.

Law is only one of many societal systems. In order to function within the society it regulates, law should fit with the other societal systems. A legal system cannot function if it does not observe basic principles of economics, politics, morals, etc. If

---

14 A 'contact', and thus at least some loss of autonomy, follows as soon as there is some territorial or personal overlap of legal systems. E.g. the territorial overlap in Europe between sub-state law, state law, European law and international law, or the personal overlap between canon law and state law.

a legal system really becomes 'autonomous' and produces rules which undermine the economic system or the political system or the predominant moral system, it will not last for long.[15] An autonomous production of legal rules is also limited from this point of view. According to the autopoietic theory, legal systems select and adapt the information coming from the outside according to their own systemic criteria. This proves to be only partly true. The selection and adaptation are also, to a certain extent, determined by the other societal systems. Eventually, it is only the technical, legal form which is completely decided autonomously by the legal system.

The same is true for another obvious link between legal systems and other societal systems: the use of *'vague concepts'* in law. When using, in the drafting of legal rules, concepts like 'fairness', 'reasonableness', 'equity',[16] 'abuse', 'torts', etc., the law implicitly refers to non-legal normative systems to substantiate the vague concept so as to fill in the actual norm a judge will or would apply to the case. Herein lies a well known link between legal systems and other societal systems, especially morals. Of course, the law still dictates when and under what conditions those social and moral rules may be brought into the legal system, but the content of the rules is left completely open. The use of vague concepts cannot be explained on the basis of some laziness or lack of competence in legislative drafting. It is a structural linkage between law and other normative systems, which aims at avoiding, both, pure gaps in law and over-regulation. In the context of great codifications in 19th century Europe and of the rise of the welfare state, legislators have often thought that it was possible and desirable to regulate as much as possible through general legislation and leave as little room as possible for individual decisions by civil officers and judges when applying the law. Meanwhile, we know the limits and disadvantages of such a top-down approach: it is not possible to foresee everything nor to adapt every Act each time a change in society would make it appropriate. Moreover, where there was a deep distrust of judges at the time of those codifications, judges, today, are sometimes considered to be the cornerstone of legal systems, whereas there is greater distrust of legislators. As a result, legislation today will more often use vague concepts, thus delegating to courts the power to 'select and adopt' moral or other social rules and to 'change' and 'translate' them into legal rules. Most prominently, this has been the case in the Dutch Civil Code of

---

15   An example of legal systems undermining the economic system is the Eastern European countries between World War II and the early 1990s. An example of a legal system, which was not observing basic rules of an acceptable, democratic political system, was the South African legal system under Apartheid. An example of an immoral legal system was Nazi Germany. Notwithstanding a strong military power which was backing these legal systems, none of them was able to last for more than a few decades.

16   In the broad sense, not in the technical sense of the common law history and the present day English legal system.

1992, where the rules very often simply refer to 'reasonableness and equity'.[17] In a way, one could present this as a 'trick' by which all social rules may become legal rules when the legal system needs them. There are no more non-legal rules: all social rules in the community are potentially legal rules; courts are explicitly empowered to label them 'legal' whenever they need them. It is a method, and an efficacious method, of closing a legal system, but at the price of a loss of autonomy. Not only is the content of the rules completely determined by other normative systems, but it becomes impossible for the legal system to control, and keep under control, the impact of other societal systems on that legal system.

The last, and most important, way in which legal systems lack autonomy vis-à-vis other societal systems is with the *interpretation* of law, which follows inevitably from adjudication. Statutory interpretation will not be discussed here. It may suffice to observe the influence of interpretation on the eventual meaning with which law is applied, and the influence of ideology on this interpretation. Bernd Rüthers, for example, has shown to what extent German law, enacted before 1933, has been perverted through an interpretation guided by national-socialist ideology.[18] But such a dramatic influence of ideology on law through judicial interpretation is not limited to such extreme political circumstances. A well known, and more sympathetic example is the concept of 'abuse of right', introduced into the legal systems by courts and legal doctrine. It not only refers to moral rules, but also limits the scope of explicitly enacted legal rules on purely moral grounds. Moreover, no secondary rule of the legal systems in question empowered the courts to limit the scope of legal rules by introducing and using such a concept. As human beings, lawyers, and more specifically judges, are not just part of the legal system, they also belong to other societal systems. Sometimes, they change their roles and change their discourse, moving into, for example a moral discourse. When combining their roles, they smuggle this moral, or other, discourse into the legal system, and suddenly it is a moral system which is determining what the law is, and not the legal system. The concept of 'abuse of right' indeed operates to render that which is 'legal' according to the legal system 'illegal' on purely moral grounds.

Autopoietic theory accepts that such role-interferences may occur, and that they are even necessary to make intersystemic communication possible.[19] This communication is considered possible because people 'speak the "languages" of various subsystems'.[20] But this role-interference and multilinguism may work in two different directions. A judge may act as part of the legal system when selecting non-

---

17 To such an extent that the Code has been severely criticised for its vagueness and lack of 'legal certainty'.

18 Bernd Rüthers, *Die unbegrenzte Auslegung* (Tübingen: J.C.B.Mohr, 1968).

19 Günther Teubner, *Law as an Autopoietic System, supra* n. 1, 99.

20 Renate Mayntz, '*Politische Steuerung und gesellschaftliche Steuerungsprobleme: Anmerkung zu einen theoretischen Paradigma*', 1 JAHRBUCH FUR STAATS- UND VERWALTUNGSWISSENSCHAFT, 1987, 89-110 (102).

legal values, norms or other data, but he might also use his position as a judge to introduce such non-legal elements *from a non-legal point of view*. He can switch to, for example a moral discourse, or an economic discourse and just adapt it technically to the extent necessary in order to enable him to label the outcome as 'legal'. The concept of 'abuse of right' is a typical example of a moral discourse introduced into the legal system and partly *replacing legal discourse*. The legal system has lost control over its content. Other societal systems have broken into the legal system and are changing its function. However, the autopoietic legal system is blind, it does not see what is happening and simply continues labelling as 'legal' whatever the judges call 'legal', just like a machine putting wine labels on every passing bottle which has the format of a wine bottle, regardless of its content. Limiting law to the structural features of legal systems in order to prove its 'autonomy' is comparable to limiting oneself to the analysis of the operation of such a labelling machine when analyzing wine and its role in society. Broadening the analysis to the content of the law, on the other hand, makes it impossible to maintain that a legal system is autonomous *vis-à-vis* other systems.

c)   *Autonomy of primary and of secondary rules*

It follows from the autopoietic theory of law, that legal systems should be considered open at the level of primary rules and closed at the level of their secondary rules. There can be no doubting that the primary rules of conduct produced by a legal system are to a (very) large extent influenced by or even borrowed from other societal systems or discourses. There is also a general agreement with the conclusion that, even when rules are borrowed from other normative systems, they are subject to some face-lift or technical adaptation in order for them to fit into legal discourse.

Secondary legal rules, however, seem to be purely legal. They organize structures and procedures through which law may be produced, including both the making and adjudication of the law. At this level, legal systems should be able to maintain their autonomy, not only with regard to form, but also with respect to the content of the rules. Unfortunately, even this is not the case. Some of the main secondary rules of a legal system are those which determine the 'sources' of the law. From several of the examples given earlier, it appeared that external influences on the legal system even altered these sources in a manner which was not regulated by the secondary rules of the system. When judges accepted international law as a source of domestic law, having even a priority over incompatible rules of the national legal system, they introduced a new source of law and a new hierarchy within these sources, without any 'secondary rule' empowering them to do so.

The same holds through for the acceptance and use of 'unwritten legal principles' as an independent source of law. The introduction of such principles has been completely determined by ideological asumptions which were not part of the legal system. The general principle of 'good faith' for example, has been introduced in several European countries by broadening considerably the scope of a rule which imposes the obligation 'to execute a contract in accordance with good faith'.[21] Even if the concept of 'good faith' could be found in one of the rules embodied in these legal systems, the idea that it could and should have an overall application in law is clearly an ideological choice, by which greater weight is assigned to a moral value than the legal system previously gave. In other cases, the moral value could not be found to be assimilated anywhere by the legal system. The most striking example is the previously discussed general principle which prohibits the 'abuse' of a right: moral values are introduced as a new source of law, limiting the scope of legal rules as produced by the legal system. This not only affects the content of the primary rules, but also considerably changes the secondary rules: a new source of law is introduced by the judiciary, notwithstanding the absence of secondary rules in the legal system empowering them to do so.

There is yet another way in which elements of the content of law co-determine the structures and procedures by which the legal system is institutionalized. The emergence of procedural rights has strongly influenced these institutions. The case law of the European Court of Human Rights, especially, has considerably changed the structures and proceedings of the national legal systems, which have had to adapt to principles such as the right of defence, the right to be judged by an independent and impartial judge, or the right to be judged within a reasonable time (art. 6 E.C.H.R.). This proves that structures and procedures are not value-free, that they cannot be created arbitrarily and completely autonomously by legal systems; non-legal values co-determine the content of these secondary rules.

If values from outside the legal system are able not only to occasionally influence the content of primary rules of conduct, but also to become an institutionalized source of law on their own, by changing the secondary rules which organize law-making, then it becomes clear that legal systems are not completely autonomous, even at the level of secondary rules. With the external world affecting not only the content of the rules produced by the legal system, but also the machinery as such, a legal system can hardly be called 'autopoietic'. Legal systems do not completely control and determine their input, nor even the channels through which an input is made possible.

III. Conclusion

What conclusions may be drawn from the above analysis as regards state organization and public governance ?

---

21   See for further details: M. Van Hoecke, '*The Use of Unwritten Legal Principles by Courts*', RATIO JURIS (1995), 248-260.

The first conclusion is that legal pluralism seems to be an inevitable result of legal development, both in Europe and on a world scale. A stronger 'juridification' of our societies has led to an increased autonomy of law, but at the price of an increased interdependence of legal systems. This is most visible in Europe, with an ever increasing intertwinement of state legal systems with one another, with European legal orders and even with non-state legal systems. A most interesting example of the degree of intertwinement is the current discussion on the adherence of the European Union (with 15 Member States) to the European Convention on Human Rights (of the Council of Europe, with 40 Member States), which would mean the structural linking together of the two European legal orders themselves and not only with their Member States.

The second conclusion is that the linear, hierarchical relationship between the making of the law and its adjudication, between the legislator and the judge, has been replaced by a circular relationship, through which those legal institutions mutually legitimate each other. Legitimation has shifted from a formal deduction of a rule or decision from some previous norm to a constant deliberation and argumentation on the acceptability and validity of a rule or decision within the framework of other legal principles, rules and decisions. A rather formal approach to democracy, in which a rule or decision is considered valid if it can be deducted from a rule, accepted by a majority in a democratically elected parliamentary body, is gradually being replaced by a more substantive approach, in which fundamental values and principles of a democratic society become more important than a sheer majority decision of a democratically elected body. However, the approach remains formal to the extent that specific legal institutions, such as constitutional courts, have the final word in this discussion: they have the ultimate power to decide about the content of the law and, by doing so, to legitimate or to invalidate rules enacted by legislative bodies.

The third conclusion is that the combination of the developments referred to in the two previous conclusions considerably increases the intersystemic interdependence of legal systems and weakens the control of one single legal system over its own components: European courts have the power to annul state legislation; new legal principles and concepts, introduced in domestic law through European Directives, influence court decisions in adjacent areas, which, strictly speaking, do not fall under the scope of that European regulation; and so on.

The fourth conclusion is that all this leads to a strengthening of the role of *legal doctrine*.

Firstly, it is to a large extent within legal doctrine that the debate on the acceptance and validity of a rule, principle, judicial decision, or of its interpretation, is carried out. This is the main forum for deliberative democracy amongst lawyers.

Secondly, in a system in which there is no final authority, at the top of some hierarchy, the generalized actual acceptance of institutions and of their decisions becomes the ultimate touchstone. This generalized acceptance is to a large extent an acceptance by the *legal profession*, and, as 'experts', the community of lawyers will strongly influence the acceptance in society at large.

Thirdly, the somewhat chaotic structure law has in this intricate intersystemic plurality of legal orders, demands a rational structuring of all those data into one coherent whole. This is the task of legal doctrine. Moreover, it should be clear that the magnitude of that legal intersystematicity makes it less and less feasible to grasp the law and to create a coherence at the level of the (European) nation states. This can only be achieved at a higher level, which may encompass the totality of the intersystemic relationships, which co-determine the content and the legitimation of each of the legal systems. Legal doctrine, in Europe, may only master this legal complexity if it becomes a *European* legal doctrine.[22]

The fifth conclusion is the loss of autonomy of the different branches of law. We have seen, in the course of the last one or two centuries, a proliferation of branches of law, which gained more and more autonomy *vis-à-vis* the one from which they developed, such as labour law as a spin-off from civil law. Without affecting the existence of such relatively autonomous areas of law, the current developments show an increasing intertwinement of different branches of law: consumer law is strongly affecting both traditional contract law and commercial law;[23] European human rights law is affecting all areas of domestic law, and most notably criminal law, procedural law and family law; EU law is affecting social security law and labour regulation,[24] and, in fact, the whole European construction leads to an intertwinement of international private law, international public (European) law, national private and public law, and comparative law. Increasing fragmentation of law is thus coupled with an enhanced intertwinement of the different areas of law.

22   For a more thorough discussion on the desirability of a European legal doctrine, see: M. Van Hoecke and F. Ost, '*Legal Doctrine in Crisis: Towards a European Legal Science*', 18 LEGAL STUDIES (1998), 197-215.

23   A strong protection of the consumer, imposed through European Directives, has run through and turned over the traditional relationships in contract law, such as vendor-buyer, or landlord-tenant.

24   In a preliminary opinion, the European Court of Justice decided that some specific obligations imposed on employers in Belgium (such as the obligation for the employer to pay contributions for loss of working days because of weather circumstances, or the obligation to draft and to keep very specific documents related to labour contracts) are unacceptable obstacles for foreign European companies offering their services on the Belgian market (ECJ 23 November 1999, cases nr. c-369/96 and C-376/96 penal cases against Arblade and Leloup – unpublished).

PART IV

THE NEW FORMS
OF WAR
IN A GLOBAL SOCIETY

Chapter 9

On Globalization:
The Military Dimension

Martin van Creveld[*]

When people talk of globalization, the aspects they have in mind are mostly technological, informational and financial. Of the three technologies, mainly that which is involved in transportation, communication, and data processing, is supposed to have created a situation in which no state can afford to be cut off from its neighbours except at intolerable cost (as illustrated, most recently, by North Korea). Carried by technologies such as satellite TV and the Internet, the flow of information has become global and has long escaped any attempts by governments to control it. Carried by technology, too, mighty flows of capital go wherever the prospect of gain is greatest, crossing national boundaries and behaving as if they did not exist. All three factors are seen as rapidly undermining the territorial state as traditionally understood; all three are seen to work in favour of organizations that are either larger or smaller than states.[1] By contrast, this chapter will explore a dimension of globalization that is only very seldom mentioned, namely its impact on war and the military.

To accomplish its purpose, the chapter is divided into four parts. Part I consists of a brief introduction to the period before the French Revolution when, in the frequent absence of a strong bond between states and their peoples, much of military life bore a markedly international character. Part II, which is almost equally brief, will explain how the period after 1789 saw the rise of nationalism in the military field, as indeed it did in any other; ending in 1939-1945 which represented both the culminating-point of the process and the beginning of a change. Part III, which introduces the main argument, examines the impact of globalization on armed forces and war since 1945. Part IV represents our conclusions.

*   I would like to thank Sean Smith for his helpful comments on this chapter.
1   See most recently M. van Creveld, *The Rise and Decline of the State* (Cambridge: Cambridge University Press, 1999), Part 6.

I.   The Invention of the Sovereign State

The modern state is a relatively new invention. To be sure, its antecedents may already be seen in the French, English and Spanish monarchies of the 15th and 16th centuries. Still, it was only towards the end of that period that government and ownership definitely separated, leading to the invention of 'politics' (and of political science). It was only towards the end of that period that the personality of the leader came to be clearly distinguished from the machinery of government, leading to the invention of the 'abstract' state. It was only towards the end of that period that the term 'sovereignty' came into vogue, forming an attribute that was possessed by states and states alone. All three developments reflected, and were reflected in, the Treaty of Westphalia which was signed in 1648 and which for the first time did away with most of the old feudal dependencies as well as the idea of a transnational empire.

At a time when states were only beginning to monopolize the right to make war, warfare bore a strong international character. For example, early in the 16th century almost every army included regiments of Swiss mercenaries (who, to make things worse, often switched form one employer to another in the midst of a campaign or battle). In spite of its name, the Spanish 'Army of Flanders' that sought to put down the Dutch Revolt during the second half of the 16th century was made up largely of Italians, Germans and Walloons.[2] Two of its best-known commanders in chief, Alessandro Farnese and Ambrosio Spinola, were Italian princes working for Philip II; a third one was John of Austria whose title speaks for itself. The Dutch Army that fought the 'Spaniards' was no different, commanded as it was by princes whose principal languages were French and German and recruiting its troops from all over Europe. At various times during the Thirty Years War as many as 80 per cent of those who served in Gustavus Adolphus' 'Swedish' army were actually German mercenaries.[3] Richelieu in his *Political Testament* considered it impossible to wage war solely with the aid of national troops.[4] All this shows not just that war was often made by foreigners, but that the very idea of foreign versus national did not carry the same significance as it does today.

Nor did the crystallization of states from the middle of the 17th century on cause the international character of war to disappear at a stroke. During the War of the Spanish Succession (1702-12) the Austrian commander-in-chief was a member of the ruling house of Savoy who, before embarking on his spectacular career in the

---

2   See G. Parker, *The Army of Flanders and the Spanish Road* (Cambridge: Cambridge University Press, 1972), Chapters 1-3.

3   On the social origins of soldiers in this period see C. Duffy, *The Thirty Years War* (London: Routledge, 1984), 194-97.

4   Quoted in G. Parker, *The Military Revolution* (Cambridge: Cambridge University Press, 1988), 42.

Habsburg Army, had offered his services to Louis XIV. During the War of the Austrian Succession (1740-48) the French commander-in-chief was Maurice of Saxe, an illegitimate son of the Elector of Saxony who also became King of Poland; at one point during this war, Frenchmen commanded both the forces besieging Prague and those defending it. During the Seven Years War (1756-63) the Hanoverian Army was made up of German mercenaries, commanded by a Duke of Brunswick, and paid for by England. During the same war Frederick the Great claimed that he preferred foreign soldiers to his native Prussians, the reason being that each one of the former represented a gain for him, a loss for the enemy, and one more Prussian to pay taxes. Frederick's actions were as good as his word. At any one time approximately a third of his forces consisted of foreigners, recruited from places as far away as Italy; he once forcibly incorporated an entire Saxon Army into his own.[5] Later during the century the British relied on German mercenaries against the American colonists. Not to be outdone, their French opponents employed regiments made up of Scotsmen and of Welsh.

Another aspect of the situation in which soldiering was considered an international occupation was the training of officers. When the first officer training schools opened their doors during the first half of the 17th century they were private establishments attached to commanders' staffs. Accordingly, they offered instruction to applicants regardless of nationality. By the later 18th century this situation had changed to the extent that each of the leading countries now had its own academy. Yet some officers continued to be trained in private institutions maintained by German princes in particular; after which they would go to wherever opportunity and fortune might take them. It remained possible for officers to transfer from one service to another, as the Swiss-born Jomini did for example when he joined the French Army and as Gerhard von Scharnhorst did when he exchanged a Hannoverian commission for a Prussian one; even as late as the 1820s it was possible for the young Moltke to change from the Danish service to the Prussian one. Conversely, when exceptional loyalty was required of certain units they were often made up of foreign personnel. When the mob stormed the Tuilleries in 1791, the troops who tried to stop it were not French but Swiss.

II.   The Rise of Patriotism and the Changed Role of the Army

The French Revolution both reflected growing national feeling and promoted it with every means available to the state. Patriotism – which Voltaire had defined as the scoundrel's last refuge – became the most important virtue of all. As part of the process, the *levee en masse* replaced standing forces. Armed forces lost their

---

5   On the international character of armies in this period see C. Duffy, *The Military Experience in the Age of Reason* (London: Routledge, 1987), 90-2.

mercenary character, at least in theory and at least to the extent that it became harder and harder to transfer from one service to the next. From now on commanders and troops were supposed to fight and sacrifice themselves because *la patrie* was in danger.

In the case of the French army itself, a regression took place under Napoleon. On the one hand, in his quest for ever-growing quantities of cannon fodder nobody trumpeted the virtues of French nationalism more vigorously than did the Emperor. On the other, the more countries he incorporated into the Empire and the more allies he gathered around him (e.g. the Kingdom of Italy, the Confederation of the Rhine, and similar short-lived political constructs), the more international the character of the army he commanded. By 1812, only about half of the troops who accompanied Napoleon to Russia were French; the rest were a miscellaneous lot of Dutch, Germans and Italians. Since they did not speak French, normally these troops served in separate units under their own commanders; at the Battle of Borodino Marshal Murat is said to have addressed his German troops with the words '*scheuss Jaeger, scheuss*'. Such heterogeneity was not without a price. Compared to the great days of 1800-1806 in particular, the *Grande Armee* was probably no longer as cohesive as it had been.

With Napoleon's enemies the direction in which development proceeded was exactly the opposite. These belligerents had entered the wars with their old, standing armies. As a result, their officer corps in particular was by no means always immune to the more universal ideals of the French revolution. As those countries began experiencing the reality of French conquest and occupation, however, their mood changed. Nationalism became the rallying cry under which they sought to liberate themselves. The change is best exemplified by Prussia where Fichte and Arendt became the prophets of a new, virulent form of nationalism under whose terms of reference anyone who so much as taught his daughter French was almost as guilty as if he had sold her to prostitution. The Prussian army, which Napoleon defeated at Jena in 1806, fought because it obeyed its orders. The one he encountered at Leipzig in 1813 was more nationally minded than any previous one in German history; the same was even truer for the Landswehr, which backed it up.[6] In Russia, too, the Napoleonic Wars helped imbue the army with a new, nationalist, spirit,[7] whereas in Italy those wars opened the door towards the national unification that was to follow.

With Napoleon and his Empire gone, the French army re-joined the general trend from 1815 on. To be sure, the details differed from one country to the next and also according to the exact period in question. Some governments felt they could trust their own people more than others did; other things being equal, the more they did so the greater their inclination, and ability, to call on nationalism as the

---

6   H. Koch, *Die Befreiugnskriege* 1807-1815 (Berg: Tuermer, 1987), 194-97.

7   On the Russian Army during this period see J. Gooch, *Armies in Europe* (London: Routledge, 1980), 69-70.

underpinning for their armed forces. Thus, from 1830 on, the only non-French component left in the French Army was the Foreign Legion, a *sui generis* organization that was deliberately kept isolated from the rest and intended solely for overseas operations.[8] By the middle of the century, the only non-British personnel left in the British Navy were the invisible Chinamen who lived in the nooks and crannies of warships and whose job was to launder and press the officers' uniforms. From 1864 on, the growing identification between the population of each state and its armed forces even began to be written into international law. The employment of mercenaries was prohibited, and so was the issuing of letters of marque. After 1870 a situation in which one's troops could be put under the command of foreign officers and where even the commander-in-chief – might not be a native had become inconceivable. As more and more countries followed the Prussian example and switched their armed forces to general conscription and reserve service, the link between people and the military was reinforced.

By 1914 in countries such as Germany, France and Italy, things had come to the point where the armed forces themselves were regarded as the greatest national institutions of all; in Britain, the Navy played a similar role. No national occasion, no official celebration, was complete without the presence of these forces, a point that was brought home even more strongly by heads of state preferring to wear uniform whenever the opportunity presented itself. In turn, the forces themselves considered themselves the repositories of patriotism. This gave them the moral right to act as 'the schools of the nation', as the saying went; their mission, apart from making war, was to forge together people from different regions and classes and imbue them with the national spirit. Nor was the close identification between nation and armed forces without its dark side. As many socialists learnt to their cost, and as the Dreyfuss affair in particular demonstrated all too clearly, to criticize those forces was *ipso facto* unpatriotic.

World War I, which soon followed, was to a large extent an outcome of these beliefs and reflected them. The war consisted of multiple clashes between mighty nation states (the only important exception, Austria Hungary, was weak for that very reason; after 1918, it disappeared). Each of those states had its regular armed forces commanded by, and made up of, its own nationals. What departures from this principle existed (in the form of the various 'Legions') were minor. They comprised perhaps a few thousand men in forces whose numbers were now counted in the million and soon disbanded after the war was over; certainly there could be no question of heads of state trusting their own security to them, as previously. Above all, each of those states claimed to represent a civilization that was unique and precious, worthy of preserving at all cost.

---

8   On the establishment of the Foreign Legion see most recently P. Montagnon, *Histoire de la legion* (Paris: Pygmalion, 1999), Chapter 1.

It is true that, even at a time when their power reached its all time high, most of the states in question were not above forming alliances with others if it suited them. However, as Lord Salisbury's dictum concerning England having neither eternal friends nor eternal enemies but only eternal interests shows, all those alliances were explicitly temporary in character. They were expected to dissolve after the conflict's end, and most did. So long as they lasted they consisted of simple partnerships; no two countries in World War I ever formed, or tried to form, a common machinery for waging war. It was only the desperate days of spring 1918 that finally compelled the leaders of the Entente to unify their forces to the extent of putting them under a single *generalissimo*, the French Marshal Foch, and even then this only applied to those parts of the forces used on the Western Front. Like the Entente itself, moreover, the arrangement was intended to be purely temporary. No sooner had the war ended than the armies concerned once again went their separate ways.

At the time it broke out, World War II looked very much like a repetition of World War I. Once again, it was a question of mighty nation states using their regular armies to fight each other for dominance and survival. Once again, some of these states had formed or were to form formal alliances with each other. Still, even those of them that considered themselves close allies – such as Britain and France – did not create a common machinery for conducting the war; let alone relinquish the precious sovereignty in whose name, after all, they had entered the fray. Some of the belligerents, notably Japan and the USSR, persisted in this attitude right down to the end of the conflict. Whether for ideological reasons or for geographical ones, they fought, triumphed, and went down to defeat in an isolation that was becoming less and less splendid.

For the remaining belligerents, things began to change during the war itself. The first governments that, willy-nilly, put their armed forces under the command of others were the exiled ones of Poland, Norway, the Netherlands and France. On the Axis side, the arrival of German forces in the North African Theatre of Operations led to the establishment of a more or less unified command organization. Under its terms the German General Rommel commanded both German and Italian divisions. Since the Mediterranean was, in principle, an Italian Theatre of War he in turn came under the control of an Italian officer, although in practice that control tended to be nominal. By way of a reciprocal arrangement, the Italian troops in Russia were put under German command. So were Slovak, Hungarian, Romanian and Spanish ones (the 'Blue Division').

To put the forces of one country under the command of another for the purpose of a specific theatre or campaign is one thing. To create an integrated command structure consisting of officers from two or more countries is entirely different. During World War II, an experiment in what was later to be called Combined Command (the very term had yet to be invented) was made in the form of SHAEF (Supreme Headquarters Allied Expeditionary Force). Established in 1942 in order to take charge of the invasion of North Africa, SHAEF was a truly international organization. Though completely dominated by the Americans and, to a lesser extent, the British, it exercised command over forces belonging to many nations. Perhaps the idea behind it was best expressed by a saying attributed to its head, General Dwight Eisenhower. He did not, he quipped, mind anybody on his staff calling anybody else a son of a bitch. What he could not and would not tolerate was anybody calling anybody else a *British* son of a bitch; or, presumably, *vice versa.*

Though SHAEF could not prevent the generals in the command structure from quarrelling with each other, on the whole the experiment was a huge success. This success could not save it from being dismantled almost as soon as the war was over; the tradition whereby one state equalled one army remained strong. It was only with the establishment of NATO four years later that the decisive break was made. Unlike any of its predecessors NATO was meant to be permanent. However much it might be dominated by the United States as the strongest member by far, as a permanent organization it was made up of officers and officials from various different Member States. Above all, NATO was not simply a partnership between nominal equals. Rather it was and remains a corporate entity with its own legal *persona* and its own secretary-general responsible for running its day-to-day affairs; it even had its own headquarters where individual members were represented by envoys carrying ambassadorial rank. In all these respects, it did not differ from the Member States themselves.

The establishment of NATO was soon followed by that of the Warsaw Pact.[9] Like NATO, it was intended to be a permanent organization with its own corporate identity as well as a supreme command (created 1956) and a military council (created 1969). Much less than NATO it was an equal partnership, being dominated by a single power that pulled all the strings. So long as the organization lasted, that dominance was not without its advantages. In point of doctrine, training, infrastructure, equipment, and presumably planning it enabled the Warsaw Pact to achieve a degree of integration greater than anything achieved by its Western counterpart.[10] NATO members often quarrelled with each other, and some would say that they never succeeded in cobbling together a coherent strategy of any kind. By contrast, leaders of Warsaw Pact countries who dared to present serious opposition to Moscow were not likely to remain leaders for long. In its own way the organization resembled NATO, reflecting the idea that war had become too important to be left to individual states. In 1968 it actually mounted a military invasion, albeit that the target was not NATO but one of its own members that had strayed from the true socialist path.

---

9   See A. Uschakow and D. Frenzke, *Der Warschauer Pakt und seine bilaterale Buendnissbertraege* (Berlin: Spitz, 1987), particularly 33-62.

10 See W. J. Lewis, *The Warsaw Pact: Arms, Doctrine and Strategy* (ed.), (New York: McGraw-Hill, 1982), Chapters 1 and 3.

As of this writing, the Warsaw Pact lies in ruins. To the surprise of many, however, NATO has survived the end of the Cold War and even expanded to include three new members. In Kosovo in 1999 it was actually able to do something for the first time ever – just in time to celebrate its fiftieth birthday. In so far as NATO includes all the most important industrial states except one (Japan), it has created a situation whereby many of the world's most powerful armed forces are now under a single command; not only that, but the exorbitant cost of modern weapon systems is increasingly forcing them to pool their resources in R&D as well as production. Thus, the 1970s saw the birth of the Franco-German Milan anti-tank missile as well as the Anglo-French-Spanish Tornado fighter-bomber project. The 1980s saw the French and the Germans co-operating to build a new attack helicopter whereas the Tornado was due to be replaced by the Eurofighter (assuming it ever flies). These facts only form the tip of an iceberg whose very existence often goes unnoticed. In 1994, in response to a survey, 54 per cent out of 800 participating European defence firms representing 70 per cent of all defence production declared they had programmes in common with other firms outside their own countries. 23 per cent had fused with such firms by buying their shares or being bought by them, and another 23 per cent had set up common branches with them.[11]

Not only military R&D, but also the armed forces of the European members of NATO are becoming more and more integrated. France and Germany have set up an army corps in common, to which most of the Belgian Army and parts of the Spanish Army are also affiliated. Most Dutch armed forces have become an extension of the Bundeswehr, and those that have not are participating in a common Dutch-British formation. Only a minority of German troops, i.e. the fourth corps at Potsdam, are still completely under national command; and, for them, integration with Czech and Polish units is being planned.[12] Unable to find enough room inside their own territories, the troops of several European countries routinely train in Canada. Not to be outdone, the Singapore Air Force is training in Australia and the Israeli one in Turkey. In this way, the situation created by the French Revolution has been turned upside down. At that time, the more powerful a state the more it insisted on the independence of its armed forces and the more it went its own way, militarily. Now, up to a certain point, the reverse obtains.

11   See J. L. Scaringella, *Les Industries de Defense en Europe* (Paris: Economica, 1998), 140-41.

12   For these arrangements see P. Klein, 'Vers des Armees Postnationales?' in B. Boenne and Christopher Dandekder (eds.), *Les armees en Europe* (Paris: la Decouverte, 1998), 163; M. J. Inacker, 'Letztes nationales Korps wird aufgeloest', *Welt am Sonntag* (9 February 1997), 4.

III. The Change of the Status of War in Modernity

In the meantime, the status of war itself has undergone a change. From the moment when the French jurist and political scientist Jean Bodin popularized the idea of sovereignty in the 1580s, the right to make war (and peace) has always been a fundamental part of it.[13] Without a higher court that would adjudicate on differences between them, war was regarded as the normal way for states to settle accounts among themselves. From the time Hugo Grotius in *Jure Belli ac Pacis* did away with the idea of just war,[14] neither legal nor moral blame could be attached to them for doing so.

The normal objective for which states went to war was to extend or defend their territory. Over the years, this led to countless occasions when territory changed hands. Thus the early wars of Louis XIV led to the occupation by France of Alsace and Lorraine. The War of the Spanish Succession caused Austria to take the place of Spain in Italy and the southern Netherlands. The War of the Austrian Succession ended by Austria signing away the province of Silesia in favour of Prussia. The Seven Years War, the French Revolutionary and Napoleonic Wars, all led to important territorial adjustments. The same was still true during the wars of the middle of the 19th century in which some states (notably Denmark and Austria) lost territories whereas others (notably France, Italy, and Prussia) gained it. War was considered a game played by states in which the prize was land. If, as sometimes happened, no land passed from hand to hand, the war was said to have been 'in vain' or 'indecisive'.

The Franco-Prussian War of 1870-71 represented both the culmination of this idea and the first indications that it was about to change. On the face of it the conflict was a 'Cabinet War' like all others, fought for limited stakes (at no time was there any question of eliminating either of the belligerents) consisting mainly of land. Like previous conflicts, it was ended by a formal peace treaty by which one state took over land and another renounced it. Not long after the end of hostilities, though, it turned out that the rules of the game had changed. On the French side, the nation simply refused to recognize the act of their government as final; instead, regarding the transfer of Alsace and Lorraine as a moral wrong, it nourished *la revanche* and devoted untold effort to prepare for it. Meanwhile, the German side also recognized that Alsace and Lorraine did not form German land in the same sense that other *Laender* constituting the Empire did. Consequently the two provinces were never allowed to form governments of their own; instead they were ruled directly from Berlin in a kind of permanent state of emergency brought about by the war itself. Thus, whatever the peace treaty might say, the newly annexed

---

13   J. Bodin, *The True Attributes of Sovereignty*, Chapter X, in M. J. Tooley (ed.), *Six Books of the Commonwealth* (Oxford: Blackwell, 1967), 40-9.

14   H. Grotius, *de Jure Belli ac Pacis* (Amsterdam, Jansunium, 1632), 2, 23, 13; 1, 3, 1.

territory was neither renounced by those who counted (the French people) nor fully integrated by its new owners.

If the war of 1870-71 for the first time cast doubt on the right of states to use force as a means for transferring territory, World War I went some way towards the delegitimization of inter-state war itself. As previously remarked, the 17th century had done away with the idea of just war, declaring war so long as it was waged by sovereign states to be just on both sides. At Versailles in 1919 that idea was revived, the victors choosing to put the blame for the conflict squarely on the shoulders of the losers. Used as the justification for the remaining provisions of the Treaty – loss of territory, disarmament, the payment of reparations – the 'war guilt' clause was rightly regarded as a new departure in international relations – so radical, indeed, that the German people proved unable to live with it. As Hitler was one day to put it, the Treaty was the most shameful one to be imposed on any people except the North American Sioux.

If the Treaty of Versailles, by distinguishing between just and unjust wars, represented one crucial step in delegitimizing war as waged by the state, the establishment of the League of Nations represented another. The idea that, given the growing weakness of Church and Empire as entities standing above individual states, those states themselves should establish an organization to arbitrate their differences had been put forward as early as the first half of the 17th century. From then on it had been in the air, so to speak, and recurrent proposals for its realization were made. The best known among them were William Penn, Jean Jacques Rousseau, Emmanuel Kant and, in the 19th century, John Stuart Mill and Johann Bluntschli; the latter's proposal strongly resembled the League of Nations as it eventually evolved.[15]

So long as war was regarded as an acceptable, even normal, instrument in the hand of the state these proposals were doomed to failure. Their incipient realization after World War I was due partly to the feeling that modern military technology had become too powerful and too destructive to be entrusted to individual states; partly, though, it was due to the idea – as embodied in the peace treaties themselves – that

---

15 For various attempts at international organization see A. Saita, *'Un Riformatore pacifista Contemporaneo de Richelieu: E. Cruce'*, RIVISTA STORICA ITALIANA, 64 (1951), pp. 183-92; W. Penn, *An Essay Towards the Present and Future Peace of Europe* (Hildesheim: Olms, 1983, originally published 1699); Abbe de Saint Pierre, *A Scheme for Lasting Peace in Europe* (London: Peace Book, 1939, originally published 1739); O. Schreker, 'Leibnitz, ses idees sur l'organization des Relations Internationales', *Proceedings of the British Academy*, 23 (1937), 218-19; E. Kant, *Plan for a Universal and Everlasting Peace* (New York: Garland, 1973, originally published 1796); J. Lorimer, *The Institutes of the Law of Nations* (Edinburgh: Blackwood, 1883-84), Chapter xiv; and J. G. Bluntschli, *Gesammelte kleine Schriften* (Nordlingen: Beck'sche Buchhandlung, 1879-81), Volume ii, pp. 293-95.

an 'aggressive' war could not be just even if it was waged by a recognized, sovereign, state. In the future, conflicts between states, instead of being settled by force of arms, should be submitted to the assembly of all states. It would be up to them to arbitrate differences and, if it were determined that 'aggression' had taken place, impose sanctions.

The third important step in the delegitimization of war as waged by individual states was taken in 1929 when the Kellogg-Briand Treaty was signed. As the name implies, the original signatories of the Treaty were the USA and France who formally renounced the right to make war as an instrument of national policy against each other. During the next few years no fewer than 61 states joined it; since there was no time limit, technically speaking the Treaty remains in effect to the present day.[16] At the time and later, some derided the Treaty as an 'international kiss' without any practical significance. Its true import was only revealed in 1946 during the War Criminals Trials, where it provided the legal basis for finding the most important German and Japanese leaders guilty of 'planning and waging aggressive war'.[17]

That the trials were not merely a fluke imposed by the victors on the losers but part of an attempt to set up some kind of new international order was made clear by the establishment of the United Nations as a permanent organization; to the contrary, in so far as they joined that organization just as soon as they were allowed to do so the losers were soon turned into supporters of that order. Like the League of Nations before it, the United Nations was intended to be a permanent body standing, in some ways, above individual states. Much more than the League of Nations, and with the consequences of World War II still vivid before its eyes, it went out of its way to prohibit 'aggressive war'. From now on the only permissible wars were those that were waged in strict self-defence. The logical consequence of this provision was that acquiring territory by means of force, which had been the normal objective of war during almost all of its history, was excluded. This idea was explicitly stated in the United Nations Charter. Later, it was reinforced by several Security Council Resolutions.

Cynics might argue, with reason, that the principle, far from being new, was merely a re-formulation of the ancient *beati sunt possedentes*. They might also argue, again with reason, that the only tangible result of the new order was to cause states to change the name of their 'war ministries' to 'ministries of defence' and that most inter-state struggles and wars went on as before. While there is much truth in such a view, in the end it is misleading. As might perhaps be expected, an agreed-upon definition of 'aggression' that could serve to separate permissible from

---

16   For these developments see. F. Porzetovcznik, '*The Illegality of the Concept of Just War under Contemporary International Law*', REVUE DE DROIT INTERNATIONAL, 70, 4 (October-December 1992), 245-94.

17   See G. Best, *War and Law since 1945* (Oxford: Clarendon Press, 1991), 181-82.

impermissible war was never discovered. Over time, and precisely for that reason, virtually any warlike act taken by a state became *ipso facto* reprehensible. To put it in a different way, the UN was an organization made up of sovereign states and full (voting) membership in it was reserved to sovereign states only. Conversely, proof of the legal status of a state increasingly consisted of its admission as full member of the United Nations. In this way the UN, having prohibited 'aggressive war' and the forceful annexation of territory, by definition turned its members into supporters of the *status quo.* This was true in theory and very often in practice as well. In today's world, the state that lays claim to land other than that which it declares to be 'its own' has become very rare indeed. Meanwhile states that are 'warlike' rather than 'peace-loving' have all but disappeared; for a ruler to tout the virtues of war, as many did before 1914 and several continued to do during the years 1919-1939, became almost inconceivable.

While individual states have progressively lost the right to wage war against other states, that right has increasingly been transferred to the international organization itself. The first time the UN as a body went to war was in Korea in 1950. Legally speaking, the move was made possible by a cardinal diplomatic error committed by Stalin who, not for the first time, misjudged the direction in which things were moving. Instead of exercising his veto-right, he withdrew from the Security Council; in this way he opened the way to the remaining permanent members to do what they pleased. It was an error that Stalin's immediate successors did not repeat. As a result, so long as the Cold War lasted the United Nations was paralysed and what wars took place were conducted without its consent. A fundamental change in the situation only came with the end of the Cold War. Since then, in one instance after another it has provided the legal basis for the conduct of war. First against Iraq, then in Somalia, then in Haiti, then in Bosnia, and finally (if only retroactively) against Serbia in Kosovo.

From 1648 on, war was something that only sovereign states could wage and then only against other sovereign states (this principle was carried to the point that, in 1861-65, the North took the decision to wage the war *as if* the enemy were a sovereign state). After 1946, however, making one's sovereignty manifest depended on joining the United Nations; and joining the United Nations increasingly meant giving up the right to wage war against other Member States. Except under the rarest of circumstances where everybody could agree on what constituted 'aggression', legally speaking the right to wage inter-state war has now become something reserved almost entirely to the United Nations and/or its main organ, the Security Council. In this way, international law has been stood on its head. At least in theory, inter-state military action is now legal *only* to the extent that it has been taken out of the hands of individual states and, to this extent, 'globalized'.[18]

18   On the transformation of the UN into an organization that can authorize war, and the problems that this creates for individual governments, see G. Picco, '*The UN and the*

IV. The 'New World Order' and the Status of War

To be sure, 'the new world order' is anything but perfect. Without exception, states continue to proclaim their right to wage war in order to defend their 'vital interests' – but then the very fact that they have to proclaim that right shows that something has changed. Some states continue to wage war without authorization by the United Nations – but, to the extent that they oppose themselves to the organization and its members, in almost every case they are made to pay a heavy price in terms of both power politics and public opinion. It is also true that the United Nations in its capacity to authorize the use of international armed force has very often acted not as an independent and impartial organization standing above its members but as an instrument of those members and, in particular, the strongest one among them. All this, and more, is freely admitted.

Legal issues apart, it is also true that most states have not yet integrated their armed forces even to the extent that NATO ones have. Yet surely it is a sign of the times that NATO is besieged by several candidates that would like nothing better than to join it and to integrate their forces with it; elsewhere, the 1997 SEATO manoeuvres conducted in Darwin Bay (which the present author had the pleasure of watching) should have been enough to convince anyone that the military of individual countries are going down, those of international alliances up. By way of another sign of the times, participating in the international exchange of officers – in other words the extent to which officers are sent to, and participate in, military training and education offered by their colleagues in other countries – has become almost synonymous with military progress. The more important a country and the greater its participation in international political and economic life, the more likely one is to meet its officers in the courses in question. Conversely, normally it is only the poorest and least important countries whose officers do not participate – in some cases, because nobody wants to visit them and because, without bilateral arrangements, they literally cannot afford the expense.

As the second millennium ends, in many way the process that started somewhere in the late Middle Ages, bore fruit in 1648, and culminated during the period 1789-1945 is being put into reverse gear. Politically speaking, many of the most powerful military states no longer operate in isolation but are grouped in alliances that, whatever the reality, are meant to be permanent and take collective action. Legally speaking, the right of individual states to declare war on other states is being lost in favour of an organization, the United Nations, which represents all states and which in recent years has mandated the use of force in Iraq, Somalia, Haiti, Bosnia,

Use of Force', FOREIGN AFFAIRS, 73, 5, (September-October 1994), 14-8; also A. Roberts, 'The United Nations: a System for Collective International Security?' in G. A. S. C. Wilson (ed.), *British Security 2010* (Camberley Staff College: Strategic and Combat Studies Institute, 1996), 65-8.

Kosovo, East Timor and, most recently, Sierra Leone. Both processes fit in with global cultural, social and economic trends and are very much part of the world in which we live. The rulers of a state who, for whatever reason, prefer to close their eyes to them are likely to pay a heavy price indeed.

PART V

THE ECONOMY
AND
GLOBAL PUBLIC GOVERNANCE

Chapter 10

The Competitive State and the Industrial Organization of Nations

Jean-Jacques Rosa[*]

I.   Introduction

Most contemporary observers of politics, governments and states suggest that the trend towards globalization spells the end of the nation-state. The rise of global markets puts new constraints on public governance – and especially on the power to tax – since capital, labour and firms become much more mobile in an open world market. States are essentially territorial in nature, so the decreasing importance of geography is deemed to make them obsolete. Some degree of control over the economy could be regained through the building of larger structures such as continental states, or the strengthening of functional worldwide organizations. In short, they propose, a world market should be balanced and controlled by worldwide political organizations.

I would like to suggest otherwise. Since Coase,[1] the economic analysis of organizations has shown that there is a fundamental trade-off between markets and hierarchies in the organization of production. Firms and markets thus evolve in opposite directions: the very forces leading to a rise of markets also explain the decline in scale of firms.

Just like firms, states are hierarchical organizations. As such, they face similar constraints and choices; their evolution parallels that of firms. The globalization of markets leads to an overall shrinking of their size. One can look at the entire population of states in the world as 'the industry of the states', a specific sector of the global economy devoted to the production of public goods, including transfers. In that framework, the downsizing of states (similar to the downsizing of firms) leads not to the disappearance of states, but to a changing structure of their industry. From an oligopolistic structure with a few very large states and a larger number of

---

*   Professor of Economics, Institut d'Etudes Politiques de Paris.
1   Ronald Coase, *The Nature of the Firm*, ECONOMICA, (1937), 386-405.

smaller states, to a competitive industry that is defined in the field of industrial organization by a large number of small firms, each of which has practically no market power. The forces leading to the globalization of markets explain the atomisation of the 'industry of states', and the rise of many small, competitive states. We do observe a significant increase in the number of independent states, from about 70 in the 1950s to 200 today. And even a powerful, rich and populated state like the US is affected by the same trend, its size, economic and demographic, is inexorably decreasing relative to that of the whole industry, compared to what it was 30 or 50 years ago.

The transition to a competitive structure is not the end of the nation state: indeed, it signals a tremendous success for this type of organization, exactly as the increase the number of firms in an industry is a mark of the success of this industry and not of failure or decline. And a competitive state is good news for the citizens of the various countries: it brings about better public services, lighter tax burdens, as well as the conditions for a durable peace between nations.

II.   The State as a Firm

Like firms, states are hierarchical institutions that produce services and use scarce resources. They serve the population that comprises a *nation*, the latter referring both to a human group with a certain cultural homogeneity and to the territory these people occupy. Just like other firms, the state's importance is measured by the volume of its production and its number of employees. And, again like firms, the state can increase its production scale and scope by either selling more services to a given customer base, or by selling a given service to a broader customer base. The first strategy results in internal (or intensive) growth of the state, within the nation and its set borders, when new activities are added to broaden the range of public interventions. This is what economists usually refer to as state growth, and it has been the prevailing trend throughout the first part of the 20th century. The state can also chose an external (extensive) growth strategy by offering its services to a larger population via territorial conquest or the control of other nations. This is the nationalistic or imperialistic strategy described by political scientists and historians.

Growth or decline strategies, as the case may be, are not altogether discretionary; they are subject to a number of constraints. Indeed, the competition between states for territories, as well as the competition between potential leaders for governance of the state within the nation itself, compel governments to be efficient in the use of the resources they manage. It therefore follows that governments must optimize their use of public resources if they want to survive and achieve their goals, whatever those may be.

The competitive state, and thus the competitive government, must be particularly careful to choose the most efficient – external, as well as internal – dimension of production. The internal size of the state (its administrative pyramid) is measured by public spending in the economy, while the external dimension is measured by the size of the territory, and thus the size of the populations, it controls.

Depending on the way in which various states optimize their geographic size and shape, a spatial equilibrium develops between these various 'political firms' in what amounts, at a planetary level, to a 'system of states'; in other words, the 'society of nations' (as a state is traditionally seen as corresponding with a nation, at least since the 19th century when the right of a people to self-government was recognized). We have continued to use the expression *nation state*, although there is not always correspondence between the two.

As state hierarchies increase their span of territorial control, they usually overlap at the frontiers, which are often sources of dispute and conflicts. In this way, the determinants of the external dimension of organizations also explain international political relations: peace or war between states, and the spatial structure of the society of nations. In other words, the dimension of organizations explains the nature of the worldwide political system, and the optimal dimensions of public and private hierarchies within a nation's geographic area determine the nature of internal political and economic systems.

We will first examine the factors that define the optimal size and shape of the nation state as a geographic area, or the size of the customer base it includes. This size and shape depends on the government's goals, whether they be productive efficiency or more growth. It also depends on production costs for collective goods. When the size of the population served is on the increase, the optimal bureaucratic size increases; there are concomitant limits to the growth of the territory governed by the state, in as much as the quality of public goods deteriorates with an increase in the size of the customer base, while the cost of administrative management finally reaches the zone of decreasing returns.

We will thus analyse how, as each state seeks its optimum size and shape, a spatial equilibrium emerges between various states of different sizes within the 'global industry of states'. This industry does not actually strive towards creating a monopoly of a single global state, as is often postulated. Instead, it has in fact been characterized by atomization and increased competition during the latter half of the 20th century.

To conclude, we will examine how such a balance may arise through military action and negotiation or through conquest and secession, as the world industry of states is mostly refashioned by war and revolution. We will also attempt to clarify the overall conditions determining peace or war.

1.   The Industry of States and the Society of Nations

The predatory state, which is also a producer and provider of a whole range of collective goods, has become the universal organizational structure amongst wealthy societies with relatively large (by historical standards) populations. Nation-states have been adopted as the primary platform of the social and political life they govern, both at national and international levels. There is no longer a space on this planet that escapes their control.

However, they do appear in different guises, through space and time, ranging from the small citystates of ancient Greece or the Renaissance to ancient and modern empires. Their size often changes over time, with periods of expansion and conquest giving way to their ultimate decline and fall. This process can be seen throughout the 20th century in the development and decline of European empires. More recently it was reflected in the transformation of the Soviet Empire.

Far from being some sort of intangible reality, the geography of states and the geopolitical balance are the contingent result of developments that need to be further explained. We therefore need to examine the factors that determine the size of each individual state, and the resulting structure within the population of the different states, or the society of nations.

A state's strategy to orient itself towards external growth in order to achieve its optimal geographic size and shape is a matter of choice. It is thus an economic problem, as economics is the science of decision and behaviour. An effective strategy is partially dependent on the decision-maker's targets, and specifically on its preference for a large or small sized firm, as well as the constraints that limit a manager's capacity to get what it wants.

2.   The State's Objectives

The state is a firm, but the state is not a person (no more so than is a firm). In this respect, the state makes no decisions and has no personal preferences. The leaders of the firm, or state, make the decisions in the name of, and under the more or less strict control of, their constituents. They are therefore in a position to pursue their own objectives to a greater or lesser degree. In a commercial firm, these leaders are the chairman or chief executive officer and the board of directors. In the state firm, decision-making is under the leadership of the Prime Minister or President and the government.

Let us nevertheless continue to use the rather convenient expression 'the state's objectives', to designate those that result from a compromise fashioned by the relationship between the power and the law, between leaders and their constituencies, and (as it may be) between the government and its citizens or subjects.

Whatever his or her ultimate motivations, the leader of the state firm is like any other individual in requiring resources. They are needed, first for his or her own personal consumption and, second, to maintain or increase the leader's power over the inhabitants of the territory as well as over adversaries and external competitors. A leader needs to be able to repel attacks by rivals.[2]

A recent current in economic literature has attempted to explain the behaviour of states in the same terms as that of other organizations subject to economic analyses, that is, to compare states to private firms.[3] For Auster and Silver,[4] the traditional analysis of the firm goes a long way toward explaining the behaviour of states fighting each other in monopolistic competition for geographic control. According to Auster and Silver, the production of states is measured by the degree of order they engender in a given territory with a population of a given size.

But all forms of production require resources. Modern states engaged in cut-throat competition have considerable financial needs, and these directly affect all their policies.[5] 'The history of revenue production by the state is the history of the state itself', writes political scientist Margaret Levi, applying Schumpeter's[6] analysis. Starting from the hypothesis that leaders are predators seeking to extract as much income as possible from the population, Levi emphasizes that the specific objectives of these governments do not affect their behaviour. They can use fiscal resources for their personal consumption needs to increase their power or to finance social policies, or even to satisfy their ideological preferences. They can be altruistic

---

2   See the description of the accumulation of public treasure by Louis XI and English sovereigns to support war in Frederic C. Lane, *Economic Consequences of Organised Violence*, JOURNAL OF ECONOMIC HISTORY, XXIV (December 1958), note 43.

3   F.C.Lane, *Economic Consequences of Organised Violence*, *supra* n. 2; Douglass C. North and Robert Paul Thomas, *The Rise of the Western World: A New Economic History* (Cambridge: Cambridge University Press, 1973); Douglass C. North, *A Neoclassical Theory of the State* in *Structure and Change in Economic History* (New York: Norton, 1981); Mancur Olson, *Toward a More General Theory of Government Structure*, AMERICAN ECONOMIC REVIEW 76 (2), (May 1986), 120-125; Richard D. Auster and Morris Silver, *The State as a Firm, Economic Forces in Political Development* (Boston: Martinus Nijhoff, 1979); David Friedman, *A Theory of the Size and Shape of Nations*, THE JOURNAL OF POLITICAL ECONOMY, Vol. 85 (1) 1977, pp. 59-77; Albert Breton, *The Economic Theory of Representative Government* (Chicago: Aldine- Atherton, 1974); Léonard Dudley, *The Word and the Sword* (Oxford: Blackwell, 1991); Norman Frohlich, Joe A. Oppenheimer and Oran R. Young, *Political Leadership and Collective Goods* (Princeton: Princeton University Press, 1971).

4   Richard D. Auster and Morris Silver, *The State as a Firm, Economic Forces in Political Development, supra* n. 3

5   Gabriel Ardant, *Histoire de l'impôt*, 2 volumes, (Paris: Fayard, 1971 and 1972); Joseph A. Schumpeter, *The Crisis of the Tax State*, Pp. in Alan T. Peacock (ed.), International Economic Papers No. 4, (Macmillan, 1954): 5-38. ; Margaret Levi, *Of Rule and Revenue* (Berkeley: University of California Press, 1988).

6   Margaret Levi, *supra* n. 5 at 1.

or egocentric, peaceful or aggressive. But no matter what their stance is, they need resources to achieve their goals. And leaders attain their personal and social goals through the state and its revenues. As a result, they seek to maximize the latter, which we can define as a form of predatory behaviour.

However, firm managers behave in very different ways, depending on whether they are seeking to maximize revenue or maximize profit. A company that seeks to optimise its revenue, or turnover, will probably not maximize its profits. By accepting a decrease in profit, it can lower its prices and, depending on the elasticity of demand, sell more and achieve a higher total turnover.

Whether the chosen strategy is to maximize sales or maximize profit will depend on the way the firm is controlled. Shareholders will prefer profit. But leaders who are independent of their shareholders can choose a growth strategy in which they play a more important social role, which enables them to support an increase in personnel costs with increased production volumes. It also allows them to increase their own level of remuneration, as leaders of large corporations are generally better paid than the leaders of small firms. Such a conflict of interests is known as the 'agency problem' in management literature, and it affects strategy in terms of both the firm's size and growth.

The state and political production suffer from the same agency conflict. A state can decide to maximize either tax revenues or added value for the service provided to the nation it governs.

3.   *Managerial State, Patrimonial State*

State turnover is measured by tax revenues. It is quite clearly in the leaders' interests to increase taxation whenever possible, irrespective of their ultimate personal goals. The state obtains the equivalent to shareholder profit in added value for services rendered to citizens and residents net of the public cost of such services. The maximum amount of this added value is not generally obtained for the same level of GDP which maximizes the tax revenue that the state can extract from the population. This is because higher taxation rates can be a disincentive for private producers and result in a drop in production of wealth.

In a sense, citizens are their state's shareholders or financial backers. If the current political constitution were to give them control over the government, their own interests and profit strategy would definitely prevail. But if the government is not controlled by the citizen and taxpayer, it tends to pursue a strategy of maximum turnover, which implies (among others) a policy of geographic expansion.

Thus a managerial (dictatorial) state tends to be expansionist. A democratic state does not seek territorial expansion for its own sake, and prefers to limit expenses at a given service level, with priority for value production and a profit strategy.[7]

---

7   This is the managerial concept of international relations. The response of specialists in

However, it must be remembered that the state could be largely the property of the leader, as in bygone monarchies. The state owner-leader – like his commercial counterpart – prefers a profit strategy (to increase assets) rather than a growth strategy (that would reduce assets). This is the meaning of Olson's distinction between a government with an 'encompassing' interest in the company it leads and one with a more limited interest, focused on the collection of taxes. The first is a manager-owner, while the second is only a temporary manager whose assets will not suffer the capitalized consequences of his strategies. He is closer to being a 'roving bandit' than a sedentary predator.

The managerial state is fundamentally strategically distinct from the two varieties of 'patrimonial' state: the dictatorial patrimonial state and the democratic State.

Political leaders always refer to the 'public good' as the object of their actions: they attempt to deny the existence of a conflict of interest between themselves and the governed. This justification is obviously invoked because it sounds more noble and reassuring to taxpayers than the pursuit of the ruler's personal interests. But it is partially true that, by pursuing his own advantage, the sovereign cannot help but provide public goods as a by-product of his quest for tax revenue. When well understood, his own self-interest leads him to care for the interests of his subjects, who are (in a certain sense) his financial backers. History has shown that, when

international relations, similar to that of those that put them into practice, the leaders of states, boils down to the objective of power – or size – pursued by a nation. It derives from the simple desire to ensure survival with respect to other nations that are more or less its rivals. This is a fundamental law of international politics, already recognized in 321-296 BC by Kautilya, first Prime Minister of India, and Chandragupta in his treatise on politics and diplomacy. He suggests a number of principles to be followed by the leader:

1. Strengthen your own country such that it becomes stronger than other states.

2. All states along your borders are potential enemies. You must vanquish and conquer them whenever possible, that is, when they are weakened and devoid of trustworthy allies.

3. Do all you can to weaken your potential enemies.

4. States that lie on the borders of your enemies but are not contiguous to your territory are potential allies. Try to enlist their aid to resist your (potential) enemies or to conquer them.

5. Once your former allies become your neighbours, they are transformed into potential enemies (Peter Bernholz, *The International Game of Power*, Mouton, 1985, pp.17-18). The immediate objective of the state or nation is thus to preserve its independence and territory, or to increase it, through alliances and diplomacy or war if necessary. Each state seeks to expand its geographic area, just as a firm seeks to develop a customer base. In both cases, these strategies will provide additional resources.

under pressure from an urgent need for resources, often in conjunction with wars against neighbours and rivals, the sovereign will not hesitate to expropriate revenue from wealthy individuals. But he cannot do this too often or too extensively, for fear of discouraging producers and innovators, reducing production and therefore limiting future tax revenues. It is clear that this could never be part of a permanent financial plan.

Frederic C. Lane – probably the first to develop an analysis of the state as a firm that specializes in violence and providing protection to a given population[8] – believes that most states throughout history have been managed in the interests of their leaders rather than those of their subjects or citizens. Thus, the state is usually a company, which economists would classify as the 'managerial' type. That is, although the leader is not the owner, he pursues his own self-interest, even to the detriment of the legitimate owners who have appointed him.

Indeed, over the course of history a large number of firms offering protection have been controlled by the upper echelons of the army and police or, in other words, by their managers. Under such conditions, the main objective of the governments was to preserve the existence of their firm; maximization of its size and shape was more important than optimizing profits. Rank and file members of the army or other administrative departments of these firms were occasionally able to take control, or were at least able to limit the discretionary power of the leaders using methods that differ from those of modern labour unions. But when the workers gained control, they were not interested in minimizing tax revenues to ensure the protection of the population. Nor were they interested in reducing the costs to the firm for the wages they were earning. They too were eager to expand the size and shape of the state corporation.

A different policy characterized governments controlled by a prince or emperor who had a sufficient degree of absolute power to consider himself the valid owner of the firm producing protection. In this case, the owner-leader of the state was well advised to maximize profit rather than turnover. This motivated him to try and reduce production costs, while still maintaining the price (taxation) of his services. Like Henry VII of England or Louis XI in France, such leaders sought to use the least expensive methods they could find to assert their legitimacy, maintain internal order and dissuade neighbouring princes from attacking them. This allowed them to lower their military expenses. By reducing costs or increasing taxation to help maintain a stable territorial monopoly, or combining these two factors, they were able to show a surplus: a sort of monopoly fund.[9]

This analysis exactly corresponds with that of a firm controlled by its manager, workers or owner. The owner can be the leader, as explained by Olson who has

---

8   See the ground-breaking article by Gustave de Molinari, *De la production de la sécurité* , JOURNAL DES ECONOMISTES (February 1849), vol. 22, pp. 277-290.

9   Frederic C. Lane, *Economic Consequences of Organised Violence, supra* n. 2 at 406.

shown that this allows state policies to directly serve the population's interest. However, the population would be even better served by a state that sought to maximize profit (as defined earlier). Lane explains that, in a democracy, a firm with a monopoly on violence should lower the fiscal cost of its services to match the level of its production and protection costs. However, a government must be controlled by its customers – the service users – in order to behave in this way. The theory of representative government postulates that the leader's control arises from competition between managers for the leadership of the firm. This contest is arbitrated by 'shareholders', comprising voters and taxpayers. The government is responsible for its policies before the general assembly of owners during elections.

However, there is another or complementary possibility: control of leaders can also arise from the mobility of voters who renounce their ownership by going into exile and becoming citizens of a competing state. In this case, governments subject to competition from other states will have to provide the best public service at the lowest price; otherwise they risk losing an increasingly large percentage of their tax base. External control – comparable to that of shareholders who sell their shares to purchase others – also plays a role in aligning governmental policies with the population's real interests.

Given competition between states, and the more or less democratic nature of the political regime, each government will continue to seek the most favourable geographic size and shape to ensure the highest level of revenue. They will pay more or less attention to costs incurred, according to the amount of control their respective populations exercise over their strategies.

4. Benefits and Costs of the External Dimension

A pure public good has a decreasing average cost that reaches zero when the number of consumers taxpayers increases to the point at which fixed production costs are paid off. National defence is an ideal example of this. But this is rarely the case in practice. States' production costs increase with the volumes produced and the size of the territory. If it were not so, there would only be one state in the world; in reality, there are a great many states and the number is constantly increasing.

This is because public goods such as national defence, the legal system and infrastructure development are not 'pure'. More money per taxpayer must be spent to ensure protection within a large territory than a small one, and police and legal systems cost more per inhabitant in large urban concentrations than in small rural towns. The cost of security is higher when it is more extensive. Additional levels of security or infrastructure equipment end up costing more and more.

In addition, administrative control is more difficult as bureaucracies increase in size. States are no different from any other firm in this respect. Finally, a heterogeneous population, and thus differentiation in demand for public services, also increases complexity and the production costs for state services. It is more difficult to depreciate production of a single, universal public service when natural, linguistic or cultural barriers separate regions.

When a state seeks to extend its area of control to gain additional resources, it compares the costs and benefits expected from further development of its production. It is in the interests of the leader, or the owner of the state, to withhold as many resources as possible from the territory he controls, and to increase his geographic area. For their part, the populations he controls prefer to pay as little as possible for the protection offered by the state.

Another determinant of a state's ideal frontier is the equality between the cost of increasing the geographic control zone and the additional tax revenue generated by this extension. A large state will not necessarily be tempted to expand its territory as to do so might cost more than the potentially available tax revenue. Imperialism is thus a self-limiting process. Each concrete state has an optimum size. But these optimal areas are not necessarily compatible with one another. Thus, competitive conflicts may arise when control is sought over a given territory.

The basic calculation of the optimal geographic size and shape of a given state involves a comparison of potentially available sources of additional revenue and the military and administrative cost of control. Several factors contribute to limiting this size and shape. First, there is the increasing cost of public services that are not 'pure' but whose quality decreases when the number of users rises, whether in the area of defence, police, justice or any other collective good, which involves development of an administrative pyramid. Second, geographic distribution of economic activity and wealth does not always allow for sufficiently high levels of revenue production. Finally, the type of management of each state, and their leaders' objectives, do not always allow the maximum size and shape to be achieved.

Geographic equilibrium also depends on the state's specific objectives, its total tax revenues or net revenue minus costs, concentration of resources and populations in a given geographic area, the rising cost of providing public services, and its administrative control of territories and populations.

5.   *The Geography of Potential 'Deposits' of Tax Revenue*

Populations and their wealth are never distributed in a spatially uniform way. It follows that a state's frontiers will be defined by geographic 'deposits' of wealth, in the form of concentrations of economic activity in certain regions. A rational predator will attempt to control the wealthiest and most easily exploited areas on a priority basis, and only later acquire less profitable ones.

Foreign trade has thus been the main source of revenue for states throughout history, because it is easier to impose tax upon foreign trade than land or internal trade. And changes in trade routes and trade flows can be considered to be a major key in understanding history.[10]

David Friedman has more specifically developed this type of thinking.[11] He shows how trade taxation in the 14th century Italian city states led to inclusion of all the trade routes within a single nation, as it would not have been efficient to levy a multitude of taxes determined by independent political authorities over a given route. A similar example can be found in the practice of road and river tolls during the Middle Ages, especially on the Rhine, which was the only trade route between the Mediterranean and the North Sea areas.

A labour tax is generally more difficult to extract if the population is mobile. It can only be maximized if labour cannot emigrate or is otherwise immobilized. As a language limits the mobility of its speakers to the areas where it is spoken, it follows that nations are no longer able to organize themselves around trade routes when a labour tax becomes an important part of a state's revenue. They must instead focus on group populations speaking the same language to reduce the external mobility of the taxed population as much as possible. Friedman explains that such issues are responsible for the regular increase in the index of linguistic homogeneity in the principal European nations from the 12th century to the present.

Various authors have emphasized the historical connection between urbanization and the development of the state, which also corresponds with the thesis about the origin of the state by the increase of population density. A high population density allows more extensive depreciation of the fixed costs of public goods; it also allows for better control of individuals than when they are dispersed over vast areas. The decline of the Roman Empire can be explained by de-urbanization, with the evolution towards feudalism resulting from contraction of the urban and trade base of the Empire's tax revenues. And it would have been the same in other civilisations. According to Auster and Silver, the barbarian raids that led to the contraction and then abandonment of Mycenean cities also caused the decline of the Mycenean state, which was replaced by a large number of small states based on rural economies. In the same way, transformations of trade routes led to extreme

---

10 The hypothesis developed by Brooks Adams cited by Gilpin who writes: 'Historically, taxation of trade was a major source of state revenue; this accounts for the importance of trade in the distribution of the economic surplus and hence of power. In contrast to other sources of state revenue, such as taxation of land or internal trade, international trade is relatively easy to administer and tax. ... It was with good reason that Brooks Adams in his provocative study *The Law of Civilisation and Decay* (1943) considered changes in trade and trade routes to be the key to history'. See, Robert Gilpin, *War and Change in World Politics* (Cambridge: Cambridge University Press, 1981) at 113.

11 David Friedman , *A Theory of the Size and Shape of Nations*, *supra* n. 3.

cases of rural deconcentration of state industry in the Dniepr basin in the 12th century, and in Prussia in the 15th century.[12]

For Sumer, urbanization apparently preceded the emergence of numerous city states and facilitated centralization of the entire region under the authority of Sargon, at Akkad in 2340 B.C. Despite sporadic interruptions due to invasions, the entire southern part of Mesopotamia remained organized in centralized and highly urbanized empires after the time of Akkad, which promoted a policy of forced settlement and urbanization of the population.

In the same way, the rapid growth of urban life in ancient Greece from 800 BC, and in Western Europe during the 11th and 12th centuries, also contributed to a re-concentration of political authority. Continued urbanization was accompanied by the rise of national monarchies and the several thousand small principalities or 'states' gradually being replaced by large protective firms, which numbered only 30 at the beginning of the 20th century.[13] The first Russian state was formed in a similar way when peasants evicted from the steppes by Tartars united and reached a sufficient degree of demographic density to found a state.

These various historical examples illustrate the influence of population density and of the concentration of resources on the profitability of the protective firm. Density of resources facilitates the process of levying tax, but also reduces the cost of public services to taxpayers. It decreases distances and increases population homogeneity. In their analysis, Ulrich Blum and Leonard Dudley[14] demonstrate how public services provided to more distant and heterogeneous populations lose their effectiveness, while the cost of military control of the territory and populations increases with distance and people's heterogeneity.

Economies of scale in production – a feature of public goods that always incites states to look for a large population implanted in a large territory – are offset by the increased administrative costs of large security firms: top-down transmission of information loses efficiency when a certain size is reached, and controls on enforcement of directives from the hierarchy become less effective as the number of organizational levels increases. Beyond a certain geographic size, the production costs of public goods inevitably increase, as do those of military control of the territory, whether by secessionists, groups seeking autonomy, or foreign powers.

12 Auster and Silver, *supra* n. 3 at 33.

13 Ibid at 35.

14 Ulrich Blum and Leonard Dudley, *A Spatial Approach to Structural Change: The Making of the French Hexagon*, JOURNAL OF ECONOMIC HISTORY (1989), 657-676 and A Spatial Model of the State JOURNAL OF INSTITUTIONAL AND THEORETICAL ECONOMICS (1991), 312-336 .

a) Local public goods

Public goods are never 'pure' in reality. The increase in the number of users tends to deteriorate the quality of the service an individual receives. This means that users are increasingly hesitant to pay tax when the demographic and geographic size of the state increases, because public services deteriorate with larger numbers, and effective service costs must increase to ensure quality.

In addition, the taxation process requires an administrative and fiscal organization whose costs rise in proportion to increasing geographic size and demographic dispersion. It follows that a state seeking to expand will, beyond a certain point, find it increasingly difficult to extract the resources it needs to function from the population it wants to control. This will be the case even if there is not a rival neighbour, and explains why states find barriers when seeking to increase their resources. At a certain point, their geographic size and shape reaches an optimal level.[15]

There are costs inherent in the large size of states, such as acquisition costs – wars with rival states – and the higher costs of managing larger administrative structures. The quality of public services also deteriorates as the number of users rises. This occurs, for example, in the field of law and order. It is more difficult to ensure this service within a very large population located in a huge metropolis (where delinquents are harder to identify) than in a town with a population of a few hundred where everyone knows everyone and their movements. In the same way, law and order are more difficult to implement in the distant, peripheral areas of a nation, or in an empire, than in its capital city. This implies that the collective service is 'impure' or 'local': its quantity and quality vary according to the number of users and their geographic remoteness.

The same difficulties are encountered in controlling a firm in which the manager, or the 'superior information available to the manager', is a 'public good' that loses part of its value when the firm increases in size, as we see in the case of mergers and acquisitions.[16]

Public goods are almost never 'pure' in the sense that consumption by some implies a reduction in consumption capacity for others, and it is more or less impossible to prevent consumers from gaining access to them. Thus, the necessarily limited number of schools and courts implies a scarcity of the service in the areas of education or justice. An additional student or trial thus erodes the quality of service available to everyone else. In the area of security – the police and justice departments – not everyone has access to exactly the same service. The service

15 Leonard Dudley develops these arguments in *The Word and the Sword* (Oxford: Blackwell, 1991).

16 See Jean-Jacques Rosa, *Le second XXème siècle, Déclin des Hiérarchies et Avenir des Nations* (Paris: Grasset, 2000), Chapter 4.

received by various people depends on their place of residence or knowledge of laws and regulations. Some will be better protected than others.

Once the customer base stretches beyond a certain size, public goods begin to resemble private goods: the quantity offered decreases while users compete to access them. Public goods are often public only at a local level. Thus the French national defence system cannot hope to serve all the inhabitants of our planet. The greater the distance of the populations from France, the less this defence system can technically be to their advantage. It follows that public goods are not 'global'. They may be national, regional, or communal, for example, depending on each situation.

There is also the concept of a 'local' – or almost public – good; that is, a public good considered within a specific geographic environment. In this case, the public good is not 'pure' in an economic sense. It is no longer available in exactly the same conditions for all users. The quality of service is not strictly the same for all, independent of the number of consumers. There will be 'overcrowding' and rivalry among users. Some take better advantage of a public good and manage to exclude some others.

Thus the quality of a collective service will vary as a result of the geographic remoteness of its operation from the centre or the place of its production. For example, a police service will be more efficient near the police station than in remote, little-frequented streets. Equipping a town centre with public infrastructures will not be of equal benefit to residents in the centre and those on the periphery, who only visit the centre occasionally. A good example is also provided by radio waves and television broadcasts. In theory, all users can receive a programme once it has been broadcast, and the broadcaster will spend the same amount of money to reach 100,000 or 500,000 additional persons. However, if these additional users are dispersed over a vast area, they will receive poor quality broadcasts, or nothing at all. Reception quality will decrease (even to the point of being non-existent) due to increased distance and natural obstacles such as mountains and valleys. It follows that a television programme, which is a 'pure' collective good in a limited geographic area, requires additional investment in infrastructure such as relay or cable stations to reach remote and dispersed populations. The cost of such equipment can be very high depending on the number and geographic dispersion of additional or marginal populations to be served. If they are too few or dispersed, the fixed costs of the additional equipment will not be covered by a sufficient number of users. The average costs will remain high. It may be too expensive to overly serve remote populations. Providers of public goods (the state, in this case) experience the economic limits of their geographic extension. National defence may also be of unequal benefit to remote parts of the territory that are more exposed than others to military action by an adversary. Border regions, for example, are often the first to be invaded and sacrificed in the event of a conflict. They thus receive less protection than the centre of the country.

b) Rising administrative costs

All public goods are subject to a centralized management system, which implies a hierarchy and thus a bureaucracy. Competition arises in the smallest or largest hierarchy (empire or commune). It all depends on the degree of scarcity or amount of information in these areas.

In a recent development, industrial economics has also studied the internal, administrative organization of the firm. The effectiveness of bureaucratic management indeed contributes to determining the firm's optimal size. The larger the firm, the more difficult it becomes to control the entire production process and each employee. Inefficiency tends to increase, and the firm's costs tend to rise. In addition to the technology used to produce goods and services, which determines the costs linked to each production level, and consequently the most advantageous production volume, it is vital to assess the firm's internal administration costs in order to determine the overall size it can achieve.

This means taking into account the size of firms that are implicated in several production processes and are active in several different sectors. 'Conglomerate firms' involve several production activities that are not necessarily situated at the same level in the process (in the range between raw material and the final user). Good examples of this are firms that manufacture televisions and automobiles. Firms are considered to be 'vertically integrated' when several consecutive activities are grouped together within the production process, such as the manufacture of clothing and its sale to the public via a chain of stores.

The performance of the internal administration in these sorts of firms is the first determining factor on the overall dimension of the various production processes, such as the total number of employees. The cost of managing this production may or may not be minimal for an optimal production level (when the average production cost is at a minimum). Minimum production costs and minimum administrative costs do not necessarily coincide.

Thus, if the optimal size for car production is greater than the firm's optimal bureaucratic dimension, a 'joint venture' between two smaller firms will arise: each firm will keep its own brand and remain independent, but they will merge production to manufacture the same model which is then marketed separately. On the other hand, if the administrative dimension is greater than the production dimension, a firm will have several different establishments with, for example, sites established in several different countries.

The same is true of state-firms. Production is decentralized if the administrative dimension is greater than the dimension responsible for producing public services. This was the case with feudalism, in which the lord of the local castle provided security at a local level. In turn, the lord recognized his obligations to the empire and to his sovereign, who supported their decisions regarding peace and war by engaging and disengaging his vassals. The contemporary trend to decentralization and autonomy is identical, with the effective production of public goods, education and the police relegated to a lower level of authority.

Conversely, military alliances can arise when the administrative dimension is smaller than the dimension of production of public goods and services. Other situations include excise payments between nations, or independent nation states' participation in international organizations in special areas such as the production of a legal order or international trade.

The state provides public services – primarily the monopoly on violence – which have a cost. Beyond a given territorial dimension, costs ultimately rise. No army benefits from such economies of scale even if its optimal production level is worldwide. In addition, a state must establish an administrative system to directly levy taxes in the territories it administers; the military system will not be sufficient to accomplish this task. The latter can seize goods through plunder, but to regularly levy taxes on all types of production requires a specialized, permanent, and sedentary organization. An army must remain mobile. Thus costs initially decrease, but subsequently rise. Altogether, the optimal territorial dimension for the state is defined by the minimum combined average cost for these two functions.

As for firms, the various functions of the state may be either fragmented or grouped together under one authority, depending on the importance of what economists call 'economies of scope'. For example, a firm manufacturing automobiles can also manufacture trucks, or two-wheel vehicles, if the combined average cost of managing these different productions by a single central department is lower than the average cost of separate firms producing each independently. A state can thus sub-contract certain functions to independent organizations and change the range of services it produces for itself. Some small states do not produce national defence capabilities, but place themselves under the protection of larger states. Some single nations produce education while others entrust this function to the private sector. However, re-organizing or modifying the usual range of public services does not necessarily impact on the geographic dimension of the nation states.

The optimal size and scale of states reflects the size of hierarchies. However, the state hierarchy can change its dimension in two different ways: it can develop by increasing its demands for resources from a given population in a given territory, which constitutes internal growth. Or, it can develop by extending its control over larger populations in larger territories, resulting in external growth. Both types of optimization can occur simultaneously, but they can be considered separately for the purposes of analysis (as done here). As I indicated in my theory of nationalization and privatization, internal growth reaches its limits when the cost of marginal taxation is superior to the marginal revenue it produces.[17] When taxation rates are

---

17   Id., *Théorie économique de la nationalisation et de la privatisation*, FINANCE Vol. 9 (December 1988), 2-ff *Nationalisation, Privatisation, and the Allocation of Financial*

higher, individuals' incentives to produce are weakened. Production will ultimately stagnate, which means that the social cost of taxation – measured in terms of earnings lost through the production of wealth – will increase. The state can then consider eliminating certain activities to reduce social costs and allow private production to resume, thus gaining tax revenue on increased production while simultaneously reducing expenses. Budgets will be less restrictive and it will again be able to attain its chosen objectives. Conversely, the state will absorb an increasingly large share of formerly private activities into its own sphere when the conditions that encourage the development of a hierarchical pyramid are given. This is nationalization and interventionism, but such internal expansion will reach its limits with the increase in the social cost of the resources that the state must levy to finance these additional activities. This returns us to the preceding analysis.

But there is a second possibility for a state with the right conditions for hierarchical development: 'external growth' provides new opportunities for taxation if the state can grow to the detriment of another state. This requires a superior capacity to control a given region. Military superiority is often evoked in this case, but it is not sufficient. It also requires administrative and management superiority, and it must complement state activities in its initial stages.

When the threshold size for efficient hierarchies has been reached, certain populations might find themselves closer to the production 'centres' of other nation states. The choice between nation states that are 'equidistant' in terms of cost and quality of collective services is then based on criteria that take into account the particular circumstances and technological change. This is the case for border areas that are repeatedly disputed over the course of history, such as the 'border country' of an empire or realm. Bordering states compete for these areas to define frontiers and the exact scope of their territorial jurisdiction.

In a group of states that all seek an optimum geographic size and space, there can only be peace if the choice of frontiers is compatible with the choices made by neighbouring states. This compatibility and simultaneous definition of compatible frontiers is the central issue of diplomacy and war. Attaining this balance is the objective of geopolitical strategies. But its achievement ultimately depends on the respective optimal dimensions of neighbouring nations.

III. Geopolitical Equilibrium

In the finite world of the 21st century, the entire planet is occupied by contiguous states. There are no more white areas on the maps, no *terra incognita* remaining to

Property Rights, PUBLIC CHOICE VOL. 75 (1993), 317-337 and *Public Choice Aspects of Privatisation Policies: Driving Forces and Obstacles* in Herbert Giersch (ed.), *Privatisation at the End of the Century* (Berlin: Springer, 1997).

be discovered by explorers and conquerors. In such a situation, what happens when the geographic optimisation for certain states implies mutually incompatible expansion? And how will the mosaic of states be structured? Will there be a large number of small states? Or a few large empires? Will a single world state arise, such as envisaged by Lenin to organize the entire Russian production into a single gigantic firm? And will the frontiers coveted by each state be compatible with the aspirations of others? Will the geographic balance of the 'industry of states' be stable or unstable, consensual or the result of conflict?

Within a given population of different states, balance results from the behaviour of each individual state. Every state tries to attain its optimal size, and the balance of each population is defined by reciprocal adjustments with residents of neighbouring states. Depending on the economic conditions driving this progression, a society of nations tends towards one of two structures. It might be a competitive structure – an 'atomistic' structure (in economic jargon) – characterized by a large number of small states, each tending towards what we may call an individual competitive state. The alternative is that it will tend towards an 'oligopolistic' or 'monopolistically competitive' structure composed of a few large states.

The explanation of the degree of concentration of the world industry of nations is based on the same analysis as that governing the structure of any industrial or service sector. When the average size of firms in a given sector rises against a given market demand, there is only room for a smaller number of firms. Thus a concentration of the population of firms arises. By contrast, the number of firms in the industry increases if the average size of the firm decreases and the population becomes subject to de-concentration.

Economic theory shows how the optimal size of a firm and its volume of production are dependent on its cost levels. The lower the production costs for a given volume, the more the firm is encouraged to increase production. The cost level for a given production is related to the technology used. Thus the production technology determines the optimal size of each firm and thus the organizational structure of the sectors of activity. This is a standard conclusion in the field of industrial economy.

The situation is exactly the same in states. Their optimal dimension will depend on the production costs of providing collective services, and especially security services (that is, military effectiveness), as well as the cost of administering the populations and territories.

The size and shape of states depends, for a given level of military technology and a given geographic situation in terms of men and wealth, on the relative size of administrative hierarchies. Thus the concentration of states worldwide will be in direct relation to the factors that determine the optimal dimension of hierarchies, especially scarcity or abundance of information in a society. When the hierarchical mechanism is seen to be more efficient than the market mechanism, the number of states decreases and their size increases. And the reverse is true where market mechanisms are more efficient than hierarchical mechanisms. This also determines the distribution of decision-making between a variable number of nations, and consequently between a variable number of state leaders on a global level.[18]

During the 'second 20th century', the population structure of states has undeniably tended towards de-concentration, as shown by the increase in the number of states. However, where the dimensions of each state remain optimally fixed, it may be that the demographic explosion dating from the beginning of the century could explain this increase. As demand for state services grows due to the rising number of 'consumers', new firms must be created to satisfy their needs if the average dimension of the ideal firm is to remain unchanged. Thus, the increase in the number of states may correspond with an unchanged optimal dimension, but also with a higher number of consumers that would imply multiplication of the number of firms and de-concentration of the industry of states.

However, several indicators show that there is probably also a decrease in the absolute optimal dimension of a state at the current time. Thus, we observe an increase in the number of states even in areas where the population has not risen, as in Europe. We might even observe a trend to separatism and secession in areas that are stagnant or in demographic decline, such as the USSR or some European nations.

This is an essential point in discussing peace and war between nations, as changes in the structure of the industry of states and the transformation of the structure of the society of nations are fundamental reasons for the overall condition of peace or war between nations.

Since the end of the 19th century, 'nationalistic' conflicts multiplied between expanding states that gradually grew into rival empires. The culminating point was reached at the end of World War II with the planet-wide conflict between the two remaining super-powers – the United States and the Soviet Union – which were locked into a 'Cold War' for half a century. At the same time, other large European empires dissolved and were replaced by a multiplicity of smaller-sized nation states.

---

18   As discussed by Auster and Silver: 'Let us view the level of concentration in any industry as resulting from an "as if" cost-minimisation decision with respect to the intermediate good *decision making*. ... In general we can conceive of two polar forms of decision mechanism: complete central planning and completely free markets, with all actual industry decision mechanisms arrayed somewhere along this centralisation of decision-making spectrum. The more concentrated an industry, the more often are its decisions made by central planning and vice versa. A comparative statistic of levels of concentration may then be generated in the familiar manner by assuming an interior solution of the cost minimisation problem (which seems to be empirical fact). In this case, factors which raise the relative costs of either polar form will lower its relative importance in the production of decisions, which can then be readily translated into a predictable effect on levels of concentration' (Auster-Silver, *supra* n. 3 at 41-42).

Then, with the triumph of the United States and the implosion of the Soviet Union, a plethora of small, independent states arose from the ruins of communism.

The nation-state system worldwide, the 'society of nations', has thus undergone profound structural changes during the last century.[19] All these nation states comprise a world sector of specific activities, a planetary industry of collective services production, or a collection of state-firms that are more or less in competition with each other depending on the period via trade, diplomacy and, sometimes, war.

The optimal structure for this sector can change over time, especially with technological development that can determine new optimal dimensions for the state-firms. To establish new frontiers in a finite space – a space completely occupied by neighbouring and rival firms – expansion by one necessarily implies the reduction of another.

Wittman's approach has clearly demonstrated that it is the firm that best increases the value of the territory contested that will be the victor, but violence need not be used as the victory can be won with peaceful exchange. However, the peaceful exchange is hardly probable in an anarchistic society of nations (that is, one without any overriding authority capable of imposing law and order to all). In several cases, exchange of territories and populations has occurred without military conflict (for example, Louisiana was handed over to the United States, Corsica was purchased by France from Genoa). But conflicts centreing on reallocation of territories are usually resolved through war.

The ideal geographic dimension of states depends on their ability to conquer and manage through their bureaucracies varying sizes of territory. An examination of this explains the conflicts that may occur when territories are coveted by two or more states, each of which seeks its optimum dimension. This implies that the optimum dimension for states constitutes the foundation of a theory of geopolitical balance, as well as for the conditions governing the negotiations or wars that determine this equilibrium. We will show that periods of geographic expansion by states that lead to increased concentration of the society of nations, inevitably result in war.

---

19 We could just as easily use the term industry of states to designate all the nations on the planet. But for many readers this expression would be confused with state industries, that is, the industrial sectors owned by the states, or firms with economic and commercial activities incorporated into the political sector via nationalization. During the first half of the 20th century, the industry of nations led to the Cold War between the equivalent of a duopoly, and then an atomization of its structure, a situation approaching the pure and perfect model of competition in economics texts. A situation extant today with the continued secessions and separatist movements affecting the entire globe, from Quebec to Kosovo and including Scotland, the Basque country, Corsica and Nigeria.

A question then arises about how to change the dimension of the nation state when the territory involved in the change is disputed. This problem is particularly obvious when the entire planet is already occupied by contiguous nation states, as has been the case since the end of the 19th century (a finite world). A reappraisal of frontiers might result in a mutual agreement – with or without compensation and payment – through the purchase of a given state's territory by another state. Another possibility is the exchange of territory (barter) or, in the case of non-compensated transfer, through the consent of previously independent populations or populations in another state (such as the Referendum joining the Savoie region to France, or the peaceful separation of the Czech and Slovak Republics).

Recourse to force cannot be excluded completely, because the world society of nations is anarchical. There is no higher authority to impose order on the society of nations. There is no monopoly of violence held by a single producer anywhere on the planet. Nor is there any recognized hierarchy that can enforce the domination of one state over all the others, or the domination of an organization other than the state (such as the United Nations or other international organizations). In such a case, as in a society composed of individuals, a mutually agreed exchange may be advantageous, but the same may be said for predatory behaviour. It all depends on the comparative superiority of each nation (or each individual) in terms of production and predatory behaviour.

IV. Conflict of Interest

The rational goal of every state-firm is to attain the optimal geographic size and shape which, depending on the respective powers of the governing forces and the governed, will either maximize tax revenue net of production cost for public services, or seek to achieve the greatest possible territorial dimension compatible with a tax rate acceptable to taxpayers.

Thus, simultaneous optimization of the territory by several states can engender conflict. If each nation reaches its optimal dimension, no conflicts should arise if their behaviour is based on rational considerations.

But there are other scenarios, which we may simplify by considering two states. The optimal dimension may be declining for both due to secessionist or separatist movements within each state. Or the optimal dimension might be growing for one and decreasing for the other. Or, the optimal dimension might be growing for both (or, in another variation, one is remaining constant while the other is growing). In the first two cases, no potential conflict exists as each state can re-organize itself independently of the other. But in the third case, we are faced with a conflict of interest.

Thus, if a given territory can enable both neighbouring states to optimize their territory, then its loss, or an inability by either state to control the territory, will undermine the well being of the state that loses the territory. This competition is a 'zero-sum-game' situation: what one wins, the other will necessarily lose.

This analysis implies that a universal increase in the optimal size of states in a finite world will necessarily give rise to generalized border conflicts: two neighbouring nations cannot both extend their territory simultaneously.

If, on the contrary, there is a universal decrease in the optimal size of nation states, there will be secessionist movements and separatist trends that will result in territorial dissolution following internal conflict. This was the case in Yugoslavia.

If several areas in a given state seek to become independent nations, they can do so by common consent, with no conflict of interest, providing they do not seek to control the same territories. The dissolution of Russia or Czechoslovakia, as opposed to the situation in Yugoslavia, is very revealing. The first two were achieved in a peaceful way, while the latter plunged the country into murderous conflict. An explanation for this contrast lies in the presence or absence of territorial and demographic disputes. In the first two cases, the populations wanted to constitute new, plainly divided states. The territories were clearly separate. However, the inextricable interpenetration of composite populations in Yugoslavia made the separation process necessarily a controversial one, implying much conflict and confusion. The overlap of areas claimed by opposed parties engendered conflict.

The geographic optimum for each state, as determined by specific factors, does change over time when the factors themselves evolve. It may result from a change in political regime following internal transformations (changes in the structure of economic activities or demography), or from a displacement of trade routes and the geographic localization of certain activities, often as a result of changes in organizational technology and, most importantly, in storage and information transmission techniques.

To be able to predict the direction a given society might take in organizational change, we must ask how the optimal size and shape of the basic organization is evolving. That is, what populations and what territories can the government or state control in an economic sense? And, as a consequence, how many independent governments can exist in the world at a given moment (that is, governments that are not in a hierarchical relationship to other states)?

The answer to such questions gives an indication of possible competitive relationships – trade disputes – between governments, and the aspects of intergovernmental co-ordination that will be handled by a higher authority. In short, it describes the problem of secession and federalism as analyzed by Donald Wittman.[20]

---

20 Donald Wittman, *Nations and States: Mergers and Acquisitions, Dissolution and Divorce*, AMERICAN ECONOMIC REVIEW PAPERS AND PROCEEDINGS (1991) (May 1991).

Wittman seeks to include general factors that influence all states simultaneously. For example, it is highly improbable that states, when faced with similar tasks such as production of order, security, and other collective goods, will encounter highly dissimilar conditions of production. In a given sector, there might be firms with extreme variations in size, but the dimensions of all these firms tend to evolve simultaneously in the same direction as production technologies. Thus, all automobile producers will generally seek to increase or decrease their size at the same time, as will all bankers or pharmaceutical firms.

Special determinants may be present that encourage growth in a single firm, leaving the optimal dimensions of all the firms unchanged. But, by definition, these special factors cannot explain the general trends observed during a major organizational cycle.

1. The Contractual Solution

David Friedman[21] and Donald Wittman[22] both envisage a contractual solution to territorial rivalry between states. The conflict may be resolved through sale or purchase. The territory becomes the property of the nation that places the most value on it, which is the case for goods and services in general. Just as the purchaser of a painting at auction is not always the richest bidder, but rather the collector who places the highest subjective value on the piece, a firm seeking to attract workers from the labour market in conditions of full employment will be the one in which the worker in question is the most useful and productive, as this will enable the firm to pay a higher salary than its less productive competitors.

In the same way, the nation that successfully wins control of a disputed border area will be the one that considers it the most useful for its economy or military strategy, such as the Golan Heights for Israel and Syria, or Alsace-Lorraine for France and Germany.

In a world in which anarchy reigns between nations, it is easy to imagine that the most powerful country will necessarily win through force, since it can, ultimately annihilate its competitor if necessary. But in a world with many nations, such a strategy seems dangerous and hardly plausible. To devote major resources to crushing a competitor in order to win a given piece of territory will weaken even the most powerful country with respect to all its other competitors, because it must consume rare resources to achieve victory. Such an increase in size and shape implies a loss of efficiency in the conquering country. This is thus a losing strategy in the medium term, unless the value of the coveted territory significantly strengthens the position of the victorious country.

---

21   David Friedman, *A Theory of the Size and Shape of Nations*, supra n. 3.
22   Donald Wittman, *Nations and States: Mergers and Acquisitions; Dissolutions and Divorces*, supra n. 20.

We must thus assume that the most powerful nation will not necessarily succeed in increasing its territory in a situation of competition between nations. Rather, the victor will be the nation for whom the disputed territory represents the greatest value. This returns us to the example of economic exchange. In this case, the value also depends on the varying capacity of the competitors to levy taxes from the coveted population. This is a capacity that in turn depends on an efficient use of violence as well as administrative management. Two predators of varying degrees of efficacy will not attribute the same value to the same territory, and the most efficient predator will thus win the competition for its control.

Under these conditions, why are all territorial disputes not solved in a peaceful way via compensatory financial transactions, where the country that places the highest value on the disputed region pays a price to the country that renounces its claim? The difference would still allow the purchasing country to reap the benefits of its acquisition, just as a collector can enjoy the painting he has purchased at a higher price than all other potential purchasers.

Under these conditions, war should not exist. We could conceive that war is a way to avoid payment of the compensatory costs to the country that renounces the territory. But this is not the case, because the costs incurred through war can easily rise to the level of what could have been a peaceful transaction. So what can explain war?

2.   *Why War?*

Several conditions must be present for a war to begin. First, a conflict of interest must exist. Second, the situation must be anarchic (that is, in addition to consensual exchange, reliance on force must be part of the strategy). Third, and finally, there must be uncertainty as to the value – net cost – of each opposing party's stakes. The first two conditions are obvious. If there is no conflict of interest, or if a higher authority can effectively forbid conflicts between subordinate political entities, there will be no war. However, in the world industry of states today, the situation is indeed anarchic. In the absence of a sufficiently powerful state – whose optimal dimension would comprise the entire world – with an ability to monopolize violence throughout the planet, violent competition will be the rule where there is more than one state. As in a society of individuals, anarchy allows both predatory behaviour and production as means to procure resources, depending on the way in which each player calculates its optimization and relative capacity for these two types of activity. Two approaches – violence or consensual negotiation – are possible, and these can be substituted for each other. This is the origin of that old adage that war is just another way of playing politics.

Nevertheless, anarchy will force all the states to consider the strategy of violence as a possible option. A potential purchaser of a territory may pay money or exchange it for another territory, or agree to military expenses to enable him to annex the territory without either monetary compensation or payment in kind. Faced with such a competitor, the current owner of the territory has no choice, and must also have recourse to violence. To renounce this option implies loss of a competitive weapon and he will always be defeated, as would be the case for any country that would refuse to use a certain type of weapon, such as the navy or aviation, in a military conflict.

No pure form of contractual negotiation is generally possible without resorting to the threat of effective violence between states that seek their geographic optimum. However, the threat of violence does not automatically imply that it will actually be used. The recourse to actual violence remains to be examined in explaining the outbreak of war.

There is thus a third condition that will cause a contractual solution to be refused and a war to ensue. If all the relevant factors operating in a competitive situation between two states for a given territory were known – the value it represents for each state and the resources available to each – the solution would be obvious to all and a contractual solution would be found without conflict, and even without negotiation. The optimal division of space would directly favour the state with the greatest need for the territory, given the military or pecuniary costs required to convince the other potential purchaser or current owner to renounce it.

This solution would prevail even in the case of a territorial division that would be to the advantage of one and the disadvantage of the other. Here, increased productivity would allow the winner to at least partially compensate the loser, whose productivity would decrease. By definition, the winner will be the state that best develops the territory and thus has the ability to compensate the loser for its loss of income, while still benefiting from a net gain due to the difference in productivity between the winner and loser.

But this assumes that one of the states has a clear managerial advantage over the other and that both protagonists are completely aware of this. In reality, there is always a degree of uncertainty and each must prove that it is prepared to develop the conquered territory better than the other. To do this, as in an auction, he must make a high offer; paying the acquisition price will effectively reveal, in a credible way, the value placed on the coveted object.

A bidder at auction promises to pay the bid price if no one makes a higher offer. Thus he truly commits his resources to the competition, with no possibility of drawing back. There is no auctioneer to enforce such commitments between states, and war requires a series of payments at an increasingly high price until one of the belligerent countries finds the cost excessive compared to the value placed on the stakes, and decides to cut its losses by proposing an armistice and negotiating peace.

Only the use of force can reveal which competing firm is more efficient, or believes itself so. The more efficient firm is that which is able to levy the maximum taxation from the population and the territory in dispute. War is high-risk spending designed to convince the adversary of one's superior capacity to develop a territory.

If it is in the interest of all nations to simultaneously increase their size and shape (for example, because military or administrative technology has changed), only a military victory will enable the victorious nation to approach its optimal size. The other nation or nations will have to remain in a sub-optimal state, that implies a cost and loss of well-being. Consequently, there is no place for negotiation or consensual transaction that could benefit both parties. Each party attempts to win through violence. Violence, as Georges Sorel said (albeit for different reasons), plays a social role, especially when anarchy is the rule. It reveals the party that places the highest value on a given resource, that is ready to pay the highest price, or that makes the most efficient use of available resources.

The industrial organization – or systemic – approach to the society of nations thus sees the overall source of wars in an increase in the optimal size and shape of nations. This is apparently the most significant common factor in the history of conflict, as we will see below, although the political regime can also be a determinant (whose influence has not yet been demonstrated because the structural and dimensional aspects analysed above have not been examined in relation to one another).

It follows that periods of general growth in the size and shapes of states, with a concentration of population among nations, are also periods characterized by wars. This is even more so when the state's internal political system is managerial rather than patrimonial, and is a hypothesis we can now test by looking at historical experience.

V.   The Territorial Hypothesis Vindicated

The traditional approach to war seeks explanatory factors in the behaviour of one or several states, especially those linked by treaties and alliances. It is true that a single state can be a 'warmongering' state that is responsible for war. War may also involve only two states in a local confrontation, while other states remain at peace with one another. But the causes of war are specific in these cases, and the conflict does not become generalized. Similarly, each company has a unique strategy. There are nevertheless important factors that will affect all the individual strategies for a given industry. Balance in a given sector depends on a plethora of individual decisions, but the latter are all affected, to varying degrees, by factors common to them all.

Taking into account the factors that apply to all conflicts between nation states is even more important when we recall that such conflicts arise from territorial disputes. In the modern world it is no longer possible to 'freely' expand frontiers.[23]

23 See William H. McNeill, *The Global Condition, Conquerors, Catastrophes, & Community* (Princeton: Princeton University Press, 1992), and especially the first section

Finally, all state pyramids of authority are simultaneously affected, in terms of optimum dimensions, by the impact of transformations in information technologies.

All the above arguments support the 'systemic' analysis of the causes of war recommended by a number of authors such as Mansfield and Gilpin,[24] as opposed to the anecdotal approach.

1. Centuries of Experience

Our vision of war has been strongly marked by the history of the construction of European nations since the 15th century. This is a history of ongoing pursuit of territorial expansion, especially for France. The optimum size and shape of nations increased throughout this period. This doubtless explains the current theory that claims that the largest, most powerful country must (barring major errors on the part of its leaders, a lack of courage and resolution, or internal dissent), invariably win the war. This also explains Kautilya's precepts[25] on the state's international strategy and the result: an obsession with size and shape, the quest for large size, the fears of certain large countries that serve to polarize the geopolitical debate as a whole.

According to Jared Diamond, who takes an historical look at agricultural societies, war has always been a tool to concentrate political entities, as proven by archaeological findings and history. And where war is absent, the threat of war determines the mergers and acquisitions of states.[26]

---

entitled: *The Great Frontier: Freedom and Hierarchy in Modern Times*.

24 Edward D. Mansfield, *Power, Trade, and War* (Princeton: Princeton University Press, 1994), and Robert Gilpin, *War and Change in World Politics* (Cambridge: Cambridge University Press, 1981).

25 See Kautilya et al., *Traité politique et militaire de l'Inde ancienne* (Paris: Les éditions du félin: Paris, 1998).

26 'The amalgamation of smaller units into larger ones has often been documented historically or archaeologically. Contrary to Rousseau, such amalgamations never occur by a process of unthreatened little societies freely deciding to merge, in order to promote the happiness of their citizens. Leaders of little societies, as of big ones, are jealous of their independence and prerogatives. Amalgamation occurs instead in either of two ways: by merger under threat of external force, or by actual conquest. Innumerable examples are available to illustrate each mode of amalgamation' (Jared Diamond, *Guns, Germs and Steel: the Fates of Human Societies* – New York: Norton, 1997 at 289.)

'All these examples illustrate that wars, or threats of war, have played a key role in most, if not all, amalgamations of societies. But wars, even between mere bands, have been a constant fact of human history. Why is it, then, that they evidently began causing amalgamations of societies only within the past 13,000 years? (Diamond, *supra* n. 26 at 291).

Like some authors cited above, Diamond suggests that population density explains the concentration of states ('Carneiro's theory'). In a low-density space, conquered populations can flee elsewhere (nomads). In a moderately populated space, they cannot flee, but they are of no use to the conqueror so everyone, except the women, is exterminated. In a densely populated space, the conquered cannot flee and are used as slaves or taxpayers (as explained by the history of slavery as an alternative to extermination).[27]

More systematic studies have been conducted by specialists in international relations to explain the circumstances under which wars occur. According to Geller and Singer,[28] a considerable number of publications on the subject began in the 1930s. However, they are primarily empirical, and their conclusions remain relatively unconvincing and somewhat limited.

These studies are based on *ad hoc* intuitive factors, such as proximity of belligerent forces, the political regime, the balance of 'power', and the psychology or pathology of leaders. Under such conditions, these attempts at empirical verification often give contradictory results and are difficult to interpret.

Geller and Singer review the main studies, seeking to identify the factors determining the outbreak of wars, and especially studies by authors who participated in the 'Correlates of War' project sponsored by the University of Michigan in 1963-1964. It is clear that social scientists feel the need to amass a vast amount of information on the factors associated with war before attempting to explain the causes.

They have looked at over 600 articles published since the end of the 1960s, all of which use data obtained from observing wars and their associated variables. In addition to these studies, all of which were published in the field's five major journals, they also examine two dozen books devoted to a rigorous and systematic analysis of international political problems in general, and armed conflict in particular.

Their main conclusions are as follows. They observe that the status of a major power is a decisive factor. By definition, great powers are usually of larger size, and thus benefit from a special initial advantage in seeking to grow.

For the overall population of states, they conclude that the factors influencing the probability and gravity of conflicts are the number of frontiers separating the nations, a polarization of state systems, and the instability of the inter-state hierarchy. A multiplicity of frontiers obviously increases the probability of friction

---

27 'Thus, food production, and competition and diffusion between societies, led to ultimate causes, via chains of causation that differed in detail but that all involved large dense populations and sedentary living, to the proximate agents of conquest: germs, writing, technology, and centralised political organization' (Diamond, *supra* n. 26 at 292).

28 Daniel S. Geller and J. David Singer, *Nations at War* (Cambridge: Cambridge University Press, 1998) at page x.

between states for reasons of control, which we present as the first cause of war. However, polarization of state systems, and the asymmetrical relationships between them, implies the concept of a concentration of resources between states, which necessarily involves a geographic aspect. Extreme polarisation results in domination by a super-state that has grown to a very large size. But less extreme degrees of polarisation result from increased concentration in the industry of states, which logically leads to friction along the borders and more opportunities for conflict. For this reason, incomplete polarization that is nevertheless pursued (explained by the instability of the hierarchy of states according to Geller and Singer) must result in increased competition for areas under control, and a more frequent use of war to allocate disputed territories and resources.

It follows that contemporary studies on wars between nations tend to confirm the idea that the general and ultimate cause of war in the world society of nations will be an increase in the average dimension of nations. However, the latter depends partly on the nature of the political regimes, as managerial (dictatorial) regimes tend to pursue growth in and of themselves, as opposed to patrimonial regimes (monarchic or democratic). This strongly supports the negative relationship between war and democracy, or war and trade, that is often observed in econometric studies but that has not yet been truly explained. Indeed, democracy develops in areas where the organizational structures are not yet too extreme, and consequently where managerial political regimes are weaker. In addition, and all other things being equal, democracy requires leaders to provide public services and depends on an economy of means that forbids the pursuit of growth and discretionary empire building.

2.   War and the World Concentration of Nations

Two other historical analyses of nations that support the territorial explanation of the origin of war are Bergesen and Schoenberg's analysis[29] on waves of expansion, and Mansfield's more precise study that concerns relations between the major national powers during a shorter period, from 1820 to 1965.[30]

Bergesen and Schoenberg begin by noting the importance of colonial expansion in the modern world system. From its beginnings during the 16th century, it included most of the surface of the globe at one time or another, until the 1960s. In 1800, about 35 per cent of the planet was, or had been, controlled by Europeans. In 1878, this figure rose to 67 per cent, to reach 84 per cent in 1914. The authors established an historical series of the number of colonies created by European nations over

---

29   Albert Bergesen and Ronald Schoenberg, 'Long Waves of Colonial Expansion and Contraction, 1415 – 1969', Chapter 10 of Bergesen, (ed.), *Studies of the Modern World-System* (New York: Academic Press, 1980).

30   Mansfield, *supra* n. 24.

these centuries. The series revealed two periods of intensive colonization: the 16th century, and the late 19th and early 20th centuries. By contrast, the 18th century (the Age of Enlightenment) and the end of the 20th century represent periods of intensive de-colonization, that is, decentralization of the world system of nation states. In passing, it is particularly interesting to note that periods of colonization are also periods of mercantilist trade policies and the decline of free international exchange, while periods of de-colonization are characterized by liberalization of world trade, first between 1820 and 1879, and later with the GATT agreement in the 1950s.

However, the most interesting observation with regard to the question at hand is the overlap between periods of strong colonization and periods characterized by major wars between European powers,[31] at the end of the 17th century, and later during the 20th century. Periods of geographic expansion controlled by European nations thus corresponded to an intensification of wars between those nations. In particular, a higher frequency of war occurred during periods of empire building. That is, during periods in which the optimal size and shape of all the European nations was growing strongly. This supports our analysis of war as a result of border conflicts between nations and expansionistic state hierarchies.

Another study, by Edward Mansfield, has resulted in a similar observation. In a systematic and statistical analysis of the period between 1820 and 1965, Mansfield seeks to determine factors governing declarations of war between major powers. He asks to what degree the distribution of forces, or powers, between nations can exert an influence on the structure of international trade and account for wars between nations.

To answer this, Mansfield begins by measuring the concentration of the 'capacities' of the five major world states, taken from among the twelve largest, at different points during the period from 1820 to 1965. These capacities were measured in terms of the economic, demographic and military dimensions of the nations concerned. The identity of some of these nations changes over time, as the identity of the five most powerful nations changed during the 19th and 20th centuries. But what is interesting is that this measurement of the 'capacities' of major powers has a direct relation to our concept of concentration of the resources of nations and thus their optimal economic, demographic and geographic size. A nation with rich economic, demographic and military resources is necessarily a 'great' nation in geographic terms as well.

Mansfield then examined the relation between this indicator of concentration of national dimensions and the degree of hegemony exercised by the most powerful nation of each period on the number of conflicts between states and the importance of international trade.

---

31   As shown in Graph 10.5 of Bergesen and Schoenberg, *supra* n. 29.

He thus demonstrates[32] that a concentration in the size and shape of major nations has a negative effect on the amount of international commerce. However, it also increases the frequency of conflicts between nations in a statistically significant way.[33] What is even more interesting is that an increase in the concentration of nations, which we interpret as a general increase in the size of nations, contributes equally and very significantly, to an increase in the probability of war between these nations. This corresponds exactly with our analysis of the probability of military conflict between nations pursuing a policy of expansion that will have to confront each other in border conflicts in territories coveted by both.

Returning to historical description, Mansfield notes that periods of low concentration of the 'capacities' of nations (that is, 'of their dimensions') were periods of co-operation between European nations, as in the early 19th century, while concentration reached its maximum level in 1946 at the beginning of the Cold War between the two empires or cartels of world nations.

3.   Conclusion

The system of nation-states evolves as a function of decisions made by each state about the optimal size and shape of its geographic area of control. When the optimal dimension of the state bureaucratic pyramid grows, states have recourse to external as well as internal growth. The world population of nation states also becomes more concentrated.

This concentration results in rivalry for control of territorial, demographic and economic resources. As there is uncertainty about the value that each protagonist places on coveted resources, and without a higher authority able to impose a peacefully negotiated solution on the competitors, war is the only way to reveal which competitor will be the most efficient in using additional resources. It follows that war will occur more frequently during periods in which the average size of hierarchies, and thus of states, is rising.

The size of the hierarchical organization is thus the key factor determining the structure of the society of nations and the conditions of war and peace between them. The current period, characterized by atomization and dissolution of major hierarchies and states, is thus a period in which the probability of war is low. While this technologically-based trend towards a decrease in the size of hierarchies and expansion of markets continues, we will experience a relatively peaceful period during which conflicts will be limited to internal wars: civil wars and wars of secession.

---

32   Mansfield, *supra* n. 24, p. 187, Table 5.4.

33   Mansfield applies this explanation to 50 per cent of conflicts between major nations between 1820 and 1965, which, in the social sciences and the early stages of geopolitics in general, is an extremely high figure.

We are also moving away from periods of hegemony during which a large country imposes its will on smaller states. The concept of the central role of hierarchical dimensions also explains differences in organization observed between small and large states. If the absolute size of the hierarchy is large, but for a variety of reasons the country cannot reach a large geographic size and shape (for example, due to the physical characteristics of the environment, such as mountains, the sea or oceans along its borders), it will tend to seek through internal growth, to optimize its capacity for organization that cannot be sought externally.

All things being equal, the smallest states will thus be characterized by a heavier taxation burden with respect to the national product. This explains Alberto Alesina's observation that states with the greatest openness to international trade are also those with the highest public expenses. Alesina explains this observation by the higher risk of instability in economies that are more open to the outside. But there is no obvious relationship between the public expenses in question and the risk of economic instability. Our explanation relies on the fact that small states are necessarily more open to international trade than larger states. This has long been a well-known fact.

The observed relationship between external trade and the importance of a state in the economy corresponds to the relation between the optimal size and shape of a state (defined in an absolute sense by the number of subordinates in the hierarchy), and the size of the economy (which is obviously small for the smallest countries). During periods in which the size of hierarchies is growing, smaller states find more new activities to invest in the economy than do larger states. This explains the strongly interventionist and socialist traditions in Nordic countries.

Finally, periods of concentration of hierarchical structures explain the change of tone in relations between nations and the intensity of conflicts between societies. The size of organizations determines the number of organizations that can survive within a given sector or society. And the number of organizations within a given sector or society defines the type of relations that will arise among them. Atomistic competition does not imply the same relationships between firms as an oligopoly or duopoly. And the perspective of an evolution of the latter towards a monopoly will determine the overall confrontation between the last two producers in a given sector: the survival of one implies the disappearance of the other.

In atomistic competition, each producer individually determines and develops his own business independently of others. Decentralization is the norm. Each consumer or user can choose his supplier. In a monopoly, a single individual decides everything. He imposes his choices on all others within and outside the firm. Order is unique, centralized and imposed on all, which results in intense conflict for control of the monopoly that decides everyone's fate.

VI. The Reasons for the Major Cycle: the Rise and Decline of Monopoly

The chaos and extreme confrontations of this totalitarian century are simply the expression of the rise of a monopolistic structure in the system of nations and in their internal systems. The first part of the 20th century was marked by a transition from competition between nations to an oligopoly, then a duopoly or, more specifically, a double cartel. In internal terms, it was marked by the shift from economic and political decentralization to a concentration of large firms, large parties and mass unions, followed by a transition towards totalitarianism and the single party system, with a single party line.

This transition leads to instability and increasingly radical confrontations, with an 'all or nothing' approach. Whereas atomistic competition allows a producer to live and leave other producers alone, only one may survive in the rise to monopoly. That survivor is the one with the motto that for him to survive, all other competitors must die. This is a total confrontation scenario.

The vision it conjures up is interestingly not in phase with current developments. The second half of the 20th century is not, contrary to what may be feared by those who still have the first half in mind, a time of hegemonic domination by a single power or organization, achieved through elimination of the main rival. It is no longer a time for globalization of a single empire, as was still possible during the times of Napoleon, Hitler or Stalin. On the contrary, it is a time of return to diversity, atomistic competition and decentralization. It is a return to a 'live and let live' philosophy.

Thus, a good understanding of the past sheds a completely new light on the present and near future.

Chapter 11

The Network Economy as a Challenge to Create New Public Law (beyond the State)

Thomas Vesting[*]

I. Personal Satellite Communication Systems and the 'Globalization' of Public Law

In recent discussion about the evolution of modern law under conditions of 'globalization', a degree of consensus has emerged regarding a significant growth in transnational rules and norms that are no longer consistent with previous state centred ideas of the production (and legitimation) of law.[1] The resulting implications for the new or – more accurately – the network economy are exemplified by the introduction and development of a new generation of personal satellite communication systems (S-PCS-systems), in which the world leaders are US-American corporations such as Motorola and particularly Qualcomm, which controls the CDMA-technology. These S-PCS-systems are operated by means of

* Professor of Law, University of Augsburg. Paper presented at the Workshop on 'Globalization and Public Governance', 17/18 March 2000, European University Institute, Florence. Translated – 'with passion' – by Jim Faulkner, Bucerius Law School, Hamburg/Germany.

1   See Gunther Teubner, 'Global Bukowina': Legal Pluralism in the World Society, in Gunter Teubner (ed.), *Global Law without a State* (Aldershot: Dartmouth, 1997), pp. 3 – 28; Karl-Heinz Ladeur, *'Towards a Legal Theory of Supra-nationality – The Viability of the Network Concept'*, EUROPEAN LAW JOURNAL, Vol. 3 (1997), pp. 33 – 54; Jean-Marie Guéhenno, *The End of the Nation-State* (Minneapolis: University of Minnesota, 1995); Niklas Luhmann, *Das Recht der Gesellschaft* (Frankfurt am Main: Suhrkamp, 1993), pp. 571 – 586; on the different meanings of 'Globalization' see e.g. Gordon Walker and Mark Fox, *'Globalization: An Analytical Framework'*, in GLOBAL LEGAL STUDIES JOURNAL, Vol. 3 (1996), pp. 375 – 411, 379 ff.

low earth orbit satellites (LEOs), and their system architecture is more highly developed and economically more efficient than the previous geo-stationary satellite systems. In the field of mobile telephones, for example, S-PCS-systems provide worldwide reachability under only one number (without roaming). In their higher developmental phases the so-called BIG LEOs combine higher performance capacity with greater flexibility, that is more connection and combination possibilities between different nets and services such as language/data, and mobile/terrestrial networks. In the long term, with the aid of so-called GIGA LEOs, S-PCS-systems should make possible a highly variable public system of network and service connections, encompassing the entire spectrum from telecommunications on the Internet to television.[2] This flexibility and the openness of their system architecture make S-PCS-systems comparable to the European Universal Mobile Telecommunications Systems (UMTS) and the technologies already used by the biggest Japanese mobile radio provider, NTT DoCoMo, for mobile Internet access. As with all information technology products, however, the ultimate commercial profitability of S-PCS-systems is highly uncertain and largely depends on the rate of demand increase among innovative companies and the achievement of a corresponding critical mass of investment. Thus, as is typical of the modern economy, this highly dynamic field of technical development is combined with a fundamental problem of timescale.

This timescale problem initially resulted in considerable pressure to act being exerted on the US-American Federal Communications Commission (FCC), the regulatory agency mainly responsible for the allocation of broadcasting frequencies. This pressure was difficult for the FCC to withstand since it had to make decisions on the basis of incomplete knowledge. Not only is it difficult to predict the technological and commercial development of S-PCS-systems, but relatively high demands are made on the management of public frequencies. Whereas technically suitable frequencies are in short supply at the moment, future requirements are difficult to estimate as progressive digitalization may make it possible to provide a multiple allocation of the same frequency to different S-PCS network operators.[3]

2   For more details see Martine Rothblatt, '*Lex Americana: The New International Legal Regime for Low Earth Orbit Satellite Communications Systems*', JOURNAL OF SPACE LAW, Vol. 23 (1995), pp. 123 – 140; Karl-Heinz Ladeur, '*Die Globalisierung der Telekommunikation und die kooperative Herausbildung einer neuen transnationalen Rechtsordnung – das Beispiel der mobilen Satellitenkommunikation*', ArchPT (1998), pp. 243 – 251; Christian Koenig and Christopher Zeiss, '*EG-Telekommunikationsrecht und Lizenzierung von satellitengestützten persönlichen Kommunikationssystemen*', EuZW (1999), pp. 133 – 139.

3   Christian Koenig and Christopher Zeiss, *supra* n.2, pp. 133 – 139, 133; Joachim Scherer, 'Innovationsoffenheit der europäischen Telekommunikations-Regulierung', in Wolfgang Hoffmann-Riem (ed.), *Innovation und Telekommunikation* (Baden-Baden: Nomos,

This situation is exacerbated by the fact that, from the outset, S-PCS-systems were oriented towards global use, whereas the responsible International Telecommunications Union (ITU), or the responsible broadcasting administration conferences WCR-92 and WCR-95, did not differentiate; they only identified and allocated frequencies for satellite communication. Thus the broadcasting frequencies for S-PCS-systems could and can only be allocated once, in view of the essential innovative nature of S-PCS technology in providing unlimited mobility and worldwide reachability with relatively small reception devices, an innovation that can only be realized with a worldwide agreement on frequencies so as to avoid resulting interferences. This need for global co-ordination and co-operation was clearly recognized by various regional regulatory agencies. Japan, for example, called in 1994 for the task of frequency allocation for S-PCS-systems to be transferred to a new international regulatory institution. However, the lead of US-American corporations and resulting variations in pressure for action between countries led to a breakdown in international co-operation, due in the final analysis to the obstructive stance of the USA (among other countries). Following consultations with US-American parties interested in LEO, the FCC as early as 1995 allocated the first licence for BIG LEOs to international corporate groups with marked American dominance, namely to Iridium, a joint venture under the leadership of Motorola (which has been wound up in the meantime), Globalstark under the leadership of Qualcomm, and Odyssey under the leadership of PRW. The FCC has also granted a licence for the third development stage, the GIGA LEOs, to an American corporation, Teledisec.

Further details can be dispensed with here, as the consequences of the licensing practice of the FCC are apparent. In a technically and economically highly dynamic field, also characterized by global competition between standards and variations in system configurations, the FCC has granted licences for the use of LEOs on a 'first come – first served' basis to the almost exclusive benefit of US-American corporations. In this, the FCC has neither made the allocation of frequencies dependent on an inter-state agreement nor has it waited for the establishment of a new international regulatory agency. Rather it has itself made decisions – as an independent regulatory agency – that were equivalent to transnational decisions, or which by virtue of their independent decision-making practice at least produced such a strong necessity for compliance that the European regulatory body for S-PCS-systems, for example, was forced to accept and fall in with the FCC licensing initiatives especially in the area of frequency harmonization.[4] If this is to be a new form of 'spontaneous' law production beyond the state, does it not in effect simply

---

2000), pp. 161- 183, 165.

4   Christian Koenig and Christopher Zeiss, *supra* n. 2, pp. 133 – 139, 133; Andreas Bartosch, '*Europäische Regulierung transeuropäischer Kommunikationssysteme*', CR (2000), pp. 214 – 220, 220.

constitute an avoidance of international law?[5] Are we not concerned with a commercially open legal form that primarily serves the interests of US-American high technology corporations? Is not the independent action of the FCC evidence that 'globalization' is little more than a conceptual vehicle aimed at strengthening the hegemony of the US-American business and legal culture?[6] With the assistance of US-American regulatory agencies, US-American corporations are strengthening their global power position and administering international law according to the standard of their own commercial interests in a way reminiscent of the application of the 19th century Monroe Doctrine. To express it even more drastically: is not the FCC introduction of S-PCS-systems evidence of a new 'legal imperialism', that is a form of law production that 'belongs to a state whose imperialistic expansion consists in the expansion of its capitalist investments and of its opportunities for exploitation'?[7]

In the context of FCC licensing practice, the international satellite communication term '*Lex Americana*' has also been applied to the case of S-PCS-systems used here as an example.[8] However, the commercially centred perspective, in which 'globalization' and 'commercialization' are seen as more or less equivalent, may fail to address the actual changes imposed on law and politics by virtue of new information technologies. If the perspective is widened to encompass development of the network economy, then it is apparent that the introduction of new information technologies is increasingly performed outside the scope of traditional forms of national legislation as practiced within the European continental model in particular. The old state model was a 'top-down' system. It was based on a pre-established and determining body of rules, the creation of aggregated sets of laws that anticipate reality and which are in practice only partially altered. The new system is a 'bottom-up' system, based on processes of flexible, heterarchic, network-like and incomplete production of rules. These emerging flexible processes of law production are in turn only loosely, if at all, connected to legislation in its previously accepted sense through task catalogues conceived at a very general level

---

5   For this argument see Christian Koenig and Christopher Zeiss, *supra* n. 2, pp. 133 – 139, which regards the one-sided action of the FCC as a potential violation of Art. 2 of the Outer Space Treaty 27th January 1967 as well as Art. 33 of the International Telecommunications Convention 25th October 1973. The Outer Space Treaty precludes laying sovereign claim to the natural resources of outer space.

6   See for example Serge Sur, '*The State between Fragmentation and Globalization*', EJIL Vol. 3 (1997), pp. 421 – 434; Paul Hirst and Grahame Thompson, *Globalization in Question* (Cambridge: Polity Press, 1996), p. 187.

7   Carl Schmitt, Völkerrechtliche Formen des modernen Imperialismus (1932), in ders., *Positionen und Begriffe im Kampf mit Weimar-Genf-Versailles 1923-1939* (Berlin: Duncker & Humblot, 1988), pp. 162 – 180, 173.

8   Martine Rothblatt, *supra* n. 2, pp. 123 – 140, 128.

(e.g. the rapid introduction of S-PCS-systems into the European Union). On the one hand, these novel law production processes are operated by various public regulatory agencies in connection with parliamentary or administratively filtered committees (e.g. European Funkausschuss – ERC). On the other hand, a wide range of semi-state and private organizations are integrated into these networks, including standardization institutions (e.g. European Telecommunications Standards Institute – ETSI), transnational work groups (e.g. CEPT[9]) or other highly organized industry specific target-groups. This pattern of private-public co-operation and network-like law production may be observed on the national level, as in Britain and Germany, with the introduction of digital television.[10] But the pattern is no less widespread on the European level, for example in the introduction of GSM or UMTS.[11] Similar forms dominate on the transnational level but are also present in other information technology contexts, in particular in the regulation of the Internet.[12] In view of this, the licensing practice of the FCC in the field of S-PCS-systems appears less an example of 'legal imperialism' on the part of the USA than the expression of a new form of 'spontaneous' transnational law production. Similarly to the way, supernational private law has liberated itself from the pressures and dysfunctionalities of the national legal order (*lex mercatoria*)[13] with the transformation of the world

9   Conférence Européenne des Administrations des Postes et Télecommunications.

10   See for example Wolfgang Schulz, Rechtssetzung in der 'Informationsgesellschaft': Renaissance für die Gesetzgebungslehre, in Kurt Imhof, Otfried Jarren and Roger Blum (eds.), *Steuerungs- und Regelungsprobleme in der Informationsgesellschaft* (Opladen: Wiesbaden, 1999), pp. 342 – 360, 352 f., on the introduction of digital TV in Great Britain and Germany; Karl-Heinz Ladeur, *'Rechtliche Regulierung von Informationstechnologien und Standardsetzung'*, CR (1999), pp. 395 – 404, on the introduction of digital TV in Germany.

11   See Andreas Bartosch, *'Europäische Regulierung transeuropäischer Kommunikationssysteme'*, CR (2000), pp. 214 - 220, 215 f., on the European GSM-regulation strategy; Jürgen Heilbock, *'UMTS – Die dritte Mobilfunkgeneration aus rechtlicher Sicht'*, MMR (1999), pp. 23 – 28, on the introduction of UMTS networks in Europe; Joachim Scherer, Innovationsoffenheit der europäischen Telekommunikations-Regulierung, in Wolfgang Hoffmann-Riem (ed.), *supra* n. 3, pp. 161 – 183, 165, on the introduction of S-PCS in Europe. For an overview on standards and standardization processes see also Paul A. David, 'The Internet and the Economics of Network Technology Evolution', in Christoph Engel and Kenneth Kellner (eds.), *Understanding the Impact of Global Networks on Local Social, Political and Cultural Values* (Baden-Baden: Nomos, 2000), pp. 39 –71.

12   For more details Michael Hutter, 'The Commercialization of the Internet. A Progress Report', in Christoph Engel and Kenneth Kellner (eds.), *supra* n.11, pp. 73 – 92.

13   See Ursula Stein, *Lex mercatoria: Realität und Theorie*, (Frankfurt am Main: Klostermann, 1995), pp. 13 – 16, 252 – 259.

economy since the 1930s, so public law is also partially liberating itself from the state-centred forms of national and international law. It is establishing law production on an independent footing and transforming it into new network-like patterns between private and public organizations. In these forms the rules and their applications are fused, and in view of the openness and indeterminability of the future, the time context dependency of law is more markedly varied than in traditional liberal law.

Even if one basically accepts the development of new co-operative, network-like legal forms beyond the state, a sober analysis cannot ignore structural weaknesses in new 'hybrid' regulatory networks compared with the previous forms. A mixture of non-binding, semi-binding and binding programming by goals predominate, whose approach to practical application is highly informal and opaque. This is because various state authorities and regulatory agencies are operating in often widely differing contexts. With the increase in operating players, more disagreements on competences and responsibilities arise (for example between sectoral regulation and competition supervision), while legal regulations are often only inadequately harmonized (for example in telecommunications law compared to traditional media law). A further problem is simply that public players in these relational networks often react very late, so that their technical knowledge often lags behind the times. In addition, regulatory or competition agencies tend to act without direction and generally lack long-term strategies for action. Thus the regulation of more complex technologies would seem to pose novel problems of knowledge. Accordingly should not public law intervene precisely here, and if so which goals and purposes in the network economy should public organizations be expected to undertake? Could this be the basis for a new public law (beyond the state)?

This chapter is intended to formulate initial responses to these rather difficult questions. The chapter should be seen as a research exercise, indicating tendencies and pointing out lines of investigation rather than giving definitive answers. To limit the potential for confusion, I deliberately narrow the scope of the questions on problems of the network economy; I also attempt to subject the inductive part of the paper to specific strands of legal theory inquiry. The intention is that both strands contribute to an alternative learning process, avoiding precipitate generalization regarding isolated individual phenomena on the one hand, and on the other making the analytical power of the theory dependent on several case examples and not only on any internal cohesion of the argumentation. Systems theory seems to me to be a particularly promising vehicle for this purpose. The new legal theoretical paradigms on network-like system creation, as built above all in the sphere of the systems theory orientated discussions of legal theory,[14] are intrinsically related to network

---

14　Niklas Luhmann, *Das Recht der Gesellschaft* (Frankfurt am Main: Suhrkamp, 1993); Karl-Heinz Ladeur, *Postmoderne Rechtstheorie* (Berlin:Duncker & Humblot, 1992); Gunther Teubner, *Recht als autopoietisches System* (Frankfurt am Main: Suhrkamp,

economy 'laws'; it is at least no coincidence that these concepts are being formulated precisely in a period in which the new global economy is poised to replace the old order of an industrial society dominated by the welfare state.[15] The innate relationship between systems theory and the global network economy is illustrated by the way systems theory provides an apparatus for conceptual differentiation by means of which autonomous systems can also be delineated. Such delineation is even possible where the territorial borders and limitations of law can no longer be taken as given, that is where the territorial concept of legal theory loses persuasive power in a way similar to the territorial concepts of sociology or state theory. This primarily legal theory perspective leads to a slight shift of emphasis away from questions of 'global governance' towards questions of the legal forms necessary for it; I shall however at an intermediary stage and in the two final sections attempt to sketch several consequences of my ideas for governance in a 'global age'.

II. Adapting Law to the 'Logic of Networking'

1. Introduction

The first step towards a new public law (beyond the state) depends on viewing present-day society in a way appropriate to its high degree of social complexity. Essential from the outset is an adequate picture of modern society from the perspective of the legal system or legal theory. This is particularly necessary in connection with the questions developed here, in that the phenomenon of 'globalization' is still seen too much from the viewpoint of the state. Society is equated with the sovereign nation state, whose unity and order is secured not least through a superior ordering of the public (the state) over the private (liberal society). Indeed, in many conceptualizations, society is first constituted through the supremacy of constitutional principles (basic rights, *rechtsstaat*, democracy, etc). The nation state, the constitutional state, *rechtsstaat* and modern liberal society become broadly the same thing, as the pluralism of the world order of states corresponds under this view to a pluralism of 'norm' oriented and territorially limited 'spatial ordering'. This fixation on the state then leads from a legal theoretical perspective to a number of premature conclusions or 'short cuts', which

1989); see also Gunther Teubner (ed.), *Autopoietic Law: A New Approach to Law and Society* (Berlin/New York: de Gruyter, 1988).

15 See the remarks on this interdependency by Kevin Kelly, *New Rules for the New Economy* (New York: Viking, 1998), p. 159; Niklas Luhmann, *Die Gesellschaft der Gesellschaft*, Bd. 1 (Frankfurt am Main: Suhrkamp, 1997), p. 31; Karl-Heinz Ladeur, *Postmoderne Rechtstheorie* (Berlin: Duncker & Humblot, 1992), p. 100.

render the production and binding nature of modern liberal law *a priori* dependent on state – generated procedures and the potential of state – guaranteed sanctions, that is ultimately on the power monopoly of the state.[16]

2. From Hierarchical to Modern Society

As early as Aristotelian times, the normative-teleological model of a 'natural unity' led in the politico-legal sphere to the conviction that human nature was such that the true purpose of the good life lay in the political community (*koinonía politike*).[17] With this close connection between politics and metaphysics it was at the same time determined that the order of the politico-legal community was not, and could not be created by mankind, because worthwhile (rational) life in the city was a product of nature striving to discover or fulfil itself.[18] Hence pre-modern society effectively oriented itself towards past circumstances, to origins, to the monarchical and aristocratic traditions, to the world which was as it was and would be ever more. Other possibilities for development were unthinkable within the past-oriented world view of the Aristotelian-Christian metaphysic. While the good life might not ultimately be attained, political action could nevertheless only serve principally worthwhile purposes or interests that were preordained politically and legally part of the 'natural unity'. This static, backward-looking character of traditional society corresponded to metaphysics and a form of awareness. Metaphysics was conceptually the core of a system of rules that, on the basis of *logical* rules, made possible the rational-demonstrative (free of contradictions) conception of being and its ultimate principles. For this reason it was, in its highest and most intensive form, nothing other than the representation of the unity of thought (form) and being (content).[19] In systems theory terms: metaphysics as epistemology consisted in the

---

16 As a brilliant example of this tradition see Martin van Creveld, *Aufstieg und Untergang des Staates* (München: Gerling Akademie Verlag, 1999), p. 205; and in this book.

17 Aristotele, Politik, 1252 a. The economy, or the house (*oikos*) is thereby seen as independent of politics, but not as initially in the 18th century as a moral science of 'political economy', but the precise opposite as apolitical; the *oikos* belonged in the world of necessity, in which the cyclical (not abstract) problem of scarcity had to be resolved; see Caroline Gerschlager, *Konturen der Entgrenzung* (Marburg: Metropolis, 1996), pp. 31, 40.

18 For more details Joachim Ritter, *Metaphysik und Politik*, (Frankfurt am Main: Suhrkamp, 1977), pp. 9 – 179; Manfred Riedel, *Metaphysik und Metapolitik* (Frankfurt am Main: Suhrkamp, 1975), pp. 11 – 105; for a brief summary see Wolfgang Kersting, *Die politische Philosophie des Gesellschaftsvertrages* (Darmstadt: Wissenschaftliche Buchgesellschaft, 1996), pp. 1 – 18.

19 Panajotis Kondylis, *Die neuzeitliche Metaphysikkritik* (Stuttgart: Klett-Cotta, 1990), p. 13.

representation of a 'rational continuum'.[20] This 'rational continuum' bound the observer into, and indeed with an immutably interpreted world, thereby rendering this world accessible for an all-knowing donor subject.

Modern liberal society shattered this natural, traditional order oriented towards a preordained state of perfection. Not overnight, not at a single stroke, but by a series of cuts together with occasional powerful blows. The attack on the past-fixated Aristotelian-Christian worldview began in the 17th century, above all with modern mathematical natural science. The mathematical science ideals of research and precision as propagated by writers such as Bacon, Descartes and Galileo, rendered obsolete the conceptual unity between thought and being and the accompanying self-legitimation of being. This was replaced under modern rationalism by methodical work according to strict rules and regular routines; for example Bacon called for a search for pure and abstract truth behind the false images and illusory apparitions (idols),[21] long before Kant in his work *Critic der reinen Vernunft* discovered 'the thing in itself' and thereby the limitations of metaphysics. In political theory the consequences of the new world view were explored above all in social contract theory in the writings of Hobbes, Locke and the Scottish Enlightenment,[22] where the politico-legal field emancipated itself from the unity of the traditional metaphysical world view and was reoriented towards self-establishing practice.[23] Thereby modern society constituted a historical break, which rendered the evolutionary theory extremely implausible and which could not be explained by liberal and Marxist laws of historical predetermination; nevertheless, the transition to modern society can at best be reconstructed 'universal-historically' as the product of entirely coincidental preconditions.[24] The process of dissolution of the traditional hierarchical society, which seen from a universal-historic perspective reached an irreversible stage *only* in England, nevertheless produced an extraordinarily intense divergence, ultimately leading to a historically unprecedented internal complexity and capacity for self-transformation. The high degree of internal complexity and the rapid transformation of modern society was then generally apparent after the industrial take-off, that is after 1820, and today, with the collapse of communism,

---

20 Niklas Luhmann, *Beobachtungen der Moderne* (Opladen: Westdeutscher, 1992), p. 53.

21 Caroline Gerschlager, *supra* n. 17, pp. 67 f.

22 'The skill of making, and maintaining Common-Wealths, consisteth in certain Rules, as doth Arithmetique and Geometry; not (as Tennis-play) on Practise onely', Thomas Hobbes (1651), *Leviathan* (Harmondsworth: Penguin, 1968), ch. 20, p. 107.

23 For more details see Karl-Heinz Ladeur, *Negative Freiheitsrechte und gesellschaftliche Selbstorganization* (Tübingen: Mohr, 2000), pp. 21 – 46; see also Wolfgang Kersting, *Die politische Philosophie des Gesellschaftsvertrages* (Darmstadt: Wissenschaftliche Buchgesellschaft, 1996), pp. 59 – 139.

24 As is well-known as a central theme of Max Weber.

this model for social (self-) organization seems to prevail as generally valid all over the world.[25]

3. *Increase of Internal Complexity of Autonomous Systems*

The idea of the increase in internal complexity should reflect the idea that from an *objectively-social* point of view modern society is a complex society which is not amenable to a centrist theoretical approach (end of metanarratives). This is primarily because in the course of its evolution modern society is gradually liberating itself from any naturally prescribed purposes. Liberal society is loosening any ties to the alien unknowable will of God and is strengthening its own internal values. This also involves a distancing from the natural existence of being, its natural 'environment'. A linguistic science standpoint views this phenomenon such that liberal society frees itself from the stable signification of the sign, and, as Hobbes pointed out, devises its own artificial signs with more signification possibilities.[26] With the liberation of society from nature (and the stable fixed 'natural' signification of the sign), and as modern society continues to evolve, a further differentiation of individual signs and sign formations *within* the society occurs, which in turn gradually stabilizes into independent and self-sufficient communications networks. The unity and accessibility of the old hierarchical society is thus giving way to the self-establishment of independent autonomous communication networks. These autonomous networks were initially described in the sociology of the turn of the century as products of the 'objective culture', as 'elementary forms', 'value spheres' or 'cultural provinces'; the Aristotelian world view – in the language of Max Weber – replaced by the concept of the 'inherent natural lawfulness of individual spheres' of 'occidental culture'.[27] In other words various *collective* (not only individual) spheres of rationality are differentiated in the modern society. The 'natural unity' of the traditional hierarchical society, the metaphysically determined hierarchical class model of traditional Europe, gives way to what Hermann Heller described in his work *Staatslehre* in 1934 as an 'objective, non-psychological coherence of the social totality'.[28] New systems theory describes this process as a reorientation in society from 'hierarchical' to 'functional differentiation'.[29] In contrast to Max

---

25 See generally Francis Fukuyama, *The Great Disruption* (New York: Free Press, 1999).

26 Thomas Hobbes, *supra* n. 22, ch. 4, pp. 12 – 17; see also Karl-Heinz Ladeur, *supra* n. 23, p. 24.

27 Max Weber, *Gesammelte Aufsätze zur Religionssoziologie* (1920), (Tübingen: Mohr, 1986), pp. 541, 11.

28 Hermann Heller, 'Staatslehre' (1934), in Martin Drath u.a. (eds.), *Gesammelte Schriften*, Bd. 3 (Berlin: Duncker & Humblot, 1977), pp. 195 – 204, 196.

29 Niklas Luhmann, *Die Gesellschaft der Gesellschaft*, Bd. 2 (Frankfurt am Main: Suhrkamp, 1997), pp. 707 – 776, 709.

Weber, Luhmann reformulates the rationality problematic of modern society in exclusively differentiation theory terms.[30] However, modern society is here divided into a number of autonomous systems orientated to function like law, politics, economy, science, mass media, etc. These primary systems orientated to function are thought of as operatively closed and, with the aid of binary codes (for example legal/illegal) and adjusted programmes (for example conditional programmes in legal systems) assume specific functions and overall responsibilities in society. Under these conditions, law and its social function can only be produced and guaranteed by the legal system, which does not exclude, but rather presupposes that the legal system takes account of the preliminary input of other autonomous systems, such as monetary payments from the economy.

It is not necessary to decide here whether the acentric and dynamic relational networks of modern society are accurately analysed under the formula of 'functional differentiation'. However Luhmann's description of the transition from the traditional to modern society as the dissolution of the traditional European 'rationality continuum' is certainly apt.[31] The concept of rationality especially becomes precarious because the closed 'holistic' conception of the Aristotelian-Christian world view is here displaced by a plurality of system rationalities and self-descriptions. This is brought about not least by scientific theories of reflection that, after the invention of the printed book, increasingly developed alongside the specific orientations and functions of different meaning systems. This happens for example through the production of new theoretical descriptions such as legal positivism, which carries forward the displacement of natural law, replacing the image of the old good law with the figure of the arbitrary production of law. The supposition that law is discovered by reference to (sacred) authority is now substituted by the image of the production of law and the possibility to change rules contained therein.[32]

4.   *The Transitional Character of Novelty*

A further characteristic of modern society, closely bound up with the idea of increased internal complexity, lies in the dynamic stability of autonomous systems and the fluid relationships that these systems enter into with each other. Modern society also destroys the old 'rationality continuum' to the extent that it is a continuum. The departure from the continuity (and authority) of tradition is manifest above all in a new time conceptualization, with whose implementation the basic orientation principles of society shift from experience (past) to expectation (future). This trend can be seen in the gradual positive re-evaluation of novelty and the

---

30   Niklas Luhmann, *Die Gesellschaft der Gesellschaft*, Bd. 1 (Frankfurt am Main: Suhrkamp, 1997), pp. 171 – 189.

31   Niklas Luhmann, *Beobachtungen der Moderne*, *supra* n. 20, pp. 51 – 91.

32   See Niklas Luhmann, *Das Recht der Gesellschaft*, *supra* n. 1, pp. 507 – 529.

supplementary concepts connected with it, such as genius, creativity, innovation, discovery, etc. For example in the 18th century the (messianic) idea of a new politically social order can already be consciously turned against tradition, as happened most significantly in the French Revolution. Here modern society at the same time succumbs to the unknownness of the future. The future is no longer experienced and lived as a mere repetition of the past (or as the fall), but as a horizon of uncertain possibilities offering opportunities and posing dangers. It is this uncertainty in the temporal dimension which makes concepts of 'bounded' and 'procedural rationality' plausible.[33]

Today the preponderance of a rapid, accelerating, and even speeding time is deeply anchored in society. The cause of this is not least that, after the end of the Enlightenment, Romanticism, Marxism, Fascism, Futurism, etc., the compulsion to produce novelty can no longer simply be put off into the future.[34] The economy in particular today sees itself as exposed to the permanent 'temporal nature of the new',[35] as shown by the constant need of the economy to substitute old money for new. The typical acceleration of time in modern society is further shown in the extreme shortening of product cycles, especially in the network economy (processors, chips, etc.). It is also seen, however, in the mass media, which have to hold attention under the conditions of an accompanying constant surplus of information, itself only possible by means of the endless production of *new* information, *new* news, *new* sports events, and *new* films. Another example is fashions, which are equally subject to a constant pressure to innovate. In short: the temporal, provisional nature of novelty has today become a way of life. Ultimately it places individuals under constant pressure to change, in which they must repeatedly show their originality and uniqueness.[36] Thereby novelty has become an incessant, everlasting event, an 'eternal present' of modern culture. With the readjustment towards future orientation an abstract (no longer space and experience related) time horizon becomes dominant,[37] which punctuates the present, that is dissolves the coherence of the given in a permanent sequence of new but equally fleeting events.

33   Herbert Simon, From Substantive to Procedural Rationality, in S.J. Latsis (ed.), *Method and Appraisal in Economics* (Cambridge: Cambridge University Press, 1976), pp. 129, 131.

34   Boris Groys, *Über das Neue* (München: C. Hanser, 1992), p. 11.

35   Caroline Gerschlager, *supra* n. 17, p. 111; for the consequences of this future-orientation see Boris Groys, *Über das Neue* (München: C. Hanser, 1992) (culture); Niklas Luhmann, *Die Gesellschaft der Gesellschaft, supra* n. 15, Bd. 1, pp. 997 – 1016 (society and semantics).

36   See Gilles Lipovetsky, *L'ère du vide. Essais sur l'individualisme contemporain* (Paris: Gallimard, 1983).

37   Manuel Castells, *The Rise of the Network Society*, Vol. 1 (Oxford: Blackwell, 1996), pp. 429 – 468, 465, talks about 'timeless time'; see also Marc Augé, *Orte und Nicht-Orte*

5. Intermediate Conclusion: From Subject to Network

In the light of these initial abstract considerations, a new public law (beyond the state) must proceed from the assumption that with the transition to modern society a network of autonomous 'cultural provinces', freed from the 'natural living space' of mankind, has arisen; an immaterial world of relations and connections whose inherent natural lawfulness is produced and reproduced over each specific selection pattern. In their respective roles for example as law professors, car mechanics, consumer, Internet user or member of the electorate, people are involved in the production and reproduction of this emergent level of the collective, but are not as the 'people' the 'cause' of society. A legal theory that started with such simplifications would be contradicted from the outset by the fact that the diversity and internal complexity of the communicative networks of society, their 'language games' and specific bodies of knowledge, have multiplied to the extent that they are no longer accessible to *one single* observer. The collective phenomenon fields, which above all emerge on the basis of the differentiation of autonomous functional systems such as politics, law, economy, mass media, etc., rather produce a *drift* which in turn leads to the dissolution of all traditional ideas of the unity of the society, the state, the nation, democracy, the people, etc., as well as the associated subject theories and all hierarchical layering related to them. *That* is meant when the end of the (sovereign) subject is talked of. Jean-Marie Guéhenno is undoubtedly correct: 'Nothing is more foreign to our age than the idea of a person-subject that could exist in and of itself, outside the network of relationships in which it is inscribed and which alone defines it'.[38]

In a networked multiplicity of rules and routines, collective 'trans-subject' relationships displace the old stable person subjects (state, people, organization, individual). This multiplicity no longer has a centre (as in the traditional European conception) and in the continuation of these collective 'trans-subject' relationships people merely are involved. This renders obsolete the idea of a stable 'subject' or 'object', which could be conceived of independently of the communicative networks and their dynamic relationships. This means for the line of questioning raised here that it can no longer be relevant today to seek *one* new stable 'person subject' like the global state or global democracy.[39] In future a new network-like thinking in terms of relations and connections will be needed, a legal-theoretical thinking which proceeds from a multiplicity of legal subjects, but which does not assume the differences and boundaries between them to be stable, but rather concentrates on how the differences and boundaries are repeatedly infiltrated,

---

(Frankfurt am Main: Fischer Verlag, 1994).

38 Jean Marie Guéhenno, *The End of the Nation-State, supra* n. 1, p. 33.

39 E.g. Otfried Höffe, *Demokratie im Zeitalter der Globalisierung* (München: Beck, 1999), makes an attempt in this direction.

deconstructed, rendered indistinguishable.[40] Thus a legal theory is needed which assumes a multiplicity of fluid distinctions and linkages. Legal theory can no longer refer to stable legal subjects, hierarchical classes and fixed relationships, but rather must develop a keener sensitivity towards the public arena and rapid self-transformational skills of autonomous systems, organizations and individuals. Like the 'objects' of ascribed legal rights and obligations, the 'subjects' of production of legal rules must be conceived of as dynamic relational networks of networks.

The readjustment of legal theory towards network-like, dynamic stability also means that in future it will not be enough to open public law to flexibility and innovativeness. This will naturally continue to be an important task of public law, but the legal-*theoretical* perspective will first require an improved understanding of the ordering function of liberal law and its autonomy against the background of *new* experiences. This brief sketch shows that the ordering function of liberal law is inadequately grasped by the widespread ideas of 'securing continuity', 'maintaining confidence' and 'securing of expectations',[41] in that, under conditions of increased social complexity and faster self-transformation capacity, it appears inconceivable that modern law will continue to be oriented towards stable social states.[42] Before we explore this area more closely, it is first necessary to explore in more detail the state and political theory consequences of such an approach for the current globalization discussion.

III.   Consequences for the Globalization Discussion

In the current globalization discussion, the new world order is still regarded as a phenomenon that undermines the sovereignty of the nation state and the territorial seclusion of their jurisdictions (and thereby in particular undermines the relatively high social standards of European societies).[43] However, if as here, one construes

40   Boris Groys, *Unter Verdacht. Eine Phänomenologie der Medien* (München: C. Hanser, 2000), p. 14.

41   See Reiner Schmidt, 'Die Reform von Verwaltung und Verwaltungsrecht', *Verwaltungsarchiv*, Vol. 91 (2000), pp. 149 – 168, 155; on the securing of expectations as involving future uncertainty, see Niklas Luhmann, *Das Recht der Gesellschaft, supra* n. 1.

42   James R. Buchanan, '*Individual Right, Emergent Social States, and Behavioural Feasibility*', in RATIONALITY AND SOCIETY, Vol. 7 (1995), pp. 141 ff.

43   With varying emphases Serge Sur, '*The State between Fragmentation and Globalization*', EJIL Vol. 3 (1997), pp. 421 – 434; Paul Hirst and Grahame Thompson, *Globalization in Question* (Cambridge: Polity Press, 1996), pp. 170 – 194; Saskia Sassen, *Losing Control? Sovereignty in an Age of Globalization* (New York: Columbia U P., 1996), pp. 1 – 30; Jürgen Habermas, 'Jenseits des Nationalstaats? Remarks on the

modern liberal society as an acentric and dynamic network of relationships of equally ranking autonomous systems, then this viewpoint requires at least partial revision. The supposition of a territorial seclusion of the legal order conceals nothing other than the idea of a *state* legal order, behind which in turn stands the equating of the nation state with modern society.[44] The above considerations, however, suggest that modern society is to be thought of as a communicatively networked global system, which in a purely formal sense can certainly be described as a 'world society' or 'worldwide communication system'.[45] Such a linguistic ruling seems to be particularly productive when less stress is placed on the unity of *the* 'world society' than on the 'heterarchic, connectist, network-like linking of communication on the level of organizations and professions'.[46] 'Globalization' is not then a principally new phenomenon, but rather the product of an increase and intensification of the global interweaving of communication systems. Such interweaving has been a feature of liberal society from its beginnings, and is continued today above all by the global development of the information economy.[47]

If one accepts the perspective given here of an acentric society, then the autonomy of primary social (function) systems must also be understood as independent of the conditions and limits of time and space. This should today be relatively plausible for the economy or mass media. But then it also is valid for the political system (and the legal system). Such a conceptual strategy would, contrary to the dominant everyday consciousness, lead to a clear shift of emphasis, but would not be a departure from the liberal tradition. All the same bourgeois thought recognized early and insisted that the generalization of the communicative

Problematic Consequences of Economic Globalization', in Ulrich Beck (ed.), *Politik der Globalisierung* (Frankfurt am Main, Suhrkamp, 1998), pp. 67 – 84, and the overview by Phillip Alston, *'The Myopia of the Handmaidens: International Lawyers and Globalization'*, EJIL (1997), pp. 435 – 448.

44 This is, for example, the approach in Anthony Giddens, *The Consequences of Modernity* (Cambridge: Polity Press, 1990); similarly Ulrich Beck, 'Wie wird Demokratie im Zeitalter der Globalisierung möglich?', in Ulrich Beck (ed.), *Politik der Globalisierung*, *supra* n. 43, pp. 7 – 66.

45 Niklas Luhmann, 'Der Staat des politischen Systems', in Ulrich Beck (ed.), *Perspektiven der Weltgesellschaft* (Frankfurt am Main: Suhrkamp, 1998), pp. 345 – 380, 373 f.

46 Niklas Luhmann, 'Der Staat des politischen Systems', in Ulrich Beck (ed.), ibid, pp. 345 – 380, 375.

47 See Manuel Castells, *The Rise of the Network Society*, Vol. 1, *supra* n. 37, pp. 66 – 151; Paul Krugman, *The Self-Organizing Economy* (Malden: Blackwell, 1998); Jonathan Perraton, David Goldbealt, David Held and Anthony Mc Green, 'Die Globalisierung der Wirtschaft', in Ulrich Beck (Hrsg.), *Politik der Globalisierung* (Frankfurt am Main: Suhrkamp, 1998); Ulrich Menzel, *Globalisierung versus Fragmentierung* (Frankfurt am Main: Suhrkamp, 1998).

relationships between people is a consequence of a liberal society possessed of uninhibited power. One only has to think of Adam Smith and his observations of the results of free trade in the last third of the 18th century,[48] or of Hegel, who some two decades later pointed out that the life-giving element for modern industry is not the earth, the ground and soil, but rather the sea, that is fluid and which knows no bounds.[49] And we know from Carl Schmitt that national macroeconomists (but not jurists) as early as 1900 clearly analysed the widespread de-territorialization, which accompanied the rise of the industrial society of the 19th century. At least the idea of 'commercial globality', that the liberal idea of free world trade and free world market was taken for granted in European thinking since the Cobden Treaty of 1860.[50]

The sovereign nation state in the sense of a territorially bound and culturally (linguistically, religiously, cultural, etc.) distinct political unity would also then have to be qualified as a historically specific form of regional political differentiation in a global communicative network of networks. *This* form of political differentiation is today dissolving. The sovereign nation state and the 'international system' based upon it are proving to an increasing degree to be an inadequate answer to cope with the increased internal complexity and capability of rapid self-transformation of liberal society. This is particularly true of the state as described in the European continental development path. The European continental state has always seen itself as the side of distinction from state and society, which has to more observe than respect the distinction. The continental European state is not a 'trust', not an institution of society which determines the tasks and boundaries of this institution, as for example with John Locke where the political society determined the end of every form of government.[51] By contrast the continental nation state has always conceived of itself as the constitutive condition and background guarantor of the entire social order. This applies to the state-fixated Hegel-derived variant as it does to the people-fixated Rousseau-derived variant. From this perspective the continental European state appears as the particular subject of history which

---

48   Adam Smith, *An Inquiry into the Nature and Causes of the Wealth of Nations* (1776), (London: Methuen, 1961), Vol. 2, p. 141.

49   Georg Wilhelm Friedrich Hegel, *Grundlinien der Philosophie des Rechts* (1821), (Stuttgart: Hg. von B. Lakebrink, 1970), 1970, § 247.

50   Carl Schmitt, *Der Nomos der Erde* (1950), (Berlin: Duncker & Humblot, 1974), p. 208. Bourgeois critical thinking early recognized the tendency in 'bourgeois society' to be driven out above itself. For Marx the tendency to create world markets was 'intrinsic to the concept of capital'. In more recent political and social science writing this insight is headed 'Pax Britannica', see Paul Hirst and Graham Thompson, *Globalization in Question, supra* n. 6, pp. 18 – 50.

51   John Locke, *Two Treatises of Government* (1698), (Cambridge: Cambridge University Press, 1967) ch. VII, §§ 77 – 94, 89, 90.

guarantees the unity of the range of interests of the *societé civile* on a higher more generalized level,[52] a theoretical pattern which is still to be encountered today in social and political science,[53] but which is particularly widespread in the German term 'Staatsrechtslehre' (state doctrine theory), and indeed among those writers who consciously distance themselves from the statist tradition of 'state law'.[54] From here public interests are and can be qualified as stable, and given by the social order, as a public good, which is implemented in society not least with the help of state law, the legislature and an administration strongly influenced by jurists. This solution and the traditional pretensions associated with it have however long been untenable.[55] But what Carl Schmitt diagnosed in the 1960s as the end of the 'statist epoch',[56] and what is referred to in recent times as the 'end of the nation state',[57] would then be no more than, and in the first place, the end of the continental European state model.

From here the thesis could be elaborated that statism and representative democracy are not identical to the continental European development path of the state, or rather – in the language of Max Weber – not with the 'institutional state' (Anstaltsstaat). The state would then be capable of outlasting the erosion of the 'institutional state'.[58] If one combines this idea with the distinction between government and state, which colours the Anglo-American tradition more strongly

---

52 For the situation in France see Francois Furet, 'Der revolutionäre Katechismus', in E. Schmitt (ed.), *Die französische Revolution* (Köln: Kiepenheuer & Witsch, 1976), pp. 46 – 88, 64; Marcel Gauchet, *Die Erklärung der Menschenrechte. Die Debatte um die bürgerlichen Freiheiten* (Reinbek: Rovohlt Verlag, 1991).

53 For an example on this perspective see Ulrich Beck, 'Wie wird Demokratie im Zeitalter der Globalisierung möglich?', in Ulrich Beck (ed.), *Politik der Globalisierung, supra* n. 43, pp. 7 – 66, 31; Helmut Willke, *Supervision des Staates* (Frankfurt am Main: Suhrkamp, 1997), p. 9.

54 Konrad Hesse, *Grundzüge des Verfassungsrechts der Bundesrepublik Deutschland* (Heidelberg: Mueller, 1995), pp. 3 –13.

55 Niklas Luhmann, 'Der Staat des politischen Systems', *supra* n. 45, pp. 345 – 380, 371; see also Thomas Vesting, *Politische Einheitsbildung und technische Realisation* (Baden-Baden: Nomos, 1990), pp. 95 – 170.

56 Carl Schmitt, *Der Begriff des Politischen* (1932), (Berlin: Duncker & Humblot, 1979), p. 10; Ernst Forsthoff, *Der Staat der Industriegesellschaft* (München: Beck, 1971), pp. 11 – 20. Stefan Breuer, *Der Staat. Entstehung, Typen, Organizationsstadien* (Reinbek: Rovohlt Verlag, 1998), pp. 298 f., correctly points out that the concept of the modern state should strictly be a *contradictio in adiecto* for Carl Schmitt.

57 Jean-Marie Guéhenno, *The End of the Nation-State, supra* n. 1, pp. 1 – 34; Martin van Creveld, *Aufstieg und Untergang des Staates, supra* n.16, pp. 371 – 463; Kenichi Ohmae, *The End of the Nation State: the Rise of Regional Economies* (London : HarperCollins, 1995).

58 In this direction Stefan Breuer, *supra* n. 57, p. 299.

than the continental European, then continental European public law would also have to orientate itself more strongly towards the idea of public government, that is a concept which is from the outset more tailored for the self-indication of the political system than is the state concept. Statism in the sense of public government would then be conceivable under conditions in which the unity of 'territorial order' and 'political order' is dissolved under the pressure of information technology development. This and similar ideas certainly are headed in the correct direction, but one must remember thereby to take into account that the increasing relationships between the states change the state itself. And even more: if one combines the emergence of supra-national and international organizations (EU, WTO, UNO) and the increasing significance of more or less autonomous public regulatory bodies (e.g. FCC, EU Commission) with the increasing significance of co-operative relationships of these authorities with private and semi-private organizations – a development which has long been observable particularly in the context of the network economy – then there is a lot to be said for the view that we are witnessing the emergence of a new world order beyond all traditions. Thus we would be facing a new political and social world, not categorized by Hobbes, Locke, Montesquieu or Max Weber.

The nation state will not disappear in this new world order. Rather it will remain indispensable for the 'international system' (and international law) for the foreseeable future, if only because the state provides a form of organized communication capability that is also relatively accessible for other states.[59] But the idea of an inter*national* political order should rather obstruct than open the view to the new in the new world order. The sovereignty of the nation state will drift further in the direction of responsibility for partial segments of regional territorial order such as for example the regulation of citizenship and its exceptions, while the dependence of the nation state on supra-national, international and transnational political networks, in Luhmann's terminology: the 'political system of the world society', will grow.[60] Beyond the level of international networks, among which are to be counted informal relations between national parliaments, governmental organizations and courts,[61] an in principle pluralistic order of overlapping regulatory networks will gain in significance, for which the terms 'global governance' or 'global public-private governance' seem to be becoming established in the political and social science literature.[62]

59	Arguments supporting this thesis collected e.g. in Michael Reisman, '*Designing and Managing the Future of the State*', EJIL Vol. 8 (1997), pp. 409 – 420.

60	Niklas Luhmann, 'Der Staat des politischen Systems', *supra* n. 45, pp. 345 – 380, 351 f.

61	Anne-Marie Slaughter, '*International Law in a World of Liberal States*', EJIL Vol. 6 (1995), pp. 503 – 538, 522 ff.

62	For an overview see the papers in Jan Kooiman, *Modern Governance. New Government-Society Interactions* (London: Sage, 1993), and Raimo Värynen, *Globalization and*

While the term 'global public-private governance' is often, perhaps justifiably, described as fuzzy, the term aptly expresses the way the new world order follows the 'logic of networking', that is a logic in which order must be generated under the conditions of displacement of earlier stable boundaries (private/public; state/non-state, etc.). The new regulatory networks will be based on time-dependent stability, will no longer be ordered territorially but *functionally,* and will largely proceed from co-operation with private actors. All in all an acentric landscape of high mobility and unravelling borders should be generated, in which public and private, national, transnational, supra-national and international components overlap to an at times varying extent.[63] Jean-Marie Guéhenno pictured the formation of such 'network-connections' using the image of the interlinked Olympic rings.[64] This image captures the new world order very well, although the rings and their connections should not be thought of as stable. The future will more probably be like a modern computer animation, like a relational network of networks based on 'iteration', in which order is not simply replaced by disorder, but in which a greater variation of figure combinations must indeed be reckoned with. The concept of democracy, for example, should also be recast in these terms.[65] Instead of simply projecting the traditional democratic image of the state coupled with a unified will onto the global (or European) level.

IV. The Ordering Function of (Public) Law

1. The Further Decoupling of law and Politics

It will also be decisive for future legal theory that the new public law, seen only in outline, is not considered equivalent to past institutional structures. Thus for example the development of the information economy will hardly lead to a 'new Middle Ages'.[66] Admittedly state legitimated organizations will not in the future be able to claim a *monopoly* over law production – a potential parallel with the Middle Ages – but there can be no talk in the new functional regulatory networks of the priority of *one* political will over other autonomous systems of the society. Also law and politics will no longer grow together, but rather both systems, which were indeed linked together in the continental European tradition, are more likely in

---

Global Governance (Lanham: Rowman & Littlefield Publishers, 1999).

63 Such a perspective is taken in Karl-Heinz Ladeur, '*Towards a Legal Theory of Supranationality – The Viability of the Network Concept*', EUROPEAN LAW JOURNAL, Vol. 3 (1997), pp. 33 – 54.

64 Jean-Marie Guéhenno, *supra* n. 1, p. 56.

65 See Karl-Heinz Ladeur in this book.

66 See e.g. Hedley Bull, *The Anarchical Society* (Macmillan: London, 1977), p. 264.

future to become more distinct from each other. This trend to a self-organizing legal system will develop the relationship between state legislation and self-organization of society further at the expense of national legislative bodies and their associated practices (judicial review, university dogmatic, journal culture, etc.) – and thereby also at the expense of traditional public law. But just as questioning the significance of the nation state is the consequence of a fully developed liberal society, so the increase of self-organization and self-regulation means neither a departure from the liberal legal tradition nor an end to public law. Karl-Heinz Ladeur recently pointed out correctly that not only the codification of law but also the judicial decision or the dogmatic always had a rather supportive *secondary* function for liberal law; whose significance could (nevertheless) be overestimated in the past because the emergence of the law of nation states in the 19th century was strongly conditioned by the antithetical fixation on local law and custom.[67] The variety and complexity of local law had to give way to the unity of a national legal system and its laws, that is the legal order of the nation state was modelled on a mechanical image. Order and rationality signified here: predictability and systematic cohesion.

2. The Self-organization of Law

Systems theory may enable a more precise delineation of the significance of the trend to self-organization of modern law. In contrast to the still widelyheld idea that law consists of a more or less ordered mass of norms derived from the prescriptions of national legislative bodies and occasionally from the 'lacuna filling' work of courts, in future the self-referential network-like closure (Geschlossenheit) of the legal system must be foregrounded. By this is meant that the legal system proceeds from the continuous use of legal communications that, for their part, link up to an existing stock of legal communications (and their corresponding forms of practice). Thus the legal system produces and reproduces a recursive structure from actually performed operations. The law[68] is not determined hierarchically from above, but rather heterarchically, that is to say collaterally, in a network of neighbourly relationships.[69] If one exploits this network-like idea fully, then the unity of modern law is not due to a 'system' which hurries on ahead of reality and which exists independently of its practical application. Rather the unity and autonomy of the legal system is realized exclusively in and through operations whose performance is a given fact, for example through the conclusion of a contract, a court ruling or the promulgation of a law. Thereby the legal system is primarily bound to the legal

---

67   Karl-Heinz Ladeur, 'Der "Eigenwert" des Rechts – die Selbstorganizationsfähigkeit der Gesellschaft und die relationale Rationalität des Rechts', in Christian J. Meier-Schatz (ed.), *Die Zukunft des Rechts* (Helbing & Lichtenhahn: Basle, 1999), pp. 31 – 56, 43.

68   See Niklas Luhmann, *Die Gesellschaft der Gesellschaft, supra* n. 15, p. 1048.

69   Niklas Luhmann, *Das Recht der Gesellschaft, supra* n. 1, p. 144.

circumstances of the present, which it carries on into the future or endeavours to vary or modify in response to corresponding negative practical experience.

Hence, the potential to orientation that the description of the social function of law generates cannot be dispensed with if one emphasizes the heterarchical, collateral, neighbour-like self-networking of law. This also applies to a theory of law that is appropriate to these developments. The previous self-descriptions of law were certainly too strongly fixated on the unity of the (national) legal system, but also a theory of the new legal pluralism will not be able to dispense with an indication of the social function of law. Legal theory must also in the future be able to identify the boundaries of the legal system; it must at least establish a concept and monitoring management that can make reliable statements on the stability of the legal system. This is also of great significance for a new public law beyond the state. Public law has always been legitimized by very specific public interests. With the rise of the welfare state, the spectrum of 'state purposes' (Staatszwecke) has however become more or less blurred. A new public law beyond the state would therefore have to attempt to jointly reflect a self-limitation of its task catalogue if it is not to force the already problematic development of constantly expanding state activity.

3. Public Law in an Order System of Distributed Decision-making Rights

As the constant pressure to produce something new has deeply penetrated the self-description of the autonomous systems of modern society, it also appears questionable from the perspective of a theory of time in modern society, whether the ordering function of liberal law is appropriately defined by the formulation 'securing expectations', that is the contra-factual stabilization of normative expectations.[70] Naturally it is beyond dispute that criminal law in particular must secure the temporal boundedness of expectations to possible self-revisions of law. But one must take into account for modern law as a whole that – in contrast to the good old law of the Middle Ages – this is no longer oriented towards the preservation of a god-given order of being, that means it does not serve the stabilization of *a specific social state*. Much more the modern society opens ever-new possibilities, which can be legitimately realized without recourse to tradition. However law cannot simply react to this dynamic self-modification of the given with the expectation that 'normative expectation will be expected normatively'.[71] It must much more – as for example in cases of liability – build into the normative structure its own mechanisms for its own judgement-modification of factual situations. The objection to the narrow delimitation of the legal function to

---

70   Ibid, pp. 124 – 164.
71   Ibid, p. 144.

expectation guarantee must remain at this point rather abstract and brief,[72] however it implies the supposition that modern law can only achieve a *limited* security of expectations. The entire problem of the concept of 'expectation guarantee' truly lies in the measure of the thereby assumed 'security'.

The function of public law should also not be lost in the idea of 'securing expectations'. This becomes clear if from the outset one includes in the legal concept social contract theory and the associated growth in significance of basic rights. This should be emphasized not least because Luhmann grossly neglects the significance of liberal social philosophy for modern law. In comparison Max Weber correctly showed in his legal sociology that the shift to modern law – in Weber's terms: to formal rational law – would not have been possible without the liberation of the individuals from the prescribed bounds of the traditional stratified society.[73] Thus liberal law is inconceivable without guaranteed subjective rights, which are beyond the arbitrary power of monarchs. Weber however only weakly stresses the break caused by modern law. Thus for example Weber sees the function of basic rights in protecting an area of legally permitted behaviour from certain forms of disturbance by third parties, and in particular by the state apparatus.[74] This still widely held view of basic rights as negative rights (Abwehrrechte) is alone rather unpersuasive because the various communication networks of modern society realize their autonomy in the form of basic rights. Modern science constantly produces *new* knowledge and claims scientific freedom for this purpose. Freedom of property, to give another example, also serves to handle property productively, that is to produce *new* property and thereby to widen possibilities of connectivity (Anschlussmöglichkeiten) in the future – and not only to be able to deal at will with a thing seated in property within certain limits (thing-ownership), as for example Max Weber supposes. The more complex the need for co-ordination and co-operation becomes resultant on this productive processing with basic rights, the more forms of self-organization and self-regulation come into their own. The function of these forms is equally interpreted too narrowly, if merely an autonomy that is schematically limited by legal transactions and derived from the state is seen therein. Much more a process of 'decentralization of legal production'[75] is concerned. This decentralization of legal production no longer permits a prioritization of the public over the private. Rather it tends to boundary drawing *and*

---

72   For more details on this argument see Karl-Heinz Ladeur, 'Der "Eigenwert" des Rechts...'., *supra* n. 67, pp. 31 – 56.

73   Max Weber, *Wirtschaft und Gesellschaft* (1922), (Tübingen: Mohr, 1980), p. 383; see also Stefan Breuer, *Bürokratie und Charisma*, (Darmstadt: Wissenschaftliche Buchgesellschaft, 1994), pp. 12 – 16.

74   Max Weber, *Wirtschaft und Gesellschaft*, *supra* n. 74, p. 398.

75   Ibid, pp. 439 f.

networking, which is to a productive, co-ordinative and co-operative relationship between the public and the private.

Against the background of these (still provisional) considerations the ordering function of public law can be defined more precisely. The function of public law is not limited to guaranteeing the predictability of state action in general and the administration of justice in particular. Therefore, its protective function is by no means directed only towards the political system. The function of public law would not be missed either if one divorces it from private law and reduces its role to the erection of a stable boundary between the public and the private. Rather public law should promote the productivity of the acentric and dynamic relational network of modern society, or in other words promote the self-co-ordination and self-production of legal capability of binding *between* organizations and individuals. The ordering function of public law is thus shifted onto a secondary level of order. As public-legal obligations are today primarily created under conditions of distributed subjective decision-making rights, that is in a context of growing significance of self-organization and self-regulation, the function of public law should consist in connecting these forms of self-organization and self-regulation and in promoting their *productive* co-ordination and co-operation. This also means that public organizations in the future can and should be involved in the production of legal capability for binding.

This applies however to the involvement role of public law in the development of information technology and information economies. This participation should be indispensable if only because the movement towards a 'knowledge society' brings with it great uncertainties. To this extent a new public law must also contribute to the establishment and trust of confidence in social and above all economic relations.[76] As coping with the uncertainty of the future in the 'knowledge society' is however no longer, as in the traditional society, a harmonious, perfection-oriented, teleological process, ordered according to the will of God (and his representatives), it cannot be ruled out that the constant quest for novelty in turn produces self-blocking effects and unproductive path-dependencies. The task of public law must consist above all in observing the innovation-driven self-modification of an acentric society in a 'secondary level of order'. It should be directed at observing the differentiated, respectively bounded rationalities of autonomous systems – and their related organizations – and possibly at drawing boundaries through public law, but also at making learning and development mechanisms available. It goes without saying that in an open society there can only be co-operative and provisional solutions. In return civil law would have to adjust not to aligning its autonomy absolutely but rather to seeing itself as the moment of a collective relational network, as the effect of the granting and conceding of distributed decision-making rights, which for their part should be used productively

76 Niklas Luhmann, *Das Recht der Gesellschaft, supra* n. 1, p. 132.

but not at will, as can be shown more exactly for the network economy through the example of patent rights and copyright law.[77]

V.   The Significance of Conventions for (Public) Law

1.   The Status of Conventions

If one accepts the considerations and conclusions drawn so far, then the significance of conventions in public law is also cast in a new light. Public law is not to be modelled so much as an 'instrument' of (state-political) 'intervention' in other autonomous systems of the society, but rather as a means of stabilizing and promoting processes of social self-organization and self-regulation. The continental European development path of legal thought has always stressed the element of 'sovereign decision' and the associated decision monopoly of the state for the creation of legal rule and order. This is shown essentially in the Kantian distinction between legality (according to law) and morality, in that there public law is associated directly with (external) enforcement by public institutions.[78] This moment appears even more clearly for example in Kelsen's reduction of the legal order to enforced normativity.[79] Thus a developmental line is involved in which the binding capability of rules is ultimately made dependent on state norm production and norm enforcement moments. In opposition to this tradition it would be necessary to point out from the perspective adopted here, that the functional capability of liberal law primarily lives and always has been derived from a functioning social infrastructure and conventions, habits (customs) standards, etc. Production of legal rules and order requires practical knowledge, which is rules rooted in knowledge experience that evolve and develop in relational networks between individuals and organizations.[80]

---

77   See *The Economist*, Vol. 355, 8-14 April 2000, pp. 85 – 89; see further M.A. Heller and R.S. Eisenberg, '*Can Patents Deter Innovation*', SCIENCE 280 (1988), pp. 280 ff.; S.A. Cohen, '*To Innovate or not to Innovate, That is the Question*', MICHIGAN TELECOMMUNICATIONS LAW REVIEW 5 (1999), pp. 1 ff.; P. Samuelson and R. Davis, *The Digital Dilemma* (Washington DC: National Academy Press, 2000).

78   Immanuel Kant, *Die Metaphysik der Sitten* (1797), AB 15, A 163, 164.

79   Hans Kelsen, *Reine Rechtslehre* (Wien: Oesterreichische Staatsdruckerei, 1960), pp. 31 – 59, 45.

80   For more details see e.g. Robert Sugden, '*Spontaneous Order*', JOURNAL OF ECONOMIC PERSPECTIVES, Vol. 3 (1989), pp. 85 – 97; Karl-Heinz Ladeur, *Negative Freiheitsrechte und gesellschaftliche Selbstorganization* (Tübingen: Mohr, 2000), pp. 72 – 80; James C. Scott, *Seeing like a State* (New Haven/London: Yale U. P., 1998), pp. 309-341.

The formation of such rules accompanies the production of 'common experience' and 'common knowledge'. By 'common experience' and 'common knowledge' we should not understand universal moral laws in the Kantian sense (or in the sense of discourse theory by Jürgen Habermas). The 'common knowledge' which is produced by conventions must rather be interpreted as 'local' or 'ecological knowledge'. It varies from place to place, is linked to concrete forms of practice and factual contexts and like these underlies constant changes. Admittedly – from the perspective of the legal system – a *pre*-existing experimental framework is concerned, but this 'framework' can itself only be conceived of as a flexible, self-changing network of bodies of practical knowledge that are distributed in society.[81] Such conventions, which initially must be formed below the level of legal rule formation (before they can then be incorporated into the legal system), fall within the field of private law as 'required level of care' or 'customs' of merchants (for example written acknowledgments between merchants). In constitutional law one thinks of the preliminary structural work of parties or mass media in the formation of a 'common will'. In administrative law the public danger concept of police law could be pointed to. Here too the attributing of loss to a perpetrator was and has been dependent on conventions and 'canonized examples'.[82] The interplay between conventions and law cannot be examined further here, but these briefly sketched interdependencies would be an indication that the evaluative and binding capability of liberal law is much more strongly dependent on self-production and self-organization processes than is acknowledged in the continental tradition of 'state law'. The functional capability of the legal system rests primarily on this distributed form of 'common knowledge' by which rules and conventions are produced, and is in the second place dependent on support by legislation, power monopoly and state administration.

Turning these ideas somewhat, previous views of sources of law must also be modified. The theory of sources of law substitutes the dependency of liberal law on experience, practice and social conventions in favour of a political constitution of law from the 'void' – and thereby implies a 'beginning' of law, which could be instrumentalized at will by a sovereign. In the context of the information economy the binding capability of liberal law is particularly dependent upon self-organization processes. As shown by our introductory example of S-PCS-systems, public law proceeds from an accompanying 'logic of networking', in which norms are generated from co-operative relations between private companies and administration officials. In consequence of this a source of law doctrine coupled with the state and

---

81 Steve Fleetwood, '*Order without Equilibrium: A Critical Realist Interpretation of Hayek's Notion of Spontaneous Order*', CAMBRIDGE JOURNAL OF ECONOMICS, Vol. 20 (1996), pp. 729 – 747; Karl-Heinz Ladeur, *Das Umweltrecht der Wissensgesellschaft* (Berlin: Duncker & Humblot, 1995), pp. 22 – 68.

82 Karl-Heinz Ladeur, *supra* n. 81, pp. 11 – 15.

its organs obstructs the view of the gain in significance of 'spontaneous law' production.[83] But from the perspective taken here it also follows that the maintenance of productivity of this 'pre-found' structural framework must become one of the central tasks of a new public law (beyond the state). The state cannot erect this framework itself, but it must observe its development and perhaps support it institutionally. This is especially so if the 'spontaneity' of convention formation is no longer conditioned by everyday habits, customs and generally shared values, but itself becomes the object of a 'heterarchic, connectivist, network-like linking of communication on the level of organizations and professions'.[84]

2.   The Significance of Technical Standards

This idea is also of great significance for the assessment of the ordering function of public law in the network economy. It is particularly important in order to be able to develop a productive view of technical standards. As mentioned in the introduction, technical standards are central to the network economy, for example in the field of mobile telecommunication technology (GSM/UMTS), in the technical linking of terrestrial and mobile networks (WAP) or in the conception of Internet protocols (TCP/IP).[85] Technical standards, which are a form of social convention,[86] do not determine the respective technical coding, but predetermine the system architecture above this, including the possibilities for linking components, levels and performances. This is especially true in the network economy, indeed in simple terms one can say that technical standards ultimately dictate the 'constitution' of the new online world, particularly whether open or closed systems will be utilized in cyberspace.[87] Here, too, further exploration must be put off until later, but a new

---

83   See on this Gunther Teubner, 'Global Private Regimes: Neo-spontaneous Law and Dual Constitution of Autonomous Sectors in World Society?', in this book.

84   Niklas Luhmann, *'Der Staat des politischen Systems'*, supra n. 45, pp. 345 – 380, 375.

85   See for an overview Paul A. David, 'The Internet and the Economics of Network Technology Evolution', in Christoph Engel and Kenneth Kellner (eds.), *Understanding the Impact of Global Networks on Local Social, Political and Cultural Values, supra* n. 11, pp. 39 – 71, and Carl Shapiro and Hal R. Varian, *Information Rules* (Boston: Harvard Business School Press, 1999), pp. 261 – 296, 305 – 309; Kevin Kelly, *New Rules for the New Economy* (New York, 1998), pp. 71 – 73.

86   On the nature and function of technical standards and their parallels with norms of social behaviour see Paul. A. David, 'The Internet and the Economics of Network Technology Evolution', in Christoph Engel and Kenneth Kellner (eds.), *supra* n. 11, pp. 39 –71, pp. 45 – 50.

87   For more details see Lawrence Lessig, *Code and Other Laws of Cyberspace* (New York: Basic Books, 1999), pp. 100 – 108; see also the overview in developments in the *'Law of Cyberspace'*, HARVARD LAW REVIEW Vol. 112 (1999), pp. 1575 – 1704, 1634 ff.

public law (beyond the state) would have to insist that the process of producing technical standards in and for the new net architectures must be an element of (public) law. The network economy is the expression of the aforementioned shift in the formation of social conventions, which no longer proceed from social habits, but rather, because of the uncertainty industry has to cope with, are made the object of explicit negotiated processes. For this reason the processes in which the common technical standards are formed must themselves become the object of strategic legal observation and possibly of legal decisions. This would also have to result in the acceptance of the normative, indeed legal character of technical standards.

In the meantime this demand has been repeatedly made.[88] Admittedly in academic literature it is just as often objected that law is an instrument for the regulation of *social* relations and therefore not transferable to technical artefacts. In the increased significance of technical standards, and of computer programs in particular, some see an indication for the dissolution of normative structures, which is a moment of the dismantling or shrinking of the *normative* order. Jean-Marie Guéhenno has targeted this supposition in this direction, that law is transformed according to the new regulatory networks into a purely economic factor of the reduction of uncertainty. Law formerly bound to state sovereignty has been downgraded to a mere 'procedural practice', a means for the reduction of business costs, while politics is losing its moral and philosophical basis. The question of the legitimacy of politics is thus just as inappropriate as the consideration of 'legality' or 'illegality' of a computer program. The 'soft humming of the social machinery is sufficient unto itself'.[89]

Here this chapter hits an important point, in that the legitimacy of a computer program is indeed difficult to assess. This is so however only if law and politics are drawn together into a unity in the tradition of continental constitutional state. If one opens one's concepts in contrast for the changes in law and order formation sketched above, as is apparently happening in the network economy at the moment, then the increased significance of technical standards is simply an indication that the pre-given structures of conventions, which liberal law makes a precondition, lose their pre-modern foundations even more than before. The traditional foundation of conventions was generated from the experience of people, practical knowledge, and above all their habits, customs and traditions, which is the 'spontaneous' order of their inter-personal relations. This traditional life-world (Lebenswelt) is now

---

88 See, e.g. Karl-Heinz Ladeur, '*Rechtliche Regulierung von Informationstechnologien und Standardsetzung*', CR (1999), pp. 395 – 404, 398; Lawrence Lessig, *Code and Other Laws of Cyberspace*, *supra* n. 87, pp. 6, 63 – 108 ('Code is law'); see more generally Joerges, Ladeur and Vos (eds.), *Integrating Scientific Expertise into Regulatory Decision-Making* (Baden-Baden: Nomos, 1997).

89 Jean-Marie Guéhenno, *The End of the Nation-State*, *supra* n. 1, p. 58; similarly Helmut Willke, *Supervision des Staates*, *supra* n. 53.

replaced even more by artificial, technically constructed worlds, for example by cyberspace, whose architecture is produced by abstract (mathematical) knowledge and which itself represents a realization of spatial real time autonomy. This leads to changes in procedures of convention formation, which now become a product of companies and private-public procedures. Hence it would be completely wrong to wish to decide the question whether technical standards and computer programs are law in accordance with pre-existing norm-typical features. More helpful is the advice of Lawrence Lessig that the Internet forces us to look behind the traditional norms.[90] However, Lessig combines this apt advice with a rather traditional conception of public law. For him regulation is roughly the same as state regulation, while in the perspective adopted here it would be important to open the concept of law itself to new modes of convention formation and thereby also for the forms of self-organization and self-regulation associated with the Internet. From this, the categorization of standards and codes as law may be explained. Precisely because the development of new information technologies is proceeding so rapidly and demands highly specialized knowledge that cannot be produced and administered by the state, a new public law must seek functional equivalents of rule and order formation. Such an equivalent is seen here on the one hand in the recognition of the new pluralism of law. On the other hand such an extension of law creation requirements would have to encompass the processes of self-organization and self-regulation, as conducted for example in the field of domain allocation (ICANN), and would be observed by public institutions with regard to the observance of particular standards (e.g. fairness). This forum of second order observation would itself have to be oriented towards the aspect of maintaining the variability and variety of connections and connection options, that is the maintenance of a plurality of development paths. At the same time this means that the production of technical standards would possibly have to be made the object of a new co-operative relationship between the state and the economy. Before examining this more closely, the concept of the 'network economy' should be sketched in the next section.

VI.   The Network Economy and the Need for New Regulatory Networks beyond Competition Policy

1.   *The Network Economy as an Academic Discipline*

The network economy, which is practised as an academic discipline under titles such as 'information economy', 'new economy' or 'Internet economy',[91] directs its

---

90   Lawrence Lessig, *Code and Other Laws of Cyberspace, supra* n. 87, p. 6.
91   See, e.g. Carl Shapiro and Hal R. Varian, *Information Rules. A Strategic Guide to the*

attention primarily to product and services markets with high knowledge and information components, such as computers, telephone systems, mobile telephones, film, music publishing, websites, books and so on. The concept 'network economy' certainly has something of a brand name effect and may be reminiscent of such difficult to grasp constructs as 'New Labour' or 'the third way'. But even if one accepts that the new network economies have predecessors in the old network economies (railways, energy provision) it is still beyond dispute that the new network economy exhibits several peculiarities and departures in comparison with industrial mass production. The concepts 'network economy', 'information economy' and 'new economy' are adopted here not so as to attract attention in the academic circles, but rather to draw attention to these peculiarities and to emphasize thereby that what we today term 'globalization' can be largely traced back to innovations in the information economy.

One peculiarity of this kind of network economy is that, unlike any other previous economy, they are driven by immaterial products and no longer by fertile soil, raw materials, energy sources or the like. Their basic elements are information and knowledge, and this makes the economies to a large degree independent of specific spatial and temporal conditions. In addition the products (and services) of the new economies are produced and distributed almost exclusively through real and virtual networks. Thereby the characteristics of elements bound to a network are changed. The 'economies of scale' become 'economies of networks',[92] in which the value of information commodities recedes into the background, while the real or virtual connection of the individual elements to a network are foregrounded. According to an oft-cited formula of Katz and Shapiro, the network effects relate to goods in which the consumer achieves a higher utility the more consumers apply that good.[93] Seen more from the network side, the value of a network depends on the number of *other* users, which are *already* connected to the network.[94] This applies in the real networks, for example the telephone network; the value of the network performance increases exponentially with the number of users at any time. The more transmitters/receivers are connected to the particular network, the more

Network Economy, supra n. 85; Kevin Kelly, *New Rules for the New Economy, supra* n. 15; Nicholas Economides, '*The Economics of Networks*', INTERNATIONAL JOURNAL OF INDUSTRIAL ORGANIZATIONS, Vol. 14 (March 1996); pp. 673 ff.; Axel Zerdick a.o., *Die Internet-Ökonomie* (Berlin: Springer, 1999); see also Manuel Castells, *The Rise of the Network Society*, Vol. 1, *supra* n. 37.

92　Carl Shapiro and Hal R. Varian, *supra* n. 85, p. 173.

93　Michael L. Katz and Carl Shapiro, '*Network Externalities, Competition and Compatibility*', AMERICAN ECONOMIC REVIEW, Vol. 75 (1985), pp. 424 – 440, 424.

94　See only Carl Shapiro and Hal R. Varian, *supra* n. 85, p. 174: 'the value of connecting to a network depends on the number of other people already connected to it'; p. 182: 'the more people using the network, the more valuable it is to each one of them'.

combination and relationship options are made available for each individual user. In the field of virtual networks, operating systems and software applications for personal computers produce the same effect: the higher the degree of dissemination of certain programs, the greater is the utility of the program for the single user.

One result of this priority of the relations over the elements themselves is that the total value of a network grows exponentially with the number of users. 'A tenfold increase in the size of the network leads to a hundredfold increase in its value'.[95] In other words information economy markets are determined by positive feedback and are subject to the law of 'increasing returns'.[96] Nothing similar may be observed in this form and to this degree in traditional markets for mass production goods. It is true that increased returns in the form of economies of scale are known to the previous markets of mass production goods, as for example the automobile industry ('Fordism'). The returns on scale which accrue here through more efficient production methods and higher level of production compared to small or 'niche' providers, however, increase in linear fashion and usually run up against organizational limits, in which the management can no longer achieve further growth of the company even through a changed enterprise concept. By contrast the network economy knows no equivalent production-related limits. This is due above all to the fact that information goods display an untypical production and cost structure, in turn resultant on the peculiarity that information goods are for all practical purposes inexhaustible. Certain information goods, such as software products, can even be used as often and by as many as required (no rivalry) and display, insofar as they are once generally accessible, also the second typical property of a 'public good', that is non-excludability – the inability to prevent third parties from use.[97] This atypical production and cost structure varies between markets, it is true, but it can still be said with the unavoidable imprecision of generalities, that information goods are characterized by high fixed costs and low variable costs, or infinitely falling average costs. The difference between first-copy costs and break-even costs in software markets is especially high. The *unikat* of

95   Ibid, p. 184; see also Kevin Kelly, *New Rules for the New Economy*, *supra* n. 15, p. 24 ('Metcalfe's Law'), and W. Brian Arthur, 'Competing Technologies, Increasing Returns and Lock-In by Historical Events', *The Economic Journal* 99 (1989), pp. 116 – 131.

96   See W. Brian Arthur, '*Increasing Returns and the New World of Business*', HARVARD BUSINESS REVIEW 74 (1996), pp. 100 – 109; Carl Shapiro and Hal R. Varian, *supra* n. 85, pp. 173 – 225 ff.; Kevin Kelly, *supra* n. 15, pp. 23 – 38; Jörn Kruse, 'Märkte für Rundfunkprogramme', in Ernst-Joachim Mestmäcker (ed.), *Offene Rundfunkordnung* (Gütersloh: Verlag Bertelsmann Stiftung, 1988), pp. 275 – 308, 279, for TV-Software especially.

97   Michael Hutter, 'The Commercialization of the Internet. A Progress Report', in Christoph Engel and Kenneth Kellner (eds.), *supra* n.11, pp. 73 – 92, 76. The Internet itself is interpreted as 'constrained' or 'impeded' public good by Hutter.

Netscape Navigator for example involved around US$ 30 million development costs, while the second copy only cost US$ 1.[98]

The positive feedback lines of the network economy lead to extremely dynamic markets, which are determined by the tendency to the formation of temporary monopolies. In place of the relatively stable oligopolistic markets of mass production goods, come markets that on the basis of their network effects tend to extreme reactions up to the economic destruction of all competitors. In the network economy there is a development dynamic that strengthens the market segment with the greatest success, resulting in a tendency to monopoly formation by the larger network with its extended connection options potential. Such an effect occurs for example when a software producer inserts ready-written program elements into other program elements and uses a strong market position in a market segment, which is characterized by network effects, to occupy other market segments ('crossover'), so as ultimately to link more and more strands and knots of a network to its own corporate technology and culture ('leveraging'). It is rather unlikely in the network economies that several big providers can survive in one market segment. It is on the contrary more likely that the market tips from a certain point and the last remaining competitor disappears if it no longer reaches the critical mass; this phenomenon is described in the literature with reference to the film industry as the 'winner-takes-all-market' effect.[99] Thus from a certain time point in its market development, the commercial success of a product is determined by its popularity; and this is precisely because the value of a product is first generated by the possibility which a real or virtual network makes available also in relation to its potential for relation-building and connection with other networks.

In this respect the network economy produces and reproduces a novel culture economic source of value, which is itself located beyond the ascribed material quality of the good. This phenomenon, in which the sheer volume in a certain way seems to suppress shortage as a source of economic value, leads in turn to path dependencies which are reversible only with difficulty. Thus the explosion-like collective growth of value, to which, for example, a certain level of dissemination software is subject, need not necessarily be the result of its technological superiority to other options. This is not comparable with oligopolistic conditions of industrial production: here competition generally leads to the continuous improvement of products and product lines and adaptation to the respective state of technology, while the monopolistic position of dominant market position in the network economy can certainly result from a disproportional advantage, which the 'first mover' is able to secure by virtue of coincidence or a chain of coincidence. The markets of the network economy are in other words characterized by lasting instability, in which initially insignificant historical events can produce an increased

---

98 For the Netscape Navigator example see Kevin Kelly, *supra* n. 15, p. 58.
99 See e.g. Carl Shapiro and Hal R. Varian, *supra* n. 85, p. 177.

divergence which influences the entire technological development and from which ultimately only one company emerges as victor.[100] This successive extension of the dominance of a company is also highly problematic to the extent that in the information economy products cannot be separated from standards, while standards are themselves inseparable from the technologies based upon them. The victor thus suppresses not only all other companies, but as a rule all other standards and technologies. The technological and economic development then becomes dependent on a single innovation source.

2. The Limitation of Antitrust Law

These few remarks on the market conditions peculiar to the network economy show that it produces a range of novel hazards and risks of self-blocking of technological and market developments. These hazards and risks cast the confidence in the 'natural' self-renewing properties of the market, widespread at the moment in US literature in particular, in a rather problematic light.[101] True the assessment of future technological and market developments from the perspective adopted here is an entrepreneurial decision, and there is no indication that public regulators could collect better knowledge on the future of the information economy than the participating companies. But on the other hand a judicial perspective must also take into account that the dispersed knowledge that is produced on the market under the specific conditions of high complexity and dynamic can equally only be a limited and provisional knowledge. Via the distributed order of decision-making rights of individual companies, this complexity and its accompanying uncertainty can only be partially coped with. The generation of information by the market is then especially precarious if, beyond already established technological paths and beyond the balance functioning market equilibrium, a faster process of basic change of technology paths *and* markets takes place, a process in which a change of the development possibilities itself is involved, that is the parameters which first lend structure to the still to be constituted markets.

These thoughts lead to the thesis that the productive self-development of dynamic markets of the network economy can in no way be taken for granted. Much more the supporting public observation and possibly national or transnational regulation of this development is needed. Here at the latest the problem is encountered that while most national jurisdictions since the last third of the 19th

---

100 Stressed particularly by W. Brian Arthur, *'Competing Technologies, Increasing Returns and Lock-In by Historical Events'*, THE ECONOMIC JOURNAL 99 (1989), pp. 116 – 131; see also W. Brian Arthur (ed.), *Increasing Returns and Path Dependence in the Economy* (Michigan: University of Michigan Press, 1994).

101 See e.g. Carl Shapiro and Hal R. Varian, *Information Rules. A Strategic Guide to the Network Economy, supra* n. 85, pp. 297 – 318, 314.

century have developed monitoring and regulatory agencies for real networks (railways, energy provision, telephones and post), regulation of virtual networks remains very uneven or even non-existent. This vacuum is filled at the moment by competition policy. However, the control of competition through antitrust law – with some exceptions – can only react in an ad hoc manner and ex post to certain market constellations, and enquires exclusively or at least primarily regarding efficiency and the functionality of markets.[102] It inquires case by case into the consequences for competition of an already existing monopoly and thereby establishes, as a foundation, a general understanding that is abstracted from particular goods and services; thus for example overlooking the particular cost structure of information goods. In addition competition law monitors the permissibility of monopolies primarily with regard to the consequences for national markets, and tends with a range of variants and various argumentation patterns to a nation-based justification of monopoly positions.

It is however decisive for the limitations of antitrust law that ideas of a functioning market in the network economy are of limited value as a starting point for a legal assessment. On the one hand information markets are subject to a completely different timescale than the traditional oligopolistic markets of mass production; the identification of a monopoly position is accordingly problematic. On the other hand the continuous transformation of information technologies constantly modifies the scope of possibilities, within which new markets arise and disappear. The network economy is – at least at the moment – characterized rather by cycles of technological innovation, temporary stabilization of technological paths and markets as well as accompanying dissolution and recombination of technological paths and markets. Such a process can only be portrayed by a disequilibrium model.[103] At any rate it lies beyond previous stable market models and can thus only with difficulty be handled on the basis of antitrust law which is based on such an equilibrium model. This is also valid from an institutional point of view. Competition regulation that decides on an individual case basis will quickly reach it limits through this dynamic, because a field of reference for the normality of a market can only be determined with extreme difficulty if at all. Further it would be unable to cope with the knowledge problems if it fails to build up a specialist competence for the long-term systematic observation of the development of the network economy. Then, though, it must operate in a way similar to a specialized public regulator which at the same time would be a departure from the hitherto concept of retrospective, situative competition policy.[104]

---

102 See only Ulrich M. Gassner, *Grundzüge des Kartellrechts* (München: Vahlen, 1999), pp. 4 f., 8 ff.

103 Kevin Kelly, *New Rules for the New Economy*, *supra* n. 15, p. 38.

104 For more details Karl-Heinz Ladeur, 'Innovation der Telekommunikation durch Regulierung', in Wolfgang Hoffmann-Riem (ed.), *Innovation und Telekommunikation*,

3.   The Example of Microsoft

The limitations of competition policy hitherto can by seen in the practices of Microsoft. In the Microsoft case the prime question was to decide whether it can be permissible from the competition point of view that Microsoft combines the Windows operating system with its own browser (Explorer) and protects this combination against competing companies (Netscape). Thereby the prime issue is the behaviour in one market. Behind the conflict lies more the competition between two quite distinct technological development paths: Microsoft pursues a strategy of vertical integration in order to bind customers to it. This initially raises the question of whether its own product is concerned or the form of combination of operating system and browser occurs in several products. This is not easy to answer by antitrust law in that the integration of the browser in the platform is economically quite efficient and in no way prevents other competitors from writing their own user programs for the Windows platform. The result is, however, that Microsoft thereby has a privileged position in part because Microsoft is always the first to learn of changes to its operating systems and can adapt its programs accordingly. By contrast, Netscape's strategy as a competitor is to promote an open standard (with the JAVA language): the program is based on a layered model of protocols and programs, within which an operating system like Windows would lose importance.[105] A further problem is the acceleration of time; markets in the network economy can change so quickly that it seems incomprehensible to establish an antitrust procedure with far-reaching consequences on a momentary apprehension, if a monopolist could have forfeited his dominant market position in the next moment with the success of a new technological option.[106]

The Microsoft conflict shows that antitrust law is hardly suitable to rule on the productivity of technology path dependencies. In extremely dynamic markets such path dependencies can however only be observed very late, and only then if anti-trust law is strengthened by a range of additional parameters that must then be administered pragmatically as 'violations' of fair competition. Nevertheless network effects can inhibit the incentive to innovate. It can even occur that on the basis of a chain of coincidences inferior technologies prevail, that not the best alternative develops into the standard and that the public technological connection and combination options are squandered. There are a number of examples of this as amply indicated in the appropriate economic literature.[107] Today too many see the operating and application programs of Microsoft as an inferior technology compared

---

supra n. 3, pp. 57 – 76.

105 Carl Shapiro and Hal R. Varian, *supra* n. 85, p. 148.

106 For more details: ibid., pp. 309 f., 323 f.

107 Examples in W. Brian Arthur, '*Competing Technologies, Increasing Returns and Lock-In by Historical Events*', THE ECONOMIC JOURNAL 99 (1989), pp. 116 – 131, 126; Id., *Increasing Returns and Path Dependence in the Economy*, *supra* n. 100, pp. 206 – 223.

for example to Linux.[108] One may accept this view or not, but the danger that unproductive technological path dependencies are entrenched by the 'winner-take-all-market' effect can hardly be denied. The Microsoft case should also not be paraded here as a blanket regulatory power, above all as it was quite customary in the past that public regulators themselves promoted unproductive development paths in order to achieve competitive advantages for 'home' companies in global information markets,[109] the (analogue) HDTV promoted by the EU Commission may suffice as an example. Nevertheless it remains that the preservation of self-renewal capacity of dynamic markets can be guaranteed neither by an unlimited trust in the market nor by a disproportionate trust in the dissemination of knowledge by public regulatory instances.

VII. Tasks of Public Law in the Network Economy

1. Fundamentals

The second and fourth sections of this investigation have shown that the function of a liberal public law may not be reduced to the establishing of a stable boundary between the public and the private. Public law not only has the task of guaranteeing the predictability of state action in general and of the jurisdiction in particular. Above all it serves the making possible and promotion of *productive* co-ordination and co-operation of divided decision-making rights in an acentric society.[110] The constant seeking of novelty under the conditions of the future-oriented modern ('capitalistic') society leads to an increase in the weight of self-organization, and in that above all is founded an increased significance of (non-state removed) forms of rules and order creation (conventions, standards, etc.). At the same time the network economy produces new forms of problems of path dependency on market and technological development, which at times can accumulate to block entire technology paths. The uncertainty of the future thus undoubtedly opens new chances for the network economy, but it equally fails to exclude new dangers and risks.

This tension should not be relaxed one-sidedly at the expense of the openness of the future. The task of a new public law could be seen more in addressing the uncertainty of the future through viable practice-appropriate structures. Essentially a liberal society can neither allow itself to plan or to 'steer' the future centrally with

---

108 Lawrence Lessig, *Code and Other Laws of Cyberspace*, *supra* n. 87, p. 105.

109 More details by Paul Krugmann, 'Increasing Returns and the Theory of International Trade', in Truman F. Bewley (ed.), *Advances in Economic Theory* (Cambridge: Cambridge University Press, 1987), pp. 301 – 329.

110 For more details see Karl-Heinz Ladeur, *Negative Freiheitsrechte und gesellschaftliche Selbstorganization*, *supra* n. 23, pp. 67 – 80.

general reliability, nor can it simply trust to unbridled evolution. Rather public law should be concerned to combine the various, but respectively bounded rationalities of autonomous system of the modern society in regulatory networks based on mutual co-operation in as productive a way as possible. It is especially necessary to facilitate a fruitful dialogue between public and private in new institutional forms. In this long-term oriented dialogue, public law would have to orientate itself more strongly than hitherto towards the 'paradoxical' effect that it produces through 'intervention' in self-regulatory private-autonomous connected networks, but on the other hand private law would have to conceive of itself as a moment of a complex collective relational network (and not as an autonomous island with intrinsic private decision-making rights). This however would depend on accepting stronger provisional solutions and experiments, the pragmatic understanding regarding 'best practice' dependent on a process of experimentation and learning.[111]

This should also apply to the ordering function of public law in the new network economy. Here there is as little to be said for an unlimited trust in the state as for an unlimited trust in the naturally growing self-renewal capacity of markets and technologies. Much more in future it will have to involve making possible and drawing together an intelligent collaboration of market, competition, autonomous rule creation, self-regulation and public regulation into functional regulatory networks. Just as in the past private law attempted with different legal instruments such as property law, patent law, copyright, company law and antitrust law in the automobile industry, to establish preconditions for forms of market economic self-organization, so must public law in future make a positive contribution to the development of the new network economy with equally new legal forms and new substantial content. Modern society has a duty in ensuring its own innovative capacity to maintain a wide range of potential surplus knowledge. And just as the co-ordination of public and private would have to orientate itself 'towards the preservation of the social knowledge pool',[112] so the most important task of a new public law (beyond the state) would lie in the preservation of such a knowledge surplus, that is the preservation of diversity and flexibility of connections and connection options of the real and virtual networks in the network economy. In other words the substantive end point, the 'meta-rule' for public law of the dynamic markets of the information economy would be the securing of variability of the networks, the guaranteeing of their openness, productivity and capacity for further development.[113]

---

111 Ibid, p. 6.
112 Id.
113 See generally Karl-Heinz Ladeur, *Postmoderne Rechtstheorie, supra* n. 14, pp. 176 – 213, 207.

2. *Differentiation and Concretization of the Concept*

This admittedly abstract description has a technological component. In view of the tendencies to technological and economic convergence of telecommunications, the computer industry and media sector (a development which we have encountered in the S-PCS example),[114] the specific task of a new public law could and should consist in maintaining and enhancing the variability of linkages between different technologies (satellite, terrestrial network, etc.). In this way public law could contribute to protecting the openness of development and renewal capacity, especially the admission of new knowledge, in the (vertically and horizontally) networked information economy. This could possibly be combined in individual areas with the positive duty to enhance the openness and flexibility of individual technology paths. In the interest of protecting the productive function of competition, this also means making the process of identifying best technology itself the object of a public-law guarantee.[115] For this the openness, compatibility, linking and further development capacity of central contact points and nodes (e.g. portals, navigation systems, digital bit rate management, etc.) must be more closely observed than hitherto and possibly promoted by public law. Thus, for example, one of the central technical strategic questions involved in introducing digital television in Germany is whether with the so-called Set-Top-Box at least optional computer and Internet compatibility is to be provided – or whether the technological development should be driven by the aim of optimization of television programme choice as well as certain additional services. The Kirch Group, the German market leader, has long favoured the second alternative, which is the television technology option. However everything points to the first alternative from the perspective taken here. The multimedia solution preserves more options and is generally more open to innovation. As such it is the preferable alternative that responds to the technological convergence of computer, telecommunications and the media by maintaining potential for learning and further development.[116]

When one defines the technological component of this regulation strategy somewhat more narrowly and refers to the Internet and the virtual networks of the computer industry (operating systems, application software, interfaces), then the central task of a new public law could and should consist in protecting the openness of protocols and programs and in enhancing the alternative options within the developmental scope of the Internet and computer programs. The Microsoft conflict is also concerned not so much with the normal harm and dangers which monopolies

---

114 On convergence of technologies see e.g. Ono and Aoki, '*Convergence and New Regulatory Frameworks*', TELECOMMUNICATIONS POLICY (1998), pp. 817 ff.

115 Karl-Heinz Ladeur, 'Innovation der Telekommunikation durch Regulierung', *supra* n. 104.

116 For more details see Thomas Vesting, '*Fortbestand des dualen Systems?*', K&R (2000), pp. 161 – 170, 164 f.

were associated with in the past, such as high prices, worse service, lack of reference to customer preferences and so on. The central problem of the Microsoft conflict, I would submit, consists in the fact that here a larger portion of the technological development becomes dependent on only one innovation source; and this speaks against Microsoft. By contrast the procedure of the FCC regarding S-PCS-systems described in the introduction seems legally rational, because a further relatively independent technology path in the field of telecommunication technologies is made possible, which contributes to the increase of links and linking options.

The preservation of diversity and changeability of links and linking options can and may not be limited to technological aspects. On the one hand technological, economic and culture-economic circumstances in the network economy cannot be sharply distinguished from one another. On the other the danger produced by network effects of a variability-reducing rush into rigid development paths of media contents may be observed. This is seen in the Hollywood film.[117] In the big Hollywood film, the prospect of huge profits results in a concentration on the blockbuster. The investment risk of these productions (which ultimately cannot be eliminated entirely) is contained by means of a flexible combination of strategies, such as a limited range of genre patterns, plot orientation, the broad opening and forming of information cascades, the use of superstars, massive expenditure on marketing, and so on.[118] In this way an incessant compression of attention throughout the media is produced,[119] which results in the 'Hollywood system' being programmed for unremitting hit productions and the destruction of national and global competition ('the-winner-takes-it-all'). Precisely the global success of Hollywood, which at times involves self-destruction, is based on a pattern which is copied increasingly by the European film industry and which ultimately results in a reduction of the pool of film ideas, of material, forms and experiments. This means that the introduction of novelty is made significantly more difficult and at times even impossible. The Hollywood system thereby consumes its own cultural raw material. It endangers the stock of new ideas and different film languages which are

---

117 Another example would be television. See e.g. Cass R. Sunstein, '*Television and the Public Interest*', CALIFORNIA LAW REVIEW, Vol. 88 (2000), pp. 499 – 564, 515.

118 For more details see e.g. David Prindle, *Risky Business: The Political Economy of Hollywood* (Boulder: Westview, 1993), pp. 18 – 34 (on risk reduction and hit producing); Arthur de Vany and W. David Walls, '*Bose-Einstein Dynamics and Adaptive Contracting in the Motion Picture Industry*', THE ECONOMIC JOURNAL (1996), pp. 1493 – 1514 (on informational cascades); Sherwin Rosen, '*The Economics of Superstars*', THE AMERICAN ECONOMIC REVIEW, Vol. 71 (1981), pp. 845 – 858. See also the chapter by Lawrence Friedman in this book.

119 See generally Georg Franck, *Ökonomie der Aufmerksamkeit* (München: Carl Hanser 1998).

indispensable to its own development; in that for example any milieu and talent reserves existent outside America are dried out, which the US-American film industry up to now has kept alive, and which indeed in the past was a cause of productivity of Hollywood. In the case of the Hollywood film too, especially if one basically accepts the development of the blockbuster cinema, consideration must be given to how maintenance of the film industry's openness and capacity for development can be supported. This is even truer because we find ourselves at the beginning of a development that will become more pronounced by virtue of the distinctive integration of the film, television and computer industries.[120]

3. Institutional Aspects

Regarding the institutional realization of these ideas the emphasis must be laid on the solving of novel knowledge and orientation problems of public institutions. For this the ordering function of public law must be more strongly conceived from the perspective of a second order observation.[121] By this is meant the perspective of an observer who observes other organizations and who utilizes the knowledge of other organizations (whether private or public) for his own strategy formulation and decision-making. Within these, neighbour-oriented private-public networks would have above all to design procedures for the creation of rules that would help to feed the knowledge of the industries being regulated back into the decision-making process. It would depend above all on developing open forms and networks with learning capacity, which are directed much more than traditional institutions towards the production of knowledge through co-operation as well as towards experimentation with hypotheses. Even if we understand the implementation of public tasks from the beginning as dependent on the dynamic of technical and market development, this does not necessarily lead to an 'arrogation of knowledge' as described by von Hayek. Precisely when we seek solutions based on co-operation with private players, new opportunities and chances present themselves for realizing public tasks that go beyond the classical aims of compensating for 'market failure'. Thus jurisprudence would have to conceive of new forms of adequate self-description for the information and network economy, forms in which the dynamic development of complex systems and the resulting self-organization problems could be constantly scrutinized, stabilized and promoted through a constant exchange of

---

120 See Neil Weinstock Netanel, '*Cyberspace Self-Governance: A Skeptical View from Liberal Democratic Theory*', CALIFORNIA LAW REVIEW, Vol. 88 (2000), pp. 395 – 498, 442.

121 On the concept of second order cybernetics (and observation) see generally Heinz von Foerster, *Observing Systems* (Seaside CA: Intersystems Publications, 1981); the consequences of this concept for politics are described e.g. in Niklas Luhmann, *Die Politik der Gesellschaft* (Frankfurt am Main: Suhrkamp, 2000), pp. 287 – 298.

knowledge and experience between public and private organizations ('sharing responsibilities').

VIII. Towards the Global Linking of 'Hybrid' Networks

The shift from nation state to transnational regulatory networks briefly sketched here, which is based from the beginning on private-public co-operation, is also an attempt to escape the usual customary either/or of the current globalization discussion: the perspective adopted here is directed on the one hand against such descriptions which dismiss 'globalization' as an epiphenomenona, but which allow for internationalization of the economy and wish to continue to depend on nation state institutions to cope with the future. On the other hand the 'post-modern' idea of overlapping functional regulatory networks is directed against such views which describe the compression of worldwide communication systems as an exclusively economic globalization, in order then to demand a globalization of politics, democracy, etc. While the first variant seeks solutions within the traditional model of the '*Rechtsstaat*',[122] the other favours calls for a raising of the control level, a 'controlling superstate' or at least the massive building up of international organizations ('transgovernmentalism').[123] Against this the perspective developed here depends on initially more readily accepting the educational processes of the self-production of transnational law and to accompany this development with new co-operative 'hybrid' regulatory networks.

The development of the network economy shows that public law has in the future to look for a connection with the processes of self-organization and self-regulation that spring up along the technological paths of modern society. A new public law (beyond the state) would have to accept not only the distinctive trend of dissolution of state sovereignty into function-oriented structures, but also the accompanying decentralization of the production of law. The old idea that each normative order is a spatial ordering must give way to the idea of global legal pluralism of overlapping regulatory networks ('global governance networks'). On the one hand this must involve improving the existing regulatory agencies in the economically advanced regions of the world, and on the other enhancing their performance by means of a better transnational co-ordination. But co-ordination

122 See e.g. Paul Hirst and Grahame Thompson, *Globalization in Question*, *supra* n. 6, pp. 170 – 194, 193.

123 See e.g. Michael Reisman, '*Designing and Managing the Future of the State*', EJIL Vol. 8 (1997), pp. 409 – 420; somewhat in between are the considerations of David Held, *Democracy and the Global Order* (Polity and Stanford University Press, 1995), who argues in favour of 'cosmopolitan democracy' which includes new governance structures, see pp. 226 – 238, 279.

does not mean integration. Rather the emphasis must be the exact opposite, on improving the efficiency of regional regulators by the construction of overlapping areas of responsibility. It makes sense at the national, as at the European or transnational levels, to accept destabilizing uncertainties and to consciously build them into regulations and institutions. In this way worldwide competition between public institutions in best practice could be stimulated[124] – for example between the regulatory authorities for telecommunications in Germany, the European Commission, the FCC and WTO. But unless one of these regulators introduces or supervises a process with transnational effect, then these decisions will have to be linked to mutual obligations regarding voting and co-ordination. Turning back full circle to our introductory example then, the FCC action regarding S-PCS-systems is perfectly acceptable. Nevertheless the FCC should be encouraged in future to make its decision-making process transparent worldwide, to inform other regions of its own future plans, and to better co-ordinate its own practice with the plans of other regions.

124 An outline of this concept is given by Lüder Gerken, *Competition among Institutions* (London: Macmillan, 1995), pp. 1 – 31.

Chapter 12

International Trade as a Vector in Domestic Regulatory Reform: Discrimination, Cost-Benefit Analysis, and Negotiations

Joel P. Trachtman*

I.   Introduction

In a variety of ways, trade values conflict with other regulatory values. In fact, by its very nature, regulation is an intervention in a conflict with the market. If the market would achieve the desired regulatory result by itself, no regulation would be needed. Certainly regulation can improve the operation of markets, and in this sense regulation may be consistent with a desire for efficient markets. However, the presumptive reason for other kinds of regulation for protective or prudential regulation is that the market itself does not sufficiently protect the relevant values. In these specific cases, political decision-making evaluates and overrides the market. This is as it should be, and it works reasonably well in domestic systems. However, in an inter-state or in an international system, the capacity to impose trade detriment on others, while enjoying the regulatory benefit at home[1] or, even less benignly, the capacity to use regulation to achieve protectionist goals, raises additional issues.

*   Professor of International Law and Dean ad interim, The Fletcher School of Law and Diplomacy, Tufts University, Medford, Massachusetts 02155. This Essay was prepared for the Organization for Economic Co-Operation and Development ('OECD') Workshop on Regulatory Reform and the Multilateral Trading System, 7-8 December 2000. I appreciate the insights offered by other participants in that workshop.
1   See, e.g. Stephen Fidler, *EU Rules 'May Cost Africa $ 700m'*, Financial Times, 25th October 2000 - citing Tsunehiro Otsuki et al., The World Bank, *Saving Two in a Billion: A Case Study to Quantify the Trade Effect of European Food Safety Standards on African Exports* (2000).

An initial analysis would suggest that in theory, cost-benefit analysis (i) encompassing all costs and benefits including 'post-material' costs, (ii) encompassing both domestic and foreign costs and benefits, and (iii) operating dynamically to seek out the unique result that maximizes net benefit (or minimizes net detriment), would be the unique best institutional structure for responding to conflicts between trade values and other regulatory values. However, I have found no instances of this type of cost-benefit analysis being used anywhere in order to address conflicts between trade and other regulatory values.

Of course, once global cost-benefit analysis begins to include in its calculation adverse effects of regulation on foreign persons,[2] either in the form of non-pecuniary externalities or pecuniary externalities, some kinds of regulation will appear more costly. On the other hand, regulation that protects foreign persons or removes externalities will appear more beneficial. Environmentalists and deregulators alike would be required to accept the consequences of thinking globally and acting locally.

This brief chapter summarizes, updates and integrates work I have done elsewhere in order to suggest, first, why cost-benefit analysis is not used in dispute settlement,[3] second, how to evaluate substitute formulae that are available for use within dispute settlement, and finally, how dispute settlement and treaty-making relate to one another in this field.[4] This chapter considers the role of international discipline by dispute resolution bodies, in comparison to multilateral treaty-making or other legislation. Treaty-making or other legislation may take the form of harmonization to one degree or another, or importantly, may take the form of agreed rules of prescriptive jurisdiction, such as mutual recognition or national treatment.

1.   Dispute Resolution Mechanisms for Disciplining National Regulation

Dispute resolution mechanisms, such as the World Trade Organization[5] ('WTO') dispute settlement system, can be given a variety of types of mandate. Tribunals may be instructed to search for discrimination (national treatment or most-favoured nation treatment – 'MFN'), to determine whether the national measure is a rational

---

2   As shown in a paper by the OECD Secretariat, *Trade and Regulatory Reform: Insights from the OECD Country Reviews and Other Analyses*, TD/TC/WP(2000)21/Final (7th - 8th December 2000), few states formally consider effects on international trade as part of their domestic regulatory review processes.

3   For an extended analysis, see Joel P. Trachtman, *Trade and ... Problems, Cost-Benefit Analysis and Subsidiarity*, 9 EUR. J. INT'L L. 32 (1998).

4   For an extended analysis, see Joel P. Trachtman, *The Domain of WTO Dispute Resolution*, 40 HARV. INT'L L.J. 333 (1999).

5   Marrakesh Agreement Establishing the World Trade Organization, Legal Instruments - Results of the Uruguay Round vol. 1, 33 I.L.M. 1144 (1994) [hereinafter WTO Agreement].

means to a legitimate end, to determine whether the national measure disproportionately impedes trade, or to determine whether the national measure is the least trade restrictive alternative reasonably available to achieve its end.

2. Domestic Regulatory Reform

a) Multilateral rules restricting discrimination: national treatment and MFN

Since 1947, the General Agreement on Tariffs and Trade[6] ('GATT') has contained requirements of national treatment and MFN treatment in regulation. These types of requirements are viewed as less intrusive on national prerogatives than requirements of proportionality, least trade restrictive alternative requirements, balancing tests or cost-benefit analysis. However, it will be shown below that anti-discrimination norms may require a rather high degree of intrusion. On the other hand, anti-discrimination norms may fail to discipline national measures that hurt other states more than they help the state that imposes the measure.

b) GATT experience and the like products problem

There seems to be little objection to anti-discrimination rules, such as the national treatment obligation contained in Article III of GATT, or the MFN obligation contained in Article I of GATT. However, these provisions, as applied, involve considerable scrutiny, sometimes quite strict, of domestic regulatory measures. They do so in two ways.

In a narrower range of cases, national treatment discipline is dependent on the product-process distinction. That is, in recent cases, where a regulation is viewed as applying to a production process, as opposed to a product as such, Article III is viewed as inapplicable.[7]

More importantly, and more generally, any prohibition of discrimination requires a prior determination that two products or services are sufficiently 'like' to merit equal treatment. The 'like products' issue can be a proxy for a judicial examination

6   General Agreement on Tariffs and Trade, 30th October 1947, 61 Stat. A-11, T.I.A.S. 1700, 55 U.N.T.S. 194 [hereinafter GATT].

7   See, e.g. United States - Restrictions on Imports of Tuna, 23rd March 1993, 39 B.I.S.D. 155 (1993), reprinted in 30 I.L.M. 1594 (1991). For discussions of the product-process distinction, see Robert E. Hudec, *The Product-Process Doctrine in GATT/WTO Jurisprudence*, in New Directions in International Economic Law: Essays in Honour of John H. Jackson (Marco Bronckers and Reinhard Quick, eds. - Boston: Kluwer Law International, 2000); Robert Howse and Donald Regan, *The Product/Process Distinction-An Illusory Basis for Disciplining 'Unilateralism' in Trade Policy*, 11 Eur. J. Int'l L. 249 (2000), and the cogent response to the Howse and Regan paper from John Jackson.

of the rationality of regulatory categories. As in the recent Asbestos WTO panel decision,[8] the determination of 'likeness' is often outcome determinative. WTO jurisprudence has so far declined to provide a very specific definition of 'like products', but perhaps the Asbestos case will provide an occasion for the Appellate Body to address this issue. The panel in that case declined to consider risk as a basis for finding products to be un-'like'. This position, if followed, would eviscerate the protection heretofore thought provided to good faith, non-discriminatory regulation under Article III of GATT. Of course, for most kinds of product standards, these types of measures would be subject to scrutiny under the Agreement on Technical Barriers to Trade[9] ('TBT Agreement') or under the Agreement on Sanitary and Phytosanitary Measures[10] ('SPS Agreement').

My point here is simply that issues of discrimination are not so simple as they are sometimes thought to be, and that they involve some difficult judgements. The judgement of whether two products are 'like' may be made using relatively discrete factors, such as characteristics of the product, end-uses, cross-elasticity of demand, etc. However, the decision whether two products are 'like' is viewed as a 'case-by-case' decision, with much latitude for judgement. Rules of national treatment are not necessarily deferential to national regulation, as shown by the experience of the recent Asbestos case, nor are they necessarily predictable in their operation.

II.   The Problems of Cost-benefit Analysis and the Alternatives

As noted above, in economic theory, at least on an initial examination, courts would be given a mandate to engage in all-inclusive, dynamic, cost-benefit analysis in order to decide questions of conflict between local regulation and global trade. Assuming that courts could perform this cost-benefit analysis accurately, this would be the first-best solution to the trade versus domestic regulation issue. (Note that international regulation does not raise the same kinds of issues.) But such cost-benefit analysis is not explicitly used anywhere. Instead, courts receive mandates to

---

8   See European Communities – Measures Affecting Asbestos and Asbestos-Containing Products, Report of the Panel, WT/DS135/R, paras. 8.130-.132 (18th September 2000) (holding that risk to health is not a factor in determining 'likeness' under article III of GATT); see also United States – Measures Affecting Alcoholic and Malt Beverages, DS23/14 (noting that 'the treatment of imported and domestic products as like products under Article III may have significant implications for the scope of obligations under the General Agreement and for the regulatory autonomy of contracting parties').

9   Agreement on Technical Barriers to Trade, 15th April 1994, WTO Agreement, Annex 1A, at http://www.wto.org/english/docs e/legal e/final e.htm.

10   Agreement on Sanitary and Phytosanitary Measures, 15th April 1994, WTO Agreement, Annex 1A, at http://www.wto.org/english/docs e/legal e/final e.htm.

apply the following types of tests, individually or in combination, and with many subtle differences within each type of test:

- National treatment rules. A national treatment rule is a type of anti-discrimination rule that examines whether different legal standards are applied to comparable cases, as between the domestic and the foreign.
- Simple means-ends rationality tests. These tests consider whether the means chosen is indeed a rational means to a purported end. Analytically, simple means-ends rationality testing is included in all of the tests described below in this list, and is sometimes used as a proxy to detect discrimination. As it imposes little real discipline, and is often included in other tests, I do not analyze the use of simple means-ends rationality testing in detail below.
- Necessity or least trade-restrictive alternative tests. This type of test inquires whether there is a less trade-restrictive means to accomplish the same end. The definition of the end is often outcome-determinative. In some cases necessity testing is qualified by requiring that the means be the least trade-restrictive alternative that is reasonably available. In addition, necessity testing is sometimes combined with limitations on the categories of ends permitted.
- Proportionality. Proportionality *stricto sensu*[11] inquires whether the means are 'proportionate' to the ends: whether the costs are excessive in relation to the benefits. It might be viewed as cost-benefit analysis with a margin of appreciation, as it does not require that the costs be less than the benefits. Proportionality may be either static or comparative, in the same way as cost-benefit analysis. A comparative approach to proportionality testing would include in its calculus the costs and benefits of alternative rules.
- Balancing tests. Balancing tests purport to decide whether a measure that impedes trade is acceptable, balancing all of the factors. Balancing may be viewed as a kind of amorphous or imprecise cost-benefit analysis.[12] More charitably, and perhaps more correctly, it may be viewed as a kind of cost-

---

11 Nicholas Emiliou, *The Principle of Proportionality in European Law: A Comparative Study* (The Hague, Kluwer Law International, 1996). A wider definition of proportionality developed in the EU context includes three tests: (i) proportionality *stricto sensu*, (ii) a least trade-restrictive alternative test, and (iii) a simple means-ends rationality test. This chapter will consider only the narrower type of proportionality.

12 See Michael E. Smith, *State Discriminations Against Interstate Commerce*, 74 CALIFORNIA LAW REVIEW 1203, 1205 (1979) (stating that 'the Justices take all relevant circumstances into account and render judgement according to their overall sense of the advantages and disadvantages of upholding the regulation'). At their most precise, balancing tests are the same as cost-benefit analysis. See Earl M. Maltz, *How Much Regulation is Too Much – An Examination of Commerce Clause Jurisprudence*, 50 GEORGE WASHINGTON LAW REVIEW 47, 59-60 (1981).

benefit analysis that recognizes the difficulty of formalizing the analysis, and seeks to achieve similar results informally.[13]

- Cost-benefit analysis. Static cost-benefit analysis in the context at hand[14] juxtaposes the regulatory benefits of regulation with the trade costs of regulation, as well as other costs of regulation, and would strike down regulation where the costs exceed the benefits. Cost-benefit analysis in this context may be viewed as stricter scrutiny than the US domestic cost-benefit analysis that has recently become popular, as it adds a cost dimension not normally included: detriments to trade. Adding trade detriments to the calculation would presumably have the marginal effect of causing some regulation to fail a cost-benefit analysis test. It is worth comparing static cost-benefit analysis, simply juxtaposing the costs and benefits of a single rule, with a more dynamic comparative cost-benefit analysis, comparing the net benefits of multiple rules, and recommending the rule with the greatest net benefits.

There are several reasons why a full cost-benefit analysis test may indeed be less than optimal, and one or more of these other tests might be preferred. In this chapter, I evaluate some of the parameters by which cost-benefit analysis might be compared with other tradeoff devices: (i) maximization of net gains of trade and regulation, (ii) administrability, (iii) distributive concerns, (iv) moral concerns, and (v) theoretical concerns. These factors are not themselves commensurable, and so we cannot place them on a simple tote board to determine when comparative cost-benefit analysis should or should not be used. Rather, these factors must be

13   'If we had a way of quantifying all the appropriate inputs, and a way of comparing them, and a theory that told us how to do so, we would not call it balancing. Rather, it would be called something like "deriving the most cost-effective solution", or just "solving the problem." Stephen E. Gottlieb, *The Paradox of Balancing Significant Interests*, 45 HASTINGS LAW JOURNAL 825, 839 (1994). See also T. Alexander Aleinikoff, *Constitutional Law in the Age of Balancing*, 96 YALE LAW JOURNAL 943, 1002-1004 (1987).

14   For more general and technical treatment of cost-benefit analysis, see, e.g. Peter S. Menell and Richard B. Stewart (eds.), *Environmental Law and Policy* (Boston : Little, Brown, 1994), 81-160; D. Pearce and C. Nash (eds.) *The Social Appraisal of Projects: A Text in Cost-Benefit Analysis* (New York: John Wiley & Sons, 1981); R. Tresch, *Public Finance: A Normative Theory* (Georgetown, Ont.: Irwin-Dorsey, 1981); Edith Stokey and Richard Zeckhauser, *A Primer for Policy Analysis* (New York: W. W. Norton, 1978); E.J. Mishan, *Cost-Benefit Analysis* (New York: Praeger 1976); H. Raiffa, *Decision Analysis: Introductory Lectures on Choices under Uncertainty* (New York: Random House 1968). See also the recent special issue of THE JOURNAL OF LEGAL STUDIES devoted to cost-benefit analysis, beginning at 29 THE JOURNAL OF LEGAL STUDIES 837 (2000) (including papers by W. Kip Viscusi, Amartya Sen, Martha Nussbaum, Richard Posner, and Gary Becker).

examined and subjected to political or deliberative analysis in order to determine which trade-off device should be used in particular circumstances.

However, very briefly,[15] it is clear that cost-benefit analysis experiences severe problems of administrability (including predictability). Cost-benefit analysis does not concern itself with the distribution of the costs and benefits, and so it could raise significant distributive issues. Cost-benefit analysis raises important moral concerns regarding the commensurability between different kinds of values, including especially between material and post-material values. Political institutions, as opposed to adjudicative or research institutions, are most appropriate to commensurate among these types of values. Cost-benefit analysis raises related theoretical concerns in economics about its implicit interpersonal comparison of utility: your valuation of the environment cannot be compared by a third party to my valuation of an SUV.

My analysis suggests that a least trade-restrictive alternative analysis overcomes some of the most difficult of these concerns, and might be worthy of consideration. First, as it only measures the detriment to trade, not the benefits of regulation, it is easier to administer. Second, it does not seek to commensurate between these values, as it simply seeks the method of satisfying the non-trade values that imposes the least detriment in trade terms. For similar reasons, it raises fewer concerns regarding interpersonal comparison of utility.

Let us be clear, though, that least trade-restrictive alternative analysis might leave in place a domestic regulation that provides benefits far smaller than the trade detriments it causes, and might strike down domestic regulation that is far more valuable than the trade detriments it causes. Thus, it is both under-inclusive and over-broad. Of course, least trade-restrictive alternative analysis has been adopted judicially in connection with the application in some circumstances of Article XX of GATT, and has been adopted 'legislatively' in both the SPS Agreement[16] and the TBT Agreement.[17]

III. 'Legislative' versus Judicial Decision-Making and Rules versus Standards

While trade diplomats and scholars have expressed pride at the Uruguay Round achievement of more binding and more 'law-oriented' dispute resolution, the same group and a variety of non-governmental organizations ('NGOs') and other

---

15 For a more extended analysis, see Trachtman, *supra* note 3.
16 See Agreement on the Application of Sanitary and Phytosanitary Measures, 15th April 1994, WTO Agreement, Annex 1A, arts. 2.2, 5.6, at http://www.wto.org/english/docse/legale/finale.htm.
17 See Agreement on Technical Barriers to Trade, 15th April 1994, WTO Agreement, Annex 1A, art. 2.2, at http://www.wto.org/english/docs e/legale/finale.htm.

commentators question the jurisdictional scope of dispute resolution. After all, should these small tribunals, lacking direct democratic legitimacy, determine profound issues confronting the international trading community, such as the relationship between trade values and environmental values? Many voices have called for greater international legislation (specific treaty-making) in these important fields. This section is intended to outline a more realistic and nuanced view, based on law and economics analytical techniques. It is intended to suggest the reasons why dispute resolution could be the appropriate place to determine these issues. Conversely, it is intended to suggest a way to determine or predict when these issues might better be subjected to more specific legislative action.

The analysis above of different 'trade-off devices' assumes that a legislative act (including the entry into a treaty) has assigned a mandate to a court. However, in addition to a choice among mandates to courts, there is a choice whether and to what extent to provide a mandate to courts. It is possible for the legislative act to provide either a broad or a narrow mandate to a court. A narrow mandate will call for less discretion to be exercised by the court. Economic analysis provides two related analytical techniques that suggest when the authors of treaties might decide to accord narrower or broader mandates to courts.

Not only do treaty-writers delegate authority to dispute resolution tribunals, they also maintain complex relationships with the dispute resolution process, both formal and informal. First, of course, is the possibility of legislative reversal: if the authors of the treaty become discontented with the manner of its application, they may change the treaty. Furthermore, they may restrain dispute resolution. Second, and relatively unusual in general international law, is a formal 'political filter' device. This political filter was much more important prior to the 1994 changes to WTO dispute resolution, but still exists in attenuated form.

The incomplete contracts literature considers the reasons for, and implications of, the fact that all contracts (like all treaties) are necessarily incomplete in their capacity to specify the norms that will be applied to particular conduct. In the rules versus standards literature,[18] a law is a 'rule' to the extent that it is specified in advance of the conduct to which it is applied. A standard, on the other hand, is a law that is farther towards the other end of the spectrum, in relative terms. It establishes general guidance to both the person governed and the person charged with applying the law, but does not specify in detail, in advance, the conduct required or

---

18 For an introduction to the rules versus standards discussion in law and economics, see Louis Kaplow, General Characteristics of Rules, in *Encyclopedia of Law and Economics* (B. Bouckaert and G. De Geest eds.), (Northampton, Ma.: Edward Elgar, 2000); Louis Kaplow, *Rules Versus Standards: An Economic Analysis*, 42 DUKE LAW JOURNAL. 557 (1992); see also, Cass R. Sunstein, *Problems with Rules*, 83 CALIFORNIA LAW REVIEW 955 (1995). In international trade law, 'standards' has a specific meaning, referring to product standards. This meaning is separate from the sense in which 'standards' is used here.

proscribed. The relativity of these definitions is critical. Furthermore, each law is comprised of a combination of rules and standards. However, it will be useful to speak here generally of rules as separate from standards.

It is worth noting that the distinction between a rule and a standard is not necessarily grammatical or determined by the number of words used to express the norm; rather, the distinction relates to how much work remains to be done to determine the applicability of the norm to a particular circumstance.

Professor Hadfield applies an incomplete contracts analysis to statutes, which we in turn can apply to treaties.[19] Treaties may be optimally incomplete with appropriate instructions to decision-makers to complete the 'contract' in particular cases. The parameters to consider include (i) the costs of advance specification, (ii) the degree to which the future is unpredictable or stochastic, (iii) the ability to customize to particular facts in specific cases, and (iv) the potential value of diversity of compliance techniques. This literature tends to treat the legislature as a unitary actor. It will be exceedingly important for us to recognize that the legislature in our case (as in Hadfield's) is a group of actors subject to strategic and social choice limitations on their ability to act.

Incompleteness of specification may not simply be a result of conservation of resources. It may be a more explicit political decision to either agree to disagree for the moment, to avoid the political price that may arise from immediate hard decisions, or to cloak the hard decisions in the false inevitability of judicial interpretation. It is important, also, to recognize that the incompleteness of specification may represent a failure to decide how the policy expressed relates to other policies. This is critical in the trade area, where often the incompleteness of a trade rule relates to its failure to address, or incorporate, non-trade policies. Thus, for example, the chapeau of Article XX of GATT may be viewed as providing a standard as to 'arbitrariness', 'justifiability', and 'discrimination'.

Laws have always referred to standards in an implicit or explicit manner. However, rules in a formal sense are less flexible and are a more demanding instrument of regulation.

1. The Costs and Benefits of Rules and Standards

Rules are more expensive to develop than standards, *ex ante*, because rules entail specification costs, including drafting costs and negotiation costs, as well as the strategic costs involved in *ex ante* specification. In order to reach agreement on specification in order to legislate specifically there may be greater costs in public

---

19 See Gillian K. Hadfield, *Weighing the Value of Vagueness: An Economic Perspective on Precision in the Law*, 82 CALIFORNIA Law REVIEW 541, 547 (1994); see also Ian Ayres and Robert Gertner, *Strategic Contractual Inefficiency and the Optimal Choice of Legal Rules*, 101 YALE LAW JOURNAL 729 (1992).

choice terms.[20] This is particularly interesting in the trade context, where treaty-making would be subjected to intense domestic scrutiny, while application of a standard by a dispute resolution process might be subjected to reduced scrutiny. On the other hand, NGOs have sought in this connection to enhance transparency in dispute resolution. Finally, rules require clear decision; standards may serve as an agreement to disagree, or may help to mask or mystify a decision made.[21] Under standards, both sides in the legislative process may claim victory, at least initially.

Rules are generally thought to provide greater predictability. There are two moments at which to consider predictability. First, is the ability of persons subject to the law to be able to plan and conform their conduct *ex ante*, sometimes known as 'primary predictability'.[22] The second moment in which predictability is important is *ex post*, after the relevant conduct has taken place. Where the parties can predict the outcome of dispute resolution where they can predict the tribunal's determination of their respective rights and duties they will spend less money on litigation. This type of predictability is 'secondary predictability'. Both types of predictability can reduce costs. While rules appear to provide primary and secondary predictability, tribunals may construct exceptions in order to do what is, by their lights, substantial justice, and thereby reduce predictability. It may be difficult to constrain the ability of tribunals to do this. Furthermore, as noted below, game theory predicts that some degree of uncertainty of unpredictability may enhance the ability of the parties to bargain to a lower cost solution. Thus, simple predictability is not the only measure of a legal norm; rather, we must also be concerned with the ability of the legal norm to provide satisfactory outcomes. In economic terms, we must be concerned with the allocative efficiency of the outcome. We consider allocative efficiency below as we consider the institutional dimension of rules and standards.

As we consider the relative allocative efficiency of potential outcomes, we must recognize that there is a temporal distinction between rules and standards. Standards may be used earlier in the development of a field of law before sufficient experience to form a basis for more complete specification is acquired. In many areas of law, courts develop a jurisprudence that forms the basis for codification or even rejection by legislatures. With this in mind, legislatures (or adjudicators) may set standards at an early point in time, and determine to establish rules at a later point in time.[23] It is

---

20   See Gillian K. Hadfield, *Weighing the Value of Vagueness: An Economic Perspective on Precision in the Law*, 82 CALIFORNIA LAW REVIEW 541, 550 (1994) (citing Linda R. Cohen and Roger G. Noll, How to Vote, Whether to Vote: Strategies for Voting and Abstaining on Congressional Role Calls, 13 POLITICAL BEHAVIOR 97 [1991]).

21   Kenneth W. Abbott & Duncan Snidal, *Why States Act Through Formal International Organizations*, 42 JOURNAL OF CONFLICT RESOLUTION 3 (1998).

22   For this use of the terms 'primary predictability' and 'secondary predictability', see William F. Baxter, *Choice of Law and the Federal System*, 16 STANFORD LAW REVIEW 1, 3 (1963).

23   See Kaplow, The General Characteristics of Rules, *supra* note 14, at 10.

clear that a rule of *stare decisis* is not necessary to the development of a body of jurisprudence by a court or dispute resolution tribunal.[24] It is also worth noting that in a common law setting, or any setting where tribunals refer to precedents, the tribunal may announce a standard in a particular case, and then elaborate that standard in subsequent cases until it has built a structure of rules for its own application.

Kaplow points out that where instances of the relevant behaviour are more frequent, economies of scale will indicate that rules become relatively more efficient. For circumstances that arise only infrequently, it is more difficult to justify promulgation of specific rules. In addition, rules provide compliance benefits: they are cheaper to obey, because the cost of determining the required behaviour is lower. Rules are also cheaper to apply by a court: the court must only determine the facts and compare them to the rule.

2. The Institutional Dimension of Rules and Standards

Another distinction between rules and standards, often de-emphasized in this literature, is the institutional distinction: with rules, the legislature often 'makes' the decision, while with standards, the adjudicator determines the application of the standard, thereby 'making' the decision. Again, it is obvious that these terms are used in a relative sense (this caveat will not be repeated). Economists and even lawyer-economists seem to assume that the tribunal simply 'finds' the law, and does not make it. Of course, courts can make rules pursuant to statutory or constitutional authority: the hallmark of a rule is that it is specified *ex ante*, not that it is specified by a legislature. However, at least in the international trade system, rules are largely made by treaty, and standards are largely applied by tribunals.

But the difference between legislators and courts is an important one, and may affect the outcome.[25] The choice of legislators or courts to make particular decisions should be made using cost-benefit analysis. Such a cost-benefit analysis would include, as a critical factor, the degree of representativeness of constituents: which institution will most accurately reflect citizens' desires? There are good reasons why such cost-benefit analysis does not always select legislatures. First, there is a public choice critique of legislatures. Second, even under a public interest analysis, legislatures may not be efficient at specifying *ex ante* all of the details of treatment of particular cases. Third, the rate of change of circumstances over time may favour the ability of courts to adjust. Finally, we must analyse the strategic relationship between legislators and courts. Thus, in order fully to understand the relationship

---

24 David Palmeter and Petros C. Mavroidis, *The WTO Legal System: Sources of Law*, 92 AMERICAN JOURNAL OF INTERNATIONAL LAW 398 (1998).

25 See Neil Komesar, *Imperfect Alternatives: Choosing Institutions in Law, Economics, and Public Policy* (Chicago: Chicago University Press, 1994).

between rules and standards, the tools of public choice or positive political theory[26] should be brought to bear to analyse the relationship between legislative and judicial decision-making.[27]

3.   *The Strategic Dimension of Rules and Standards*

It is not possible to consider the costs and benefits of rules and standards separately from the strategic considerations that would cause states to select a rule as opposed to a standard. Johnston analyses rules and standards from a strategic perspective, finding that, under a standard, bargaining may yield immediate efficient agreement, whereas under a rule, this condition may not obtain.[28] Johnston considers a rule a 'definite, *ex ante* entitlement' and a standard a 'contingent, *ex post* entitlement'. Like Kaplow, he does not consider the source of the rule, whether legislature or tribunal.

Johnston notes the 'standard supposition in the law and economics literature ... that private bargaining between [two parties] over the allocation of [a] legal entitlement is most likely to be efficient if the entitlement is clearly defined and assigned *ex ante* according to a rule, rather than made contingent upon a judge's *ex post* balancing of relative value and harm'.[29] Johnston suggests this supposition may be incorrect,[30] 'When the parties bargain over the entitlement when there is private information about value and harm, bargaining may be more efficient under a blurry balancing test than under a certain rule'.[31] This is because under a certain rule, the holder of the entitlement will have incentives to 'hold out' and decline to provide information about the value to him of the entitlement. Under a standard, where presumably it cannot be known with certainty *ex ante* who owns the entitlement, the person not possessing the entitlement may credibly threaten to take it, providing incentives for the other person to bargain. Johnston points out that this result is obtained only when the *ex post* balancing test is imperfect, because if the balancing were perfect, the threat would not be credible. This provides a counter-intuitive

---

26   See, e.g. John Ferejohn and Barry Weingast, *A Positive Theory of Statutory Interpretation*, 12 INTERNATIONAL REVIEW OF LAW AND ECONOMICS 263 (1992).

27   Robert Cooter and Josef Drexl, *The Logic of Power in the Emerging European Constitution: Game Theory and the Division of Powers*, 14 INT'L REV. L. & ECON. 307 (1994).

28   Jason Scott Johnston, *Bargaining under Rules versus Standards*, 11 JOURNAL OF LAW ECONOMICS AND ORGANISATION 256 (1995).

29   Ibid.

30   See also Carol Rose, *Crystals and Mud in Property Law*, 40 STANFORD LAW REVIEW 577 (1988); Joel P. Trachtman, Externalities and Extraterritoriality, in *Economic Dimensions in International Law: Comparative and Empirical Perspectives* (Jagdeep Bhandari and Alan O. Sykes [eds.] - New York : Cambridge University Press, 1997).

31   Johnston, *supra* note 24, at 257.

argument for inaccuracy of the application of standards.[32] Interestingly, further research as to the magnitude of strategic costs under rules and under standards might suggest that over time, rules provide some of the strategic benefits of standards. This might be so if tribunals develop exceptions to rules in a way that introduces uncertainty to their application. This increased benefit would of course be countervailed to some extent by the reduction of predictability that the development of exceptions would entail.

I do not, in this brief chapter, give examples of how these considerations might apply to actual cases.[33]

IV. Improving 'Legislation'

There are several problems with the international treaty system: with international legislation. First, it is functionally Balkanized: trade, environment, health, competition, tax, etc., are all dealt with separately, and there is insufficient co-ordination. Second, legislation takes place largely through new treaty-making, and this generally requires unanimity. Thus, international legislation is slow to respond to many emerging, overlapping issues. By default, many of these issues are referred to dispute resolution in the WTO. The WTO dispute resolution system seems to bear too much responsibility, compared to the international legislative system. This section considers how the legislative capacity of the international regulatory system can be improved.

1. Improving Functional Integration Through Horizontal Institutional Co-ordination

There is already much co-operation between the WTO and the United Nations Environmental Program ('UNEP') and Multilateral Environmental Agreements ('MEAs'). There needs to be more co-operation, and at some level, the relationship between trade norms and other norms needs to be worked out more definitively, and more formally. For example, the European Union has recently argued that greater clarification of the validity of MEA norms within the WTO legal system would be useful, while the United States has argued that the WTO dispute resolution system has set forth an adequate test for the validity of MEA norms that may conflict with trade norms. Functional integration could take the form of choice of law and/or choice of forum rules, when these norms come into conflict, rules regarding supremacy of norms, later in time rules, interpretative rules that seek to avoid conflict, or at the extreme, joint formulation of norms, as we would expect within a

---

32 Ibid at 272.
33 See Trachtman, *supra* note 4.

domestic system. For example, a type of 'choice of law' rule might specify that certain MEAs override certain trade law obligations.

2. *Request-Offer Negotiations Regarding National Regulation*

How would more specific international law regarding domestic regulation be made; how would rules regarding the interplay between trade and other norms be legislated? There may also be room for further elaboration of standards in certain areas.[34] Rules can be developed by courts through the application of standards over time. Rules are more often made by legislatures. Sometimes judicial action can act as a pathfinder for legislation: legislative action can respond, positively or negatively, to judicial action.

Thus, the United States, having lost in the Shrimp-Turtle case,[35] might seek new treaty action, either within or without the WTO, to approve its action. Now that the Appellate Body has spoken in that case, the onus is on the United States to seek 'legislative reversal'. However, the Appellate Body has not provided an extremely clear response: this is why the EU is seeking greater legislative clarification. In accordance with the strategic rules-standards perspective, the lack of perfect clarity promotes negotiation. This is an example of the problem of 'asset ownership' in this field: if it were clear that WTO law never permits process standards as barriers to import, it would be for those states that wish to impose such barriers to negotiate for exceptions. Given some ambiguity, both sides have some incentive to negotiate. Negotiations take place in the shadow of judicial action.

It is important to recognize that there is a distributive aspect to these norms. In order to achieve greater specificity in order to legislate rules – it will be necessary to negotiate transactions between states. The original WTO style of tariff negotiations request/offer may be appropriate for use in the regulatory field. That is, states could request exceptions for their regulation, or alternatively, states could request liberalization of another state's regulation, in exchange for another concession. The advantage of this type of transaction – a rule-based transaction – is that states would know in advance what types of modifications of their domestic regulation would be required, or what kinds of liberalization in other states they had achieved. These modifications could then be legitimated as part of the trade negotiations, instead of being left to the dispute resolution process.

Negotiations in the WTO context may provide an advantage over negotiations in a MEA or UNEP, or other functional international organization, context: the greater

---

34 On 24th December 1998, the WTO Committee on Trade in Services adopted the Disciplines on Domestic Regulation in the Accountancy Sector, S/L/64, developed by the WTO Working Party on Professional Services.

35 United States – Import Prohibitions of Certain Shrimp and Shrimp Products, Report of the Appellate Body, WT/DS58/AB/R (12th October 1998).

possibility of linked package deals. While linkages may be made across functional organizations, it is easier to do so, both administratively and in terms of legitimation, within a single organization. The WTO already contains much scope for package deals. Thus, there is a network externality argument for inclusion of additional subject matter in the WTO.

3. High-Powered Incentives to Negotiate: Selective (and Weighted?) Majority Voting as a Means to Redress the Adjudication/Legislation Imbalance

In order to provide even stronger incentives to negotiate than those existing with simply a judicial prod, states could agree on selective, and possibly weighted, majority voting. The incoming Director-General of the WTO, Thai Trade Minister Supachai, has already broached this issue. For an example of selective majority voting, states could agree that MEAs, perhaps with a specified minimum number of parties, might in the future be exempted from WTO prohibitions by majority vote. If majority voting were the applicable legislative rule, states would have greater incentives to come to terms on unanimously agreed resolution of trade versus regulation problems. Furthermore, majority voting would redress the current imbalance in the capacity to act between WTO adjudication and multilateral treaty-making.[36]

4. Reducing the Problem of Private Information: The Potential Role of International Organizations in Evaluating Regulatory Barriers

One of the most serious obstacles to negotiations regarding regulatory barriers to trade is lack of knowledge. This ignorance exists on several dimensions: (i) what are the trade costs associated with the relevant regulation; (ii) what are the full regulatory benefits associated with the relevant regulation; (iii) is there a less trade-restrictive alternative? An independent party may assist negotiations by serving as an independent source of this information, overcoming information asymmetries between the parties. Private information may impede negotiation toward the reduction of barriers.

5. Legitimating Adjudication

As indicated above, trade versus regulation decisions put a good deal of pressure on the adjudicator. Mandates that do so explicitly would help to legitimate this allocation of responsibility, while alleviating some of the criticism of the dispute settlement process. In addition, as noted above, a more effective structure for

36 For a story of a similar imbalance in the European Union context, see Joseph Weiler, *The Transformation of Europe*, 100 YALE LAW JOURNAL 2403 (1991).

legislation would reduce concern about the legitimacy of adjudication. If legislative reversal were more readily available, adjudication would be more responsive.

V. Conclusion

Current arrangements for addressing the interface between trade and domestic regulation may not be satisfactory. National treatment standards may not be as unintrusive as advertised, and may leave in place measures that should be disciplined. Decisions to assign responsibility for disciplining national regulation must consider various alternative mandates. However, these decisions must be examined in comparison to decisions to provide greater treaty or legislative guidance. This chapter considers the choice among general standards that can form the basis for a mandate to dispute resolution bodies in juxtaposition to the choice to provide more specific treaty rules.

Chapter 13

Public Governance and the Co-operative Law of Transnational Markets: The Case of Financial Regulation

Pedro Gustavo Teixeira[*]

I.   Introduction: The Law and Regulation of Transnational Markets

The limitations of nation states' political and legal frameworks in tackling phenomena arising from globalization are increasingly evident.[1] Of more consequence, reality is ahead of theory in that the transnational markets seem to sustain and develop themselves without having to refer their ordering to the constitutional organization of the nation state and to judiciary adjudication. The awareness of a commonality of fears, like the uncertainty of risk and the growing complexity of transactions,[2] has led public authorities and private parties to put together mechanisms of trust with a view to creating order and governance among themselves. In this context, the legal significance of relations which, for example,

*   Researcher, Law Department of the European University Institute, Florence, Italy, and Expert in Prudential Supervision, European Central Bank, Frankfurt am Main, Germany. The views expressed in this chapter are personal to the author. This chapter is a revised version of that presented in the workshop on 'Public Governance in the Age of Globalization' (Florence, March 2000). The author gratefully acknowledges the comments of the participants.
1   See G. Teubner, '"Global Bukowina": Legal Pluralism in the World Society', in Teubner (ed.), *Global Law Without a State* (Aldershot: Dartmouth, 1997), pp.3-28 at p.5; K.F. Röhl and S. Magen, *'Die Rolle des Rechts im Prozeß der Globalisierung'*, ZEITSCHRIFT FÜR RECHTSSOZIOLOGIE, vol.17 (1996), pp.1-57; and K. Ronit and V. Schneider, 'Private Organizations in Global Governance', Paper prepared for the conference 'Problem Solving Capacity of Transnational Governance Systems', Max-Planck-Institut für Gesellschaftsforschung, (Köln, 1996), p.9.
2   See for instance, C. Stanley, *'Speculations on the Conflict of Discourses: Finance, Crime and Regulation'*, JOURNAL OF FINANCIAL REGULATION AND COMPLIANCE, vol.4, n.3 (1996), pp.239 ff.

range from relational contracting to complex associations, such as networks, should be established to a high degree.[3] They represent a main source of the regulatory regimes that govern global economies.

Against this background, this chapter discusses how forms of 'co-operative law'[4] elaborated by public authorities within co-operative regulatory bodies provide governance to the international and European financial markets. It gives an overview of the current arrangements allowing co-operative law-making to take place and of the sort of rules being produced. The aim is to grasp the nature of this co-operative law, its regulatory features, its circular effect on co-operative regulatory bodies, and whether it may be perceived as having a legal character. The final step is to assess the procedural and non-procedural features of a transnational order whose shortcomings are far less than apparent.

1.　*Market Relations in the Global Economy and the Implications for Legal Theory*

The evolution of the international economy and of modern capitalist structures, is leading to both the spatial and sectoral segmentation of market relations across national boundaries.[5] Small, specific and specialized groups of merchants or business communities are being established.[6] Systems of production and of supply of services are diverging in their features, rather than converging, as a result of globalization. Economies are being built around alternative modes of production, as both current institutional arrangements and natural knowledge constraints do not allow for a consistent first-best solution for a given production problem. These circumstances and others determine a pattern of an indefinable multiple causality between market phenomena that severely restrains, if it does not undermine, the potential reach of public regulation as paradigmatically issued and adjudicated by the nation state.[7]

3　See T.L. Fort, '*Trust and Law's Facilitating Role*', AMERICAN BUSINESS LAW JOURNAL, vol.34 (1996), pp.211ff.

4　See, on the concept of co-operative law, K.-H. Ladeur, '*The Theory of Autopoiesis as an Approach to a Better Understanding of Postmodern Law - From the Hierarchy of Norms to the Heterarchy of Changing Patterns of Legal Inter-relationships*', EUI Working Paper LAW No. 99/3 at p.42; and 'Towards a Legal Concept of the Network in European Standard-Setting', in Joerges and Vos (eds.) *EU Committees: Social Regulation, Law and Politics* (Oxford: Hart, 1999), pp.151-170 at 167.

5　See R. Boyer and J. R. Hollingsworth, 'From National Embeddedness to Spatial and Institutional Nestedness', in Hollingsworth and Boyer (eds.), *Contemporary Capitalism: The Embeddedness of Institutions* (Cambridge: Cambridge University Press, 1997), pp.449ff.

6　See R.D. Cooter, '*Decentralized Law for a Complex Economy*', SOUTHWESTERN UNIVERSITY LAW REVIEW, vol.23 (1994), p.445.

7　See K.-H. Ladeur, '*Post-Modern Constitutional Theory: A Prospect for the Self-Organising Society*', MODERN LAW REVIEW, vol.60 (1997), pp.617ff.

An important implication of this state of affairs to be brought to legal theory is that legal pluralism, the qualitative multiplicity of the sources and discourses of law, has been used as the concept to be more appropriate to define transnational ruling.[8] Such pluralism is not rooted in hierarchical assumptions, such as the one between the public and the private sphere or any others based on power relations. Hierarchies, if at all in existence, get blended in the way that market actors, independently of their original nature (be it public authorities or market participants) functionally distribute tasks in order and governance, namely using private law instruments, such as economic organization, to have such distribution effective, running and evolving.

This being so, the contention is that, other than mere public regulation, the concept of legal centralism is put at stake as the source of market governance. This is because the formal rationality that informs hierarchical power depends on the possibility of making clear causal connections in order for rules to be produced. In a complex economy this is simply not feasible as markets are numerous and technically manifold (i.e. extremely product- and process-specific), based on the search for and holding of restricted or innovative information, thus revealing themselves to be quite hermetic to external observation from, and consequently regulation by, a central authority.

The concept of a '*lex mercatoria*' has been the support of a private legal order that validates international transactions in the lack of a supra-national uniform system of adjudication.[9] It has been, however, a concept historically related to a society of merchants as individuals. They trade across national borders having their contracts self-validated by their own will to be bound to a commercial agreement. Repetitive and cross-contracting led to the establishment of business practices among the community of international traders. This circumstance, the fact of 'tradition' in trade usages, is then recognized to be a validating criterion through which the legal/non-legal distinction is asserted. Arbitration courts have accordingly been issuing their awards in a way to continuously reinforce the safe and perennial values of fair trade (e.g. *pacta sunt servanda*).

In a transnational and complex economy, traditional values and principles may no longer be deemed sufficient to order market relations. Markets are founded on diversity and specialization of trading among economic organizations, revolving around the competitive search for knowledge and solutions for production or supply of services problems. Furthermore, market evolution is not simply reduced to the expansion of trade and contracting. It is instead linked to forms of co-operative and

8   On the elaborate concept of 'legal pluralism', see G. Teubner, 'Global Bukowina', pp.5-8, and L.M. Friedman, '*Emerging Sociology of Transnational Law*', STANFORD JOURNAL OF INTERNATIONAL LAW, vol.32 (1996), pp.66 ff.

9   See B. Sousa Santos, *Toward a New Common Sense* (New York: Routledge, 1995), pp.288-92.

co-ordinated action institutionalized between market participants through means other than merely contractual. One finds that 'highly specialized overlapping networks of relationships' structure markets in a way not easily grasped by external agents, such as public authorities.[10] Such networks underlie the intricate regulatory regimes that purport to be the meta-structures of law in transnational and complex contexts. Examples of this kind are certainly environmental regulations, telecommunications and media law, and financial regulation.

The new regulatory regimes involve increasingly original dynamics of processes of rule-making, interpretation and adjudication of rules. Legal principles and norms have to be adapted to a reality in constant change, where risks are uncertain and scientific knowledge is bounded.[11] As a result, the concept of 'transnational commercial law' has to be adjusted to the activities developed by economic organizations. This implies that the debate on the validity and legitimacy of transnational economic orders is to be re-directed and founded on grounds other than mere contractual self-validation or substantial legal values. In this sense, the adoption of procedural principles, for instance guaranteeing the learning capacity of organizations, may prove to be the paradigm to which transnational commercial law must conform.

2. Market Participants and Regulators as Economic Organizations

Merchants are no longer individuals attending local fairs. Market participants are elaborate organizations, business firms with an internal structure accommodating different interests of individuals and apt to pursue a given activity. They have the power to act externally as legal persons, for instance, by contracting between one another or with other entities. At the same time, and due precisely to their internal and external facets, they are also bound to gather, preserve, and exchange information and knowledge. The constraints of modern business make firms more and more dependent on their ability to learn and be flexible to learning.[12]

10   See K.-H. Ladeur, 'A Legal Theory of Supranationality', *European Law Journal* (1997), vol.3, p.53.

11   See ibid, p.53, stating that 'Rule-making is possible only in the form of a co-operative modelling of the heterarchical linkage of various elements: public regulatory issues, self-regulation. control and self-control, evaluation and self revision on the basis of knowledge generated through experimental processes'.

12   See H.A. Simon, 'Designing Organizations for an Information-Rich World', in Greenberger (ed.), *Computers, Communications, and the Public Interest*, pp.38-52 (Baltimore: Johns Hopkins Press, 1971), pp.194ff.; M. Crozier, *L'Entreprise a l'Ecoute: Apprendre le management post-industriel* (Paris: InterEditions, 1991), pp.211ff.; C.F. Sabel, 'Learning by Monitoring: The Institutions of Economic Development', in N.J. Smelser and R. Swedberg (ed.) *Handbook of Economic Sociology* (Princeton: Princeton University Press, 1994), pp.137-65, pp.137ff.; A.A. Alchian and H. Demsetz, 'Production, Information Costs, and Economic Organization', in P.J. Buckley and J.

With these characteristics, business firms certainly express some sort of social control. Their work rules, besides exerting self-control, discipline and monitor their individual agents. Furthermore, the contract rules in which they engage not only bring self-restraint, but also provide the possibility to monitor and direct the behaviour of the other market participants.[13] Finally, their comparative advantage in the selective possession of information and knowledge provides them with a relative political emancipation for problem- and dispute-solving, allowing the effective decentralization of power and even the firms' self-governance.[14] At a parallel level, market authorities also fashion themselves in decentralized forms of public administration, like independent administrative agencies, emulating firms and economic organizations in order to procure the social control with which these are favoured.[15]

The context depicted here implies that a modern conception of transnational commercial law will have to be constructed around the social control inherent to organizations, and not simply around individuals' actions as before. Business firms, functioning already as social contracts or constitutions[16] (restricted however to conforming their own activities), definitely add a vital substance to the ordering of market relations as they may well prove to be the building blocks and a factor for the sophistication of the more comprehensive social contract underlying transnational commercial law.

Therefore, given the difficulties in establishing legal centralism for a complex economy, especially out of a nation state, law-making in transnational markets is assuming very distinct and innovative features. A most salient one is the role that transnational regulatory organizations, made out of co-operative initiatives between national regulators, have been gradually acquiring. As market participants are themselves organizations, regulators secure co-operation and co-ordination between

Michie (eds.), *Firms, Organizations, and Contracts* (Oxford: Oxford University Press, 1996), pp.75-102 at 93-4.

13 See R. Coase, *The Firm, the Market, and the Law* (Chicago: University of Chicago Press, 1988), pp.33ff; R.C. Ellickson, *Order without Law* (Cambridge: Harvard University Press, 1991), pp.248-9; O. Williamson, 'The Modern Corporation: Origins, Evolution, Attributes', JOURNAL OF ECONOMIC LITERATURE, vol.XIX (1981), pp.1547 ff.

14 See C.F. Sabel, 'Design, Deliberation, and Democracy: On the New Pragmatism of Firms and Public Institutions', in Ladeur (ed.), *Liberal Institutions, Economic Constitutional Rights, and the Role of Organizations* (Baden-Baden: Nomos, 1997), pp.101ff.; and B. Sousa Santos, *Towards a New Common Sense, supra* n. 9, pp.25 ff.

15 See C.F. Sabel, *'Bootstrapping Reform: Rebuilding Firms, the Welfare State, and Unions'*, POLITICS & SOCIETY, vol.23 (1995), pp.15ff.

16 See A. Gifford Jr., '*A Constitutional Interpretation of the Firm*', PUBLIC CHOICE, vol.68 (1991), pp.92ff.; V.J. Vanberg, *Rules & Choices in Economics* (London: Routledge, 1994), pp.135ff.; C.F. Sabel, 'Constitutional Orders: Trust Building and Response to Change', in Hollingsworth and Boyer (eds.), *supra* n. 5, pp.154 ff.

themselves through the means of mimicked sort of economic organizations.[17] Such organizations are imbued with social control mechanisms that were referred to before. Their rules discipline their structure and members (i.e. a specific group of market regulators). In addition, their capacity to act externally and represent common interests will avoid self-closure and provide the possibility of intervention on how market relations get structured, for instance by co-operating and negotiating with market participants in policy and regulation matters. In this way, and performing the function of social controllers, these co-operative regulatory bodies, often referred to as 'regulatory *fora*', are effectively decentralized bodies of law-making.

For the purposes envisaged in this chapter, and taking into account that its focus will be on transnational regulatory organizations (that is, action which does not depend on political territorial boundaries and thus particularly on national legal preferences), the legal relevance of regulatory *fora* has been looked for in any mode of collective action that entails voluntary co-operation involving reciprocal trust and exchange of knowledge between the associated regulators in accordance with certain procedural rules.[18] In other words, what have been sought are social contracts as established by market regulators in order to organize collective action, independently of the specific goal to be pursued. These contracts distinguish themselves from pure exchange contracts which are limited to making explicit the terms of a market transaction between counterparties and have it performed successfully. Social contracts, on the other hand, are inclusive in the sense that their intent is to truly constitute a group and keep it cohesive and functioning indefinitely, in both explicit and implicit terms.[19] Moreover, the relationships and dialogue established between associated parties, at the same time that they produce

---

17   J.R. Macey puts forward the argument that market processes, such as the emergence of truly transnational markets, may lead also to obsolescence of national financial regulators in the form of administrative agencies. This may be deemed as a strong incentive to international co-operation and co-ordination among these agencies. See J. R. Macey, '*Administrative Agency Obsolescence and Interest Group Formation: A Case Study of the SEC at Sixty*', CARDOZO LAW REVIEW, vol. 15 (1994), p. 909.

18   This is an approximation to the constitutional paradigm of organizations as proposed by V.J. Vanberg, *supra* n. 16, pp.135-7. In a certain sense it is also close to M. Oakeshott's conception of the 'civil condition' according to which civil association is an 'association in terms of rules' that 'begins and ends in the recognition of rules', 'where the terms of relationship are exclusively the rules of a practice which may concern any and every transaction between agents and is indifferent to the outcome of any such transaction', as distinct from 'enterprise association' whose rules are 'instrumental to the pursuit of what is already recognized as a common purpose' (*On Human Conduct* [Oxford: Clarendon Press, 1975], pp.124-41).

19   See for the comparison of paradigms in organization theory and a thorough evaluation of the constitutional paradigm, V.J. Vanberg, *supra* n. 16, pp.135-143.

knowledge,[20] may unveil a deliberative-binding capacity which clearly enables a regulative function.

3. *The Role of Transnational Regulatory Organizations*

The regulatory organizations with which this chapter is concerned have as their object 'specialized business communities'. They look into a particular market segment, such as a particular financial sector, which is of a technical and complex nature. From here, there is the perception, arising from all interested parties (market regulators, market participants, and even the public in general) that a public good[21] is at stake (e.g. financial stability) in the arrangement of specific market relations. Where a central authority is lacking, it should follow that the members of such communities create and then align with a special set of rules, norms and strategies, which will ideally conform to the public good or benefits involved in the market-exchanges.[22] As a result, the formation of new, overlapping regulatory organizations seems to be an appropriate means for the market regulators and market participants to select, develop and issue the norms that will consensually regulate their relations.

The work developed by transnational regulatory organizations cannot be immediately identified with elements of a legal order. As in the case of contractual validation, legal character may only be attributed to what will substantiate the rights and claims arising from the activity of the members of the business communities, as well as the activity itself, in accordance with criteria ascertaining legal validity and legal regulation. Such criteria surface precisely from the communication, and then negotiations and agreements, which organizations enable and stimulate between interested parties (such as the market participants and the market authorities), from which is determined what should and what should not be legal norms.[23]

This circumstance certainly adds an additional feature to the law of a complex economy: besides being a decentralized law, in the sense that the legal order does not depend on a central authority, it is also a 'plural law', given that it is based on the confrontation of multiple discourses originating from entities and 'communicative processes' of various qualities.[24] A main cause for this legal

---

20 See A. Gifford Jr., *supra* n. 16, pp.94-5.
21 See R.D. Cooter, *supra* n. 6, pp.447-9; and K. Ronit and V. Schneider, *supra* n. 1, pp.3-12.
22 This is, for example, the conclusion reached by R.C. Ellickson in his study on the resolution of cattle-trespass disputes in small rural communities, *Order without Law*, *supra* n. 13, pp.280 ff.
23 See S. Zamora, '*Is There Customary International Economic Law*?', GERMAN YEARBOOK OF INTERNATIONAL LAW, vol.32, 1989, pp.34 ff.; and M. Bothe, '*Legal and Non-Legal Norms - A Meaningful Distinction in International Relations?*', NETHERLANDS YEARBOOK OF INTERNATIONAL LAW, vol.XI (1980), pp.90 ff.
24 See G. Teubner, *supra* n. 1, pp.11-15.

pluralism is the proliferation of a sequence of localized social contracts forming specialized business communities. At the same time, there are those other international organizations, either formed or not out of the private sphere, and also national legislative, regulative and adjudicative bodies that continue to be eminent providers of law and order to transnational market relations.

As transnational commercial law is developed out of the interaction of all these very diverse legitimized and legitimizing structures without hierarchical dependence, a natural conflict comes to light: how to make compatible the competing claims of such structures. As in classic private international law, where norms are intended to co-ordinate the application of national laws in international legal cases, it seems imperative that a body of rules of conflict stand at the core of the fundamental principles underlying modern transnational commercial law. The design of these rules should meet and thus prevail over the difficulties that 'inter-systemic conflicts' may provoke in the consistent interpretation and application of the qualitatively distinct legal norms ordering transnational market relations,[25] the tautology being that their origin will also rest in the same processes that construct the systems they will regulate.

To conclude this section, co-operative regulatory organizations constitute a new parameter in the law of transnational market relations. The implications of their potential influence in their problem-solving capacity should not be downplayed. Going beyond previous fragilities of the *lex mercatoria*, they may provide, in a certain context, constancy and continuity to legal ordering and public governance. Being catalysts and repositories of information and knowledge, they have, from the start, a legitimacy of their own. Their role in the selection and design of market rules is a factor to counter-balance and supplement the innate spontaneity of market order.[26] There is evidence that the elaboration and re-elaboration of legal principles and norms is and has been furthered, particularly as the law of specific market segments.[27] Additionally, the emergence and ascendancy of what has been called 'associational governance'[28] indicates that private law mechanisms, especially contract and economic organization, are gaining prominence over the classic public law and public international law means of regulating the markets. Finally, this move towards private law also means that legal ordering is seemingly less structured in comparison to the norms originating from the public sphere. One finds an accompanying move from 'hard law' to 'soft law', meaning that interpretation,

25   See ibid, pp.7-8.
26   See the non-interventionist argument of F.A. Hayek, *Law, Legislation, and Liberty* (London: Routledge, 1976), vol.I, p.51, and, vol.II (1976), pp.128-9.
27   See K.P. Berger, *Formalisierte oder 'schleichende' Kodifizierung des transnationalen Wirtschaftsrechts* (Berlin: de Gruyter, 1996), pp.194ff.
28   This is the term used by W. Coleman, 'Associational Governance in a Globalizing Era: Weathering the Storm', in Hollingsworth and Boyer (eds.), *supra* n. 5, pp.127-53, pp.145-8.

application and enforcement is less articulated and systematic given the inexistence of a cardinal jurisdiction. 'Soft law is not weak law',[29] however, as the law of a complex economy should by definition conform to the markets' intrinsic characteristics, such as diversity, swift change or innovation.

The following sections provide an overview of the international co-operative *fora* dealing with the regulation and supervision of financial markets, primarily in the sectors of banking and securities markets. These groups mainly comprise the national regulators of those countries with the most developed financial centres. They somewhat differ in their institutional structure, even though it is usually the case that they function on the basis of a permanent secretariat, which organizes the work being developed and the regular meetings of the groups.

The technical areas of financial law and regulation, which are the object of the work of these *fora*, go beyond the distinction between municipal (or territory-based) law and international law. They appear as autonomous and independent rules in the sense that they are distinguishable and comparable not from the territory they serve but from the market relations which constitute their object. Moreover, the market relations in question are of a technical and sophisticated nature, with a strict and identifiable number of participants and authorities sharing a common knowledge (which may be referred to as 'epistemic communities').[30] In this sense, there may be the risk that regulation is captured by the reality it serves and thus relatively immune to outside intervention or integration within an inclusive framework.

4. The Basle Committee on Banking Supervision

The Basle Committee on Banking Supervision was established under the aegis of the Bank for International Settlements (BIS) after the collapse of the Herstatt Bank at the end of 1974, with the central banks of the G-10 countries.[31] The aims were of comparing supervisory methods and establishing privileged channels of communication between banking authorities, and also to co-ordinate joint policy on the supervision of international banking. With the Basle Concordat of 1975, a first visible result of the Basle Committee, the building principles of legal integration that were to follow for international banking markets became to some degree explicit. They related to the rules of conflicts for supervisory competences. The agreement was that a banking authority should have the responsibility to oversee the

---

29 See G. Teubner, *supra* n. 1, p.21; and see the case for public international law in D. Thürer, '*Soft Law'-eine neue form von Völkerrecht?*, ZSR, vol.104 (1985), p.433ff.

30 See P. Haas, '*Epistemic Communities and International Policy Coordination*', INTERNATIONAL ORGANIZATION, vol.46 (1992), pp.1ff.

31 See 'History of the Basle Committee and its membership', in *Compendium of documents produced by the Basle Committee on Banking Supervision*, Bank for International Settlements, (Basle: BIS, 2000). The Basle Committee's documents cited henceforth are available at http://www.bis.org.

activities (but especially the solvency) of the banking groups established in their respective countries with the inclusion of foreign branches: *the principle of home-country control*.[32] Accordingly, there should be *mutual recognition* between country authorities of such competences.[33]

To supplement these basic principles of home-country control and mutual recognition, the subsequent revisions of the Basle Concordat (motivated by banking crises such as of the Banco Ambrosiano and the Bank for Credit and Commerce International), suggest the progressive institutionalisation of multilateral co-operation as an option to a central supra-national authority or to mere bilateral assistance.[34]

The Basle Accord of 1988 on the 'International Convergence of Capital Measurement and Capital Standards' [of international financial institutions] (hereinafter 'the Accord'), effective at the end of 1992, is the significant achievement, up until now, of such multilateral co-operation.[35] This agreement, in the form of a report endorsed by the majority of countries with international financial centres, set a regulatory standard, that is, a level playing field to be applied to international banks. This had the clear rationale of ideally decreasing the eventuality, first, of unfair competition between international banks and also,

---

32 See Basle Committee, *The Supervision of Cross-Border Banking* (1996).

33 See G. Majone, on the method of mutual recognition as a strategy of international regulatory co-ordination: '[i]t requires that jurisdictions accept for domestic purposes certain regulatory determinations of other jurisdictions, even though those determinations and the criteria on which they are based are not harmonized'. 'International Regulatory Cooperation: a Neo-institutionalist Spproach', in Bermann, Herdegen and Lindseth (eds.), *Transatlantic Regulatory Co-operation* (Oxford: Oxford University Press, 2000), pp.120-145 at 124-126.

34 See E.B. Kapstein, 'Supervising International Banks', in C. Stone/A. Zissu (eds.), *Global Risk Based Capital Regulations*, vol.I 'Capital Adequacy', (New York: Irwin Professional Publishers, 1994), pp.44ff.; G.R.D. Underhill, 'Private Markets and Public Responsibility in a Global System: Conflict and Co-operation in Transnational Banking and Securities Regulation', in Underhill (ed.), *The New World Order in International Finance* (New York: St. Martin's Press, 1997), pp.23ff.; W.R. White, *International Agreements in the Area of Banking and Finance: Accomplishments and Outstanding Issues*, BIS Working Papers (Basle: BIS, 1996), pp.24ff.; A.K. Shah, '*The Dynamics of International Banking Regulation*', JOURNAL OF FINANCIAL REGULATION AND COMPLIANCE, vol.4 (1996), pp.373ff.; D.E. Alford, '*Basle Committee Minimum Standards: International Regulatory Response to the Failure of BCCI*', GEORGE WASHINGTON JOURNAL OF INTERNATIONAL LAW & ECONOMY, vol.26 (1992), pp.252ff.; and R. Dale, 'International Banking Regulation', in Steil (ed.), *International Financial Market Regulation*, pp.167-96 (Chichester: John Wiley & Sons, 1994), pp.168 ff.

35 On the process of achieving agreement for the Basle Accord, see E.B. Kapstein, 'Supervising International Banks', pp.103ff. In June 1999 the Basle Committee issued a proposal to replace the 1988 Accord. The final version of the Accord should be published by the end of 2002 and implemented in 2005.

secondly, of a low level of financial safety resulting from states' global regulatory competition and their failure in taking collective action for appropriate financial rules.[36]

The Accord purported to establish a common standard of supervisory regulations governing the capital adequacy of international banks, which is the proportion of capital needed, and deemed appropriate, to balance the risks incurred by these banks in their financial transactions. A compelling reason for regulating the international banks' capital adequacy at the time was the national regulators' perception that these financial institutions were incurring more and more risks, without necessarily having the perception of such risks, especially in the case of innovative financial instruments and transactions.[37] The concern, however, was not so much of protecting the individual institutions' financial soundness, as it was to create safety measures against the systemic risk posed by the activity of financial firms in integrated global financial markets. Capital adequacy regulations, in fact, do not ensure that a particular firm goes bankrupt, but instead tend to guarantee that, if a firm goes bankrupt, no losses will spread throughout the market as the minimum capital requirements will cover the substantial amounts outstanding.[38]

Rational and well-founded as they may appear to be, the provisions on capital adequacy were far from being neutral when applied to national contexts. Capital requirements imply that a restraint be put on the banks' lending capacity and general risk-taking in other financial transactions, affecting thus their overall competitiveness in the global markets. National market authorities could then benefit from the Basle Committee's lack of enforcement powers of the provisions of the Accord, therefore engaging in regulatory competition to lessen its restrictive implications on financial activity.

The implementation of the Accord is a matter for national discretion, which implies that a selective application of rules may turn out to be the token by which

---

36 See A.K. Shah, 'The Dynamics of International Banking Regulation', pp.376ff; R. Dale, *supra* n. 34, pp.172ff; W.I. Conroy, '*Risk-Based Capital Adequacy Guidelines: A Sound Regulatory Policy or a Symptom of Regulatory Inadequacy?*', FORDHAM LAW REVIEW, vol.63 (1995), pp.2399ff.; R.J. Herring and R.E. Litan, *Financial Regulation in the Global Economy* (Washington D.C.: The Brookings Institution, 1995), pp.107ff.; and E.J. Kane, 'Incentive Conflict in the International Regulatory Agreement on Risk Based Capital', in Stone and Zissu, *supra* n. 34, pp.106 ff.

37 See H.T.C. Hu, Swaps, '*The Modern Process of Financial Innovation and the Vulnerability of a Regulatory Paradigm*', UNIVERSITY OF PENNSYLVANIA LAW REVIEW, vol.138 (1989), pp.366ff.

38 See W. White, *supra* n. 34, pp.18-9, stating that the main purpose of international agreement in the area of banking and finance is to enhance financial stability, more specifically by stimulating the overall resilience of the financial system to any kind of shocks (thus preventing the so-called systemic risk), and not so much to prevent any bankruptcies of market participants.

national action is taken.[39] The good intention of having more appropriate legal decisions for each national context could give rise to a bias towards national industry, which could hinder fair competition between international banks. The conflicts arising from the space given for regulatory competition were however ironed out in the case of the Accord. National banking regulators provided for a consistent implementation of the Accord. This is said to have occurred due to the confluence of two factors: first, the mutual pressure that market authorities imposed between themselves;[40] second, and most significantly, the fact that market participants were to some extent persuaded of the validity of the regulatory standards proposed by the Accord to the point of observing them unprompted by nothing else than market discipline (for example, the use that rating agencies commonly make of such standards).[41] Accordingly, this latter factor is reinforced in the forthcoming revision of the Accord, which emphasizes market discipline, through enhanced disclosure by banks, as the 'third pillar' of the new framework for supervisory policies.[42]

The achievements of the Basle Accord and the successive transnational regulatory arrangements in implementing measures which are complex in their design and debatable on their appropriateness to procure certain results, such as minimizing financial risks, stem from the particular association between national banking authorities institutionalized in the Basle Committee.

First, this Committee allowed for a certain consensus on what the basic objectives of international banking regulation should be among national supervisory authorities: financial stability in relation to banks' propensity for risk-taking, through home-country control and supervision of financial institutions in accordance with certain minimum regulatory standards. In addition, it has fostered a common agreement on such regulatory standards and on the basic institutional requirements for effective banking regulation and supervision, both at the national and cross-border level, in the so-called 'Basle Core Principles for effective banking supervision'.[43] This regulatory framework, on which the market authorities progressively start to depend when facing the liberalisation of financial markets, is being substantiated in formally diverse instruments, from international agreements

---

39   For a comparative study of the implementation of the rules on capital adequacy, see M.J. Hall, *Banking Regulation and Supervision, A Comparative Study of the UK, USA and Japan* (Aldershot: Edward Elgar, 1993), pp. 188ff.

40   See, in this sense, J.R. Macey, 'The Demand for International Regulatory Cooperation: a Public Choice Perspective', in Bermann, Herdegen and Lindseth (eds.), *supra* n. 33, pp.147-165 who argues at p. 165 that '[...] the increasing globalization of markets [...] has increased the incentives of regulators to enter into international accords by raising the loss of power to bureaucrats who do not enter into such accords'.

41   See W.R. White, *supra* n. 34, p.25.

42   See Basle Committee Consultative Paper, *Pillar 3 (Market Discipline)*, 2001.

43   See Basle Committee, *Core Principles for Effective Banking Supervision* (1997).

to technical recommendations, or policy guidelines, or mere research papers, which accordingly result from the associative activity and the contacts established with other entities, such as market participants.

Second, the Basle Committee manages to flexibly surpass the difficulties for and challenges to international regulatory effectiveness. Regulatory competition among states, the obsolescence of international agreements and the inherent difficulties to revise and update them (for example, facing financial innovation), or even the non-binding force of many legal instruments such as recommendations have not hindered considerably the efforts of the Basle Committee. On the contrary, these factors provide the very motivation for the continuing activities of the Basle Committee. What started therefore as a mere technical committee ended up by becoming a regulatory structure for international finance. It consists of an elaborate form of market governance which develops through 'transnational associative ruling', based essentially on the co-operation and the exchange of information between the interested parties. This creates, at the same time, a certain self-enforcing dependency between market authorities for the generation of knowledge and for the effectiveness of market regulation.

5. The International Organization of Securities Commissions

The paradigm of the US 'Securities and Exchange Commission' as an independent and technocratic market authority was followed by the vast majority of administrative national systems as a first-best solution to regulate securities markets, in spite of divergences in national laws.[44] This phenomenon of administrative agency standardization contributed to easing a natural co-operation between the autonomous regulatory bodies of securities markets. Such co-operation has become institutionalized in the International Organization of Securities Commissions (IOSCO). Since 1983, IOSCO has been a transnational organization grouping securities markets authorities with the primary aims of enhancing regulatory co-operation, providing means of exchange of information and experiences, setting international regulatory standards, observing international securities transactions, and ensuring the authorities' mutual assistance in the implementation and enforcement of securities regulation.[45]

---

44   A.Hirsch, 'Worldwide Legal Harmonization of Banking Law and Securities Regulation', in Buxbaum, Hertig, Hirsch and Hopt (eds.), *European Business Law. Legal and Economic Analyses on Integration and Harmonization* (Berlin: de Gruyter, 1991), pp.349-50.

45   See IOSCO, *Resolution on Commitment to Basic IOSCO Principles of High Standards and Mutual Co-operation and Assistance*, 1994; R. Dale, *supra* n. 34, pp.143ff.; G.R.D. Underhill, '*Keeping Governments Out of Politics: Transnational Securities Markets, Regulatory Cooperation, and Political Legitimacy*', REVIEW OF INTERNATIONAL STUDIES, vol.21 (1995), pp.251-78, at 252 ff.

What is significant in this organization is its working dynamics and the particular manner by which it attains a certain level of market governance. The close-knit group of banking authorities of the G-10 countries composing the Basle Committee which allowed for, among other things, the formalization of transnational legal instruments and its implementation in the core banking centres, has no equivalent in IOSCO. Although a distinction can be made between the jurisdictions that turn out to more or less drive deliberations, the processes involved in IOSCO's regulatory activity are mostly of an informal nature. IOSCO includes 120 securities and futures markets authorities. A multilateral regulatory standard-setting agreement like the Basle Accord may be hard to conceive as one of the most feasible initiatives. The network structure which IOSCO establishes among its members is more important.[46] As the complexity of today's financial markets does not allow for an immediate perception of the legal problems at stake, on how to tackle them, and who to address for such a purpose, the market authorities' reaction is to rationalize their administrative procedures so as to increase the opportunities for information-gathering and knowledge-generation.[47]

IOSCO presents itself, therefore, as a transnational expression of the ongoing administrative procedural rationalization. Through it, national securities markets authorities become involved in co-operative relationships between themselves, with no specific purpose other than essentially to develop each others' learning potential on market transactions and their desirable regulation. On the other hand it also serves to improve the possibilities for the enforcement of national regulations across jurisdictions by mutual assistance.

Several means serve as components of such procedural rationality. For instance, IOSCO's members should commit themselves to the 'principles of maintaining high regulatory standards and providing the fullest mutual assistance and co-operation'. In addition, they should perform a self-evaluation of their own aptness to 'provide assistance to foreign securities and futures regulators' by means of a written assessment to be deposited at IOSCO's secretariat for free consultation by its members.

Going beyond these revealing self-referential elements, the structure of IOSCO, served by a General Secretariat, is composed fundamentally of interwoven committees: the Presidents' Committee (the formal governing body which establishes the guidelines of the organization's activity); the Executive Committee (which executes such guidelines); the Regional Standing Committees (grouping the markets of specific areas of the globe: Africa/Middle-East, InterAmerican,

46   A similar network effect is also a main advantage of the *Financial Action Task Force on Money Laundering*, comprising 31 members, which describes itself as an intergovernmental and policy-making body which develops and promotes policies to combat money laundering at the national and international level.

47   W.D. Coleman, *supra* n. 28, pp.8ff.; K-H. Ladeur, 'Post-Modern Constitutional Theory', *supra* n. 7, pp.627-9.

European, and Asia-Pacific); and the Self-Regulatory Organizations' Consultative Committee (grouping, for consulting purposes, the private self-regulatory organizations which are affiliate members of IOSCO).[48] The Executive Committee has, in addition, established two specialized committees: the Technical Committee and the Emerging Markets Committee. The former comprises the regulatory agencies of the most developed and international markets. Its objective is to review major regulatory issues related to international securities and futures transactions and to coordinate practical responses to these concerns. The latter promotes the development and improvement of efficiency of emerging markets by establishing principles and minimum standards, preparing training programmes and facilitating exchange of information and transfer of technology and expertise.

The Technical Committee is the pivot of IOSCO's regulatory activity. It decentralizes its work through the constitution of working groups in charge of reporting on special issues of capital market law, such as the regulation of secondary markets or the regulation of market intermediaries.[49] The members of such working groups meet several times during the year to tackle the mandates that they receive from the Technical Committee.

Therefore, with this procedure of selectively grouping market authorities, IOSCO surmounts the difficulties of having too many members to cope with for achieving its aims. In reality, IOSCO attempts to promote what one may call 'co-operative clusters'[50] among market authorities, which are only feasible with a small number of parties, so as to facilitate negotiations and consensus on particular issues, the exchange of information, and the blending of knowledge or mutual experiences. Following this, the material results of such selective grouping, in the form of guidelines, resolutions, recommendations, technical reports, or other documents, are divulged among all the members, mostly through IOSCO's international annual conferences. In this way, by grouping and divulging, IOSCO manages to demonstrate how effectively and productively can the co-operation between market authorities be secured to the point of achieving some sort of transnational governance. This is in effect, to some extent, accomplished, even without the support of a hierarchical structure or strict compliance powers on the provisions issued.

A sign of the effectiveness of IOSCO's regulatory structure also arises from the fact that it serves as a convenient forum for the negotiation of agreements between securities markets authorities. In international law, it is solely under the strict terms

---

48 See G.R.D. Underhill, 'Keeping Governments Out of Politics', *supra* n. 45, pp.260ff.; P. Guy, 'Regulatory Harmonization to Achieve Effective International Competition', in Edwards and Patrick (eds.), *Regulating International Financial Markets: Issues and Policies*, pp.291-7 (Boston: Kluwer Academic Publishers, 1992), pp.292 ff.

49 See G.R.D. Underhill, ibid, p.262; P. Guy, ibid, pp.294ff.

50 See V.J. Vanberg, *supra* n. 16, pp.68 ff.

of the Hague XX Convention on the Taking of Evidence Abroad in Civil and Commercial Matters (concluded 18th March 1970) that market authorities can seek assistance in obtaining evidence 'for use in judicial proceedings, commenced or contemplated' (art.1).[51] To circumvent the limitations of the Hague Convention, which may hinder effective cross-border legal action in securities markets, national market authorities have to reach precise compromises on reciprocal agreements to provide assistance, for instance in the form of disclosure of information. As diplomatic negotiation processes for formal agreements between states are, as a rule, cumbersome, both in the time spent and in the intricacies of consensus, IOSCO and its procedures surface as catalysts for agreement on common regulatory issues and on the viable and acceptable solutions to lay on the negotiation table.

Evidence suggests that a growing number of 'soft law' instruments such as Memoranda of Understanding (non-legally binding statements of intent), and other kind of informal agreements such as co-operative arrangements, declarations, exchange of letters or of diplomatic notes, are in part due to the networking activity implemented by IOSCO's mechanisms.[52] Interestingly enough, IOSCO, in turn, and in a self-referential move, also provides to have such agreements disclosed, in order to promote their application and compliance between the parties, and also to give incentives for the spread of practices of the same kind among its members.[53]

Many of IOSCO's features conform to what is described as law-making in a complex economy. IOSCO is based on a plurality of discourses surfacing from the communication it enables between its members and to which legal validity may be attached, in spite of having to be ultimately considered as being 'soft law'. At the same time, the surge of such a global network of technocracy provides clear evidence for the thesis of the 'fragmenting state' and its legal implications should thus be discussed from various stances, one being the constitutional legitimacy of a structure which escapes public control and monitoring in the way that it is self-enclosed in its own object of regulation.

IOSCO is therefore a singular kind of organization of market authorities. As a form of administrative rationalization, it is the starting point for a transnational technocracy which sublimates the common interests of national independent regulatory bodies in achieving their aims in global markets. This implies that it is also a structure which keeps national political preferences away from market governance, as only technical legal issues are apparently at stake in the communicative processes of its members. In a certain sense, IOSCO may seem to

---

51   For an analysis of the scope and limits of the Hague Convention in securities law enforcement, see C.A.A. Greene, '*International Securities Law Enforcement: Recent Advances in Assistance and Cooperation*', VANDERBILT JOURNAL OF TRANSNATIONAL LAW, vol.27 (1994), pp.639ff.

52   See, for instance, G.R.D. Underhill, 'Private Markets and Public Responsibility in a Global System', *supra* n. 34, pp.32ff.

53   See the list of agreements at IOSCO's homepage: http://www.iosco.org.

present itself as a private organization, an NGO representing the interests of the specialized community regulating securities markets, for instance in the way it co-operates in a similar manner with both the Basle Committee and organizations of market participants.[54]

6. Co-operation Between Transnational Regulatory Organizations

The need for comprehensive regulation of financial markets, together with shared views on risk-awareness and the possibilities of risk-observation by market authorities, have also led to co-operation between banking supervisors, as grouped in the Basle Committee, and securities markets regulators, grouped under IOSCO.[55] In particular, they declared that '[b]oth organizations share the *common goal of improving the quality of supervision worldwide and responding to financial market developments* in a timely, effective and efficient manner' (italics in the original).[56] This co-operation has in the meantime been in the final form of joint regulatory proposals in matters such as those of capital adequacy or regulation of financial derivatives.[57] In addition, together with the International Association of Insurance Supervisors (IAIS), they have institutionalized their co-operation on the supervision of financial conglomerates through the creation of the Joint Forum on Financial Conglomerates. The main tasks of this transnational group of market authorities are to facilitate the exchange of information and to enhance the supervisory co-ordination between supervisors of different sectors, developing at the same time principles towards the more effective supervision of regulated firms within financial conglomerates.[58]

Being distinct in their respective configurations, internal procedures, and the expression of regulatory measures, the Basle Committee and IOSCO may complement each other in their public governance of transnational capital markets, in order to provide a certain consistency to treatment of common issues. Harmonization and convergence of capital market law have in fact been proceeding

---

54 G.R.D. Underhill, 'Keeping Governments out of Politics', *supra* n. 45, pp.253ff.

55 See the basic document of the Basle Committee, *Exchanges of Information Between Banking and Securities Supervisors* (1990).

56 *Basle Committee /IOSCO Joint Statement for the Lyon Summit*, 1996, which presents the main principles for co-operation between the Basle Committee and IOSCO.

57 See for instance IOSCO's Technical Committee and Basle Committee, *Recommendations for Public Disclosure of Trading and Derivatives Activities of Banks and Securities Firms*, 1999.

58 See *Joint Forum on Financial Conglomerates*, 1998.

at a significant pace,[59] even if it is debatable which organization, and therefore which configuration, proves to be more effective in its own context.

The Basle Committee can function more flexibly and more swiftly as the range of informal contacts is limited to a core group of regulatory authorities with autonomous political and bargaining powers *vis-à-vis* their home countries, which in addition also allows for reaching binding agreements like the Basle Accord. IOSCO's activity, on the other hand, in spite of its 'selective grouping technique' (which seems to mimic the Basle Committee), relies basically on the workability of the inclusive network which it attempts to institutionalise among its members, and on the 'soft law' character of what it issues. Results emerge progressively and are often contingent on the will of the interested parties.[60] This implies that agreement on precise and significant rules and standards, such as the Basle Committee's capital regulations, is problematic within IOSCO and has not so far been reached.

7. The Law of Co-operation and the Development of Co-operative Law

Commitments among the authorities of different states are becoming numerous and more prone to be agreed upon. Basic reciprocal declarations of intent develop into complex multilateral agreements on pursuing certain regulatory undertakings in consistent manner across borders and within national jurisdictions. Such commitments are being mainly promoted by the activities of transnational *fora* of regulators and of other administrative agencies. The activities of these *fora* typically involve regular meetings, informal discussions on matters of common interest, the elaboration of technical papers stemming from their joint generation of knowledge, and may extend to the expression of regulatory commitments. In practice, the informal deliberations that such co-operative organizations are originally meant to promote often lead to common understandings and mutual expectations between their members. As organizations, the groupings of regulatory authorities provide the procedural infrastructure for reaching agreement, for instance via meetings, recording of minutes, endorsement of papers and declarations, or signing of concrete agreements or contracts, such as the so-called Memoranda of Understanding. Moreover, it may be argued that participation in the organization, particularly in restricted groupings such as the Basle Committee, may embody from the outset the commitment to co-operate and to commit further *vis-à-vis* the other members. In this manner, *fora* may have the potential to function as quasi-legislatures with specific purposes regarding the governance of market relations.

---

59   A.Hirsch, *supra* n. 44, pp.349-350, stating that 'for banking and securities regulation, [harmonization by administrative agencies] is the most important [method of legal harmonization]'.

60   See P. Guy, *supra* n. 48, p.297; R. Dale, *supra* n. 34, p.147.

In order to structure the evolving corpus of transnational co-operative law, the participants in regulatory groupings have defined certain fundamental assumptions as the basis to proceed with co-operation itself. The perception that transnational groupings of regulators may feature as 'quasi-legislatures' has apparently led to the definition of a constitutional backbone of principles and rules which serve to further co-operative law- and regulation-making. This means that the preliminary step to commitments among the authorities of different states involves the agreement on a framework of principles on co-operation. In this sense, the elaboration of 'co-operative law' on the transnational regulation of markets presupposes a pre-determined, self-referential, 'law of co-operation' among the authorities of different states.[61] Therefore, the institutional law of co-operation has as addressees the regulators themselves. The resulting 'co-operative law' is addressed to regulate market relations.

The law of co-operation typically comprises a framework of principles and rules agreed multilaterally on co-operation and information-sharing among national administrative agencies. This framework is essentially designed for addressing the classical co-ordination problems in international relations. For instance, before engaging in any sort of international commitments, national authorities wish to ensure that their statutory constraints as imposed by national law are respected on a cross-border basis, that their competences and prerogatives within their respective jurisdictions are preserved, that a reciprocity of treatment is provided, or ideally that the performance of their statutory functions is enhanced. These conditions may additionally warrant a certain degree of institutional similarity or standardization among the authorities involved in co-operation.

In the case of financial regulatory authorities, the law of co-operation has materialized in requirements on confidentiality of privileged information, on broadly agreed distribution of tasks (such as between the home and host supervisors of a financial institution), or on essential standards for financial regulation and supervision, which should be implemented by those wishing to 'join the group'. These ground principles for cross-border co-operation can be found in the general guidelines and principles for financial supervision issued by some of the above mentioned international regulatory organizations. They are included in publications such as the *Basle Core Principles for Effective Banking Supervision* (February 1997); IOSCO's *Guidance on Information Sharing* (November 1997); IOSCO's *Objectives and Principles of Securities Regulation* (September 1998); the *G-7 Ten Key Principles for International Financial Information Exchange* (May 1998);[62] *The*

---

61 See R.D. Cooter, *The Strategic Constitution* (Princeton: Princeton University Press, 2001), Chapter 15, on how problems of government may require co-operation among states within a framework for exchanging information.

62 These principles are included in the G-7 Finance Ministers report on 'Financial Stability – Supervision of Global Financial Institutions'. They cover: the authorization to share supervisory information with foreign supervisors; cross-sector information sharing both

Five Guiding Principles for Supervisory Information Sharing of the Joint Forum on Financial Conglomerates (February 1999); or the over-arching International Monetary Fund's *Code of Good Practices on Transparency in Monetary and Financial Policies* (September 1999). The common denominator to these international guidelines is, briefly, that there should not be any obstacles of substance for co-operation and information-sharing between financial regulators and supervisors of different countries. A pre-condition to supervisory information-sharing is however the preservation of confidentiality requirements and the observance of professional secrecy. It is also asked of national regulators that they should also take a proactive stance towards co-operation, both as providers and requestors of assistance and information. In this manner, supervisors should not be bound by legal restrictions or obliged to follow formal legal channels to co-operate and share information. They should have the authority to take an autonomous decision on whether to enter into, for instance in crisis situations, cross-border contacts and information flows. Lastly, some of the guidelines also refer to the ideal national institutional arrangements for the conduct of financial regulation and supervision, in order that a certain degree of administrative standardization among agencies is achieved.[63]

In addition to general guidelines, the law of co-operation between regulatory authorities is also defined by international agreements. In particular, there is a profusion of specific agreements, dealing with administrative cross-border co-operation between regulatory authorities, known as 'Memoranda of Understanding' (MoU). MoU are used as secondary agreements specifying the practical application of a certain transnational framework of principles.[64] They are administrative

---

internationally and domestically; supervisors should be able to share objective information about individuals as they can about firms and other entities; confidentiality of shared information; the use of formal agreements and written requests should not be a prerequisite for information-sharing; reciprocity requirements should not be a prerequisite for information-sharing, but may be considered; the removal of laws preventing supervisory information exchange.

63 For instance, the Basle Core Principle no. 1, under the heading of 'Precondition for effective banking supervision', stipulates that '[a]n effective system of banking supervision will have clear responsibilities and objectives for each agency involved in the supervision of banking organizations. Each such agency should possess operational independence and adequate resources. A suitable legal framework for banking supervision is also necessary, including provisions relating to authorization of banking organizations and their ongoing supervision; powers to address compliance with laws as well as safety and soundness concerns; and legal protection for supervisors [...]'.

64 For instance, Memoranda of Understanding are usually the means used by the banking supervisory authorities of Member States to specify co-operation arrangements among them within the framework of the banking directives. See the reference to these agreements, and also to the need to harmonize their basic elements, in the recent

agreements, not legally binding under public or private international law, which are therefore designed to provide for flexible international legal and administrative regimes.[65] In this context, they usually set out co-operation provisions and common principles for cross-border co-ordination and co-operation between national authorities.[66] In addition, MoU may serve to bridge the performance of different regulatory functions, both domestically and cross-border.[67] Against the background of the framework provided by regulatory standards and by other more general expressions of co-operative law, MoU may be seen as derivative or secondary administrative agreements, which provide effectiveness to co-operative law.

The co-operative law regulating transnational market relations, on the other hand, also finds its source in multilateral understandings and agreements among regulatory agencies. Its effectiveness is however dependent on the extent to which regulatory authorities actively comply with their self-imposed principles and rules on co-operation, as referred to above. Co-operative law is as effective as such compliance. This is because co-operative law has no direct effectiveness and hinges on the intermediation of national authorities. The ultimate stage of effectiveness of transnational co-operative law corresponds to the commitment by national authorities to implement it within their jurisdictions through national legislatures. For instance, the key provisions of the Basle Accord have been incorporated in several national laws and also in Community law.[68] Otherwise, co-operative law may be sufficiently effective by providing the motivation or inspiration of national legislation and regulatory activities. For instance, this is the spirit underlying certain

Economic and Financial Committee's *Report on Financial Crisis Management*, Economic Papers No. 156, (Brussels: European Commission, July 2001), p.28.

65   This is also in fields other than international finance. For the environment, see C. Shine, 'Selected Agreements Concluded Pursuant to the Convention on the Conservation of Migratory Species of Wild Animals', in Shelton (ed.) *Commitment and Compliance: The Role of Non-binding Norms in the International Legal System* (Oxford: Oxford University Press, 2000), p. 204.

66   See, in this regard, *Essential Elements of a Statement of Co-operation Between Banking Supervisors* (Basle: Committee on Banking Supervision, May 2001), which sets out the basic and main elements of a Memorandum of Understanding in the field of banking supervision. The main elements relate to duties of information-sharing, mutual assistance in carrying out inspections, confidentiality provisions on the information being shared, and ongoing co-ordination between national authorities to ensure the effectiveness of the administrative agreements.

67   See, for instance, the 'Memorandum of Understanding on Co-operation between Payment Systems Overseers and Banking Supervisors in Stage Three of Economic and Monetary Union', described in a press release dated 2 April 2001, available, among other websites, at http://www.ecb.int.

68   See, for instance, Council Directive 93/6/EEC of 15 March 1993 on the capital adequacy of investments firms and credit institutions OJ L 141 , 11.06.1993 p.1-26. See also M.J Hall, *supra* n. 39, pp. 188ff; and W. White, *supra* n. 34, pp.18.

provisions of the *Basle Core Principles for Effective Banking Supervision* and of IOSCO's *Objectives and Principles of Securities Regulation*.

Primarily, co-operative law may involve formal written agreements between regulatory authorities which are somewhat similar in nature to actual international treaties. The main example in this respect is the Basle Accord, as mentioned above, in which the parties comprising the Basle Committee commit themselves, but also *vis-à-vis* one another, to implement their provisions within their national jurisdictions.[69]

Further to explicit international agreements, co-operative law may also be expressed in different degrees of formalism and, accordingly, be more of a 'soft law' nature or integrate hard law features in the sense mentioned above that national authorities may commit themselves to be more or less involved in ensuring its effectiveness. In terms of formal presentation, co-operative law may be, first, implicit in the regular activities of a certain grouping or organization, for instance as revealed by internal working documents. This does not represent so much an expression of precise principles and rules, which would be ultimately enforceable, but may serve instead to further and consolidate among regulatory authorities their joint generation of 'regulatory' knowledge. It may also signal to market participants the possible direction of regulatory developments. Secondly, the deliberations of a regulatory grouping may be presented and disclosed to the public as technical guidelines, declarations of intent, or desirable 'best practices' and 'standards', which should be followed by market participants and implemented by regulatory authorities within their jurisdiction. This relates, in particular, to the emergence of the concept of 'regulatory standards', which has provided an element of textual recognition of co-operative law. Regulatory standards are principles and rules, which are agreed by groupings sometimes designated as 'standard-setting bodies',[70] and which are meant to provide a regulatory benchmark to assess and further develop national policies regarding financial regulation.[71] The main standards,

---

69   The precise text of the Basle Accord, which takes the form of a Basle Committee report, regarding the commitment of regulatory authorities to implement its provisions, is: '[t]he present paper is now a statement of the Committee agreed by all its members. It sets out the details of the agreed framework for measuring capital adequacy and the minimum standard to be achieved which the national supervisory authorities represented on the Committee intend to implement in their respective countries'.

70   For G. Teubner, global standard-setting bodies may be seen as an example of 'linkage institutions', since they create new laws directly without a political sovereign, which are not translated into political issues; the activities of such bodies results however in the linking of technical issues with legal discourse. See 'The King's Many Bodies: the Self-deconstruction of Law's Hierarchy', manuscript (1996), on file with the author.

71   See a collection of regulatory standards, and the reference to the current standard-setting bodies in *International Standards and Codes to Strengthen Financial Systems* (Washington D.C.: Financial Stability Forum, 2001), available at http://www.fsforum. org.

which also correspond to the most recognizable texts of co-operative law in the field of financial regulation, are structured under the heading of *Twelve key standards for sound financial systems*. They are so designated and compiled by the Financial Stability Forum, which is the focus of the next section.[72]

II.   The Codification of Co-operative Regulatory Standards by the Financial Stability Forum

The Financial Stability Forum (FSF) was established in April 1999, by the Finance Ministers and Central Bank Governors of the G-7 countries, to promote international financial stability through information exchange and international co-operation in financial supervision and surveillance. This forum was established following the recommendations put forward in the Tietmeyer report, which dealt with the appropriateness of the arrangements for co-operation between the international financial regulatory and supervisory bodies.[73] The FSF comprises the national authorities (Treasury, Central Bank and Financial Supervisor) responsible for financial stability of the main international financial centres; the transnational regulatory organizations for each specific sector of the financial system (Basle Committee, IOSCO and IAIS); the international institutions responsible for the surveillance of financial systems and the monitoring of the implementation of standards (International Monetary Fund, World Bank, BIS and the Organization for Economic Co-operation and Development); and the committees of central bank experts concerned with market infrastructure.[74] Given its composition, the FSF aims at co-ordinating the efforts of these various bodies in order to promote international financial stability, improve the functioning of markets, and reduce the risks to the financial system as a whole.

---

72   See next section on the codification of standards undertaken by the Financial Stability Forum. The 'twelve key standards for sound financial systems' include: the IMF's Code of Good Practices on Transparency in Monetary and Financial Policies, Code of Good Practices in Fiscal Transparency, Special Data Dissemination Standard and General Data Dissemination System; the OECD's Principles of Corporate Governance; the International Accounting Standards; the International Standards on Auditing; the Core Principles for Systemically Important Payment Systems; the Forty Recommendations Anti-Money Laundering of the Financial Action Task Force; the Core Principles for Effective Banking Supervision; the Objectives and Principles of Securities Regulation; and the Insurance Core Principles.

73   See *International Co-operation and Co-ordination in the Area of Financial Market Supervision and Surveillance*, Report by Hans Tietmeyer, President of the Deutsche Bundesbank (February 1999).

74   Committee on the Global Financial System and the Committee on Payment and Settlement Systems, established by the central banks of the G-10 countries.

A first initiative of the FSF was to codify the existing transnational regulatory standards in a 'Compendium of Standards'. This is referred to as a means to provide a common reference for the various standards and codes of good practice that are 'internationally accepted as relevant to sound, stable, and well-functioning financial systems'. The Compendium, which is available in the form of world-wide-web links on the website of the FSF,[75] is designed to allow financial regulators and market participants to access in a structured manner the standards which are currently agreed upon by international *fora*. In accordance with the FSF, the Compendium is also meant to signal the importance attached by the international community to the implementation of such standards and practices, and to facilitate the dissemination of information on them. Therefore, it is being constantly updated, since technical standards have not the nature of lasting rules.

The method of codification is quite straightforward. Standards are basically divided into broad subject matters relating to 'macroeconomic policy and data transparency', 'institutional and market infrastructure' and 'financial regulation and supervision' and within these into more specific sub-sets. Moreover, the FSF also makes a qualitative distinction between standards by pointing out the twelve standards that the FSF designates as the 'key standards for sound financial systems'.[76] It is noteworthy that the standards issued by groupings of private parties are also included to the extent that they have attained a 'regulatory' relevance.[77]

The codification of regulatory standards introduced by the FSF, as any codification of legal norms, has both descriptive and prescriptive aims. As a description of financial co-operative law, the Compendium pieces together into a coherent whole the scattered materials issued by transnational groupings of regulatory authorities and market participants. This attempt for coherence may help to resolve potential conflicts among the various communicative sources of such a 'plural law', as has been the quest of private international law. The FSF goes on to acknowledge that many of the standards it codifies are 'functionally overlapping or interdependent'. Despite being issued by a variety of institutionally diverse groups, standards should be seen as a system of interlocking rules and principles. They may ultimately represent the corpus of a virtual international treaty for the financial system. On the other hand, the prescriptive function of the Compendium relates to having the standards complied with and actually implemented within national jurisdictions. The Compendium makes explicit the existence of an 'order' of standards, as probably the ignorance of their existence should not justify their non-

75   http://www.fsforum.org/Standards/Home.html.

76   See above the previous section.

77   For instance, the International Accounting Standards of the International Accounting Standards Committee, and the International Standards on Auditing of the International Federation of Accountants, are included in the FSF's Compendium of Standards.

observance. This is particularly so with regard to the 'twelve key standards for sound financial systems', which deserve 'priority implementation'.

In its prescriptive tone, the FSF cares to mention the several implementation modes of transnational regulatory standards. Depending on their degree of 'specificity', standards may be 'principles', which are general but basic, 'practices', which are more specific, and 'methodologies' or 'guidelines', which provide quite a detailed guidance. To the extent that the FSF comprises all the relevant parties to the transnational process of devising and implementing regulatory standards for the financial system, this structure represents the understanding of the hierarchical structure of a normative system. It is a system comprising both primary rules and secondary rules, with the former providing the links between the latter. Their 'normative' emphasis is however not so much in their legal/non-legal value as it is in the possibilities for their actual enforcement and implementation. The legal/non-legal distinction seems therefore to be asserted more with regard to 'procedural' aspects (implementation) rather than to substantial regulatory values. Notwithstanding, this virtual codification initiated by the FSF, as in previous instances in the evolution of transnational law, may be seen as reinforcing the customary nature of the rules being agreed for the management of the international financial system. In the same manner, it also serves to establish the legal validity of such rules.

1. The Community Law of Co-operation Between Financial Regulators

The Community law of the single market for financial services is based on the three principles of minimum harmonization of national laws through Community directives, home-country control of financial institutions by national regulators and mutual recognition of national competences. As for international markets, the effectiveness of this framework is mostly dependent on the establishment of co-operative relations between the financial regulators of Member States. The institutional structure for co-operation between authorities relies on three sets of mechanisms. First, Community directives provide for obligations of co-operation and stipulate the appropriate rules and safeguards, which therefore correspond to the core of the Community 'law of co-operation'. Second, financial regulators negotiate and establish between themselves, bilaterally or multilaterally, ad hoc agreements, for instance in the form of Memoranda of Understanding, which govern their mutual relations with regard to the regulation and supervision of markets and individual institutions. Third, several groupings of regulators are currently established within the Community which increasingly contribute to the effectiveness of the Community's regulatory process, either to law-making through comitology procedures, or to implementation and enforcement of rules, for instance through exchange of information, convergence of practices, monitoring and generation of knowledge.

The Community legislation regarding banking services, which is for the most part consolidated under the Codified Banking Directive,[78] provides the main examples regarding the features of the law of co-operation between European financial regulators.

First, with regard to specific legal norms on co-operation, the main provision in Community banking legislation regarding cross-border co-operation and exchange of information between national regulators and supervisors is under Article 28 of the Codified Banking Directive. This imposes collaboration and exchange of information between supervisors in relation to institutions operating in their jurisdictions.[79] This provision is supported by the duty of professional secrecy, imposed on banking supervisors by Article 30 (1) of the Codified Banking Directive, which contains the general principle that no confidential information may be divulged to any person or authority whatsoever, except in summary or collective form, such that individual institutions cannot be identified. The exception to this principle for the purpose of cross-border exchange of information between national banking supervisory authorities is that information may be exchanged on the basis of legal provisions of directives applicable to credit institutions (Article 30 [2] of the Codified Banking Directive). In this manner, if a certain provision of a directive provides for the exchange of information in certain cases, this should be always allowed, without prejudice however to the observance of professional secrecy. Article 30 (4) of the same Directive restricts the use of the information received on such basis to the exercise of concrete supervisory functions.[80] In the context of the relationship between home- and host-country banking supervisors, the Codified Banking Directive stipulates that the exercise of the right of establishment of branches of a credit institution and the exercise of the freedom to provide services involve a necessary communication between these authorities (Article 20 [3] and 21

78   Directive 2000/12/EC of the European Parliament and of the Council relating to the taking up and pursuit of the business of credit institutions, OJ L 126, 26.5.2000, p.1.

79   Article 28: 'The competent authorities of the Member States concerned shall collaborate closely in order to supervise the activities of credit institutions operating, in particular by having established branches there, in one or more Member States other than that in which their head offices are situated. They shall supply one another with all information concerning the management and ownership of such credit institutions that is likely to facilitate their supervision and the examination of the conditions for their authorisation, and all information likely to facilitate the monitoring of such institutions, in particular with regard to liquidity, solvency, deposit guarantees, the limiting of large exposures, administrative and accounting procedures and internal control mechanisms'.

80   Article 30 (4): 'Competent authorities receiving confidential information may use it only in the course of their duties: - to check that the conditions governing the taking-up of the business of credit institutions are met and to facilitate monitoring, on a non-consolidated basis or consolidated basis, of the conduct of such business, especially with regard to the monitoring of liquidity, solvency, large exposures, and administrative and accounting procedures, and internal control mechanisms (…)'.

[2] respectively). In addition, Article 22 (3) and (4) of the same Directive provide that the home- and host-country supervisory authorities should co-operate and exchange information in the particular case that a credit institution or its branch is not complying with the legal provisions adopted in the host state pursuant to the provisions of the Directive involving powers of the host Member State's competent authorities. For the purposes of the mutual recognition principle, Article 12 of the Codified Banking Directive imposes the obligation for the competent authorities of different Member States to consult each other prior to the authorization of a credit institution which is a subsidiary of a credit institution authorized in another Member State, or a subsidiary of the parent undertaking of a credit institution authorized in another Member State, or controlled by the same persons, whether natural or legal, as control a credit institution authorized in another Member State. This provision is significant, as its aim is to avoid forum shopping by credit institutions, which would be prejudicial for the workability of mutual recognition. Lastly, Article 53 (4) of the Codified Banking Directive imposes the obligation for the competent authorities for consolidated supervision to agree on 'procedures for co-operation and for the transmission of information such that the objectives of the Directive [supervision on a consolidated basis] may be achieved'.

Second, on the basis of the obligations provided by the Codified Banking Directive, the authorities of Member States have also concluded specific written agreements among them in order to govern their relationships as home- and host-country regulators. The object of these agreements, which for the most part take the form of Memoranda of Understanding,[81] is of detailing the arrangements foreseen by the above mentioned provisions of the Codified Banking Directive.

Third, with regard to regulatory groupings,[82] the 'Banking Advisory Committee' (BAC) was established by the First Banking Co-ordination Directive[83] to assist the Commission in the implementation of the banking directives and in the preparation of new proposals to the Council concerning further co-ordination in the sphere of credit institutions. This committee comprises representatives of national banking regulators and supervisors, of Finance Ministries of the Member States, and of the Commission. On the one hand, the BAC is an element of the Community law-making process for banking services with both an advisory and regulatory role. With regard to the former, the deliberations of BAC lead to advice on the need to update or adjust the Community banking legislation, on the consistency of the implementation and interpretation by Member States of the banking directives and

---

81   See, on the institutional framework for co-operation in banking supervision in the euro area, 'EMU and Banking Supervision', European Central Bank, Monthly Bulletin (April 2000), pp.57 ff.

82   See, for an overview of the web of *fora* of regulators and supervisors in the field of financial services, 'Institutional Arrangements for the Regulation and Supervision of the Financial Sector', European Commission, January 2000.

83   The BAC is now described under Article 57 of the Codified Banking Directive.

on the possible need for further convergence of regulatory practices. With regard to the latter, certain technical provisions of the banking directives can be amended according to a comitology procedure, which committee has the same composition as that of the BAC. On the other hand, the BAC also furthers co-operative relations among banking supervisors by providing an arena for exchange of information and the production of joint technical work among banking supervisors and regulators.

The development of co-operative relations among financial regulators of Member States as the basis for the deliberation, preparation, implementation and enforcement of Community law and regulation of financial services has received a fresh impetus from the Report of the Committee of Wise Men on the Regulation of European Securities Markets.[84] This report, in view of the shortcomings of the current regulatory procedures of the Community, recommends a 'four-level approach' to the Community regulation of securities markets, which may be deemed as valid and thus extended to all the fields of financial regulation. First, the current legislative procedures for the adoption of Community law should be limited to the definition of 'framework principles', which would correspond to regulation at Level 1. Second, two new committees, a European Securities Committee and a European Securities Regulators Committee, would assist the Commission in defining the details of Level 1 legislation, which would correspond to regulation at Level 2. Third, the securities regulators of Member States should enhance co-operation and networking among them as the regulatory Level 3, namely through the European Securities Regulators Committee, in order to ensure consistent and equivalent transposition of Level 1 and Level 2 legislation. Lastly, at Level 4, the enforcement of Community law would be supported by the co-operation between the Member States, their regulators and the private sector.

2.   Findings: A Procedural Legal Order for Transnational Financial Markets?

Proceduralization of legal and regulatory decision-making is becoming the paradigm of law in a complex society. Issues that do not conform to the causality and scientific principles which underlie the values of 'experience' or 'tradition', have to be managed within a process devised for the generation of knowledge. This will potentially lead to a revisable rational outcome acceptable for most of the parties involved.[85] The consequence is that the justification of law, i.e. of legal principles and legal rules, will be derived mostly (but certainly not only) from the way the

---

84   See *Final Report of the Committee of Wise Men on the Regulation of European Securities Markets*, February 2001, available at http://europa.eu.int.

85   See K.-H. Ladeur, *Post-Moderne Rechtstheorie*, (Berlin: Duncker & Humblot, 1995), pp.194-7; 'Proceduralization and its Use in Post-Modern Legal Theory', EUI Working Paper LAW No 96/5 (Florence: European University Institute, 1996), pp.20ff. See also R. Wiethölter, 'Materialization and Proceduralization in Law', in Teubner (ed.) *Dilemmas of Law in the Welfare State* (Berlin: de Gruyter, 1986), pp.221-49 at 31ff.

successive learning processes that deliver legal decisions are contrived,[86] and not as previously from substantive ideas on what is right or from the mere choice between alternative policy guidelines. This implies furthermore that the dynamics within and between public and private organizations towards the development of legal rules will have to conform to procedural principles prone to guarantee rational strategies and decisions.

Mechanisms such as those of association and organization, institutionalized co-operation and participation or consultation, besides justifying binding rules, will prove to be effective means to modify and update the ever provisional legal rules of complex markets, and this in the most flexible way.[87] One becomes aware that the simplistic tit-for-tat based values which made up much of the *lex mercatoria* of individual merchants are to be replaced by elaborate give-and-take principles of negotiation and deliberation in the society of economic organizations. Consequently, certain areas of transnational commercial law, such as the one relating to financial regulation, develop primarily out of learning processes, knowledgeable persuasion and flexible bargaining. Law and regulation may emerge as seemingly unstructured and their commands of a 'soft law' nature,[88] but evolving at a pace still comparable to the one of the complex reality supposed to be ordered. Furthermore, regulators grouped in co-operative *fora* may also act as mediators or 'translators'[89] of the plural legal discourses that conflict in transnational markets. In this sense, co-operative fora may play the role of discovering the 'rules of conflict', as in classic private international law, which provide transnational order to market transactions.

This being so, a procedural legal order, somewhat in accordance with the Hayekian idea on the general rules of a spontaneous order,[90] is the starting point

---

86   See J.R. Macey, *'Public and Private Ordering and the Production of Legitimate and Illegitimate Legal Rules'*, CORNELL LAW REVIEW, vol.82 (1997), p.1123, on the relevance of procedure as a 'filter against illegitimate rules', at pp.1143 ff.

87   See for instance J. Black, *Rules and Regulators* (London: Oxford University Press, 1997), pp.30-45, on how 'regulatory interpretive communities' are emerging in the financial services sector.

88   See on the concept of 'soft economic law' applied to the Basle Committee's activity, J.J. Norton, *Devising International Bank Supervisory Standards* (London: Kluwer, 1995), pp.255 ff.

89   See the analysis on the role of regulators as mediators of deliberation by J. Black, *'Proceduralizing Regulation: Part II'*, OXFORD JOURNAL OF LEGAL STUDIES, vol.21, no.1 (2001), pp.33-58, at pp.46 ff.

90   See F.A. Hayek, *supra* n. 26, p.50, and see, accordingly, V.J. Vanberg, *supra* n. 16, pp.77-94, stressing the need for a continuous search for alternative rules: 'one has to engage in institutional or constitutional economics, analysing how alternative rules affect, and are affected by, private as well as public choices' (p. 94). See also an empirical assessment of the merits of common law, as an example of spontaneous order, for economic growth, P.G. Mahoney, *'The Common Law and Economic Growth: Hayek Might be Right'*, Working Paper 00-8, University of Virginia School of Law (2000).

from which to unveil the market as a continuous discovery process. The new paradigm to which transnational commercial law and regulation is to apply should therefore be that of a self-organizing market system which does not incorporate any expectations of leading to a natural and scrutinizable stability (e.g. in efficiency terms). As is already striking in the process of law-making and regulation of transnational finance, including what is foreseeable within the European Union and already acknowledged within the institutional framework of the Economic and Monetary Union,[91] it is instead a structure based on the necessity for a reinforcing co-operative search for knowledge through self- and mutual observation of, and between, market authorities, market participants, and other market institutions.

In this sense, one may start to observe that the spread of co-operative regulatory bodies may correspond to the rise of single-purpose governments for the economy.[92] As non-majoritarian institutions, Majone would argue that non-majoritarian standards of legitimacy should apply to these co-operative regulatory *fora*. These are standards of expertise, procedural rationality, transparency, and accountability by results, which should be sufficient to justify the delegation by political institutions of the necessary powers.[93]

However, this can only be true to a certain extent. International and European standard-setting and regulation do not refer to a precise polity. Their constituencies are first, the national regulators themselves and, second, internationally active banks and securities firms rather than the domestic institutions for which national regulators are primarily accountable. Transnational co-operative law serves in a way diffuse interests through diffuse means. It does not rely so much on the clarity and transparency of procedures and decision-making as on the moral suasion of the private club spirit that the principle of mutual recognition brings in its developed stages. Accountability of decisions seems therefore almost a non-issue as there is no precise polity to be accountable to. This may not represent a serious problem to the extent that the objective of co-operative law is standard-setting in accordance with a *de minimis* principle. The problem is important enough, though, in policy areas where a clear definition and implementation of market policies is necessary, for instance in crisis situations (the main example is the spread of financial crises in the 1990s). This may mean that co-operative law serves mainly liberal impulses, facilitating market forces, with no critical scrutiny of policies of market restraint. The rules of co-operative law may then be ultimately described as the outcome of

---

91   See J.-V. Louis, '*A Legal and Institutional Approach for Building a Monetary Union*', COMMON MARKET LAW REVIEW, vol.35 (1998), pp.33-76 at 72 ff.

92   The expression is from R. D. Cooter, 'The Optimal Number of Governments for Economic Development' (April 1999), Working Paper available at www.berkeley.edu.

93   See Majone, '*Europe's "Democratic Deficit": The Question of Standards*', EUROPEAN LAW JOURNAL, vol. 5, pp. 5 and 28.

'second-order decisions', which according to Sunstein and Ullmann-Margalit[94] 'involve the strategies that people use in order to avoid getting into an ordinary decision-making situation in the first instance'. In this context, certain authors start to suggest the constitutionalisation of international law[95] as means to provide legitimacy to transnational co-operative law.

The latest developments in the public governance of transnational markets through co-operative law relate to an increasing focus on effectiveness and compliance. It is argued that the standard-setting role of transnational regulatory *fora* needs to be complemented by a much stronger emphasis on compliance, by firms and regulators themselves, with standards.[96] Such compliance would involve, first, an independent assessment of whether standards are complied with, and, second, the publication of such assessment. This assessment is currently under way, but not particularly through co-operative means. Instead, international financial institutions, the IMF and the World Bank, are conducting such assessments, which correspond to the adjudication of the standards elaborated as co-operative law. This, as a preliminary conclusion, seems to hint that co-operative law may be, after all, an intermediate stage for legal centralism, for instance in the form of the creation of 'global authorities'.

94   C.R. Sunstein & E.Ullmann-Margalit, 'Second-Order Decisions', Chicago Public Law and Legal Theory Working Paper No. 01 (1999), p.3.

95   See the proposals of A.-M. Slaughter, including of a 'transgovernmental constitution', 'Agencies on the Loose? Holding Government Networks Accountable', in Bermann/ Herdegen/Lindseth (eds.), *supra* n. 33, pp.521-546, at p.535 ff. See also in the same volume, E-U. Petersmann, 'Globalization and Transatlantic Regulatory Cooperation: Proposals for EU-US Initiatives to Further Constitutionalize International Law', pp.615-627 at 616-617.

96   H. Evans, '*Plumbers and Architects: A Supervisory Perspective on International Financial Architecture*', Financial Services Authority Occasional Paper 4 (2000).

Index